GUIDE TO

WILD
FLOWERS
OF BRITAIN AND NORTHERN EUROPE

BOB GIBBONS AND PETER BROUGH

THE AUTHORS

Dr Bob Gibbons worked for the Nature Conservancy Council for seven years before becoming a freelance writer and photographer, specialising in botany and wildlife. He has written and provided photographs for many books, as well as numerous magazines and journals. He has travelled extensively in Europe while studying wild flowers, and now leads wildlife tours to many regions in Europe. He lives in Dorset.

Dr Peter Brough is an enthusiastic naturalist, conservationist and medical practitioner. His broad knowledge of natural history, gained over many years, includes a long experience of field botany in Britain and Europe. He plays an active role in promoting conservation, not least for the wildlife trust in his home county of Hampshire.

COMMISSIONING EDITOR *Steve Luck*

EXECUTIVE ART EDITOR *Mike Brown*

DESIGNER *Caroline Ohara*

PRODUCTION *Aggeliki Rabaouni*

First published in 2008 by Philip's, a division of Octopus Publishing Group Ltd, www.octopusbooks.co.uk
2–4 Heron Quays, London E14 4JP
An Hachette Livre UK Company
www.hachettelivre.co.uk

FRONT COVER : *clockwise from tl* Peony (*Hamlyn*), Early-purple Orchid (*Hamlyn*), Sheep's-bit (*Hamlyn*), Beaked Hawks-beard (*Hamlyn*), Harsh Downy-rose (*Hamlyn*), Purple Saxifrage (*Hamlyn*), Greater Celandine (*Hamlyn*)
BACK COVER : *l to r* Large-flowered Butterwort (*Hamlyn*), Wild Strawberry (*Hamlyn*)
SPINE : Orange Hawkweed (*Hamlyn*)

Other titles from Philip's

Philip's publish a range of natural history titles in the same format as this book, including:

Details of other Philip's titles and services can be found on our website
www.philips-maps.co.uk

Contents

INTRODUCTION

The area covered by the *Philip's Guide to Wild Flowers of Britain and Northern Europe* comprises northern Europe, including Scandinavia, and as far south as central France and southern Germany, excluding the Alps. In practice, the useful coverage extends more widely since the vegetation tends to change gradually as you move to different areas, and many of the flowers in this book can be found farther south and east. However, the farther away one is from this core area, the less comprehensive the book becomes.

The Philip's Guide to Wild Flowers of Britain and Northern Europe is not intended to be a comprehensive guide to the flowers of this vast area. If all the species of the area were included, their number would make it unsuitable as a portable field guide. Instead, we have selected around 1,000 species that are most likely to be encountered by virtue of their abundance or distinctive appearance; thus, most species that the average user will notice, within the core area of the book, are included.

The order of the species and families within the book in general follows that adopted in *Flora Europaea*. Since the publication of *Flora Europaea*, many changes in scientific names have taken place, and there has been much new work on plant relationships as a result of DNA research. We have retained the order of families followed in *Flora Europaea*, but updated individual names (both scientific and common) in accordance with the *New Flora of the British Isles* by Clive Stace, 2nd edition (1997, Cambridge University Press), and subsequent updates on the Botanical Society of the British Isles checklist (www.bsbi.org.uk). Where new family names are now in use (such as Apiaceae instead of Umbelliferae) we have used these, but have not followed the subdivision of families into new ones that some authorities now favour.

Using the book

The primary source of information for many users will be the illustrations. A quick scan through these will often quickly show what a plant is, or at least in what group or family it is to be found. Some species, such as Motherwort (*Leonurus cardiaca*), stand out instantly as being different from almost everything else; other species will be much more difficult. The illustrations have been annotated to draw attention to some of the key features used in the identification of each species. These should be looked at in conjunction with the species descriptions.

To achieve accurate identification, the text provides general introductions to the characteristics of each family and descrip-

tions of each species. The species descriptions are written to emphasise the differences between closely related or similar-looking species. The format of the book does not allow for the provision of dichotomous keys to difficult groups, but, where appropriate, we have divided larger groups into sub-groups sharing distinctive characteristics, and there is a general illustrated key to the families on pp. 12–21.

Spring flowers on the rocks at Stumble Head, Pembrokeshire, including Cowslips and Spring Squill.

The species descriptions themselves have been written in a standardised way to make it easier to find facts and to compare species. However, it is not possible, nor useful, to describe all species in exactly the same way. For example, the colour of the hairs on the filaments is of key importance in identifying mullein species, but not for many other groups.

In addition to the straightforward anatomical information on leaf shape, height, flower colour and so on, which is largely self-explanatory, there is also information on the distribution, abundance and flowering time of each species. In addition, where appropriate there is also specific information on the distribution within the British Isles (**Br Is dist**). When trying to identify a

rare or scattered distribution

widely naturalised

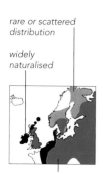

main area of distribution

species, all this information should be taken into account. It is, for example, very unlikely that a species will be found well outside the range indicated on the maps or in the text, though some species are extending their range, and others are occasionally discovered in new localities.

The precise distribution of many species of flowering plants throughout Europe is still uncertain and therefore maps have only been included for those where this reasonably accurate information is available. Also, we have in most cases only mapped those species that are not found throughout the region.

The colour codes on the maps are as follows: dark green indicates the main area of distribution; pale green indicates where the plant has a scattered distribution or where it is comparatively rare; black indicates where it is widely naturalised.

Flowering time (**Fl**) must be taken as a guide only. Apart from variations from year to year according to the weather, there is also a wide variation in flowering time over such a large range of altitude and latitude as is found in northern Europe. In a few cases, flowering time is one of the first aids to identification, such as in distinguishing Spring Squill (*Scilla verna*) from Autumn Squill (*S. autumnalis*).

The habitat in which a plant occurs is often important. Unfortunately, over such a large area, the chosen preferences of plants may vary, so it is difficult to be precise for any given area. Nevertheless, it is worth taking this information into account when trying to identify a species; for example, it is highly unlikely that a plant recorded as occurring on heaths and heathy woods will be found on a salt-marsh or a chalk downland.

THE STRUCTURE OF FLOWERS

Flowers vary enormously in shape and other characteristics, relating to how they are pollinated and the environment in which they live. These are the general rules of flower structure, but there are exceptions.

Flowers generally consist of several whorls or circles of parts, which may or may not be symmetrical. The outermost whorl, which is often (but not necessarily) green, is known as the **calyx** and is made up of individual **sepals**, which may be separate or fused into a tube with just the terminal teeth revealing their number. Their function is to protect the developing flower, though in many species they are adapted to form part of the mechanism for attracting insects. The next whorl towards the centre is the **petals**, which are usually highly coloured and conspicuous, forming the main part of the visual means of attracting insects. The petals may be separate or fused into a tube, such as in bellflowers. As with sepals, there are usually a number of teeth at the end of the tube, indicating the number of original petals. In flowers normally pollinated by wind, the petals may be reduced or completely invisible. In some flowers, especially those of Monocotyledons, the petals and sepals are so similar in form or colour that they are collectively called the **perianth**, with individual parts known as **tepals**. The number of sepals and petals, and the degree to which they are fused, is important in identification.

Simple dicotyledon
Buttercup (*Ranunculus* sp)

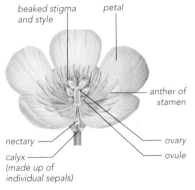

beaked stigma and style
petal
anther of stamen
nectary
calyx (made up of individual sepals)
ovary
ovule

Specialized dicotyledon
Sweet Pea (*Lathyrus odoratus*)
Family Fabaceae

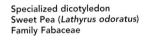
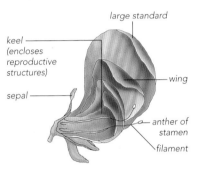

large standard
keel (encloses reproductive structures)
wing
sepal
anther of stamen
filament

Specialized monocotyledon
Orchid (*Dactylorhiza* sp.)

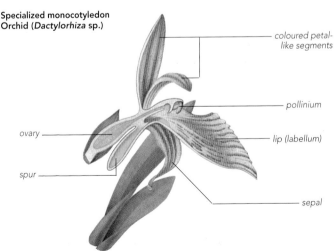

coloured petal-like segments
pollinium
ovary
lip (labellum)
spur
sepal

Symmetry

Flowers with simple concentric symmetrical whorls, such as the Buttercup opposite, are **regular** or **radially symmetrical**. However, many flowers are more irregular in shape and are symmetrical in one plane only from front to back, such as those from the pea (Fabaceae) or dead-nettle (Lamiaceae) families. They are highly adapted for insect pollination. In the pea family, the petals are distinctive enough to have separate names, with the single **large standard** at the back, and a pair of **wings** which enclose the two central petals that form the boat-shaped **keel**. Orchid flowers are similarly irregular, often even more highly adapted, and in some species such as the Bee Orchid (*Ophrys apifera*), the lower petal is wholly different to the upper two petals, mimicking the body of a bee-like insect.

Parts of a flower

At the centre of most flowers lie the female parts, collectively known as the **gynaecium**. Commonly this consists of one or more **carpels**, each containing one or more **ovaries**, and these may be quite separate and distinct or have several carpels tightly fused together. Normally a carpel has a stalk-like **style**, which ends in a **stigma** where **pollen** settles and germinates. These features may assist in the identification of families, genera and species. It is also important whether the ovary is **superior** or **inferior**: if the gynaecium sits on the **receptacle** (the swollen end of its supporting stem) above where the petals, sepals and stamens are inserted, then the

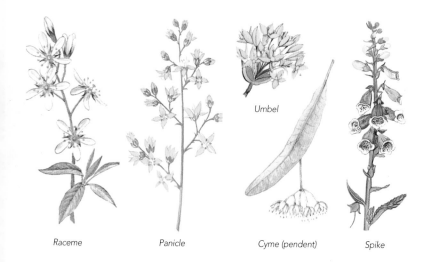

Raceme   Panicle   Cyme (pendent)   Spike

Ovate

Lanceolate, tip sharply pointed

Spoon-shaped, tip blunt

Round

Linear, tip shallowly notched

Tip tapering to a slender tip, margin double-toothed

Margin lobed, base with auricles

Margin toothed, base heart-shaped

Palmate

Pinnate, leaflets elliptic

Twice-pinnate

Leaves diamond shaped, arranged in alternating pairs at right angles

Arrangement whorled

ovary is superior. If the petals and other parts are clearly attached on top of the ovary, then the ovary is inferior. This is always a useful character to look for, and may be crucial in distinguishing plants from similar families – for example, bellflowers (Campanulaceae) have inferior ovaries, while members of the gentian family (Gentianaceae) have superior ovaries.

Finally, it is important to note how the flowers are held and grouped. They may be solitary and well separated or grouped in an **inflorescence**. Inflorescences take different forms, such as **spikes**, **racemes** or **cymes** (*see* p. 8 and glossary pp. 22–3); these distinctions may be important for identification. In the Daisy family (Asteraceae) and several others, numerous flowers are grouped tightly together in a structured head, which often resembles a single flower especially in plants such as Oxeye Daisy (*Leucanthemum vulgare*) where regular symmetrical **ray florets** surround the central tightly grouped mass of fertile flowers. Such flowers may be surrounded by sepal-like structures, which are actually bracts, since they surround an inflorescence rather than a single flower.

Leaves

The shape and arrangement of a plant's leaves are also often used to identify a particular species of wild flower. The main examples are shown opposite. As well as the form and arrangement of the leaves, the species description may also indicate whether the leaves are 'toothed' or 'untoothed', 'hairy' or 'hairless'; this information may be helpful in distinguishing one species from another.

Wet meadows dominated by Yellow Flag; in the distance lie the Twelve Pins of Connemara, Galway, Ireland.

USING THE KEY

To assist with identification, by accurately placing any given plant in its family, we have provided an illustrated key to all the families in the book. Keys such as this work by asking a series of questions about the plant, the answers to which gradually take you closer to a precise identification. To make this a simpler process, the key takes the form of paired questions (occasionally 3), answers to which lead the user in a different direction. The first part of the key, the **Key to Plant Groups**, separates the plants out by 1 or more steps into 12 distinct groups according to their characteristics; this section leads the user onto the **Group Key** where simple short keys are provided to the families within each of the groups.

Here is an example of how the key works, using the plant illustrated to the right, which is a widespread yellow-flowered herb that grows in wet places. In the Group Key, the first question is **1**, asking whether the plant has green parts or not. It does, so go to **2**; this plant grows on land, so proceed to **4**; the flowers are obvious and coloured, leading to **5**; since there are 5 petals, so go to **6** and from there to **7**; a careful check will show that the petals are completely unjoined or free, so proceed to **8**; this flower has more than one plane of symmetry (it is radially symmetrical, *see* p. 8) unlike a pea flower or a dead-nettle, leading to **Group H**. From here, proceed to the second stage of the Group Key, starting at Group H.

Group H begins with three options, demanding a detailed examination of the flower parts, preferably using a lens. In this plant, the flower parts (the sepals, petals and stamens) are attached below the ovary, so the ovary is superior (*see* right); in addition, there is a single ovary but with 3 styles projecting, which suggests that there are three fused carpels, so proceed to **H6**. This plant has numerous stamens, many more than 10, so you go to **7**; the leaves are in opposite pairs and there are no stipules (*see* glossary), so go to **8**. As already mentioned there are three styles, and further examination reveals that the stamens are indeed attached in little groups, confirming that the plant is in the Clusiaceae, the St John's-wort family.

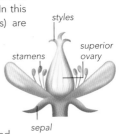

styles

stamens

superior ovary

sepal

Turn to pp.152–4, and check the various options, using both the text and the illustrations. The combination of square stem and lack of hairs leads to the Square-stemmed St John's-wort (*Hypericum tetrapterum*) and the details of habitat, distribution and other information should confirm this identification.

Although it can be slow using a key, especially at first if you are unfamiliar with some of the terms, it does have many advantages.

Horizontal section through 3 fused carpels

It quickly teaches you what the various botanical terms mean, and you soon get a clear appreciation of the characteristics of each of the main families.

Whenever possible, **take the book to the plant** when attempting an identification. If absolutely necessary, collect a small sample only (unless there are very few individuals present) without uprooting it, or make notes and sketches or take digital photographs, concentrating on obtaining the full range of its features from basal leaf to fruit, as well as flowers. This will make later identification much easier. Plants are under threat everywhere throughout Europe, mainly from habitat loss, and we should not add to this stress by unnecessary collecting. In addition, there are laws in many countries that outlaw collecting of plants by uprooting, or even by picking with rarer species and in certain protected areas.

Key to plant groups

		Proceed to
1	Plants with no green parts	Group A
1b	Plants green	2
2a	Growing in water	3
2b	Growing on land	4
3a	Floating aquatics, not rooted in mud	Group B
3b	Aquatica, rooted in mud	Group C
4a	Individual flowers inconspicuous, may be in clusters, e.g., catkins, colour green or brown	Group D
4b	Flowers obvious, coloured	5
5a	5 or more petals or petal-like parts	6
5b	Fewer than 5 petals	10
6a	5 petals	7
6b	6 or more petals	Group L
7a	Petals free (not joined together)	8
7b	Petals joined together	9
8a	Flowers radially symmetrical	Group H
8b	Flowers symmetrical about 1 axis only	Group J
9a	Flowers radially symmetrical	Group I
9b	Flowers symmetrical about 1 axis only, hooded, lipped or spurred	Group K
10a	0, 2 or 3 petals or petal-like parts	Group E
10b	4 petals	11
11a	Petals free	Group F
11b	Petals joined at least at base	Group G

Group Key

Group A Plants with no green pigment

1a	Plant erect	2
1b	Plant twining around another species. **Convolulaceae pp. 220**	
2a	Flowers radially symmetrical, drooping. **Pyrolaceae p. 188**	
2b	Flowers not radially symmetrical	3
3a	Flowers 2-lipped, tubular below. **Orobanchaceae p. 266**	
3b	6 free petal-like structures, prominent lower lip. **Orchidaceae p. 346**	

Group B Floating aquatics, not rooted in mud

1a	Plant small (less than 10mm), not disk-like or lobed. **Lemnaceae p. 344**	
1b	Plant larger than 10mm, not disk-like.	2
2a	Leaves finely divided, has small bladders. **Lentibulariaceae (Utricularia) p. 268**	
2b	Leaves not divided	3
3a	Flowers with 4 petals. **Trapaceae p. 160**	
3b	Flowers with 3 petals. **Hydrocharitaceae p. 320**	

Group C Aquatic plants, rooted in mud

1a	Plant erect, tall, emerging from water	2
1b	Plant not erect, usually immersed or floating	7

2a	Flowers conspicuous, individual flowers greater than 10mm. **Butomaceae p. 320** or **Alismataceae p. 318**	
2b	Individual flowers small, inconspicuous, but may be in dense, obvious clusters.	3
3a	Leaves whorled. **Hippuridaceae p. 166**	
3b	Leaves not whorled	4
4a	Inflorescence surrounded by a sheath (spathe). **Araceae (Calla) p. 342**	
4b	Inflorescence without encircling sheath	5
5a	Inflorescence cylindrical	6
5b	Inflorescence globular **Sparganiaceae p. 344** or **Eriocaulaceae p. 342**	
6a	Plant sweet-smelling inflorescence to one side **Araceae (Acorus) p. 342**	
6b	Plant not scented, inflorescence terminal. **Typhaceae p. 346**	
7a	Flowers conspicuous, white or yellow	8
7b	Flowers inconspicuous, but may be in dense spikes, green or brown	10

13

8a	Petals free. **Nymphaceae** p. 56	
8b	Petals united	9
9a	Flowers radially symmetrical, white. **Menyanthaceae** p. 212	
9b	Flowers symmetrical about 1 axis only, yellow. **Lentibulariaceae** (*Utricularia*) p. 270	
10a	Leaves whorled. **Ceratophyllaceae** p. 58 or **Haloragaceae** p. 164 or **Najadaceae** p. 324	
10b	Lower leaves in opposite pairs. **Callitrichaceae** p. 230 or **Najadaceae** p. 324	
10c	Lower leaves alternate **Zosteraceae** p. 324 or **Potamogetonaceae** p. 322 or **Ruppiaceae** p. 322	

Group D Terrestrial plants. Flowers inconspicuous, green or brown, but often arranged in prominent clusters

1a	Flowers in catkin-like structures	2
1b	Flowers not in catkins	3
2a	Erect or creeping shrubs	3

2b	Erect herbs or climbers **Salicaceae** p. 10 or **Myricaceae** p. 10	
3a	Plant parasitic on trees **Viscaceae** p. 26	
3b	Plant not parasitic on trees	4
4a	Leaves compound	5
4b	Leaves simple	8
4c	Leaves absent, stems cylindrical, succulent **Chenopodiaceae** (*Salicornia*) p. 38	
5a	Flowers in dense heads	6
5b	Flowers not in dense heads	7
6a	Flowers in heads of 5, flowers at right angles to each other **Adoxaceae** p. 274	
6b	More than 5 flowers per head **Rosaceae** p. 100	
7a	No petals, 4 stamens **Rosaceae** (*Alchemilla*) p. 112 or (*Aphanes*) p. 112	
7b	4–5 petals, many stamens **Ranunculaceae** (*Thalictrum*) p. 70	
8a	Inflorescence a dense spike with sheath (spathe) **Araceae** p. 342	
8b	Not so	9

9a Milky juice, flowers in umbels **Euphorbiaceae p. 144**		
9b No milky juice present, flowers not arranged in umbels	10	
10a Opposite or whorled leaves	11	
10b Alternate leaves	14	
11a Low, creeping stems	12	
11b Plant erect	13	
12a 5 sepals and petals **Caryophyllaceae p. 40**		
12b **Saxifragaceae** (*Chrysosplenium*) **p. 98**		
13a Stinging hairs, 4 stamens **Urticaceae p. 26**		
13b No stinging hairs, many stamens **Euphorbiaceae** (*Mercurialis*) **p. 140**		
14a Leaves with sheaths around base **Polygonaceae p. 28**		
14b No sheaths at leaf bases	15	
15a Flowers in dense, narrow spikes, leaves linear, not fleshy **Plantaginaceae p. 270**		
or		
Ranunculaceae (*Myosurus*) **p. 68**		

15b Flowers not in narrow spikes, often fleshy and/or mealy **Chenopodiaceae p. 34**		
Group E Terrestrial plants. Flowers conspicuous, 0, 2 or 3 or petals		
1a Petals absent, flowers in dense, reddish heads **Rosaceae** (*Sanguisorba*) **p. 106**		
1b Petals present, flowers not in dense heads	2	
2a 2 petals **Onagraceae** (*Circaea*) **p. 160**		
2b 3 petals	3	
3a Petals joined in a tube **Aristolochiaceae p. 26**		
3b Petals free **Alismataceae p. 318**		
Group F Terrestrial plants. Flowers conspicuous, 4 petals or petal-like parts, not joined together at their base nor in a tube		
1a Leaves undivided	2	
1b Leaves divided into segments	7	
2a More than 8 stamens **Resedaceae p. 92**		
2b Fewer than 8 stamens	3	
3a Fe4 sepals	4	
3b 2 sepals, soon falling **Papaveraceae p. 70**		
4a Ovary inferior	5	
4a Ovary superior	6	

15

5a	Flowers with large, whitish, petallike bracts **Cornaceae** p. 166	
5b	Flowers with true petals **Onagraceae** p. 160	
6a	Ovary 1-celled **Caryophyllaceae** p. 40	
6b	Ovary 2-celled **Brassicaceae** p. 74	
6c	Ovary 5- or 6- celled **Linaceae** (*Radiola*) p. 140	
7a	More than 8 stamens, leaves palmately lobed **Rosaceae** (*Potentilla erecta*) p. 110	
7b	Usually 6 stamens, leaves not palmate **Brassicaceae** p. 74	

4a	Leaves opposite, 5 stamens **Gentianaceae** p. 206	
4b	Leaves alternate, more than 5 stamens	5
5a	Sepals petal-like, no true petals **Thymelacaceae** p. 150	
5b	Green sepals and coloured petals present **Ericaceae** p. 190	
6a	Flowers in dense heads, whorled bracts beneath **Dipsacaceae** p. 276	
6b	Flowers not in dense heads	7
7a	2 stamens, ovary 1-celled **Fumariaceae** p. 72	
7b	4 stamens, ovary 2-celled **Scrophulariaceae** p. 246	

Group G Terrestrial plants. Flowers conspicuous, 4 petals or petallike parts, joined together at their base or in a tube

1a	Flowers radially symmetrical	2
1b	Flowers not radially symmetrical	6
2a	Leaves in whorls	3
2b	Leaves not in whorls	4
3a	4 or 5 stamens **Rubiaceae** p. 214	
3b	8 stamens **Ericaceae** p. 190	

Group H Terrestrial plants. Flowers conspicuous, 5 petals or petallike parts, not joined together

1a	Ovary superior, carpels free	2
1b	Ovary superior, carpels fused	6
1c	Ovary inferior	21
2a	More than 10 stamens	3
2b	10 stamens or fewer	4
3a	Stipules present **Rosaceae** p. 100	
3b	Stipules absent **Ranunculaceae** p. 58	

4a	Succulent (fleshy) leaves **Crassulaceae p. 94**		10a	2 sepals **Portulacaceae p. 38**	
4b	Leaves nor succulent	5	10b	More than 2 sepals	11
5a	Leaves divided into lobes **Rosaceae (Sibbaldia) p. 110**		11a	Leaves opposite or whorled	12
			11b	Leaves alternate or in a basal rosette	14
			12a	Leaves simple, unlobed	13
5b	Leaves not divided into lobes **Polygonaceae p. 28** or Ranunculaceae (*Myosurus*) p. 68		12b	Leaves palmately or pinnately lobed **Geraniaceae p. 134**	
			13a	Ovary 1-celled **Caryophyllaceae p. 40** or **Frankeniaceae p. 158**	
6a	More than 10 stamens	7	13b	Ovary, 4–5-celled **Linaceae p. 140**	
6b	10 stamens or fewer	10			
7a	Leaves alternate, stipules present	8	14a	Leaves with sticky glands, insectivorous **Droseraceae p. 92**	
7b	Leaves opposite, no stipules	9			
8a	Leaves palmate, stamens fused in a ring **Malvaceae p. 148**		14b	Not so	15
			15a	Leaves with 3 lobes **Oxalidaceae p. 134**	
8b	Leaves not palmately lobed, stamens free **Rosaceae p. 100**		15b	Not so	16
			16a	5 stigmas	17
9a	Single style, stamens free **Cistaceae p. 158**		16b	Fewer than 5 stigmas	19
			17a	Leaves entire (not lobed)	18
9b	Several styles, stamens in bundles **Clusiaceae p. 152**		17b	Leaves pinnate or palmately lobed **Geraniaceae p. 134**	

18a	Many stem leaves present **Linaceae p. 140**		2b	5 stamens	5
	or		3a	Woody plants, usually evergreen **Ericaceae p. 190**	
18b	Leaves confined to basal rosette **Plumbaginaceae p. 204**				
19a	1 style **Pyrolaceae p. 188**		3b	Succulent, roundleaved herb **Crassulaceae (*Umbilicus*) p. 94**	
19b	2–4 styles	20			
20a	5 stamens alternating with feathery 7 structures **Saxifragaceae (*Parnassia*) p. 98**		4a	Stamens opposite the petals	5
			4b	Stamens alternating with the petals	6
20b	10 stamens **Saxifragaceae p. 94**		5a	Single stigma and style **Primulaceae p. 198**	
21a	More than 5 stamens	22	5b	5 stigmas **Plumbaginaceae p. 204**	
21b	5 stamens, flowers in umbels	23			
22a	More than 10 stamens **Rosaceae p. 100**		6a	Leaves opposite	7
			6b	Leaves alternate	8
22b	10 stamens **Saxifragaceae p. 94**		7a	2 free carpels with a single style **Apocynaceae p. 212**	
23a	Herbs **Apiaceae p. 166**		7b	Single ovary with 2 styles or 1 style, 2 stigmas **Gentianaceae p. 206**	
23b	Woody climber **Araliaceae p. 166**		7c	Single ovary and style, 3-lobed stigma **Diapensiaceae p. 188**	

Group I Terrestrial plants. Flowers conspicuous, 5 petals joined together, radially symmetrical

			8a	Ovary strongly 4-lobed **Boraginaceae p. 222**	
1a	Ovary superior	2			
1b	Ovary inferior	12			
2a	10 stamens	3	8b	Not so	9

9a Flowers in a terminal inflorescence	10	16a Leaves opposite	17	
9b Flowers axillary or in axillary clusters	11	16b Leaves alternate	19	
10a Leaves simple **Scrophulariaceae p. 246**		17a Creeping, with flowers in pairs **Caprifoliaceae (*Linnaea*) p. 272**		
10b Leaves pinnate **Polemoniaceae p. 218**		17b Erect, with small flowers in clusters	18	
		18a Milky sap, ovary with 2 carpels, 2-celled **Asclepiadaceae p. 212**		
11a Sepals free **Convolvulaceae p. 222**		18b No milky sap, single-celled ovary **Valerianaceae p. 274**		
11b Sepals united in a tube **Solanaceae p. 244**		19a Twining climber **Cucurbitaceae p. 160**		
12a 8–10 stamens **Ericaceae p. 93**		19b Not climbing **Campanulaceae p. 278**		
12b 5 or fewer stamens	13	or		
13a Flowers in dense heads	14	**Primulaceae (*Samolus*) p. 202**		
13b Flowers not in dense heads	16			
14a Stamens completely free	15			

14b Stamens united by their anthers into a tube **Asteraceae p. 284**	**Group J** Terrestrial plants. Flowers conspicuous, 5 petals but flowers symmetrical about 1 axis only	
	1a More than 8 stamens	2
	1b 8 stamens or fewer	3
15a 5 stamens, alternate leaves **Campanulaceae p. 278**	2a 10 stamens, no spur to flower **Fabaceae p. 112**	
15b 2 or 4 stamens, opposite leaves **Dipsacaceae p. 276**	2b Many stamens, flowers spurred **Ranunculaceae p. 58**	

3a	5 stamens, flowers spurred **Violaceae p. 154**	
3b	8 stamens, flowers not spurred **Polygalaceae p. 146**	

Group K Terrestrial plants. Flowers conspicuous, 5 joined petals, flowers hooded, lipped or spurred, symmetrical about 1 axis

1a	Flowers in dense heads	2
1b	Flowers not in dense heads	3
2a	Leaves opposite **Dipsacaceae p. 276**	
2b	Leaves alternate **Globulariaceae p. 264**	
3a	Flowers spurred	4
3b	Flowers not spurred	5
4a	Sticky, insectivorous leaves in rosette **Lentibulariaceae p. 268**	
4b	Leaves not sticky, present on fleshy stem **Balsaminaceae p. 146**	
5a	Stamens joined in a tube by their anthers **Campanulaceae** (*Lobelia*) **p. 282**	
5b	Stamens free	6
6a	Woody, twining climber, 5 stamens **Caprifoliaceae p. 272**	

6b	Not a climber, 2 or 4 stamens	7
7a	Ovary 2-celled **Scrophulariaceae p. 246**	
7b	Ovary 4-celled **Lamiaceae p. 230**	
	or	
	Verbenaceae p. 228	

Group L Terrestrial plants. Flowers conspicuous, 6 or more petals or petal-like parts

1a	Petals free	2
1b	Petals joined together	13
2a	More than 12 stamens	3
2b	12 or fewer stamens	5
3a	Stipules present, clear area round ovary **Rosaceae p. 100**	
3b	Stipules absent, no clear area round ovary **Ranunculaceae p. 58**	
4a	Ovary superior	5
4b	Ovary inferior	10
5a	3 stamens (may be joined together)	6
5b	More than 3 stamens	7

6a	Leaves linear, flowers stalked in leaf axils **Empetraceae p. 198**		12a	6 stamens **Liliaceae p. 324**	
6b	Leaves broad, pointed, stiff, flowers stalked in centre of leaflike structure **Liliaceae (*Ruscus*) p. 336**		12b	3 stamens **Iridaceae p. 338**	
7a	Leaves with sticky glands (insectivorous) all in basal rosette **Droseraceae p. 92**		13a	Climber with heart-shaped leaves **Dioscoreaceae p. 338**	
7b	Leaves without stick glands	8	13b	Not a climber	14
8a	Leaves cylindrical, succulent **Crassulaceae p. 94**		14a	No obvious sepals or sepals petallike	15
			14b	Green, leafy sepals present	18
8b	Leaves not succulent	9	15a	Flowers in dense heads, surrounded by whorls of bracts **Asteraceae p. 284**	
9a	2 whorls of 3 petallike parts, no green sepals **Liliaceae p. 324**		15b	Flowers not so arranged	16
			16a	Ovary superior **Liliaceae p. 324**	
9b	Single whorl of petals, sepals green	10			
10a	Flowers pink or red **Lythraceae p. 160**		16b	Ovary inferior	17
			17a	6 stamens **Liliaceae p. 324**	
10b	Flowers yellow/green or white **Resedaceae p. 92**		17b	3 stamens **Iridaceae p. 338**	
11a	Flowers radially symmetrical	12	18a	Stamens opposite petal lobes **Primulaceae p. 198**	
11b	Flowers symmetrical about only one axis **Orchidaceae p. 346**		18b	Stamens alternating with petal lobes **Gentianaceae p. 206**	

GLOSSARY

achene 1-seeded dry fruit, not splitting
acute Sharply pointed
adpressed See *appressed*
alternate Not opposite each other, eg. leaves
annual Life-cycle that is complete within 12 months
anther Pollen-bearing tip of stamen
apex Tip (of leaf or stem)
appressed Pressed closely to another part eg. hairs to stem
ascending Curving upwards
auricle Rounded lobe projecting backwards at leaf-base
awn Stiff, bristle-shaped projection
axil Angle between upper surface of leaf base, or its stalk, and stem
axillary In axil
basal leaves Leaves at base of stem
base-rich soil or rock rich in calcium, magnesium or other calcareous substances
berry Fleshy fruit with several seeds without a stony outer layer
biennial Taking 2 years to complete life-cycle: usually germinating and forming leaves in first year; then flowering, bearing seeds and dying in second year
bract Modified leaf at base of flower stalk or stalks
bracteole Small bract at base of each individual flower-stalk
bulb Swollen underground structure comprising short stem, leaf-bases and next year's bud
bulbil Small bulb-like structure developing asexually on a plant and after falling being capable of growing into a new plant
calcareous Containing calcium, eg. chalk or limestone
calyx Outer part of flower, often divided into sepals
carpel Division of female reproductive part of flower, consisting of ovary, stigma and style
casual Introduced plant, neither planted nor permanently established
cell Cavity in ovary or fruit
clasping Leaf-base stalkless with backward-projecting lobes around stem
compound leaf Having a number of separate leaflets
corm Swollen underground-stem of 1 year's duration, the new one growing on top of old
corolla Collective term for petals
corona Trumpet-like outgrowth, between the petals and the stamens, particularly applied to Daffodil flowers

cyme Repeatedly divided inflorescence, with succession of lateral flowers on either one side or both sides
decumbent Lying on ground and rising towards the tip
dicotyledon Division of plants with 2 first leaves on germinating seedling
digitate Having more than 3 finger-shaped leaves arising from the same point
dioecious With male and female flowers on separate plants
endemic Native in only one country or small area
epicalyx Outer calyx additional to the true (inner) calyx
epichile Front part of flower lip of some orchids, e.g. helleborines
epiphyte Plant growing on another plant but not parasitic
escape Plant which has spread from cultivated stock
floret Small flower
free Not joined together
fruit Seeds with surrounding structures
gland Either (1) small globular sticky structure at tip of hair, or (2) in spurges, the fleshy, yellowish bracts that alternate with the leafy bracts at the base of flower-clusters
globose Rounded like a globe
halberd-shaped Shaped like a medieval pike-head
herb Non-woody vascular plant
herbaceous Green with soft, leaf-like texture
hermaphrodite Male and female organs in same flower
hybrid Plant derived from cross-fertilisation between 2 different species
hypochile Rear part of flower lip of some orchids, e.g. helleborines
hypogynous Of flowers with stamens beside or beneath ovary
inflorescence Combination of flowers, bracts and their branches
involucre Ring of bracts surrounding 1 or more flowers
irregular flower One that is not radially symmetrical with equal petals, but is only symmetrical in one plane
keel In pea family, the 2 lower petals that join together
labellum Lip of orchid flower, usually on the lower side but occasionally the upper
lanceolate Lance-shaped
latex Milky juice in stem or leaf
lax Not dense (see loose)
leaflet Separate segment of a leaf that resembles a leaf but has no associated bud or stipule

linear Long, narrow and parallel-sided

lip Part of the corolla of an irregular flower, usually the lower part but occasionally the upper

lobe Projection or division of leaf

loose Not dense or tightly packed

membrane Thin structure, not green but either opaque or transparent

membranous With membrane

midrib Central vein of leaf

monocotyledon Division of plants with 1 first leaf on germinating seedling

monoecious With male and female flowers on same plant

nectary Organ secreting nectar

node Part of stem where a leaf or leaves arise

notch Small indentation at tip of leaf

oblong Leaf shape, central part parallel-sided

ochrea (pl. ochreae) Membranous stipules forming a tubular sheath around stem, in dock family

opposite Leaves or stalks arising in pairs at same level

ovary Central part of the flower containing the ovules which later develop into seeds

ovate Leaf shape, like an egg

ovoid 3-dimensional equivalent of ovate, ie. ovate in cross-section

palmate With 3 or more lobes arising from the same point

panicle Branched inflorescence

pappus Tuft of hairs on a fruit, eg. Dandelion

parasite Plant deriving all its nourishment from another living organism, to which it is attached

perianth Collective name for sepals and petals

perennial Plant which lives for more than two years, usually flowering each year

petals Inner whorl of perianth segments, often brightly coloured

pinnate Leaf composed of more than 3 leaflets arranged in 2 rows on opposite side of main axis

pinnatifid Pinnately cut, but not as deeply as pinnate

pollen Tiny grains produced by anthers, containing male sex cells

pollinium Pollen grains aggregated into substantial mass

procumbent Lying loosely along the ground surface

prostrate Lying tightly along the ground surface

raceme Spike-like inflorescence, with flowers distantly stalked

ray One of the stalks of an umbel

ray floret Outer florets of a composite flower, with part elongated into a strap-like structure

receptacle Part of the stem from which the floral organs arise

reflexed Curled or bent abruptly at more than a right angle

rhizome Underground or ground-level stem, lasting more than one season, often swollen

rosette Radiating cluster of leaves, usually lying close to the ground

runner Above-ground stem that roots at the nodes to form new plants

saprophyte Plant which lacks chlorophyll and lives by absorbing food from decaying organic matter

sepal See *calyx*

silicula Fruit of Cruciferae that is less than 3 times as long as wide

siliqua Fruit of Cruciferae that is more than 3 times as long as wide

simple Leaves that are not compound, or unbranched stems

spadix Erect tightly-packed spike of florets in the arum family

spathe Large bract (or pair of bracts) sometimes surrounding inflorescence, as in eg. in arum family

speculum Shiny, shield-like patch, eg. on the lip of *Ophrys* species

spike Simple elongated inflorescence with individual flowers unstalked

spur Hollow cylindrical projection from petal or sepal, usually containing nectar

stamen Male parts of a flower, made up of a stalk (filament) and pollen-containing anther

standard Uppermost petal of a pea-family flower

sterile Not producing fertile seeds or variable pollen

stigma Receptive surface of a style, to which pollen grains adhere

stipule Leaf-like or scale-like appendage at the base of a leaf stalk

stolon Short-lived creeping stem from the base of a rosette plant, usually above ground

style Part of the female organ linking the stigma to the ovary

ternate In 3 parts

thallus Plant body, if not clearly separated into leaf, stem etc.

trifoliate Leaf with 3 separate leaflets

tomentose Densely covered with short cottony hairs

tuber Swollen portion of stem or root, lasting less than 1 year

tubercle Wart-like swellings

umbel Umbrella-shaped inflorescence

whorled 3 or more organs (eg flowers or leaves) arising at the same point on the stem

wing Lateral petals of flower, especially in pea family

winged stem Stem with longitudinal narrow outgrowths

Dwarf Willow

a

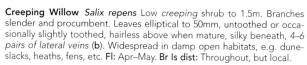

b

ORDER MAGNOLIIDAE (DICOTYLEDONS)

Major division of the angiosperms having two first leaves on the germinating seedling. Dicotyledons usually have net-veined leaves and flower parts in 4s or 5s.

WILLOW FAMILY Salicaceae

Deciduous trees or shrubs. Leaves simple and usually alternate. Flowers in catkins, dioecious (male and female on different plants). Seeds surrounded by long silky hairs, aiding wind dispersal.

Dwarf Willow *Salix herbacea* Dwarf under-shrub, prostrate and patch-forming to a few centimetres high with rhizomess. Leaves rounded to 20mm, *toothed* (**a**), shiny green above, slightly paler beneath and with *veins prominent on both sides*. Locally frequent on mountains and tundra. **Fl:** Jun–Jul. **Br Is dist:** Frequent on the higher mountains from N Wales northwards, down to 100m in N Scotland.

Creeping Willow *Salix repens* Low *creeping* shrub to 1.5m. Branches slender and procumbent. Leaves elliptical to 50mm, untoothed or occasionally slightly toothed, hairless above when mature, silky beneath, *4–6 pairs of lateral veins* (**b**). Widespread in damp open habitats, e.g. dune-slacks, heaths, fens, etc. **Fl:** Apr–May. **Br Is dist:** Throughout, but local.

BOG-MYRTLE FAMILY Myricaceae

Shrubs or trees, deciduous or evergreen. Leaves alternate, simple and aromatic. Flowers usually dioecious and in catkins. Fruit fleshy or a nut.

Bog-myrtle *Myrica gale* Deciduous shrub to 2.5m, suckering. Twigs red-brown. Leaves oblong-lanceolate, producing strong resinous smell when bruised. Male catkins reddish-brown, oblong; female catkins reddish, oval. Plants usually dioecious, but sometimes monoecious or hermaphrodite, and can change sex from year to year. Widely scattered in bogs, wet heaths and fens. **Fl:** Apr–May. **Br Is dist:** Widespread throughout, locally common in Ireland and from N Wales and N England to N Scotland, but rare or absent in many parts of S and C England and SE Scotland.

HOP FAMILY Cannabaceae

Dioecious herbs with leaves usually lobed. Female flowers unstalked with perianth undivided; male flowers stalked with perianth in 5 parts. Fruit an achene.

Hop *Humulus lupulus* Roughly hairy, climbing perennial, with annual, square aerial stems twining in a clockwise direction. Leaves long-stalked and deeply palmately divided into 3–5 coarsely toothed lobes. Male flowers greenish-yellow in panicles, female flowers pale green and in conical catkins. Widespread and common in woods, scrub and hedgerows. **Fl:** Jul–Aug. **Br Is dist:** Common. Introduced in Scotland and Ireland, but native in England and Wales; often an escape from cultivation where it is grown for brewing beer.

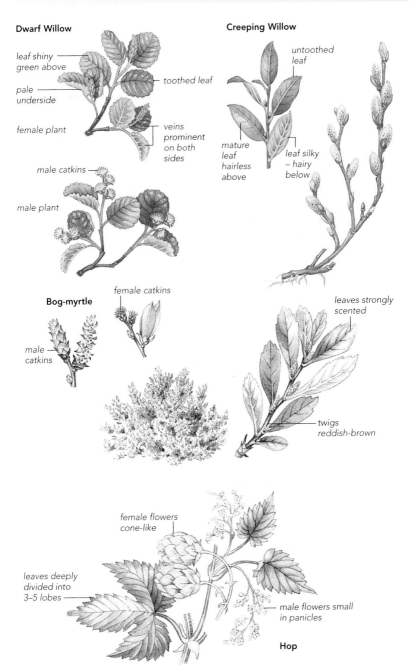

Dwarf Willow

leaf shiny green above

toothed leaf

pale underside

female plant

veins prominent on both sides

male catkins

male plant

Creeping Willow

untoothed leaf

mature leaf hairless above

leaf silky – hairy below

Bog-myrtle

female catkins

male catkins

leaves strongly scented

twigs reddish-brown

female flowers cone-like

leaves deeply divided into 3–5 lobes

male flowers small in panicles

Hop

Pellitory-of-the-wall

Mistletoe

Asarabacca

NETTLE FAMILY Urticaceae

Herbs with simple leaves, opposite or alternate, often with stinging hairs and stipules. Flowers unisexual, male and female on same (monoecious) or separate (dioecious) plants. Perianth with 4–5 parts. Fruit an achene.

Common Nettle *Urtica dioica* Coarsely hairy perennial with square stems and creeping rhizomatous yellow roots. Leaves to 80mm, pointed, toothed and in opposite pairs with sharp hairs which sting by releasing formic acid and histamine-like substances. *All leaves longer than their stalks (see* Small Nettle). Dioecious; male flowers in long drooping catkins, female in shorter heads. Widespread, common and often abundant. Prefers disturbed or enriched soils. **Fl:** Jun–Oct. **Br Is dist:** Common throughout.

Small Nettle *Urtica urens* Similar to Common Nettle, except that it is annual; the leaves are shorter to 40mm, but more deeply toothed, the *lower leaves shorter than their stalks*; monoecious. Widespread and common in gardens, waste areas and arable land. **Fl:** Jun–Oct. **Br Is dist:** Widespread and locally common; rare in W Scotland.

Pellitory-of-the-wall *Parietaria judaica* Spreading and *much-branched* perennial herb, softly hairy and with reddish stems. *Leaves to 50mm*, ovate, untoothed and alternate. Flowers in clusters on stems and leaf stalks, male and female separate within each cluster. Widespread and frequent near coasts, locally common inland on walls and hedge banks; a predominantly western species, absent from Scandinavia and the east. **Fl:** Jun–Oct. **Br Is dist:** Locally common; absent in N Scotland.

MISTLETOE FAMILY Viscaceae

Semi-parasitic small shrubs with opposite leaves and sticky berries.

Mistletoe *Viscum album* Rather woody, parasitic shrub to 1m, forming roundish clumps on tree branches when mature. Leaves leathery and in pairs, widest towards tip. Flowers dioecious. Fruit is a sticky white berry, ripening long after flowers. Locally common, becoming rarer in the north and absent from most of Scandinavia. Parasitic on a variety of deciduous trees, especially Apple, Poplar and Lime. **Fl:** Feb–Apr. **Br Is dist:** Locally frequent fom Yorkshire southwards; most frequent in the south.

BIRTHWORT FAMILY Aristolochiaceae

Herbs with alternate untoothed leaves, no stipules and flowers tubular due to tripartite perianth being united below. Fruit a capsule.

Asarabacca *Asarum europaeum* Distinctive evergreen perennial with a creeping, hairy stem. Dark green, kidney-shaped leaves, with a prominent network of veins; bell-shaped, purplish-red flowers, about 15mm long, ending in 3, pointed petal-like lobes. Locally common in woodland margins, grassy banks and scrub. **Fl:** May–Aug. **Br Is dist:** Native but rare and decreasing, with localities to S Scotland; also naturalised.

Birthwort *Aristolochia clematitis* Erect perennial to 80cm, tufted with unbranched stems. Leaves heart-shaped and deeply veined. Flowers in clusters at base of leaves, yellowish and tubular, 20–30mm long, with a smell of carrion and shape reminiscent of tiny Arum Lilies. Globose swelling at base of flower traps insects which aid pollination. Fruit pear-shaped. Formerly cultivated for medicinal aid in midwifery, and long naturalised in scattered localities; possibly native towards the south. **Fl:** Jun–Sep. **Br Is dist:** Rare and declining in widely scattered spots from S England to S Scotland.

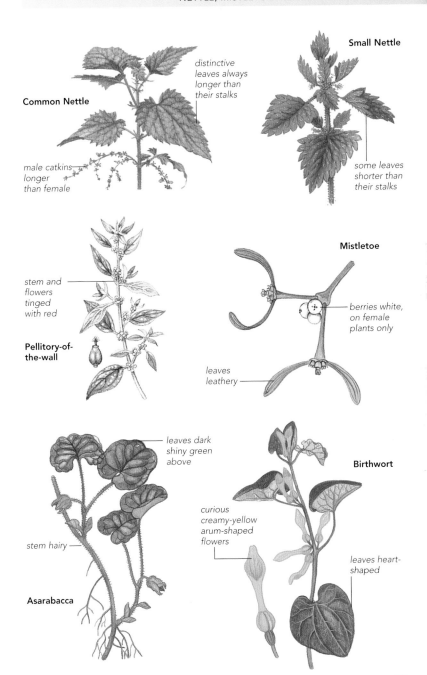

Small Nettle

distinctive leaves always longer than their stalks

Common Nettle

male catkins longer than female

some leaves shorter than their stalks

stem and flowers tinged with red

Pellitory-of-the-wall

Mistletoe

berries white, on female plants only

leaves leathery

leaves dark shiny green above

Birthwort

curious creamy-yellow arum-shaped flowers

leaves heart-shaped

stem hairy

Asarabacca

Alpine Bistort

a

KNOTWEED FAMILY Polygonaceae

Herbs with stipules usually united into a tubular membranous sheath (ochrea) around stem at base of leaf stalk; leaves usually alternate and flowers small with 3–6 petals or sepals and 6–9 stamens. Fruit a 3-angled or rounded nut.

Knotgrass *Polygonum aviculare* Spreading or erect, hairless annual with wiry stems and alternate lanceolate leaves. Can be to 2m tall but is usually much less. Leaves over 5mm wide, those on main stem obviously larger than those on branches. Ochreae silvery (brown below), about 5mm long, with few unbranched veins, *surrounding the leaf stalks*. Flowers pink and greenish, solitary or in clusters in leaf axils giving stem a knotted effect. Fruit completely covered by perianth. Widespread and common throughout; in a variety of open habitats. **Fl:** Jun–Nov. **Br Is dist:** Common throughout.

Water-pepper *Persicaria hydropiper* Erect, branched annual to 80cm, with narrow lanceolate leaves (10–25mm wide) and greenish or pinkish flowers arranged in slender spikes, nodding at the tip. Ochreae not fringed. Lower flowers in leaf axils never open. *Perianth segments covered in yellow glands* when viewed under lens (a). Fruit dull. Widespread and common almost throughout, but absent from the far north; in damp habitats or shallow water. **Fl:** Jul–Sep. **Br Is dist:** Common except in the far north.

Redshank *Persicaria maculosa* Erect or somewhat sprawling *hairless annual* to 70cm, branched and with stems reddish below and swollen at the leaf nodes. Leaves lanceolate, tapering to the base and usually with a dark central blotch. *Flowers pink* and in dense terminal or axillary spikes. Widespread and common in waste areas, arable or bare ground, damp places. **Fl:** Jun–Oct. **Br Is dist:** Common throughout.

Pale Persicaria *Persicaria lapathifolia* Similar to Redshank, but *rather hairy*, stems greenish, flower stalk with scattered yellowish glands and *flowers usually greenish-white* (rarely pink). **Fl:** Jun–Oct. **Br Is dist:** Common throughout.

Bistort *Persicaria bistorta* Erect and often patch-forming, unbranched, almost hairless perennial to 1m. Leaves triangular, the lower ones abruptly contracted into the long-winged leaf stalk; upper leaves almost stalkless and often arrow-shaped. Flowers pink in a dense cylindrical terminal spike. Widespread, common in some areas, rare in others; in damp grassland and meadows. **Fl:** Jun–Oct. **Br Is dist:** Locally common in the north, rare in the south.

Amphibious Bistort *Persicaria amphibia* Perennial to 75cm with 2 distinct forms: (1) aquatic form hairless with floating stem and leaves, the latter truncate at the base; (2) land form with erect stem and roughly hairy leaves narrowed and rounded at the base. Both forms have deep pink flowers in dense oval terminal spike. Widespread and frequent; aquatic form in ponds and ditches, land form on riverbanks, in damp grassland and sometimes arable or waste areas. **Fl:** Jul–Sep. **Br Is dist:** Widespread and locally frequent.

Alpine Bistort *Persicaria vivipara* Erect unbranched hairless perennial to 30cm. Leaves narrow lanceolate, lower ones tapering at the base into unwinged stalk, the upper ones unstalked; leaf margin downturned. Flowers white or pale pink, in slender terminal spikes, but flowers in the lower part of the spike replaced by purplish bulbils which are a means of vegetative propagation. Locally frequent in mountain grassland, to 2,000m. **Fl:** Jun–Aug. **Br Is dist:** Locally frequent from N Wales northwards; rare in W Ireland.

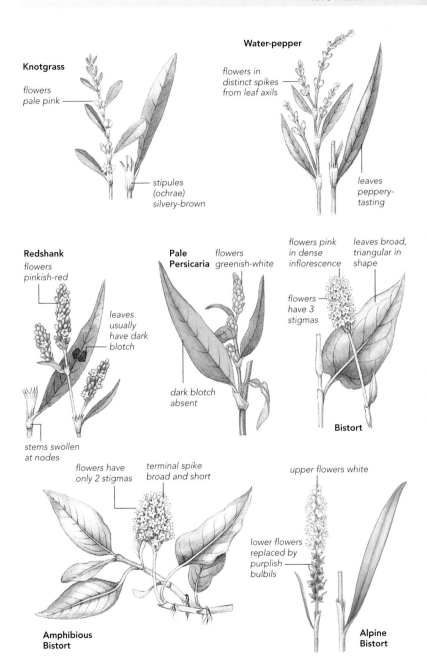

Knotgrass

flowers pale pink

stipules (ochrae) silvery-brown

Water-pepper

flowers in distinct spikes from leaf axils

leaves peppery-tasting

Redshank

flowers pinkish-red

leaves usually have dark blotch

stems swollen at nodes

Pale Persicaria

flowers greenish-white

dark blotch absent

flowers pink in dense inflorescence

leaves broad, triangular in shape

flowers have 3 stigmas

Bistort

flowers have only 2 stigmas

terminal spike broad and short

Amphibious Bistort

upper flowers white

lower flowers replaced by purplish bulbils

Alpine Bistort

Mountain Sorrel

Black-bindweed *Fallopia convolvulus* Annual, clockwise-twining plant, prostrate or climbing to 1.2m. Stem angular. Leaves heart- or arrow-shaped, pointed and rather mealy beneath. Flowers greenish-white or greenish-pink in loose spikes arising from leaf axils. Fruit a dull black triangular nut on *short stalk to 3mm*. Differs from the true bindweeds (*see* p. 220–22) in twining clockwise and having angular stems. Widespread and common throughout; in arable and waste areas. **Fl**: Jul–Oct. **Br Is dist**: Common throughout.

Japanese Knotweed *Fallopia japonica* Tall, rampant perennial to 2m, often forming extensive thickets. Stems reddish or bluish-green, rather zigzagging. *Leaves broadly triangular*, pointed and abruptly truncated at the base. Flowers whitish in loose branched spikes from axils of upper leaves. Introduced to Europe as a garden plant in the 19th century. Now widely naturalised and a serious pest on riverbanks, roadsides, railway embankments, etc. **Fl**: Sep–Oct. **Br Is dist**: Common throughout.

Mountain Sorrel *Oxyria digyna* Erect hairless stout perennial to 30cm. Stem almost leafless. Basal *leaves rounded and kidney-shaped*. Flowers greenish with red edges in loose branched spikes. Outer perianth segments 4. Fruit flat and broadly winged. Locally common in damp rocky places or streamsides in mountains, descending to low altitudes in Arctic and sub-Arctic areas. **Fl**: Jul–Aug. **Br Is dist**: Locally common in Scottish mountains; rare in N Wales, Cumbria and W Ireland.

DOCKS *Rumex* These differ from *Polygonum* and *Persicaria* in having branched spikes of flowers with 6 (as opposed to 5) outer perianth segments in 2 whorls, the outer tiny and thin, the inner enlarging and hardening to form the so-called 'valves' which envelop the fruit. Features of the valves, notably the presence or absence of teeth and tubercles (warts), are an important part of identification, for which a hand lens is needed.

Common Sorrel *Rumex acetosa* Variable erect perennial to 1m (usually less). Leaves lanceolate, *arrow-shaped at the base;* basal leaves long-stalked, upper leaves unstalked and clasping the stem. Flowers dioecious and reddish. Widespread and common in grassy places. **Fl**: May–Jun. **Br Is dist**: Common throughout.

Sheep's Sorrel *Rumex acetosella* Variable erect perennial, differing from Common Sorrel in being shorter, to 30cm. Differs also in having *basal lobes of leaves spreading or forward-pointing*, and upper leaves stalked and not clasping the stem. Flowers greenish in loose panicles. Widespread and common on well-drained acid soils, heaths and sand-dunes. **Fl**: May–Aug. **Br Is dist**: Common throughout. 2 subspecies are recognised: ssp *acetosella* Perianth segments form a loose covering around fruit, and are easily separated by rolling between fingers. Ssp *pyrenaicus* Perianth segments not easily separated from fruit.

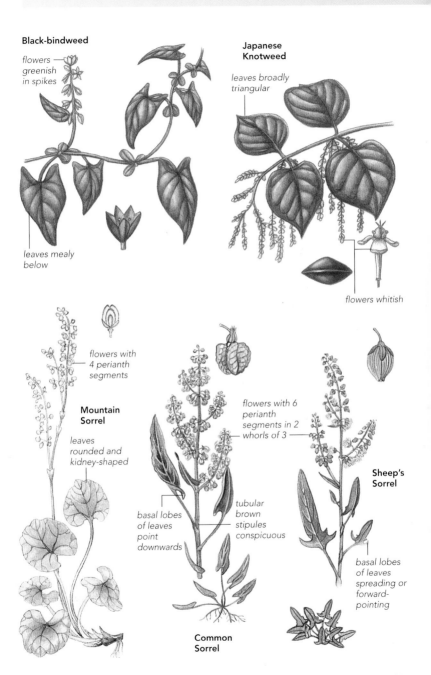

Black-bindweed

flowers greenish in spikes

leaves mealy below

Japanese Knotweed

leaves broadly triangular

flowers whitish

flowers with 4 perianth segments

Mountain Sorrel

leaves rounded and kidney-shaped

flowers with 6 perianth segments in 2 whorls of 3

basal lobes of leaves point downwards

tubular brown stipules conspicuous

Sheep's Sorrel

basal lobes of leaves spreading or forward-pointing

Common Sorrel

31

Water Dock *Rumex hydrolapathum* Very tall erect perennial to 2m. Basal leaves leathery and lanceolate, *very long* to 1m and tapering to *short stalk*. Flowers in dense whorls in much-branched inflorescence, leafy below. Fruit perianth segments with an elongated tubercle on each side (a). Frequent in wet habitats: marshes, ditches, rivers, streams, canals, etc; absent from the far north. **Fl:** Jul–Sep. **Br Is dist:** Locally frequent; rare in Scotland.

Scottish Dock

Scottish Dock *Rumex aquaticus* Similar to Water Dock, but basal leaves *long-stalked* and *triangular with a broad base*, and fruit has *no tubercles* (b). Local by lake and streamside; mainly in the east. **Fl:** Jul–Aug. **Br Is dist:** Found only by Loch Lomond.

Curled Dock *Rumex crispus* Variable erect perennial to 1m. Leaves to 30cm, oblong-lanceolate with *markedly wavy edges*. Flower spikes branched and dense. Valves untoothed and *each with a tubercle*, often 1 larger than the others on plants by the sea. Ubiquitous as a common weed of waste areas, arable land and roadsides. **Fl:** Jun–Oct. **Br Is dist:** Very common throughout.

Shore Dock

Wood Dock *Rumex sanguineus* Like Curled Dock, but with leaf margins not strongly wavy, and sometimes red-veined. Flower spikes not leafy except lower down, and *only 1 fruit valve possessing a swollen tubercle* (c). Widespread and often common in grassy places and woodland margins; absent from most of Scandinavia. **Fl:** Jun–Oct. **Br Is dist:** Common northwards to mid-Scotland.

Fiddle Dock

Shore Dock *Rumex rupestris* Recognisable by its *blunt greyish leaves*, erect branches and *inflorescence leafy only at the base*. Local in a variety of coastal habitats, from rocky shores to dune-slacks. **Fl:**. 6–Aug. **Br Is dist:** Very local in SW England and S Wales.

Fiddle Dock *Rumex pulcher* Low, *spreading* perennial plant to 50cm, *branches making a wide angle with the main stem* to give a characteristic appearance. Lower leaves small, to 10cm (but usually less), and *waisted* to give a violin shape (**d1**). Branches often tangled in fruit. Fruit valves toothed and all with tubercles (**d2**). Very local on well-drained soils in open grassy places, often near the coast; absent from the north and east. **Fl:** Jun–Aug. **Br Is dist:** Local by the coast in S and SE England and Wales.

Broad-leaved Dock *Rumex obtusifolius* Stout erect perennial to 1m, with large lower leaves to 25cm, *heart-shaped at the base* and often with a slightly wavy edge. Branched flower spikes leafy below. *Fruit valves with several long teeth*, and at least 1 with a tubercle. Widespread and very common in a variety of habitats, particularly farmed areas where there is nitrogen enrichment. **Fl:** Jun–Oct. **Br Is dist:** Very common throughout.

a

b   c

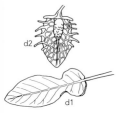

d2

d1

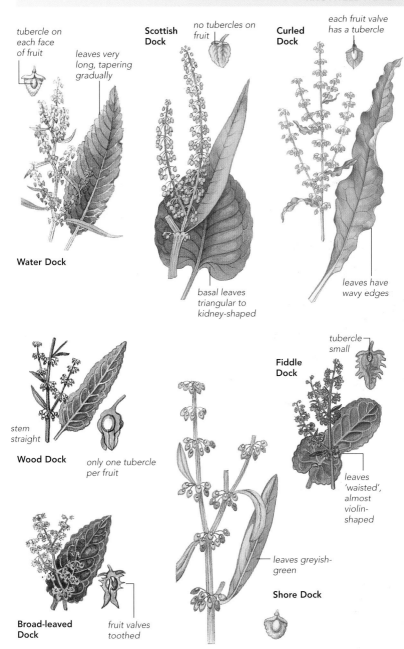

tubercle on each face of fruit

leaves very long, tapering gradually

Water Dock

Scottish Dock

no tubercles on fruit

basal leaves triangular to kidney-shaped

Curled Dock

each fruit valve has a tubercle

leaves have wavy edges

stem straight

Wood Dock

only one tubercle per fruit

Fiddle Dock

tubercle small

leaves 'waisted', almost violin-shaped

leaves greyish-green

Shore Dock

Broad-leaved Dock

fruit valves toothed

Marsh Dock *Rumex palustris* Erect branched annual or biennial to 70cm, with spreading branches and lanceolate pointed leaves. Flower spikes consist of dense whorls of flowers, leafy throughout. Plant a characteristic yellow-brown colour in fruit, and *fruit valves have long bristle-like teeth* in addition to a tubercle, *the teeth shorter than the valves* (a). Local on the bare mud of lakesides and rivers. **Fl:** Jun–Sep. **Br Is dist:** Very local in the south, otherwise rare northwards to Yorkshire.

Marsh Dock

Golden Dock *Rumex maritimus* Erect annual similar to Marsh Dock, but *golden yellow in fruit* and *bristle-like teeth on fruit valves longer than the valves* (b). Widespread but local in similar habitats to Marsh Dock; not only near the sea but also far inland. **Fl:** Jun–Sep. **Br Is dist:** Local in C and S England; rare elsewhere and extending northwards to S Scotland. Very local in Ireland.

GOOSEFOOT FAMILY Chenopodiaceae

A variable family of herbs usually growing on open ground, with the common features of tiny, usually greenish, 3- to 5-lobed flowers. Goosefoots (*Chenopodium*) and oraches (*Atriplex, see* pp. 36–8) are usually annuals with alternate, often mealy, leaves. Oraches have male and female flowers on separate plants. In goosefoots they occur on the same plant. Oraches have fruits surrounded by 2 swollen bracts, goosefoots by 3–5 sepals. Glassworts (*Salicornia, see* p. 38) are succulent with indistinct leaves.

Beet

Beet *Beta vulgaris* Erect or sprawling perennial to 1m with red-striped stems and shiny dark green, untoothed and leathery leaves. Basal leaves triangular and wavy, upper stem leaves oblong. Flowers green, in dense, leafy and often branched spikes. Perianth often becomes prickly in fruit, several fruits sticking together as a result. Locally common on sea-cliffs, shingle and edges of salt-marshes. **Fl:** Jun–Sep. **Br Is dist:** Frequent on coasts in the south, much more local in the north.

GOOSEFOOTS *Chenopodium* Recognised by their alternate often mealy leaves and perianth with 2–5 segments. Annuals except for Good-King-Henry. Flowers small, in clusters. Lower leaf shapes (left) help separate species.

Good-King-Henry *Chenopodium bonus-henricus* Erect branched perennial with stiff *stems often streaked red*. Leaves mealy at first, later *dark green. Lower leaves triangular*, to 10cm (c). Frequent in waste areas, arable land, on old walls and hedge banks. **Fl:** May–Aug. **Br Is dist:** Introduced and naturalised; locally frequent.

Red Goosefoot *Chenopodium rubrum* A variable fleshy plant, erect or sprawling to 60cm and often tinged red. Leaves to 60mm, *not mealy but shiny*, variably diamond-shaped and coarsely toothed (d). Locally common in waste areas, arable land, dried pond margins and marshes. **Fl:** Jul–Sep. **Br Is dist:** Common in S England; rare in the north, Wales and Ireland.

Many-seeded Goosefoot *Chenopodium polyspermum* Spreading or erect, to 60cm, not usually mealy (except sometimes underleaves) with *stems square* and usually red. Leaves to 80mm, *untoothed* (occasionally asymmetric basal tooth) (e). Locally common in waste areas and arable land. **Fl:** Jul–Oct. **Br Is dist:** Locally abundant in England; rare elsewhere.

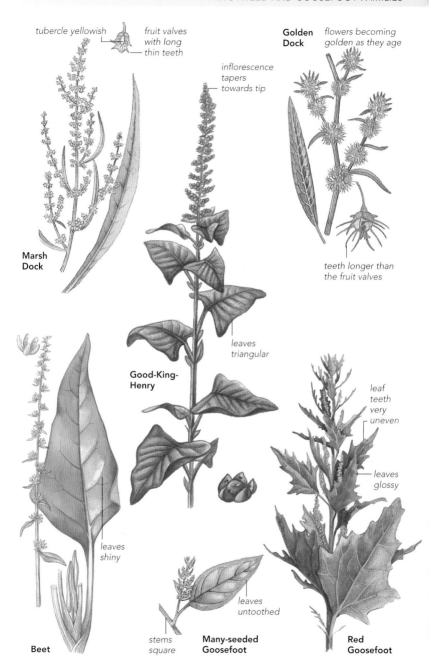

tubercle yellowish

fruit valves with long thin teeth

Golden Dock

flowers becoming golden as they age

inflorescence tapers towards tip

Marsh Dock

teeth longer than the fruit valves

leaves triangular

Good-King-Henry

leaf teeth very uneven

leaves glossy

leaves shiny

stems square

Many-seeded Goosefoot

leaves untoothed

Red Goosefoot

Beet

35

Stinking Goosefoot *Chenopodium vulvaria* Erect or prostrate, branched, grey and mealy plant to 30cm. Leaves diamond-shaped, to 30mm, with a pair of basal lobes (**a**). *Plant smells strongly of rotten fish when bruised.* Very local in waste areas, coastal bare places. **Fl:** Jul–Sep. **Br Is dist:** S England, very rare.

Stinking Goosefoot

Nettle-leaved Goosefoot *Chenopodium murale* Erect, *slightly mealy plant* to 70cm. *Leaves rarely turn red* and have coarse irregular forward-pointing teeth, reminiscent of nettle leaves (**b**). Inflorescence spreading with flower spikes leafy at the top, and short branches (compare with Fat-hen, which can have similar leaves). Locally frequent in waste areas, sand-dunes, arable land on sandy soils. **Fl:** Jul–Oct. **Br Is dist:** Scattered and local in England and Wales; casual elsewhere.

Nettle-leaved Goosefoot

Fat-hen *Chenopodium album* Tall, erect, *deep green* and rather *mealy plant* to 1m. Stems stiff and *often streaked red*. Leaves ovate or *diamond-shaped*, to 80mm, coarsely and bluntly toothed (**c**). Common in arable and waste areas. **Fl:** Jul–Oct. **Br Is dist:** Common throughout.

ORACHES *Atriplex* Annuals similar to goosefoots with alternate leaves and inconspicuous flowers in spikes; male and female flowers separate, with female flowers surrounded by a pair of bracts which swell in fruit. Leaves have strong lateral veins. Diagrams are of lower leaves.

a

Grass-leaved Orache *Atriplex littoralis* Erect plant to 1m, with ridged stems and linear leaves 20–30 times longer than broad, untoothed or slightly toothed (**d1**). Bract triangular, entire or toothed (**d2**). Common on bare muddy ground near the sea. **Fl:** Jul–Oct. **Br Is dist:** Locally common on the coast of England and Wales; local in Scotland and Ireland.

b

Common Orache *Atriplex patula* Very variable, much-branched plant, erect or more often prostrate, to 60cm. Stems ridged and often reddish. Leaves mealy, the lower ones usually diamond-shaped or arrow-shaped and coarsely toothed (**e1**), the upper ones narrow, linear and slightly toothed. Lower leaves have *basal teeth forward-pointing*. Greenish flowers in long spikes either from leaf axils or terminal. *Bracts diamond-shaped, untoothed, or slightly, toothed* (**e2**). Common in waste areas inland or by the sea. **Fl:** Jul–Sep. **Br Is dist:** Common throughout.

c

Babington's Orache *Atriplex glabriuscula* Usually prostrate, mealy plant, very similar to Common Orache, with reddish stems, but plant to only 20cm long, basal leaves less toothed (**f1**), bracts thick, diamond-shaped (**f2**) and united to half-way up, *silvery white when fruit is ripe*. Widespread on coastal shingle. **Fl:** Jul–Oct. **Br Is dist:** Frequent throughout on the coast.

d1 d2

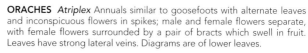

e1 e2

f1 f2

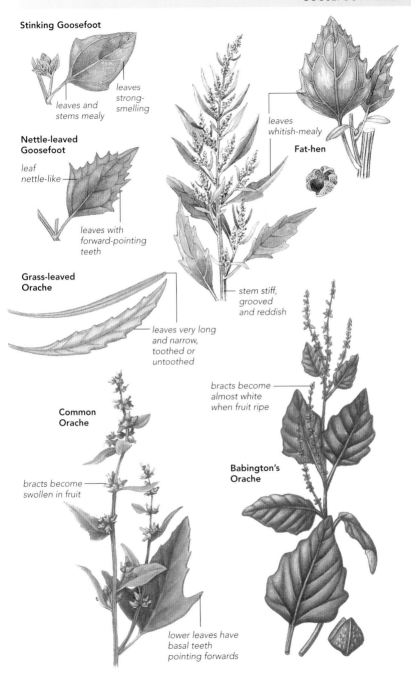

Stinking Goosefoot

leaves and stems mealy

leaves strong-smelling

Nettle-leaved Goosefoot

leaf nettle-like

leaves with forward-pointing teeth

leaves whitish-mealy

Fat-hen

Grass-leaved Orache

leaves very long and narrow, toothed or untoothed

stem stiff, grooved and reddish

bracts become almost white when fruit ripe

Common Orache

bracts become swollen in fruit

Babington's Orache

lower leaves have basal teeth pointing forwards

37

Sea-purslane

Halimione These differ from oraches in that the bracts do not swell in fruit, are united almost totally and leaves have lateral veins less obvious than central vein.

Sea-purslane *Atriplex portulacoides* Mealy spreading perennial under-shrub to 1m, with woody brown stems and lower leaves opposite, untoothed. Flowers are yellowish-green, in interrupted branched spike; fruit unstalked. Widespread and frequent on the drier parts of coastal salt-marshes; absent from the far north. **Fl:** Jul–Oct. **Br Is dist:** Common in England and Wales; rare in Scotland and Ireland.

GLASSWORTS *Sarcocornia* and *Salicornia* A very distinctive group of succulent herbs with slender finger-like segmented branches and stems, with indistinct leaves and flowers.

Common Glasswort, Marsh Samphire *Salicornia europaea* To 40cm, bright green but flushed red when flowering. *Fruiting segments only slightly swollen*, joints not waisted. Scarious margin at apex of segment fairly inconspicuous. Coastal mud or sand; upper salt-marshes. **Fl:** Aug–Sep. **Br Is dist:** Locally common. Glaucous, matt-green plants are sometimes called *Salicornia obscura*.

Annual Sea-blite *Suaeda maritima* Succulent annual to 50cm with pros-trate or ascending stems, and distinct, rather *pointed, alternate, fleshy leaves* ranging from bluish green to purplish red; leaves slightly *concave above in cross-section*. Flowers tiny, green, 1–3 together in axils of upper leaves. Common in muddy salt-marshes. **Fl:** Jul–Oct. **Br Is dist:** Common on coasts.

Prickly Saltwort *Salsola kali* ssp *kali* Semi-prostrate prickly annual to 60cm. Stems markedly branched with pale green or reddish stripes, often rough to touch. Leaves succulent, rather flattened and abruptly narrowed at the tip into a short spine. Flowers solitary in leaf axils. Widespread and frequent on sandy shores near drift-line; occasionally inland on waste areas and sides of regularly salted roads. **Fl:** Jul– Sep. **Br Is dist:** Frequent all round the coasts.

BLINKS FAMILY Portulacaceae
Annual or perennial herbs, sometimes rather fleshy. Flowers are hermaph-rodite, always with only 2 opposite sepals (in contrast to Caryophyllaceae, *see* p. 34) and 3–6 petals (usually 5). Fruit is a capsule.

Blinks *Montia fontana* Very variable but often inconspicuous, tiny pale green plant (often patch-forming) with stems often reddish, and narrow oval opposite leaves. Flowers tiny, white and in small loose clusters with stalks lengthening when in fruit. Widespread and fre-quent on bare or damp ground, or submerged in water. **Fl:** May–Oct. **Br Is dist:** Frequent throughout. Several subspecies described.

Springbeauty *Claytonia perfoliata* Short hairless annual, 10–30cm, char-acterised by rather fleshy stem leaves being fused in a pair surrounding the stem, and with small white flowers in a cluster just above them. Flowers 5–8mm with 5 white petals, un-notched or hardly notched. Introduced from N America, and now widespread on bare sandy soils. **Fl:** May–Jul. **Br Is dist:** Scattered and often abundant throughout.

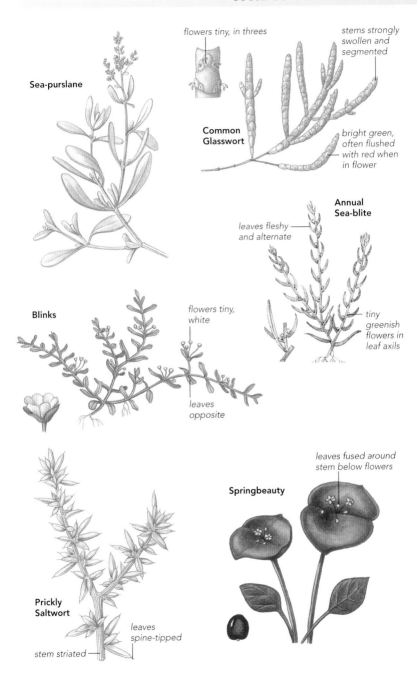

Sea-purslane

flowers tiny, in threes

stems strongly swollen and segmented

Common Glasswort

bright green, often flushed with red when in flower

Annual Sea-blite

leaves fleshy and alternate

tiny greenish flowers in leaf axils

Blinks

flowers tiny, white

leaves opposite

leaves fused around stem below flowers

Springbeauty

Prickly Saltwort

leaves spine-tipped

stem striated

39

Pink Purslane *Claytonia sibirica* Annual or perennial to 15–40cm, with opposite unstalked and distinctly veined stem leaves and long-stalked basal leaves. Flowers 15–20mm in diameter, 5 notched petals, pink with darker veins. Introduced from N America, very widespread; often abundant in damp, shady places. **Fl:** Apr–Jul. **Br Is dist:** Naturalised almost throughout.

Fringed Sandwort

PINK FAMILY Caryophyllaceae

A large and diverse family of plants, all characterised by having flowering shoots repeatedly forked, 4–5 pink or whitish petals and, unlike purslanes, 4–5 sepals which may be free or fused into a tube. Stems have a characteristic swelling at their junction with the usually opposite and untoothed leaves. Fruit is usually a capsule, rarely a berry.

SANDWORTS These are often small or slender plants. Most have white flowers with 5 unnotched petals, ununited sepals and 3 styles, the exceptions being Cyphel and Sea Sandwort which have greenish-white flowers. There are four main genera: *Arenaria*, *Moehringia*, *Minuartia* and *Honkenya*.

Spring Sandwort

Fringed Sandwort *Arenaria ciliata* Similar to Arctic Sandwort, but stems rough to the touch, and prostrate then ascending. *Leaves very obviously single-veined*, and with hairs on the lower margins. Flowers to 16mm with white anthers; sepals hairy. Very local to rare on calcareous soils in mountains. **Fl:** Jul–Aug. **Br Is dist:** Found in 1 locality at Ben Bulben in Ireland.

Three-nerved Sandwort *Moehringia trinervia* Weak often straggling annual to 40cm with *petals shorter than sepals* like Common Chickweed (*see* p. 42), but unlike that plant it has *stems hairy all round, leaves 3- to 5-veined* and petals undivided. Flowers about 6mm in diameter. Widespread and frequent in woods and hedge banks. **Fl:** Apr–Jul. **Br Is dist:** Frequent throughout, especially in ancient semi-natural woodlands on rich soils.

Cyphel

Spring Sandwort *Minuartia verna* Low, loose, cushion-forming perennial 5–15cm tall. Leaves 3-veined, flowers 6–8mm with purplish anthers and petals slightly longer than sepals. Similar to Knotted Pearlwort (*see* p. 46), but the latter has petals twice as long as sepals and 5 styles. Very local in dry grassy or rocky places, especially on limestone or spoil from old lead workings. **Fl:** May–Oct. **Br Is dist:** Very local scattered localities in W and N Britain, with a few localities in Ireland.

Cyphel *Minuartia sedoides* Dense and compact, cushion-forming perennial with crowded fleshy leaves, to 15mm, and greenish-yellow flowers, 4–5mm in diameter, which often lack petals. Local on damp mountain ledges. **Fl:** Jun–Aug. **Br Is dist:** Local in Scottish Highlands and Islands.

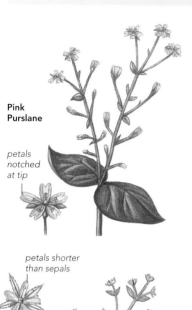

Pink Purslane

petals notched at tip

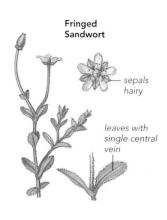

Fringed Sandwort

sepals hairy

leaves with single central vein

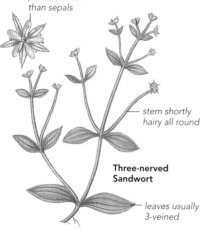

petals shorter than sepals

Three-nerved Sandwort

stem shortly hairy all round

leaves usually 3-veined

petals broad, not notched; slightly longer than sepals

Spring Sandwort

Cyphel

leaves very crowded on stems

41

Marsh Stitchwort

STITCHWORTS and CHICKWEEDS *Stellaria* Annual or perennial herbs with white flowers that have petals cleft so deeply that there appears to be twice the number, 5 sepals and 3 styles. Capsules oval. (Mouse-ears usually have 5 styles and cylindrical capsules.)

Common Chickweed *Stellaria media* Prostrate or semi-prostrate annual to 40cm with *stems hairy on alternate sides between leaf nodes.* Lower leaves long-stalked, upper almost unstalked. Flowers 5–10mm in diameter, petals equalling sepals and with *3–8 red-violet stamens.* Widespread, very common and often abundant on disturbed or waste ground. **Fl:** Jan–Dec. **Br Is dist:** Very common throughout.

Greater Stitchwort *Stellaria holostea* Perennial to 60cm, with weak square stems, rough at the angles; leaves rigid with a characteristic lanceolate shape tapering from a broadish base to a fine point. *Leaf edges and midrib very rough.* Flowers 18–30mm in diameter, petals divided to half-way and twice as long as sepals. Widespread and common in woodlands and hedgerows on all except very acid soils. **Fl:** Apr–Jun. **Br Is dist:** Common throughout.

Lesser Stitchwort *Stellaria graminea* Similar to Greater Stitchwort, but has smooth stems, *leaves with smooth edges* and flowers only 5–18mm in diameter, with petals divided to more than half-way, and stamens often grey-violet. Widespread and common on acid soils, heathy grassland and open woods. **Fl:** May–Aug. **Br Is dist:** Common throughout.

Marsh Stitchwort *Stellaria palustris* Similar to Greater Stitchwort but stems smooth at the angles, *leaves greyish green* and smooth-edged, and *bracts with a broad membranous margin.* Flowers terminal, 12–20mm in diameter, and stamens often blackish violet or reddish. Local to locally frequent in marshes and fens, often supported by tall vegetation. **Fl:** May–Aug. **Br Is dist:** Local and decreasing; scattered throughout except N Scotland.

MOUSE-EARS *Cerastium* Similar plants to stitchworts and chickweeds but usually much more hairy, and flowers usually have 5 instead of 3 styles. Leaves always unstalked. Capsules are cylindrical, not ovoid. Petal length in relation to sepals helps to separate species.

Field Mouse-ear *Cerastium arvense* Rather variable perennial to 30cm, slightly hairy and with flowers 12–20mm in diameter. The only lowland *Cerastium* species with such large flowers and relatively tall height. Widespread but often very local in dry grassland, especially on calcareous soils. **Fl:** Apr–Aug. **Br Is dist:** Locally common in E England; much more local or rare elsewhere.

Alpine Mouse-ear *Cerastium alpinum* Low, mat-forming, greyish-green perennial, noticeable for the *long white hairs on leaves and stem*, and large white flowers 18–25mm in diameter. Leaves broadest above middle, *bracts with narrow membranous margins* and petals deeply cleft. On rock ledges in mountains, to 2,500m. **Fl:** Jun–Aug. Ssp *lanatum* is white woolly due to a dense cover of hairs; occurs throughout the range of Alpine Mouse-ear in Europe. **Br Is dist:** Local in N Wales, NW England and Scottish Highlands.

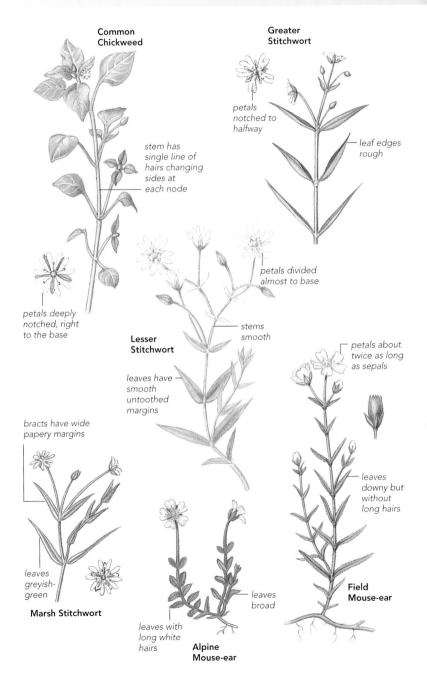

Common Chickweed

stem has single line of hairs changing sides at each node

petals deeply notched, right to the base

Greater Stitchwort

petals notched to halfway

leaf edges rough

petals divided almost to base

stems smooth

Lesser Stitchwort

leaves have smooth untoothed margins

petals about twice as long as sepals

leaves downy but without long hairs

bracts have wide papery margins

leaves greyish-green

Marsh Stitchwort

leaves with long white hairs

leaves broad

Alpine Mouse-ear

Field Mouse-ear

43

Sea Mouse-ear

Upright Chickweed

Water Chickweed

a1   a2

b

Common Mouse-ear *Cerastium fontanum* Very variable hairy green or greyish-green perennial, at first glance similar to Common Chickweed (*see* p. 42) but stiffer and with *longer petals in relation to sepals*. Both non-flowering and longer flowering shoots present, the latter to 45cm tall but usually much shorter. Leaves to 25mm, densely covered with whitish non-glandular hairs. Flowers small, in loose clusters, with petals deeply cleft. Widespread and common in a variety of grassy places and disturbed ground, with several different varieties described for certain habitats. **Fl:** Apr–Nov. **Br Is dist:** Common throughout.

Sticky Mouse-ear *Cerastium glomeratum* Short yellowish-green rather *glandular-hairy* and sticky annual to 45cm, with characteristic *compact heads of flowers*. Sepals hairy to tip (**a1**); bract with hairy margin (**a2**). Upper stem leaves rather broadly ovate. Flower stalks remain short in fruit, not exceeding sepals. Fruit stalk never drooping. Widespread almost throughout, and common in a variety of dry or bare places. **Fl:** Apr–Oct. **Br Is dist:** Common throughout.

Little Mouse-ear *Cerastium semidecandrum* Low, *glandular,* hairy and sticky annual 1–20cm tall. *Bracts with broad transparent margins* (**b**). Flowers 5–7mm in diameter, with 5 stamens and styles, and petals only slightly notched. Fruit stalks drooping initially, then erect, exceeding sepals. Locally common on dry or bare sandy ground. **Fl:** Apr–Jun. **Br Is dist:** Locally common throughout, but mainly coastal in Ireland.

Sea Mouse-ear *Cerastium diffusum* Densely *glandular* and sticky annual with prostrate or ascending stems 5–30cm tall. Upper leaves and *bracts dark green, the latter without transparent margins*. Flowers 3–6mm in diameter, usually with *parts in 4s* or occasionally 5s and with petals cleft to no more than a quarter of their length. Fruit stalk drooping initially, then erect, exceeding sepals. Locally common in dry places usually near the coast, but occasionally inland especially on old railway tracks. **Fl:** Apr–Jul. **Br Is dist:** Locally common all around the coast, much more local inland.

Upright Chickweed *Moenchia erecta* Usually tiny annual, but sometimes to 12cm tall, with a characteristic waxy grey colour to the leaves. *Flowers with 4 white petals, not cleft,* and only opening in very sunny conditions. Sepals white-edged, slightly longer than petals. Rare or locally common in dry grasslands, often on sandy or gravelly soils. **Fl:** Apr–Jun. **Br Is dist:** Very local in S England and S Wales.

Water Chickweed *Myosoton aquaticum* Rather straggling perennial with prostrate overwintering stems from which the flowering shoots arise to 1m tall. Leaves characteristic, *broadly heart-shaped and opposite,* the upper ones unstalked and somewhat wavy edge. Flowers in loose clusters, white with *petals cleft to base and much longer than sepals*. Widespread in damp grassy places by streamsides, ditches, woodland margins, marshes and similar habitats. **Fl:** Jun–Oct. **Br Is dist:** Locally frequent in England and Wales, especially in the south.

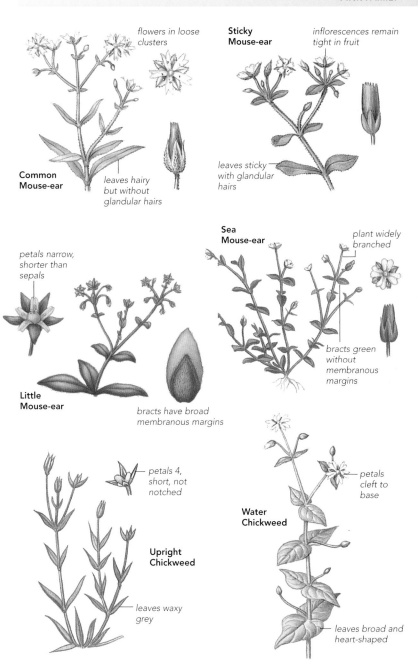

flowers in loose clusters

Sticky Mouse-ear

inflorescences remain tight in fruit

Common Mouse-ear

leaves hairy but without glandular hairs

leaves sticky with glandular hairs

petals narrow, shorter than sepals

Sea Mouse-ear

plant widely branched

Little Mouse-ear

bracts have broad membranous margins

bracts green without membranous margins

petals 4, short, not notched

Water Chickweed

petals cleft to base

Upright Chickweed

leaves waxy grey

leaves broad and heart-shaped

45

Sea Pearlwort

Coral-necklace

Four-leaved Allseed

PEARLWORTS *Sagina* Characterised by small size, short awl-shaped fleshy leaves without stipules, most with entire white petals (minute in some species, absent in others) and 4–5 styles.

Knotted Pearlwort *Sagina nodosa* Perennial to 15cm, and characterised by a *knotted feel to the stem* caused by tufts of shorter leaves at the leaf junctions. The largest-flowered pearlwort (flowers to 10mm in diameter) and *the only one with petals twice as long as sepals*. Can be confused with Spring Sandwort (*see* p. 40) but distinguished by knotted feel to stems and 5 styles, not 3. Locally frequent in damp sandy ground, heaths or mountain habitats. **Fl:** Jul–Sep. **Br Is dist:** Local but most frequent in the west and north.

Procumbent Pearlwort *Sagina procumbens* Low mat-forming perennial with *central non-flowering leaf rosette* from which arise *numerous creeping stems* rooting at intervals and from which ascend the erect flowering stalks. Leaves long-awned, with non-hairy edges (**a**). Widespread and very common in a variety of damp bare places, ranging from lawns to walls. **Fl:** May–Sep. **Br Is dist:** Common Throughout.

Sea Pearlwort *Sagina maritima* Annual often with central leaf rosette and *fleshy blunt leaves* (**b**). Sepals purple-edged, not spreading in fruit. Locally common in bare open habitats such as dune-slacks and cliffs, usually near the sea but occasionally inland. **Fl:** May– Sep. **Br Is dist:** Local on the coast; rare in Scottish Highlands.

Annual Knawel *Scleranthus annuus* Small, rather wiry or spiky-looking greyish annual or biennial, to 10cm high. Leaves linear and pointed, united in opposite pairs around stem. Flowers minute, in terminal or axillary clusters and with 5 *pointed green sepals* with *very narrow white border*, but no petals. Widespread and locally frequent in dry sandy or arable areas. **Fl:** May–Oct. **Br Is dist:** Local to locally frequent throughout.

Smooth Rupturewort *Herniaria glabra* Low, prostrate, bright green annual or biennial, with shoots to 20cm long, *hairless or slightly hairy all round*. Leaves to 10mm, elliptical and usually hairless. Flowers about 2mm in diameter, with 5 minute green petals, shorter than sepals. Sepals not hairy. Fruit pointed, much longer than sepals. Local to locally frequent in bare chalky or sandy soils. **Fl:** May–Sep. **Br Is dist:** Rare in Breckland and elsewhere in E England.

Coral-necklace *Illecebrum verticillatum* Low, prostrate, hairless annual with square pinkish stems up to 20cm long, bearing bright green, oval, opposite leaves which have basal clusters of tiny, bright white flowers. Sepals 5, thick, corky and hooded; petals minute. Very local on damp sandy or gravelly soils, especially if seasonally flooded, and sometimes on sandy margins of ponds. **Fl:** Jun–Oct. **Br Is dist:** Very rare in S and SW England; rarely naturalised elsewhere.

Four-leaved Allseed *Polycarpon tetraphyllum* Small much-branched annual to 15cm with oval leaves stalked and grouped in 4s and 2s. Flowers in branched heads, tiny, whitish and with 5 white petals which soon fall and 5 longer, white-edged sepals. Local in sandy ground, often by the sea. **Fl:** Jun–Aug. **Br Is dist:** Very rare in SW England and local in Channel Isles.

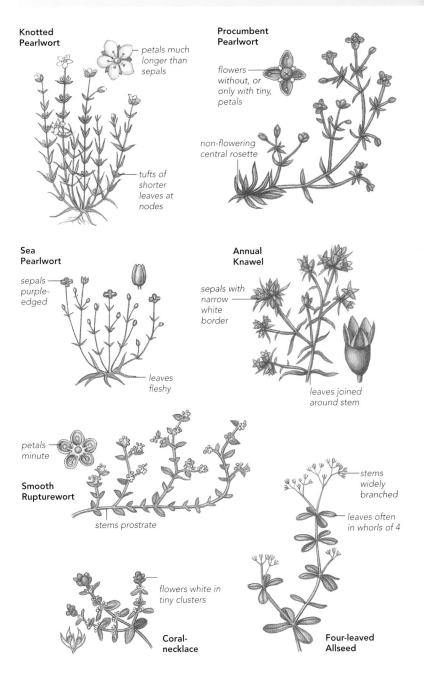

Knotted Pearlwort

petals much longer than sepals

tufts of shorter leaves at nodes

Procumbent Pearlwort

flowers without, or only with tiny, petals

non-flowering central rosette

Sea Pearlwort

sepals purple-edged

leaves fleshy

Annual Knawel

sepals with narrow white border

leaves joined around stem

petals minute

Smooth Rupturewort

stems prostrate

stems widely branched

leaves often in whorls of 4

flowers white in tiny clusters

Coral-necklace

Four-leaved Allseed

Sticky Catchfly

Alpine Catchfly

SPURREYS *Spergula* Characterised by being much-branched at base and having cylindrical fleshy leaves which appear to be in whorls (they are actually in pairs with the rest in axillary tufts). Stipules white and chaffy; flowers with 5 unnotched petals. 5 styles.

Corn Spurrey *Spergula arvensis* Rather straggling annual to 30cm with stems stickily hairy above and *leaves furrowed beneath*, blunt-tipped. Flowers 4–7mm in diameter, with white petals slightly longer than sepals. Common weed of arable ground, especially on sandy soils. **Fl:** May–Sep. **Br Is dist:** Frequent throughout; much less common than formerly, because of herbicide usage.

LYCHNIS *Lychnis* Erect perennials with upper leaves opposite and flowers in 5 parts. Petals narrowed at the base into a long claw, often with scales at the base of the limb. Sepals united into a tube with 10 veins. 5 styles.

Ragged-Robin *Lychnis flos-cuculi* Distinctive perennial to 70cm, often branched. Leaves narrow-lanceolate, rough to the touch. Flowers pink, petals divided into 4 narrow lobes with a ragged appearance. Widespread throughout and common in moist grassland, fens, wet woodlands, etc. **Fl:** May–Aug. **Br Is dist:** Frequent throughout but decreasing along with other plants of damp grassland due to agricultural 'improvement'.

Sticky Catchfly *Lychnis viscaria* Perennial to 60cm, with stems often purplish and very sticky below leaf nodes. Leaves almost hairless and lanceolate. Flowers 18–20mm in dense spikes, with petals red or purplish-red, slightly notched. Locally frequent in dry sandy grasslands or rocky places. **Fl:** May–Aug. **Br Is dist:** Very rare, on volcanic rock in Wales and Scotland.

Alpine Catchfly *Lychnis alpina* Tufted perennial to 15cm, with most leaves in dense basal rosettes some of which bear the erect flowering stems; leaves narrow and spoon-shaped. Flowers 6–12mm in diameter, in dense rounded terminal clusters, petals rose-red and deeply notched. Local in rocky places, usually metal-rich, in mountains. **Fl:** Jun–Jul. **Br Is dist:** Very rare; in Cumbria and Scottish Highlands.

Corncockle *Agrostemma githago* Annual to 1m, covered with appressed greyish hairs. Leaves narrow-lanceolate and pointed. Flowers pale reddish-purple, with shallowly notched petals shorter than the linear sepals. Formerly locally abundant as an arable weed, but rapidly decreasing with the use of herbicides. **Fl:** May–Aug. **Br Is dist:** Rare and sporadic in a number of counties; sometimes introduced or naturalised.

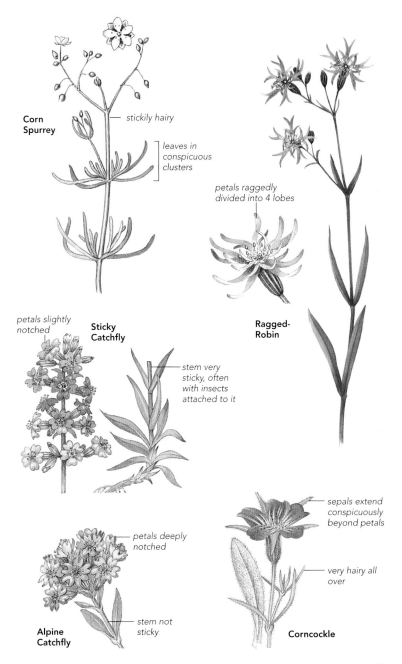

Corn Spurrey

stickily hairy

leaves in conspicuous clusters

petals raggedly divided into 4 lobes

Ragged-Robin

petals slightly notched

Sticky Catchfly

stem very sticky, often with insects attached to it

petals deeply notched

Alpine Catchfly

stem not sticky

sepals extend conspicuously beyond petals

very hairy all over

Corncockle

White Sticky Catchfly

Night-flowering Catchfly

Silene Annuals or perennials with similar characters to Lychnis (*see* p. 48), but flowers usually have 3 styles (rarely 5) and calyx tube has up to 30 veins.

Nottingham Catchfly *Silene nutans* Perennial to 80cm, stems downy below and sticky above. Basal leaves spoon-shaped and stalked; stem leaves oblong, pointed and unstalked. *Flowers drooping*, 18mm in diameter, in 1-sided panicle. Petals whitish, sometimes slightly pinkish or greenish beneath, *deeply cleft into narrow lobes which are rolled inwards during the day*, but roll back during evening when flower is fragrant. Calyx 9–12mm long with 10 purplish veins. Widespread throughout; in dry, often bare, calcareous habitats such as chalk grassland, shingle beaches and limestone cliffs. **Fl:** May–Aug. **Br Is dist:** Very local, north to Angus.

White Sticky Catchfly *Silene viscosa* Biennial, more robust than Nottingham Catchfly, *densely stickily hairy* throughout. Leaves lanceolate, pointed, the lower ones with wavy margins. *Flowers large* (to 22mm in diameter), arranged in whorls in a dense panicle. Petals white and deeply cleft. Calyx green, 14–24mm long. Very local in dry, grassy places. **Fl:** Jun–Jul. **Br Is dist:** Absent.

Bladder Campion *Silene vulgaris* Greyish, generally hairless perennial to 90cm. Leaves pointed-oval, sometimes wavy-edged with a hairy margin. *Flowers drooping*, 16–18mm, with deeply cleft white petals, not overlapping. *Calyx very inflated* like a bladder. Widespread and often common in dry grassy places, preferring sandy or calcareous soils. **Fl:** May–Sep. **Br Is dist:** Widespread throughout, but more common in the south and absent from much of the north.

Sea Campion *Silene uniflora* Differs from Bladder Campion in being *cushion-forming* with ascending flowering shoots to 25cm. *Leaves waxy-looking* and rather fleshy. Flowers erect, 20–25mm, petals overlapping. Locally abundant on sea-cliffs and shingle, and occasionally on mountains and inland lakes. **Fl:** Jun–Aug. **Br Is dist:** Frequent on coasts; rarely inland.

Night-flowering Catchfly *Silene noctiflora* Softly hairy annual to 60cm, sticky above. Lower leaves ovate-lanceolate and stalked; upper leaves narrower and stalked. Flowers similar to White Campion (*see* below) but petals yellowish beneath and pink above. 3 *styles are present*, and unlike White Campion, the *flowers are hermaphrodite*. Like Nottingham Catchfly, petals roll inwards during the day, and only roll back in the evening when the flowers become heavily fragrant to attract pollinating moths. Locally frequent, but decreasing, in arable fields, especially on chalk or sandy soils. **Fl:** Jul–Sep. **Br Is dist:** Local and decreasing as a result of herbicide usage; mainly in the south.

White Campion *Silene latifolia* Softly hairy short-lived perennial (occasionally annual) to 1m, rather sticky above. Leaves ovate-lanceolate, lower ones stalked and upper ones unstalked. Flowers few, 25–30mm in diameter, in branched clusters. Petals white, deeply notched; *flowers dioecious*, male smaller and with calyces 10-veined, female larger and 20-veined with 5 styles. Female flowers drop readily if not pollinated early. Fragrant in the evening. Widespread and common in hedgerows and on roadsides, arable land and waste areas. **Fl:** May–Oct. **Br Is dist:** Common throughout.

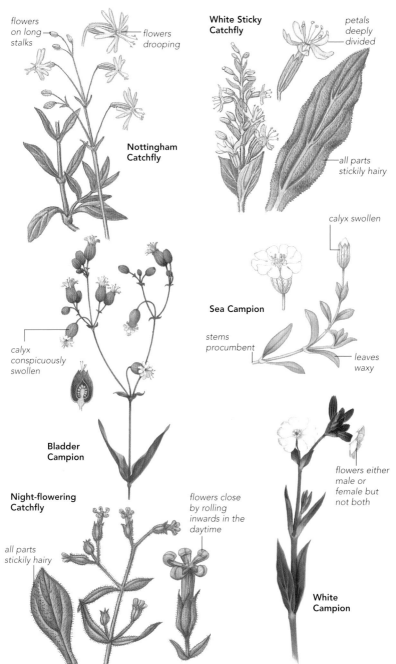

flowers on long stalks

flowers drooping

White Sticky Catchfly

petals deeply divided

Nottingham Catchfly

all parts stickily hairy

calyx swollen

Sea Campion

stems procumbent

leaves waxy

calyx conspicuously swollen

Bladder Campion

Night-flowering Catchfly

flowers close by rolling inwards in the daytime

all parts stickily hairy

flowers either male or female but not both

White Campion

Spanish Catchfly

Moss Campion

Sand Catchfly

Red Campion *Silene dioica* Similar to White Campion (*see* p. 50), with which it often hybridises. Biennial or perennial, softly hairy, sometimes sticky above. Flowers numerous, dioecious, unscented with deep rose-pink petals; male flowers smaller than female. Widespread throughout; in shady places, hedgerows, woodlands and on roadsides, especially on basic soils. **Fl:** Mar–Oct. **Br Is dist:** Mostly common except in some parts of E England, N Scotland and Ireland.

Forked Catchfly *Silene dichotoma* Distinctive annual to 1m, sparsely hairy, branched above and with numerous horizontal flowers in character-istic *1-sided forked spikes*. Flowers 15–18mm in diameter, petals white (rarely pink), deeply notched. Arable weed; native in Poland, introduced elsewhere. **Fl:** May–Sep. **Br Is dist:** Introduced, casual and rare.

Spanish Catchfly *Silene otites* Distinctive biennial or short-lived perennial to 90cm, stickily hairy near the base. Basal leaves spoon-shaped and stalked; upper stem leaves oblong and stalked. Flower heads unlike any other catchfly: loose, branched clusters of tiny greenish-yellow flowers, 3–4mm in diameter, with undivided narrow petals. Local on dry sandy soils and heaths. **Fl:** Jun–Sep. **Br Is dist:** Very local and rare in Breckland.

Northern Catchfly *Silene wahlbergella* Very distinctive but rather incon-spicuous, *slightly hairy, unbranched perennial* to 25cm. Flowers solitary and nodding at first. Calyx tube 14–18mm, inflated and almost complete-ly concealing the purplish petals which only just become visible at the calyceal opening. Damp meadows to 1,900m; in Scandinavia. **Fl:** Jun–Aug. **Br Is dist:** Absent.

Moss Campion *Silene acaulis* Distinctive cushion-forming perennial with moss-like habit. Leaves bright green, linear and pointed. Flowers pale or deep pink, 9–12mm in diameter, solitary on short stalks and often covering the cushions, the petals notched. Locally frequent on damp rocks, screes and short turf in mountains, to 2,500m, descending to low altitudes in Arctic and sub-Arctic areas. **Fl:** Jun–Aug. **Br Is dist:** Locally frequent in mountains from N Wales to N Scotland, and in W Ireland.

Rock Catchfly *Silene rupestris* Distinctive, hairless, erect, greyish perennial to 30cm, with lanceolate leaves and small (7–9mm) white or pale pink flowers with shallowly notched petals. Dry screes and rocky places in mountains; locally frequent in Scandinavia; absent from the north-west of the range. **Fl:** Jun–Sep. **Br Is dist:** Absent.

Sand Catchfly *Silene conica* Stickily hairy, greyish annual to 35cm. Leaves narrow and downy. Flowers only 4–5mm in diameter, in loose clusters, and distinctive; petals deep pink or whitish, shallowly notched; calyx strongly ribbed, at first cylindrical but soon swelling below to become markedly flask-shaped. Widespread but rather local in dry, sandy areas. **Fl:** May–Aug. **Br Is dist:** Local, mainly on the S and E coasts of England and Scotland; often casual and introduced elsewhere.

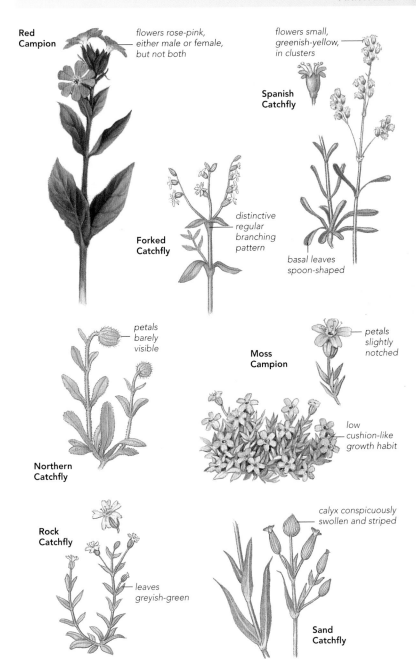

Red Campion

flowers rose-pink, either male or female, but not both

flowers small, greenish-yellow, in clusters

Spanish Catchfly

Forked Catchfly

distinctive regular branching pattern

basal leaves spoon-shaped

petals barely visible

Moss Campion

petals slightly notched

low cushion-like growth habit

Northern Catchfly

Rock Catchfly

leaves greyish-green

calyx conspicuously swollen and striped

Sand Catchfly

53

Alpine Gypsophila

Annual Gypsophila

Tunicflower

Carthusian Pink

Alpine Gypsophila *Gypsophila repens Sprawling* hairless perennial to 30cm, with greyish-green linear-lanceolate leaves to 30mm long. Flowers 8–10mm in diameter, in loose clusters, petals pink or white and slightly notched. Locally frequent in damp woods and meadows; mainly a C and E European plant, becoming much more local westwards towards France and Sweden. **Fl:** Jun–Oct **Br Is dist:** Rare casual.

Annual Gypsophila *Gypsophila muralis* Annual to 30cm, *hairless above* and with linear greyish-green leaves to 25mm long. Flowers 4mm in diameter in loose much-branched clusters arising from axils of leaves. Petals pink or white, slightly notched. Locally frequent in damp woods and meadows; mainly a C and E European plant, becoming much more local westwards towards France and Sweden. **Fl:** Jun–Oct. **Br Is dist:** Rare casual.

Soapwort *Saponaria officinalis* Hairless perennial to 1m, often rather straggling. Leaves ovate, pointed and strongly veined. Flowers large, 25–38mm in diameter; petals pink, unnotched with the limbs standing well clear of the reddish calyx. Widespread throughout; by roadsides, hedges, waste areas and damp woods; possibly native only in the south of its range where it grows in damp woodlands; naturalised elsewhere. **Fl:** Jun–Sep. **Br Is dist:** Possibly native in parts, or long naturalised; locally frequent, but rare in Scotland.

PINKS *Petrorhagia* and *Dianthus* Characterised by being annual or perennial, with 5, usually pink, petals and base of calyx surrounded by an epicalyx of paired bracts; flowers have 10 stamens and 2 styles. *Petrorhagia* species differ from *Dianthus* species in having a scarious membrane in the gaps between the calyx teeth.

Tunicflower *Petrorhagia saxifraga* Hairless mat-forming perennial to 35cm with decumbent, then ascending, flowering shoots. Leaves linear, pointed and rough-edged. *Flowers solitary* on long stalks, petals notched and pale pink or white. Local in dry, sandy habitats. **Fl:** Jun–Aug. **Br Is dist:** Introduced, rare.

Deptford Pink *Dianthus armeria* The only annual *Dianthus* in this list, to 60cm tall and hairy. Characterised by its dark green leaves, clusters of bright reddish-pink flowers, 8–13mm in diameter, subtended by *long leafy green bracts*, and with *rather pointed, toothed petals*, the epicalyx having a pair of long scales equalling the sepals. Widespread throughout on dry sandy or calcareous soils; more frequent towards the south. **Fl:** Jun–Aug. **Br Is dist:** Local and rare; absent from Ireland.

Carthusian Pink *Dianthus carthusianorum* Hairless perennial to 60cm. Leaves green, leaf sheaths 4 times longer than diameter of stem. Flowers 18–20mm in diameter bright pink or red in dense clusters subtended by *short brownish-green bracts, petals blunt* and toothed; epicalyx scales half as long as sepal tube. More frequent towards the south and east of its range; local elsewhere in dry grassy places. **Fl:** May–Aug. **Br Is dist:** Occasional garden escape.

Alpine Gypsophilia

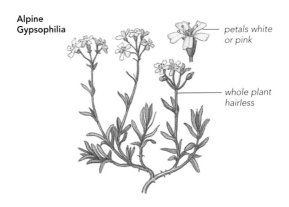

petals white or pink

whole plant hairless

Annual Gypsophilia

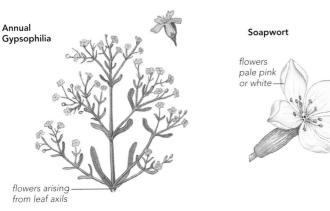

flowers arising from leaf axils

Soapwort

flowers pale pink or white

Tunicflower

Deptford Pink

petals spotted with white

long green bracts and epicalyx scales

Carthusian Pink

petals unspotted

epicalyx scales and bracts papery brown

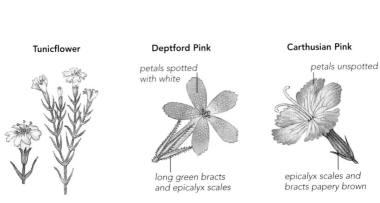

Cheddar Pink

Jersey Pink

Cheddar Pink *Dianthus gratianopolitanus* Hairless tufted perennial to 20cm, with long creeping runners. Erect flowering stems have greyish, *rough-edged linear leaves*, 20–60mm long. Flowers solitary, 20–30mm in diameter with toothed pink petals, *the teeth not more than a sixth the length of petal limb*; epicalyx scales about a quarter the length of calyx. Very local on open limestone grassland and rocks. **Fl:** May–Jul. **Br Is dist:** Restricted to the Cheddar Gorge; occasionally naturalised elsewhere.

Jersey Pink *Dianthus gallicus* Differs from Cheddar Pink in being often loosely tufted, hairy towards the base, with leaves to only 15mm long and *petals toothed to a third of their limb length*. Very local on coastal sand-dunes. **Fl:** Jun–Aug. **Br Is dist:** Jersey only, possibly naturalised.

Maiden Pink *Dianthus deltoides* *Roughly hairy perennial* with short creeping runners from which arise the erect flowering stems to 20cm. Leaves greyish green with rough edges. Flowers solitary or up to 3 in a group, 17–20mm in diameter; petals toothed, deep pink (occasionally pale pink) with *pale basal spots above a dark band*. Epicalyx scales half the length of calyx. Plants occasionally grow in tufted clumps. Widespread and locally frequent throughout, especially in the south of its range; in dry, often sandy places. **Fl:** Jun–Sep. **Br Is dist:** Widely scattered and varying from local to rare. Absent from the extreme north.

WATER-LILY FAMILY Nymphaeaceae

Aquatic perennials of either still or moving fresh water. Stems root in basal mud, leaves float or remain submerged and are oval or circular in outline. Flowers are terminal with 3 to many petals and 3–6 sepals (the 2 main genera can be separated by sepal numbers: *Nymphaea* has 4 sepals, *Nuphar* 5–6). If only leaves are available, *Nuphar* leaves have veins which fork near the leaf margin, but do not re-join each other. Conversely, the veins on *Nymphaea* leaves fork and then re-join one another, forming a reticulum. The terminal flowers separate the Nymphaeaceae from other aquatic plants with floating leaves, such as Fringed Water-lily (*see* p. 212) which has flowers in axillary clusters. Frogbit (*see* p. 320) differs by not having roots buried in mud.

White Water-lily *Nymphaea alba* Conspicuous for its large rounded leaves, 10–30cm in diameter and its large white flowers 10–20cm in diameter only opening in bright sunshine. Basal lobes of leaves parallel or diverging. Flowers have 20 or more petals. Widespread throughout and often common; in still or slow-moving fresh water. **Fl:** Jun–Sep. **Br Is dist:** Common throughout.

Yellow Water-lily *Nuphar lutea* Like White Water-lily, has conspicuous large leathery floating leaves to 40cm in diameter, but also has thinner submerged leaves. *Flowers yellow*, 60mm in diameter, held on stalks above water level. *Stigma disc not wavy when viewed from above*. Petals partially concealed by the much longer yellow sepals, which markedly overlap each other. Widespread and generally common in similar habitats to previous species, often in more nutrient-rich water. **Fl:** Jun–Sep. **Br Is dist:** Throughout, mostly common, but rare in N Scotland.

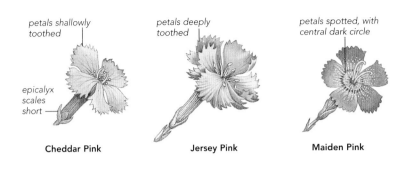

petals shallowly toothed

epicalyx scales short

Cheddar Pink

petals deeply toothed

Jersey Pink

petals spotted, with central dark circle

Maiden Pink

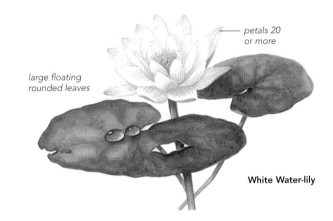

large floating rounded leaves

petals 20 or more

White Water-lily

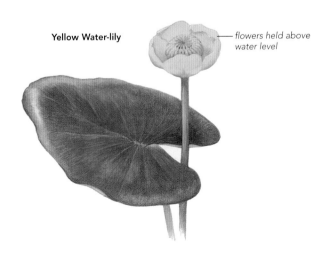

Yellow Water-lily

flowers held above water level

HORNWORT FAMILY Ceratophyllaceae

Aquatic perennials, submerged and with whorled leaves divided into multiple narrow linear segments. Male and female flowers are separate on the same plant, alternating at the leaf nodes. The stems of hornworts often become encrusted with calcium during the summer, and these deposits fall to the bottom of the water as the stems and leaves decay.

Rigid Hornwort

Rigid Hornwort *Ceratophyllum demersum* Stems flexuous, up to 1.5m long, bearing whorls of dark green, rigid, minutely toothed *leaves, forked once or twice*. Flowers tiny at leaf nodes. Fruit has 2 basal spines. Widespread throughout, but often local in freshwater habitats or occasionally brackish water; can colonise or spread very rapidly. **Fl:** Jul–Sep. **Br Is dist:** Local in England; rare elsewhere.

Stinking Hellebore

BUTTERCUP FAMILY Ranunculaceae

A large and variable family with a broad range of characters, but virtually all members can be recognised by their very numerous, free hypogynous stamens and their distinct carpels. Most are perennial herbs with alternate leaves and 5–6 sepals. Leaves usually divided or palmately lobed (but linear in Mousetail, *see* p. 68, and unlobed in some *Ranunculus* species, *see* pp. 64–6) and stipules absent. Although many members of the Rose family have numerous free stamens, there is always a gap between the ovary and the insertion of the other flower parts (*see* pp. 100 ff), and stipules are usually present.

Green Hellebore

Stinking Hellebore *Helleborus foetidus* Rather robust, fetid bushy perennial to 80cm, with dark green, overwintering basal leaves. All leaves palmately divided into numerous narrow toothed lobes, *arising from 2 or 3 arched stalks* and not from the same point at the top of the leaf stalk. Flowers cup-shaped, 10–30mm in diameter; sepals blunt, bright yellowish-green with purplish edges; petals small, hidden by sepals. Local in open woods on calcareous soils. **Fl:** Jan–May. **Br Is dist:** Very local in S England and Wales; sometimes naturalised farther north.

Globeflower

Green Hellebore *Helleborus viridis* Similar to Stinking Hellebore, but does not have evergreen leaves; *leaf lobes arise from a single point* and are often further lobed; flowers have spreading pointed sepals without purplish margins. Widespread but only locally frequent in moist calcareous woods. **Fl:** Feb–May. **Br Is dist:** Local in S England, rare in the north and sometimes naturalised.

Winter Aconite *Eranthis hyemalis* Very distinctive low perennial to 12cm with erect stems, each bearing a single, cup-shaped, bright yellow flower, to 15mm in diameter, subtended by a collar of 3 palmately divided leaves which protect the growing flower in bud. Flower has 6 conspicuous yellow sepals, whilst the petals are reduced to horn-like structures from which nectar is secreted. Widely naturalised in woodlands, churchyards and roadsides, etc. **Fl:** Jan–Apr. **Br Is dist:** Naturalised widely as far north as S Scotland.

Globeflower *Trollius europaeus* Perennial to 60cm, with palmately divided, toothed leaves and distinctive lemon-yellow, globe-shaped flowers. The 10–15 sepals overlap and curve inwards, producing the orbicular shape and concealing the diminutive nectar-bearing petals. Widespread in damp upland meadows, ditches and by upland streams. **Fl:** May–Aug. **Br Is dist:** Locally frequent From Wales to N Scotland, and in NW Ireland.

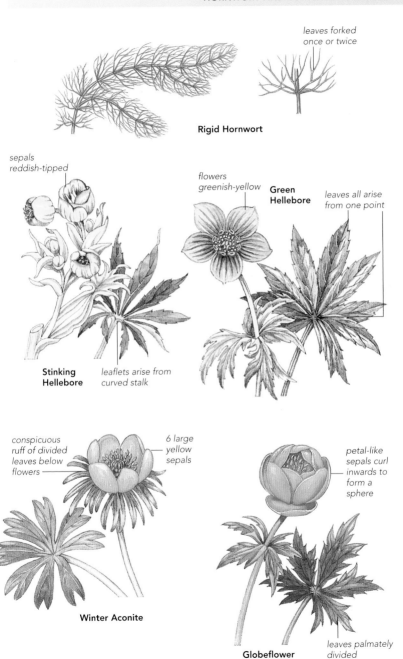

leaves forked once or twice

Rigid Hornwort

sepals reddish-tipped

flowers greenish-yellow **Green Hellebore**

leaves all arise from one point

Stinking Hellebore *leaflets arise from curved stalk*

conspicuous ruff of divided leaves below flowers

6 large yellow sepals

Winter Aconite

petal-like sepals curl inwards to form a sphere

Globeflower *leaves palmately divided*

Baneberry

Baneberry *Actaea spicata* Perennial, almost hairless, fetid herb to 70cm. Basal leaves large, like an umbellifer, the leaf stalk divided into pinnately arranged branches, with the leaflets coarsely toothed and often 3-lobed. Flowers in spikes, with 4–6 white petals and sepals and numerous long white stamens which give the flower spikes a feathery appearance. Fruit a shining berry, green at first then black when ripe, 12–13mm in diameter. Local to locally frequent; in woodlands on limestone and on limestone pavements. **Fl:** May–Jun. **Br Is dist:** Very local in N England.

Monk's-hood

Marsh-marigold *Caltha palustris* Hairless perennial with stout hollow stems, and broad heart-shaped or kidney-shaped leaves to 10cm. Distinctive when flowering, with its large bright yellow, buttercup-like flowers, to 50mm in diameter. As with many of the buttercup family, petals are absent so the 5 sepals provide the splash of colour. Widespread throughout and common; in a variety of wetlands ranging from calcareous fens to wet woodlands. **Fl:** Mar–Aug. **Br Is dist:** Still common throughout, but decreased in the lowlands along with other wetland plants because of agricultural drainage.

MONK'S-HOODS *Aconitum* Distinctive genus of herbs with spirally arranged, much-divided leaves and flowers with 5 coloured sepals, the 2 upper ones forming a prominent helmet-like hood.

Monk's-hood *Aconitum napellus* Minutely downy perennial to 1m with lower stem leaves deeply divided into 3–5 lobes, each segment further divided into narrow, linear segments. Flowers blue or violet, to 20mm, with rounded *helmets equally broad as tall and pubescent pedicels*. Often confused with the garden escapes which have much less narrowly divided leaves and hairless pedicels. A local plant of damp woodlands or by shady streams. **Fl:** May–Sep. **Br Is dist:** Rare in the south and south-west.

Forking Larkspur *Consolida regalis* Distinctive downy annual to 30cm with leaves much divided as with the Monk's-hoods, but the blue flowers are in loose spikes, not hooded, and possess 5 perianth segments and a backward-pointing spur. Flower stalks are much longer than bracts. Widespread as a casual of arable fields. **Fl:** Jun–Aug. **Br Is dist:** Introduced and a rare casual.

ANEMONES *Anemone* Perennials with 3 palmately lobed stem leaves in a whorl beneath the flower, the fruit a cluster of achenes.

Wood Anemone *Anemone nemorosa* Perennial to 30cm with erect, slightly hairy flowering stems. Stem leaves long-stalked in a whorl below flower, palmately divided into 3 lobes further divided into pointed toothed segments. Basal leaves appear after flowering. Flowers 20–40mm in diameter, terminal, *solitary* with 6–12 white or pink-tinged petal-like sepals. Fruit a globular cluster of beaked achenes. Widespread almost throughout, and common in woodlands, old hedgerows and sometimes meadows. **Fl:** Mar–May. **Br Is dist:** Common throughout, but absent from some of the Scottish islands.

Narcissus-flowered Anemone *Anemone narcissiflora* Very similar to Wood Anemone, but differs in having 3–8 *flowers together* in an umbel. Local in woodlands and grassland, in mountains in the south and east, usually on limestone. **Fl:** Jun–Jul. **Br Is dist:** Absent.

Baneberry

flowers white and feathery-looking

berries black and shiny when ripe

leaves kidney-shaped, undivided

Marsh-marigold

tall helmet-like upper petal-like sepals

pedicels downy

Monk's-hood

long backward-pointing spur

long flower stalks

Forking Larkspur

flowers solitary

all sepals white and petal-like

Wood Anemone

flowers white in an umbel

Narcissus-flowered Anemone

61

Yellow Anemone

Liverleaf

Pasqueflower

Small Pasqueflower

Pale Pasqueflower

Traveller's-joy

Yellow Anemone *Anemone ranunculoides* Differs from Wood Anemone (*see* p. 60) in having stem leaves only very short-stalked, and flowers with 5–8 bright yellow petal-like sepals. Widespread and locally frequent in deciduous woodlands. **Fl:** Mar–May. **Br Is dist:** Rarely naturalised.

Snowdrop Anemone *Anemone sylvestris* Differs from Wood Anemone (*see* p. 60) in being hairy and having large white flowers, 40–70mm, and only 5 petal-like sepals; fruit woolly, elongated and strawberry-shaped. Widely scattered in dry woodlands and scrub; absent from Scandinavia and NW France. **Fl:** Apr–Jun. **Br Is dist:** Absent.

Liverleaf *Hepatica nobilis* Hairless or slightly hairy perennial to 20cm with very distinctive 3-lobed evergreen fleshy leaves, untoothed, dark green (often mottled), purplish below. Flowers bluish violet (occasionally pink or white) with 6–9 petal-like sepals and 3 sepal-like bracts beneath. Locally frequent in woods on calcareous soils. **Fl:** Mar–May. **Br Is dist:** Introduced and rarely naturalised.

PASQUE FLOWERS *Pulsatilla* Leaves pinnately divided and fruits with elongated feathery styles. The coloured petal-like flower segments are really sepals.

Pasqueflower *Pulsatilla vulgaris* Hairy with erect flowering stem to 30cm, usually much less. Basal leaves silky when young, twice pinnately divided into long linear segments. Stem leaves 3, unstalked and divided into narrow segments. Flowers 50–80mm in diameter, *erect at first*, later drooping. Petal-like sepals 6, purple-violet; anthers bright yellow. Local and declining on dry calcareous grasslands. **Fl:** Apr–May. **Br Is dist:** Very local in S and E England.

Small Pasqueflower *Pulsatilla pratensis* Very like Pasqueflower, but differs in having smaller bell-shaped flowers, 30–40mm, *always drooping* and with sepals recurved at the tips, often greyish-violet or yellow. Local to locally frequent; in turf on sandy soils, and in mountains. **Fl:** Apr–Jun. **Br Is dist:** Absent.

Pale Pasqueflower *Pulsatilla vernalis* Has basal leaves broadly lobed, and is *evergreen*, with flowers 40–60mm *sepals white inside* and tinged pinkish or purplish on the outside, often with a downy covering of yellow hairs. *Stem leaves unstalked*, like Pasqueflower. Local in mountain grassland or hills, often on sandy soils and near melting snow. **Fl:** Apr–Jun. **Br Is dist:** Absent.

CLEMATIS *Clematis* Perennial woody climbers or herbs with opposite leaves and 4 petal-like sepals. Fruits conspicuous bearded structures formed by clusters of 1-seeded achenes with persistent feathery styles.

Traveller's-joy, Old Man's Beard *Clematis vitalba* Woody climber to 30m with pinnate leaves divided into pointed leaflets. Flowers creamy or greenish white, fragrant, in terminal or lateral loose clusters. Widespread and common; in hedgerows, woodland margins and scrub, on calcareous soils. **Fl:** Jul–Sep. **Br Is dist:** Common from Lancashire and Yorkshire southwards. Introduced in Ireland.

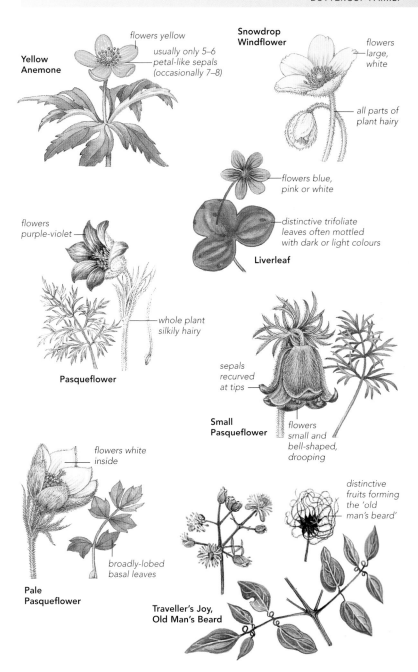

Yellow Anemone

flowers yellow

usually only 5–6 petal-like sepals (occasionally 7–8)

Snowdrop Windflower

flowers large, white

all parts of plant hairy

flowers blue, pink or white

distinctive trifoliate leaves often mottled with dark or light colours

Liverleaf

flowers purple-violet

whole plant silkily hairy

Pasqueflower

sepals recurved at tips

Small Pasqueflower

flowers small and bell-shaped, drooping

flowers white inside

broadly-lobed basal leaves

Pale Pasqueflower

distinctive fruits forming the 'old man's beard'

Traveller's Joy, Old Man's Beard

Pheasant's-eye

Summer Pheasant's-eye

Corn Buttercup

a1   a2

b

PHEASANT'S-EYES *Adonis* Annuals or perennials with feathery pinnate leaves like the pasqueflowers but pheasant's-eyes have both petals and sepals, with fruits elongated heads of non-feathery wrinkled achenes. Petals do not have a basal nectary.

Pheasant's-eye *Adonis annua* Erect hairless annual to 40cm, with stems often branched. Leaves 3 times pinnate with very narrow segments, the *lower leaves unstalked.* Flowers terminal and erect with 5–8 bright scarlet petals, blackish at the base. Sepals spreading, *hairless.* Widespread, but decreasing; on arable and disturbed, calcareous soils. **Fl:** Jun–Aug. **Br Is dist:** Rare and decreasing on arable land in S England.

Summer Pheasant's-eye *Adonis aestivalis* Unlike Pheasant's-eye, has adpressed sepals, which are *hairless* and *lower leaves are stalked.* On arable land. **Fl:** Jun–Sep. **Br Is dist:** Absent.

Yellow Pheasant's-eye *Adonis vernalis* Erect perennial to 30cm with typical *Adonis* twice to 3 times pinnate feathery leaves but with large showy *yellow flowers* 40–80mm in diameter, with 10–20 long shiny petals. Local or rare in dry grassland, and occasionally open woodland; absent from the north and north-west. **Fl:** Apr–May. **Br Is dist:** Absent.

BUTTERCUPS and CROW-FOOTS *Ranunculus* Annuals or perennials, sometimes aquatic. Leaves entire or divided. Flowers yellow or white. Petals 5 or more, sepals 3–5. Each petal has a basal nectary.

Meadow Buttercup *Ranunculus acris* Softly hairy perennial to 1m, often much less. Basal leaves long-stalked and rather rounded in outline, divided into 3–7 unstalked and wedge-shaped coarsely toothed lobes (**a1**). Lower stem leaves similar, but upper stem leaves unstalked and more deeply cut into narrower linear lobes. Flowers bright golden yellow, 18–25mm in diameter, *on long unfurrowed stalks.* Achene with a hooked beak (**a2**). Very common throughout; in grassland of roadsides, meadows and ditches. **Fl:** Apr–Sep. **Br Is dist:** Throughout.

Creeping Buttercup *Ranunculus repens* Variable hairy perennial to 60cm with creeping runners above ground, rooting at the nodes. Basal and lower stem leaves stalked, rather triangular in outline and 3-lobed, the *middle lobe stalked* (**b**). Upper stem leaves unstalked with narrower lobes. *Flower stalks furrowed.* Very common throughout in grassy places, especially on heavier clay soils. **Fl:** May–Sep. **Br Is dist:** Very common throughout.

Corn Buttercup *Ranunculus arvensis* Annual to 60cm. Leaves stalked and pale green, *basal leaves with paddle-shaped lobes,* stem leaves with numerous narrow linear lobes. Flowers a characteristic pale lemon yellow. *Fruits very distinctive large spiny achenes.* Arable weed, now much decreased due to herbicides. **Fl:** May–Jul. **Br Is dist:** Now very local or rare, and found mainly in the south.

Pheasant's-eye

sepals well separated from petals

lower leaves unstalked

Summer Pheasant's-eye

petals pressed against sepals

lower leaves stalked

numerous yellow petals

Yellow Pheasant's-eye

flower stalk smooth and ungrooved

Meadow Buttercup

flower stalk grooved

Creeping Buttercup

stem creeping

flowers pale lemon yellow

fruit spiny

Corn Buttercup

Goldilocks Buttercup *Ranunculus auricomus* Slightly hairy perennial to 30cm with basal leaves rounded, kidney-shaped, or deeply 3-lobed; *stem leaves with 3–6 very narrow segments.* Flowers distinctive, 15–25mm in diameter usually *with 1 or more petals absent or imperfectly developed. Achenes slightly hairy.* Widespread throughout; in damp woodlands or grasslands, often on rather basic soils. **Fl:** Apr–Jun. **Br Is dist:** Rather local throughout, decreasing northwards.

Celery-leaved Buttercup *Ranunculus sceleratus* Pale green hairless or slightly hairy annual to 60cm. Basal leaves stalked, deeply 3-lobed with the lobes further divided into narrow segments; lower stem leaves often shiny, short-stalked and divided into 2–3 narrow segments. *Flowers pale yellow*, 5–10mm in diameter, numerous in branched clusters. *Fruit heads distinctly elongated.* Widespread throughout, and varying from local to common; in wet places, streamsides and ditches. **Fl:** May–Sep. **Br Is dist:** Locally common, mainly in the south; absent from parts of the north.

Bulbous Buttercup *Ranunculus bulbosus* Hairy *perennial* to 40cm with markedly swollen stem-base underground. *Hairs are appressed above, spreading below.* Flower stalks stalked and 3-lobed. Flower stalks furrowed; flowers 20–30mm in diameter, *bright yellow*. After flowering, vegetative parts often disappear for a short period during the summer. Widespread and often very common; in dry grassland, often on calcareous soils. Absent from the far north. **Fl:** Mar–Jul. **Br Is dist:** Common throughout, but more so in the south.

Lesser Celandine *Ranunculus ficaria* Hairless perennial to 25cm with fleshy triangular or heart-shaped leaves having wavy margins. Sometimes has bulbils in axils of leaf stalks. Flowers bright yellow, paling with age and 20–30mm in diameter, with 8–12 petals and 3 sepals. Widespread and very common in bare damp ground; absent from much of Scandinavia and also Iceland. **Fl:** Feburary–May. **Br Is dist:** Common throughout.

Lesser Spearwort *Ranunculus flammula* Variable perennial to 50cm, erect or decumbent with lower stems often reddish. Basal leaves oblong, often sparsely toothed; stem leaves lanceolate. Flowers few, bright yellow and *7–18mm in diameter*, on furrowed and *slightly hairy* stalks. Widespread and common, but absent from much of Scandinavia and also Iceland; in a variety of damp or wet places. **Fl:** May–Sep. **Br Is dist:** Common throughout.

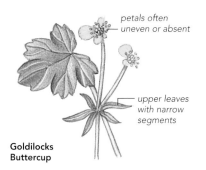

petals often uneven or absent

upper leaves with narrow segments

Goldilocks Buttercup

Celery-leaved Buttercup

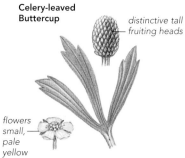

distinctive tall fruiting heads

flowers small, pale yellow

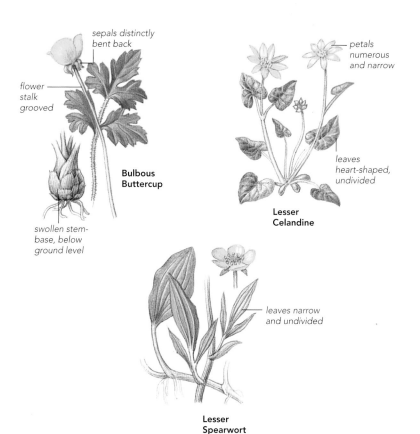

sepals distinctly bent back

flower stalk grooved

Bulbous Buttercup

swollen stem-base, below ground level

petals numerous and narrow

leaves heart-shaped, undivided

Lesser Celandine

leaves narrow and undivided

Lesser Spearwort

67

Large White Buttercup

Large White Buttercup *Ranunculus platanifolius* A tall white-flowered buttercup with 5- to 7-lobed leaves, with *the lobes not divided to the base*. Widespread in marshes and damp woodland, usually at low altitudes; in southern central part of area and W Scandinavia. **Fl:** May–Aug. **Br Is dist:** Absent.

CROWFOOTS and WATER-CROWFOOTS A group of mainly aquatic plants, or sometimes growing on bare mud, all with white petals usually having a yellow base. In aquatic species, 2 types of leaves can be present: floating ones which are palmately lobed, and submerged ones which are very finely divided, or sometimes just the latter can be present especially in species which grow in fast-moving water.

Glacier Crowfoot

Glacier Crowfoot *Ranunculus glacialis* Hairless perennial to 20cm. Distinctive with its thick 3- to 5-lobed basal leaves, upper unstalked leaves with narrow lanceolate lobes and *large flowers 25–40mm in diameter*, pink-tinged with age. Local in rocky or stony places in mountains, often near snow patches. **Fl:** Jul–Oct. **Br Is dist:** Absent.

Ivy-leaved Crowfoot *Ranunculus hederaceus*
Creeping annual or biennial with numerous leaves, all kidney- or heart-shaped and shallowly lobed to look (**a**). Flowers 3–6mm in diameter, *petals equal to or slightly longer than sepals*. Locally common in bare muddy places or sometimes ditches. **Fl:** May–Sep. **Br Is dist:** Rather local throughout.

Ivy-leaved Crowfoot

Common Water-crowfoot *Ranunculus aquatilis* Annual or perennial aquatic usually with both floating (**b1**) and submerged (**b2**) leaves, the latter occasionally absent. *Floating leaves deeply divided into 3–7 straight-sided segments with teeth at the tips.* Flowers 12–18mm in diameter, petals 5–10mm; fruit stalk up to 50mm. Widespread and often common in still or slow-moving shallow water. **Fl:** Apr–Aug. **Br Is dist:** Frequent throughout.

River Water-crowfoot

River Water-crowfoot *Ranunculus fluitans* Robust perennial with only submerged leaves *10–30cm long*, the segments greenish black and almost parallel. Flowers 20–30mm in diameter; petals 5–10, overlapping. Stems to 6m long. Widespread and locally frequent in fast-flowing streams and rivers; absent from most of Scandinavia. **Fl:** May–Aug. **Br Is dist:** Locally frequent north to S Scotland, but rare in Wales and Ireland.

Mousetail

Mousetail *Myosurus minimus* Distinctive, but easily overlooked, low annual from 5–12cm. Leaves rather fleshy, linear and in a basal tuft. Flowers tiny, to 5mm in diameter, pale greenish yellow and solitary on long stalks; petals and sepals 5–7. Fruit a characteristic elongated, to 70mm, head of tiny achenes, resembling a 'tail'. Widespread but decreasing in bare, often sandy, soils and arable field-margins; absent from the far north. **Fl:** Mar–Jul. **Br Is dist:** Increasingly rare, now mainly in S England.

a

b1   b2

Columbine *Aquilegia vulgaris* Hairless erect perennial to 1m, with twice trifoliate basal leaves on long stalks and nodding flowers, 30–50mm long, usually blue but rarely white or bluish red. Petals 5, with distinctive long hooked spurs bearing nectaries; *stamens not or hardly protruding beyond petals*. Widespread, but local or absent in the north; in a variety of habitats, including damp open woods, scrub and fens. **Fl:** May–Jul. **Br Is dist:** Rather local northwards to S Scotland; very local in Ireland.

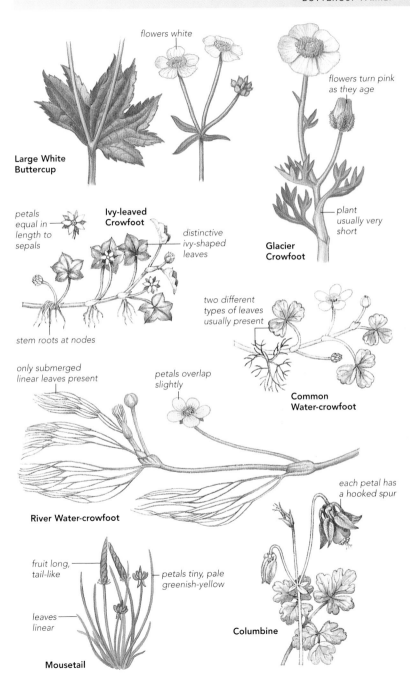

flowers white

Large White Buttercup

flowers turn pink as they age

plant usually very short

Glacier Crowfoot

petals equal in length to sepals

Ivy-leaved Crowfoot

distinctive ivy-shaped leaves

stem roots at nodes

two different types of leaves usually present

Common Water-crowfoot

only submerged linear leaves present

petals overlap slightly

River Water-crowfoot

each petal has a hooked spur

fruit long, tail-like

petals tiny, pale greenish-yellow

leaves linear

Columbine

Mousetail

69

Alpine Meadow-rue

Peony

Long-headed Poppy

MEADOW-RUES *Thalictrum* Perennials with rather fern-like compound leaves and flowers having 4–5 petal-like sepals and a feathery appearance as a result of the multiple protruding stamens.

Alpine Meadow-rue *Thalictrum alpinum* Slender, easily overlooked, plant *to only 15cm tall*, with twice trifoliate dark green leaves and tiny rounded leaflets. Flowers in a terminal raceme, the lower flowers drooping, all with purplish sepals and stamens and yellow anthers. Local in damp mountain-ledges and turf. **Fl:** May–Jul. **Br Is dist:** Very local from N Wales to N Scotland; rare in W Ireland.

Common Meadow-rue *Thalictrum flavum* To 1m tall with leaves twice to 3 times pinnate, *the end-leaflet being longer than broad* and *toothed*. Flowers erect in dense clusters, and appearing yellowish despite white sepals because of the feathery, protruding, erect stamens. Widespread and frequent in damp meadows, fens or by streams and lakes, especially on basic soils, but absent from mountainous areas. **Fl:** Jun–Aug. **Br Is dist:** Frequent throughout, except extreme N Scotland.

Lesser Meadow-rue *Thalictrum minus* Very variable species to 1.5m tall (less tall in drier places). Leaves 3 to to 4 times pinnate, with *end-leaflets as broad as long*. Flowers not densely clustered, *drooping at first then erect*; stamens pendulous. Widespread and locally frequent in a variety of habitats, including dry grassland, dunes and rocky places, but generally on base-rich soils. **Fl:** Jun– Aug. **Br Is dist:** Local throughout, but absent from most of CS England.

PEONY FAMILY Paeoniaceae

Perennial herbs or shrubs with alternate leaves, and fruits consisting of a group of up to 8 follicles, each follicle bearing several seeds.

Peony *Paeonia mascula* Stout perennial herb to 50cm, with twice trifoliate leaves, dark green and shiny. Flowers solitary, 8–12cm in diameter with up to 10 shiny petals. Follicles 3–5, recurved with seeds first red, then blue and finally black. Mainly a S European species, in rocky places and cliffs; in NC France; introduced elsewhere. **Br Is dist:** Introduced and well established on Steep Holm in Bristol Channel.

POPPY FAMILY Papaveraceae

Herbs with milky or slightly coloured latex and leaves usually deeply divided. Flowers with 4 petals and 2 sepals which fall early; stamens numerous. Fruit a capsule opening by pores or splitting into valves.

Common Poppy *Papaver rhoeas* Annual to 60cm, often with *spreading hairs*. Leaves deeply divided into narrow segments. Flowers 7–10cm with 4 overlapping scarlet *petals often having a dark blotch at the base*. Capsule ovoid. Common in arable and waste areas; absent from the far north. **Fl:** Jun–Sep. **Br Is dist:** Common but declining in England; local in N Scotland, Wales and W Ireland.

Long-headed Poppy *Papaver dubium* ssp *dubium* Similar to Common Poppy, but has *appressed hairs*; flowers 30–70mm in diameter with orange-red overlapping *petals which do not have a dark blotch at the base*; anthers purplish-tinged. Capsule more than twice as long as wide, gradually narrowing downwards from the top. Locally common in arable and waste areas. **Fl:** Jun–Aug. **Br Is dist:** Locally common throughout.

Alpine Meadow-rue

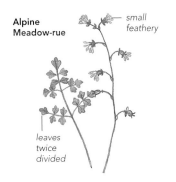

small feathery

leaves twice divided

Common Meadow-rue

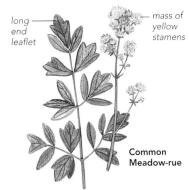

long end leaflet

mass of yellow stamens

Lesser Meadow-rue

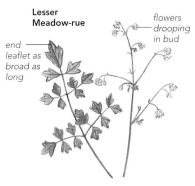

end leaflet as broad as long

flowers drooping in bud

Peony

large solitary flowers

Common Poppy

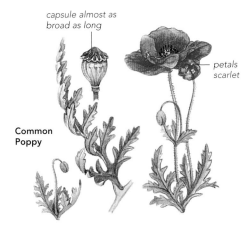

capsule almost as broad as long

petals scarlet

Long-headed Poppy

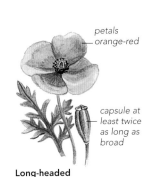

petals orange-red

capsule at least twice as long as broad

Prickly Poppy *Papaver argemone* Annual with bristle-pointed leaves. Flowers 20–60mm in diameter with pale red petals not usually overlapping at base but having *a dark blotch*. Capsule narrowly oblong and *ribbed with erect bristles* (**a**). Local in arable and waste areas, usually on sandy soils; absent from the north. **Fl:** May–Sep. **Br Is dist:** Local, mainly in the south.

Papaver radicatum

Papaver radicatum Extremely variable, tufted perennial to 25cm, with yellow latex and *leaves acutely pinnately lobed*. Flowers 30–50mm in diameter, usually yellow but occasionally pinkish or white. Capsule elliptical, widest about the middle. Gravelly or bare rocky places, screes to 1,800m; in Scandinavia. **Fl:** Jun–Aug. **Br Is dist:** Absent.

Welsh Poppy *Meconopsis cambrica* Perennial to 60cm, with pinnate *long-stalked basal leaves*, the *segments coarsely toothed*. Flowers 50–80mm in diameter with overlapping petals orange-yellow on opening but soon changing to yellow. Capsule 4- to 6-ribbed and splitting above to form 4–6 valves. Atlantic distribution in moist, semi-shaded, often rocky places. **Fl:** Jun–Aug. **Br Is dist:** Locally frequent in Wales, SW England and Ireland.

Welsh Poppy

Yellow Horned-poppy *Glaucium flavum* Greyish biennial or perennial with waxy leaves. Basal leaves long-stalked, deeply pinnately lobed, the lobes progressively longer towards the tip. Flowers 60–90mm in diameter with overlapping yellow petals. *Capsule very distinctive, greatly elongated, slender and curved* to 30cm. Rather local plant in coastal shingle and dunes. **Fl:** Jun–Sep. **Br Is dist:** Locally common round most of the coasts.

Yellow Horned-poppy

Greater Celandine *Chelidonium majus* Perennial to 90cm with brittle stems. Leaves irregularly pinnate with ovate, blunt, coarsely toothed segments. Flowers 20–30mm in diameter with 4 bright yellow petals not overlapping. Fruit a narrow elongated capsule to 50mm, splitting on 2 sides from below. Frequent in hedge banks, open woods and waste areas, often near habitation; native in most areas but also widely introduced; absent from the far north. **Fl:** Apr–Oct. **Br Is dist:** Throughout, but most frequent in the south.

Climbing Corydalis

FUMITORY FAMILY Fumariaceae

Delicate herbs with much-divided leaves, and spikes or racemes of 2-lipped flowers which have 2 small sepals, 2 outer petals (1 or both spurred) and 2 narrower inner petals. Fruit an oblong many-seeded capsule in *Corydalis* species or a rounded 1-seeded nutlet in *Fumaria* species (*see* p. 74).

a

Climbing Corydalis *Ceratocapnos claviculata* Delicate pale green climbing annual to 80cm, with twice pinnate leaves ending in a branched tendril. Flowers 5–6mm long, pale creamy-white, in racemes opposite leaves. Fruit a 2- to 3-seeded capsule. Local in woodlands, rocky areas or heaths, usually on acid soils or peat. **Fl:** May–Sep. **Br Is dist:** Locally common, especially in W Britain, but rare in Ireland.

Yellow Corydalis *Pseudofumaria lutea* Perennial to 30cm, with twice to 3 times pinnate leaves and bright yellow flowers, 12–18mm long, in racemes opposite leaves. Naturalised on old walls and rocky places. **Fl:** May–Sep. **Br Is dist:** Scattered throughout.

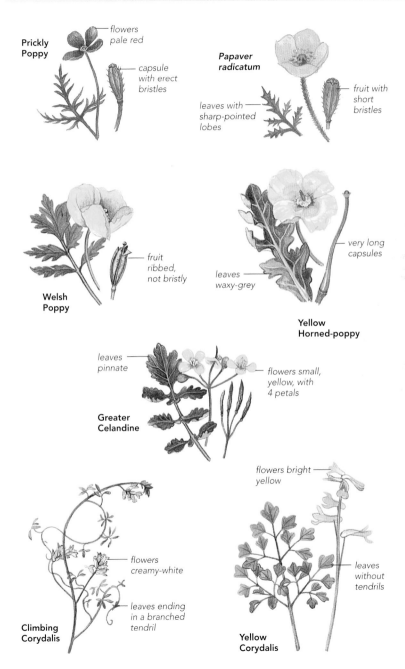

Prickly Poppy
flowers pale red
capsule with erect bristles

Papaver radicatum
fruit with short bristles
leaves with sharp-pointed lobes

Welsh Poppy
fruit ribbed, not bristly

Yellow Horned-poppy
very long capsules
leaves waxy-grey

Greater Celandine
leaves pinnate
flowers small, yellow, with 4 petals

Climbing Corydalis
flowers creamy-white
leaves ending in a branched tendril

Yellow Corydalis
flowers bright yellow
leaves without tendrils

Bird-in-a-bush *Corydalis solida* Perennial to 20cm with *stem bearing an oval scale near the base.* Leaves twice or 3 times trifoliate and flowers purplish, 15–30mm long, in dense racemes. Lower *flower stalks more than 5mm. Bracts large and toothed.* Widespread, but local, in open woods, hedgerows and disturbed ground; absent from the north. **Fl:** Mar–May. **Br Is dist:** Introduced and naturalised in a few places.

FUMITORIES *Fumaria* A difficult genus of very closely related annuals.

Common Fumitory *Fumaria officinalis* Weak or robust, spreading or climbing. Inflorescence dense first then loose (*20–40 flowers*), longer than its stalk. Flowers 7–8mm, pink with dark tips (**a1**). Lower petal (**a2**). Upper petal flattened, with wings concealing keel. Sepals at least a quarter the length of flower. Bracts shorter than fruit stalks. Fruit (**a3**). Widespread and often common in arable areas. **Fl:** May–Oct. **Br Is dist:** Common generally but less so in the west.

CABBAGE FAMILY Brassicaceae (Cruciferae)
A large family of distinctive herbs with 4 free sepals, 4 free petals, 6 stamens and a superior ovary with 2 carpels. The old family name is derived from the appearance of the flowers which have the 4 usually equal petals separated and in the form of a cross. The fruit is in the form of a pod, called a siliqua when long and linear (**b1**), or a silicula when less than 3 times as long as broad (**b2**). The presence or absence of a beak at the top of the pod helps to separate genera.

SISYMBRIUMS *Sisymbrium* Distinguished by having slender fruit (siliqua) not beaked (compare with *Sinapis* (*see* p. 90)) and valves of pod 3- to 7-veined (veins often indistinct); seeds never extend beyond ends of valves. Stem leaves often have a halberd-shaped larger terminal lobe.

Hedge Mustard *Sisymbryum officinale* Stiff, erect annual or biennial to 90cm. *Upper part characteristically branched.* Basal leaves deeply pinnatifid (**c**); stem leaves with halberd-shaped, longer terminal lobe. Flowers yellow, 3mm in diameter, in terminal rounded clusters, overtopping the *short fruits (10–20mm) which are closely pressed to the stem.* Widespread and common on waste ground or roadsides. **Fl:** May–Oct. **Br Is dist:** Common throughout.

London-rocket *Sisymbryum irio* Erect annual to 60cm, leaves deeply pinnately lobed with the terminal lobe larger and halberd-shaped (**d**). *Flowers 3–4mm*, with petals longer than, or equal to, sepals. Fruit 30–50mm long, *overtopping the open flowers.* Introduced and naturalised in waste places and docks. **Fl:** Jun–Aug. **Br Is dist:** Rare, mainly around London and Dublin.

Flixweed *Descurainia sophia* Hairy grey-green annual or biennial to 80cm. Leaves twice to 3 times-pinnatifid, the segments narrow and linear. Flowers 3mm in diameter, pale yellow; *petals equal sepals, or slightly shorter.* Fruit to 50mm. Widespread on waste areas and roadsides, often on sandy soils. NB Amongst yellow crucifers, only this species, London-rocket (sometimes) and *Rorippa* species (*see* p. 78) have petals equal to sepals. **Fl:** Jun–Aug. **Br Is dist:** Native or long-introduced casual, locally frequent in E England; uncommon elsewhere.

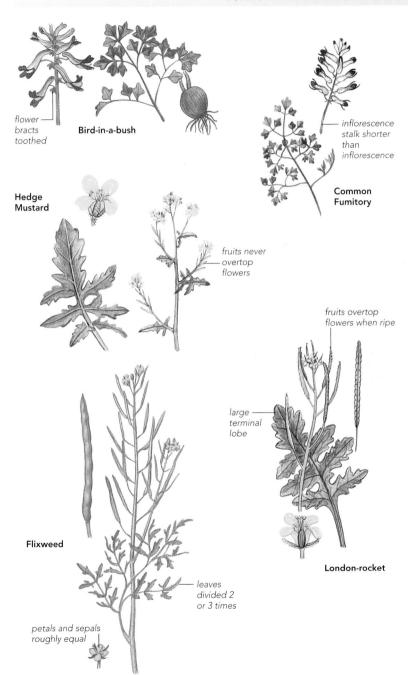

flower bracts toothed

Bird-in-a-bush

inflorescence stalk shorter than inflorescence

Common Fumitory

Hedge Mustard

fruits never overtop flowers

fruits overtop flowers when ripe

large terminal lobe

London-rocket

Flixweed

leaves divided 2 or 3 times

petals and sepals roughly equal

75

Garlic Mustard *Alliaria petiolata* Biennial to 1.2m. Leaves thin, pale green, heart-shaped and toothed; *smelling strongly of garlic when crushed.* Flowers white, 6mm in diameter, petals twice length of sepals. Widespread in hedgerows, roadsides and woodland margins. **Fl:** Apr–Jun. **Br Is dist:** Common almost throughout, less so in N Scotland and Ireland.

Woad

Thale Cress *Arabidopsis thaliana* Annual or biennial to 50cm, roughly hairy below and with a *basal rosette of elliptical, toothed or untoothed leaves.* Flowers 3mm in diameter, white. Fruit a *siliqua to 20mm long,* not flattened (compare with *Arabis* species *see* pp. 82–4), and obliquely erect on long stalks; valves 1-veined. Widespread and common in disturbed places on dry sandy soils, or on old walls. **Fl:** Mar–Oct. **Br Is dist:** Fairly common except in upland areas, and uncommon in Ireland.

Sea Stock

Woad *Isatis tinctoria* Biennial or perennial to 1.2m, with downy lanceolate basal leaves in a rosette. Stem leaves greyish, arrow-shaped, clasping the stem, yielding a blue dye when dried and crushed. Flowers yellow, 4mm in branched panicle. *Fruit distinctive, broadly winged, purplish brown and pendulous.* Naturalised in dry, often rocky or chalky places. **Fl:** Jun–Aug. **Br Is dist:** Rare and established in a few places in Gloucestershire and Surrey.

a

TREACLE-MUSTARDS *Erysimum* Difficult genus of plants characterised by being hairy with branched hairs; leaves usually simple or only shallowly lobed; flowers yellow; sepals erect; fruit a 4-angled siliqua, less than 3mm wide with each valve usually strongly 1-veined.

Treacle-mustard *Erysimum cheiranthoides* Annual to 90cm, with angled stem. Basal leaves simple, shallowly toothed, short-stalked (**a**), in a rosette, withering before flowering; stem leaves similar, often unstalked. Flowers 6–10mm in diameter. Flower stalks 4–8mm, longer than sepals. Fruit to 25mm. In waste and arable areas. **Fl:** Jun–Sep. **Br Is dist:** Possibly introduced but long naturalised, most frequent in SE England.

Wallflower *Erysimum cheiri* Perennial to 60cm, with woody stem base and branched hairs. Leaves narrow-lanceolate, untoothed. Flowers 20–30mm in diameter, orange-yellow, in racemes; erect sepals half the length of petals. Fruit a flattened siliqua to 70mm. Introduced and widely naturalised on old walls and cliffs. **Fl:** Mar–Jun. **Br Is dist:** Locally common throughout.

Sea Stock *Matthiola sinuata* An erect biennial to 40cm; lower leaves wavy-edged and toothed or lobed; fruit with obvious glands. Very local on sea-cliffs and dunes. **Fl:** Jun–Aug. **Br Is dist:** Very rare in SW England, S Wales and Channel Islands.

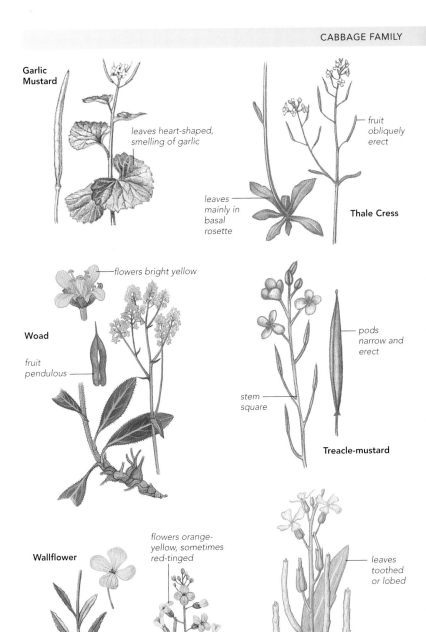

Garlic Mustard

leaves heart-shaped, smelling of garlic

fruit obliquely erect

leaves mainly in basal rosette

Thale Cress

flowers bright yellow

Woad

fruit pendulous

pods narrow and erect

stem square

Treacle-mustard

Wallflower

flowers orange-yellow, sometimes red-tinged

fruit flattened

leaves toothed or lobed

Sea Stock

77

Water-cress

Coralroot

a

WINTER-CRESSES *Barbarea* Biennials or perennials with angled stems, yellow flowers and clasping leaves. Fruit a 4-angled siliqua with convex valves having strong midrib.

Winter-cress *Barbarea vulgaris* Hairless biennial or perennial to 90cm. Lower stem leaves shiny and lobed with characteristic *large terminal lobe which is shorter than rest of leaf*; upper leaves clasping, progressively less lobed and uppermost leaves undivided. Flowers 6–9mm in diameter, in dense racemes. Fruit a 4-angled siliqua to 30mm. Widespread and common in a variety of damp habitats. **Fl:** Apr–Aug. **Br Is dist:** Common in the south, decreasing farther north.

YELLOW-CRESSES *Rorippa* Annual to perennial herbs with yellow flowers and fruit valves always convex, without a strong midrib. Seeds usually in 2 rows in each cell.

Great Yellow-cress *Rorippa amphibia* Perennial to 1.2m, with runners and stout, erect, *hollow stems*. Lower leaves short-stalked and sometimes lobed, upper ones unstalked and never lobed. Flowers 5–7mm in diameter, petals twice length of sepals. Fruit elliptical, 3–6mm long, on spreading stalks. Widespread and often common in wet habitats; absent from the far north. **Fl:** Jun–Sep. **Br Is dist:** Locally common in England; rare in S Scotland and E Wales; scattered localities in Ireland.

Marsh Yellow-cress *Rorippa palustris* An erect perennial up to about 60cm tall. Leaves pinnately divided, usually with an auricle at the base Flowers small, about 3mm across, yellow. Widespread in wet places. **Fl:** Jun–Oct. **Br Is dist:** Widespread and frequent.

Water-cress *Rorippa nasturtium-aquaticum* Perennial with hollow creeping or floating stems, rooting below. Leaves pinnate with rounded lobes untoothed or sinuate-toothed, persisting green over winter. Flowers 4–6mm in diameter in dense racemes. Fruit a siliqua 14–18mm, spreading or ascending on stalks 8–12mm; *seeds in 2 rows per cell* (a). Widespread and often common, in freshwater habitats such as ditches and streams. **Fl:** May–Oct. **Br Is dist:** Common except in mountains. NB Fool's Water-cress (see p. 180) has finely toothed leaves, flowers in umbels and leaf stalks sheathing the stems.

BITTER-CRESSES *Cardamine* Leaves pinnate or trifoliate, and, if pinnate, the basal leaves have the lateral leaflets stalked (unlike other crucifers). Pods long with veinless valves which coil spirally from the base when ripe, often releasing the seeds explosively.

Coralroot *Cardamine bulbifera* Perennial to 70cm with no root leaves and pinnate stem leaves having 1–3 pairs of leaflets; upper leaves simple, and characteristically *bearing purplish-brown reproductive bulbils in their axils*. Flowers 12–18mm in diameter, pale rose-pink, in short terminal racemes. Fruit to 35mm, but often not ripening, especially in the north of its range. Locally frequent in semi-shaded woods on calcareous or sandy soils, but absent in many areas. **Fl:** Apr–May. **Br Is dist:** Very local or rare; SE England only.

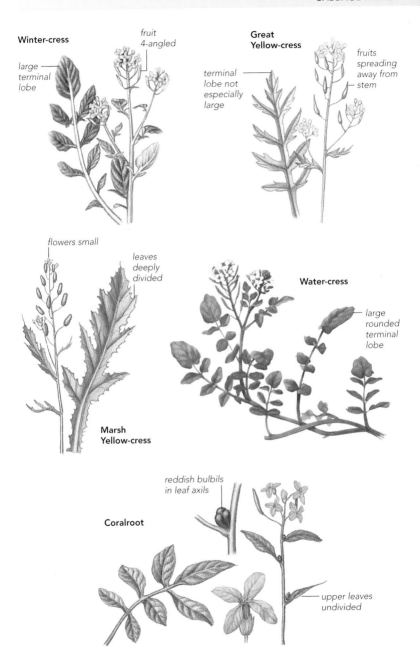

Winter-cress

fruit 4-angled

large terminal lobe

Great Yellow-cress

terminal lobe not especially large

fruits spreading away from stem

flowers small

leaves deeply divided

Water-cress

large rounded terminal lobe

Marsh Yellow-cress

Coralroot

reddish bulbils in leaf axils

upper leaves undivided

79

Hairy Rock-cress

Large Bitter-cress *Cardamine amara* Perennial to 60cm, with pinnate leaves not in a basal rosette, leaflets obscurely toothed and elliptical; terminal lobe longer than broad. *Flowers white*, 12mm in diameter, *violet anthers*. Fruit to 40mm. Widespread and locally abundant; in wet woodlands, flushes, marshes and streamsides. **Fl:** Apr–Jun. **Br Is dist:** Locally abundant, especially in SE, N and C England, and S and E Scotland.

Cuckooflower, Lady's Smock *Cardamine pratensis* Variable perennial to 60cm, with basal leaves pinnate and in a rosette, leaflets rounded but terminal lobe kidney-shaped; upper stem leaves with *very narrow unstalked* linear leaflets. *Flowers lilac or white*, 12–18mm in diameter, *with yellow anthers*. Fruit to 40mm. Widespread and common in a variety of damp, open or semi-shaped habitats. **Fl:** Apr–Jun. **Br Is dist:** Common throughout.

Hairy Bitter-cress *Cardamine hirsuta* Annual to 30cm, with *straight*, erect, *hairless* stems. Leaves pinnate, mainly in basal rosette; leaflets rounded or oval, terminal leaflet kidney-shaped. *Stem leaves 1–4* on main stem (compare with Wavy Bitter-cress). Flowers white, 3–4mm in diameter, petals often absent. Fruit to 25mm, curving upwards and markedly overtopping flower heads. Widespread in a variety of damp, often disturbed, places and old walls. **Fl:** Feb–Nov. **Br Is dist:** Common throughout.

Wavy Bitter-cress *Cardamine flexuosa* Similar to Hairy Bitter-cress, but taller, to 50cm; *stem wavy, hairy*, often branched above. *Stem leaves 4–10* on main stem. Fruit only slightly overtopping flower head. Widespread in damp or wet habitats and waste areas. **Fl:** Mar–Sep. **Br Is dist:** Common throughout.

Arabis Characterised by having numerous unstalked stem leaves and a strongly flattened siliqua with indistinct midribs on valves.

Hairy Rock-cress *Arabis hirsuta* Extremely variable biennial or short-lived perennial to 60cm. *Stems and leaves markedly hairy.* Basal leaves ovate, scarcely toothed, in a rosette; stem leaves untoothed (sometimes with a few teeth), *half-clasping*, erect and close to stem. Flowers many, white, 3–5mm in diameter, in compact inflorescence. Fruit to 35mm, erect. Widespread and locally frequent in calcareous grasslands. **Fl:** May–Aug. **Br Is dist:** Local throughout. Ssp *brownii* is *hairless except for leaf margins.* **Fl:** May–Aug. **Br Is dist:** Endemic to W Ireland, in sand-dunes.

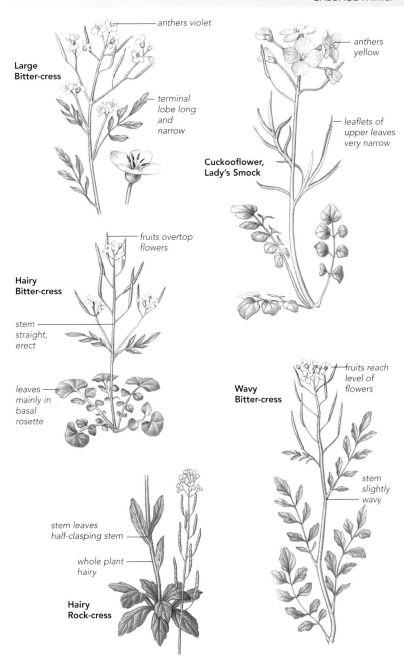

Large Bitter-cress

anthers violet

terminal lobe long and narrow

anthers yellow

leaflets of upper leaves very narrow

Cuckooflower, Lady's Smock

fruits overtop flowers

Hairy Bitter-cress

stem straight, erect

leaves mainly in basal rosette

fruits reach level of flowers

Wavy Bitter-cress

stem slightly wavy

stem leaves half-clasping stem

whole plant hairy

Hairy Rock-cress

Alpine Rock-cress

Small Alison

Yellow Whitlowgrass

Alpine Whitlowgrass

Tower Cress *Arabis turrita* Hairy biennial or perennial to 70cm, with *stems often reddish below*. Basal leaves oblong, sinuate-toothed in rosette; stem leaves 30–50mm, irregularly toothed and *clasping with rounded bases. Flowers pale yellow*, 7–9mm in diameter. *Fruits very distinctive, to 15cm long and all arching over to 1 side* (**a**). Local in rocky places and on old walls. **Fl:** Apr–Jul. **Br Is dist:** Introduced and rarely established on old walls, as at Cambridge.

Alpine Rock-cress *Arabis alpina* Hairy perennial to 40cm, creeping and mat-forming. Basal leaves oblong, coarsely toothed, in a rosette; stem leaves similar but *clasping stem with rounded lobes* (*see* Northern Rock-cress). Flowers white, *6–10mm* in diameter. Fruit to 35mm, spreading and curved upwards. On wet rock ledges and screes in mountains. **Fl:** May–Jul. **Br Is dist:** Very rare and confined to Skye.

Perennial Honesty *Lunaria rediviva* Perennial to 1.5m, with *hairy stems, both lower and upper leaves stalked*. Flowers 20–25mm, reddish-purple, and flattened fruit elliptical in outline, pointed at tip. Widespread in damp, shady woodland, especially on calcareous soils; absent from the north and west. **Fl:** May–Jul. **Br Is dist:** Introduced; rare garden escape.

Small Alison *Alyssum alyssoides* Greyish-hairy annual or biennial to 25cm. Leaves to 30mm, lanceolate, stalked and untoothed. *Flowers pale yellow fading to whitish*, 3mm in diameter, in dense *compact* racemes. Fruit a rounded silicula, 3–4mm in diameter; sepals persistent in fruit. Local on open sandy or calcareous grassland or arable land. **Fl:** Apr–Jun. **Br Is dist:** Rare and probably introduced in S and E England and E Scotland.

WHITLOWGRASSES *Draba* Leaves simple. Stem leaves few or none; occasionally numerous (Hoary Whitlowgrass, *see* p. 84). Fruit (**b**) a many-seeded silicula with valves flat, midrib in lower part only. Petals not deeply cleft (Common Whitlowgrass, *see* p. 84).

Yellow Whitlowgrass *Draba aizoides* Tufted perennial to only 15cm. Leaves only in basal rosettes, *linear-lanceolate* and stiff with marginal bristles; tip of leaf has long white bristle. Flowers bright yellow, *8–9mm* in diameter, in dense terminal clusters. Fruit 6–12mm long. Very local on cliffs, rocky places in mountains and on old walls; mainly a S and C European species. **Fl:** Mar–May. **Br Is dist:** Very rare, and mainly confined to limestone rocks in S Wales where it is probably native; also introduced and naturalised on old walls.

Alpine Whitlowgrass *Draba alpina* Variable, densely tufted, hairy perennial to 20cm. Leaves only in basal rosettes, *elliptical*. Flowers bright yellow, *4–8mm* in dense terminal clusters. Fruit 4–10mm. Very local in rocky and gravelly places; in Arctic and sub-Arctic. **Fl:** Jul–Aug. **Br Is dist:** Absent.

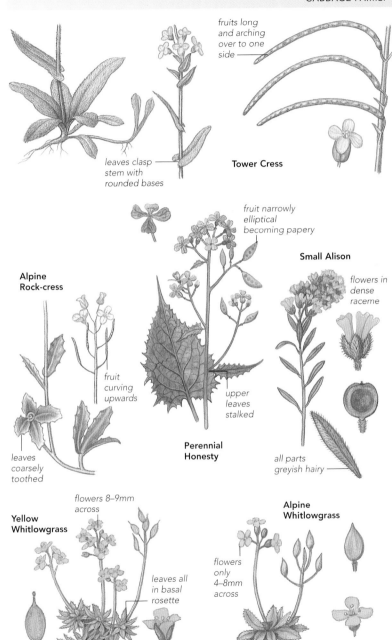

fruits long and arching over to one side

leaves clasp stem with rounded bases

Tower Cress

fruit narrowly elliptical becoming papery

Small Alison

Alpine Rock-cress

flowers in dense raceme

fruit curving upwards

upper leaves stalked

leaves coarsely toothed

Perennial Honesty

all parts greyish hairy

Yellow Whitlowgrass

flowers 8–9mm across

leaves all in basal rosette

Alpine Whitlowgrass

flowers only 4–8mm across

Hoary Whitlowgrass

Hoary Whitlowgrass *Draba incana* Robust biennial or perennial, to 35cm, *usually with numerous stem leaves*. Basal leaves in a rosette, lanceolate, hairy, slightly toothed or untoothed; stem leaves lanceolate, usually coarsely toothed, *densely hairy*. Flowers white, 3–5mm in diameter, in 10- to 40-flowered terminal cluster; *petals slightly notched*. Fruit hairless to 9mm, twisted when ripe. Very local on rocks and cliffs, especially on limestone; usually in mountains, but occasionally on dunes. Fl: Jun–Jul. **Br Is dist:** Very local from N Wales to N Scotland.

Danish Scurvygrass

Common Whitlowgrass *Erophila verna* Annual to 20cm, slightly hairy below. Leaves only in a basal rosette, elliptical or lanceolate. Flowers white, 3–6mm in diameter, with petals deeply cleft (this distinguishes *Erophila* from the *Draba* species). Fruit to 9mm. Widespread and common in bare places, on walls and rocks, but absent from much of Scandinavia. Fl: Mar–Jun. **Br Is dist:** Common throughout.

SCURVYGRASSES *Cochlearia* Annuals or perennials with simple, often fleshy, leaves; flowers white or reddish with 6 stamens; fruit a swollen, rounded silicula. Often coastal.

Common Scurvygrass

Danish Scurvygrass *Cochlearia danica* Annual to 20cm. Basal leaves long-stalked, roundish with a heart-shaped base; upper stem leaves stalked, the lowest ivy-shaped with 3–7 lobes. Flowers white or pale mauve, 4–6mm in diameter. Fruit ovoid, to 6mm. Locally frequent on coastal cliffs, sandy ground or walls; occasionally on disturbed ground inland. Fl: Jan–Aug. **Br Is dist:** Frequent all round the coasts.

English Scurvygrass

Common Scurvygrass *Cochlearia officinalis* Very variable biennial or perennial to 50cm, with kidney-shaped *basal leaves more than 20mm long*, and oblong stem leaves, often coarsely toothed with the upper ones clasping the stem. *Flowers white, 8–10mm.* Fruit ovoid 4–7mm, longer than its stalk. Widespread and locally common on coastal salt-marshes, walls and mountains inland (especially on basic rocks). Fl: Apr–Sep. **Br Is dist:** Locally common. Two subspecies are now recognised: Ssp *officinalis* Stems to 30cm or more, petals 4–8mm, usually white. Widespread on salt-marshes, and inland by salt-treated roads. Ssp *scotica* Stems to only 10cm, petals 2–4mm, often lilac. Leaves (**a**). Mainly coastal. **Br Is dist:** Endemic.

a

Pyrenean, or Alpine, Scurvygrass *Cochlearia pyrenaica* Differs from Common Scurvygrass in having *smaller basal leaves (under 20mm)*, *smaller flowers (5–8mm)* and elliptical fruit, narrowed above and below, shorter than its stalk. Local inland species of mountains, rocky places, stream margins, spoil heaps or meadows. Fl: Jun–Sep. **Br Is dist:** Widely scattered but often local. Sometimes separated into ssp *pyrenaica* found on lead- or zinc-rich spoilheaps; and ssp *alpina* found in rocky places in W and N Britain.

English Scurvygrass *Cochlearia anglica* Biennial or perennial to 35cm, with rather stiff stems, and oblong basal leaves narrowed at the base, often with a few teeth; upper leaves clasping the stem. Flowers white, 10–14mm in diameter. Fruit elliptical and compressed, 8–15mm. Locally common; coastal muds and estuaries. Fl: Apr–Jul. **Br Is dist:** Locally common on most coasts.

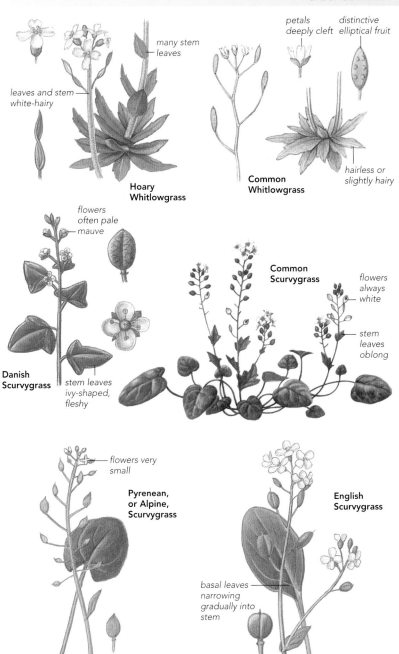

petals deeply cleft

distinctive elliptical fruit

many stem leaves

leaves and stem white-hairy

Hoary Whitlowgrass

hairless or slightly hairy

Common Whitlowgrass

flowers often pale mauve

Common Scurvygrass

flowers always white

stem leaves oblong

Danish Scurvygrass

stem leaves ivy-shaped, fleshy

flowers very small

Pyrenean, or Alpine, Scurvygrass

English Scurvygrass

basal leaves narrowing gradually into stem

85

Dittander

a1   a2

Shepherd's-purse *Capsella bursa-pastoris* Annual or biennial to 40cm, dull green. Basal leaves oblong-lanceolate, varying from deeply lobed to unlobed; upper leaves usually toothed, clasping the stem. Flowers white, 2–3mm in loose racemes; petals up to twice the length of sepals. Fruit distinctively triangular, flattened and notched. Widespread and often abundant in disturbed places or tracksides. **Fl:** Jan–Dec. **Br Is dist:** Common throughout.

Shepherd's Cress *Teesdalia nudicaulis* Annual or biennial to 25cm, with few or no stem leaves and basal rosette of pinnately lobed leaves. Flowers distinctive, 2mm, with white petals, *2 much shorter than the other pair*. Fruit heart-shaped, notched above, 3–4mm. Local to locally common in dry sandy places or shingle. **Fl:** Apr–Jun. **Br Is dist:** Local in the south, rare in the north and Ireland.

PENNY-CRESSES *Thlaspi* Stem leaves unstalked and often clasping. Flowers white or occasionally lilac. Fruit a flattened silicula with an apical notch and the valves winged and keeled. Seeds 2 or more per cell (compare with pepperworts, *see* below).

Field Penny-cress *Thlaspi arvense* Hairless annual to 50cm, emitting a fetid smell when crushed. No basal rosette of leaves; stem leaves lanceolate, toothed and *clasping with arrow-shaped base*. Flowers white, 4–6mm, with *yellow anthers*. Fruit a circular silicula, 10–15mm in diameter with a deep notch. Widespread and common as weed of arable and waste areas. **Fl:** May–Jul. **Br Is dist:** Common throughout.

PEPPERWORTS *Lepidium* These resemble penny-cresses, but fruits have only 1 seed per cell as opposed to 2 or more.

Field Pepperwort *Lepidium campestre* Greyish, hairy annual or biennial to 60cm. Basal leaves ovate-lanceolate, untoothed and soon withering; stem leaves arrow-shaped, *clasping stem*. Flowers white, 2mm, with *yellow anthers*. Fruit shaped like a coal-shovel when viewed from the side, 5–6mm, notched and *covered with small white vesicles*; style equals notch; fruit stalk spreading, but fruit erect. Widespread, and locally common, on dry grassland, arable or disturbed ground. **Fl:** May–Aug. **Br Is dist:** Fairly common, less so in the north.

Dittander *Lepidium latifolium* Stout perennial to 1.2m with *large (to 30cm) oval, toothed leaves* (**a1**), the lower ones stalked, and a dense pyramidal panicle of white flowers, 2–3mm in diameter. Fruit rounded, 2mm, unnotched or hardly so (**a2**). In salt-marshes and wet sandy areas. **Fl:** May–Jul. **Br Is dist:** Very local as both native and introduction.

Shepherd's-purse

fruit distinctive triangular and notched

stem leaves clasping

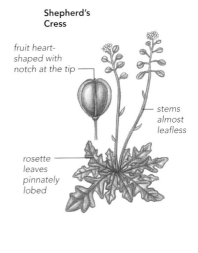

Shepherd's Cress

fruit heart-shaped with notch at the tip

stems almost leafless

rosette leaves pinnately lobed

fruit round, winged and notched

Field Penny-cress

fruit rounded – triangular, notched

Field Pepperwort

stem leaves clasping stem

flowers in branched inflorescence

Dittander

leaves large

Swine-cress *Coronopus squamatus* Prostrate annual or biennial to 30cm, with ascending stems bearing pinnate, light green leaves, the leaflets coarsely toothed. Flowers white, 2.5mm in diameter, in dense racemes opposite leaves or in axils of branches. Fruit kidney-shaped, pointed above and with network of raised ridges (**a**). Locally common in waste and disturbed areas and paths. **Fl:** May–Oct. **Br Is dist:** Common throughout S and E England, locally frequent elsewhere; usually near coast.

Annual Wall-rocket,
Stinkweed

Lesser Swine-cress *Coronopus didymus* Very similar to Swine-cress, but flowers usually have no petals (or, if present, they are shorter than sepals), and fruit is notched above and below, shaped like a dumb-bell (**b**). Locally common in waste and disturbed areas; absent from many inland areas. **Fl:** Jun–Oct. **Br Is dist:** Naturalised throughout, but rarely abundant.

WALL-ROCKETS *Diplotaxis* Flowers yellow or lilac and fruit (siliqua) with single vein on each valve and 2 rows of seeds per cell.

Wild Cabbage

Annual Wall-rocket, Stinkweed *Diplotaxis muralis* Annual to 60cm, with erect or ascending stems branched mainly below. Leaves mainly in basal rosette, pinnatifid with oblong lobes, very fetid when bruised. Flowers yellow, 10–15mm in diameter. Fruit to 40mm. Locally common in waste areas and arable land, on sandy soils and walls. **Fl:** May–Sep. **Br Is dist:** Naturalised or casual, widespread in England and Wales but rare in Scotland and Ireland.

a

BRASSICAS *Brassica* Leaves undivided or pinnately lobed; petals yellow or white; fruit a beaked siliqua with 1 row of seeds, and valves rounded on back with only 1 strong vein (**c**).

b

Wild Cabbage *Brassica oleracea* Biennial or perennial to 1.5m, greyish-green with a thick woody stem below bearing obvious leaf scars. Basal leaves fleshy and large, to 30cm, wavy, lobed and with winged stalks; upper stem leaves to 70mm, unstalked, unlobed and clasping. Flowers pale yellow, 30–40mm in elongated racemes. Fruit to 90mm, ascending. Coastal, usually on calcareous cliffs and often near sea-bird colonies which disperse the seeds. **Fl:** Apr–Sep. **Br Is dist:** Local and possibly intro-duced in S and SW England and Wales.

c

Black Mustard *Brassica nigra* Tall annual to 2m, often greyish and hairy below. Leaves all stalked, the lower ones pinnately lobed. Flowers yellow, 12–15mm in diameter. Fruits to only 30mm, flattened and distinctively pressed close to stem (unlike any other *Brassica* species). Frequent on riverbanks and sea-cliffs; casual in arable and waste areas. **Fl:** May–Sep. **Br Is dist:** Native and locally frequent in England and Wales; rare in S Scotland; also a frequent casual.

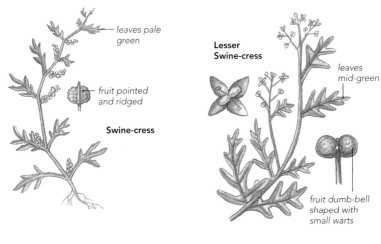

leaves pale green

fruit pointed and ridged

Swine-cress

Lesser Swine-cress

leaves mid-green

fruit dumb-bell shaped with small warts

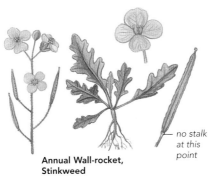

no stalk at this point

Annual Wall-rocket, Stinkweed

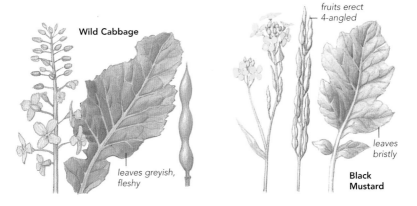

Wild Cabbage

leaves greyish, fleshy

fruits erect 4-angled

leaves bristly

Black Mustard

Hairy Rocket

Sea Rocket

Sea-kale

a

SINAPIS *Sinapis* Differ from *Brassica* in that the fruit valves (**a**) have 3–7 strong veins, not 1.

Charlock *Sinapis arvensis* Tall annual to 2m, dark green or purplish, hairy below. Lower leaves large, stalked, coarsely toothed, often lyre-shaped; upper leaves stalked or unstalked, and unlobed. Flowers yellow, 15–20mm, in crowded terminal clusters; sepals usually spreading or down-turned. Fruit beak rounded (compare with White Mustard). Common in arable and waste areas. **Fl:** Apr–Oct. **Br Is dist:** Common throughout.

White Mustard *Sinapis alba* Differs from Charlock in having upper leaves pinnately lobed and fruit beak flattened. Locally common casual of arable and waste areas; absent from much of the extreme north. **Fl:** May–Sep. **Br Is dist:** Frequent in SE; scattered elsewhere.

Hairy Rocket *Erucastrum gallicum* Hairy annual to 60cm, with *bipinnatifid leaves*. Flowers pale yellow, 10–15mm in diameter, in crowded terminal heads; lower part of flower stalk has *pinnately lobed bracts*. Fruit to 45mm, with seeds in 1 row and valves with 1 strong vein. Uncommon in dry waste areas and docks. **Fl:** May–Nov. **Br Is dist:** Rare to occasional casual.

Sea Rocket *Cakile maritima* Annual to 30cm with sprawling stems and shiny green hairless and succulent leaves, pinnatifid or shallowly lobed. Flowers white, pink or lilac, 6–12mm in diameter, in crowded racemes. Fruit erect, to 20mm, with 2 segments, 1 above the other, the lower with 2 shoulder-like projections. Frequent on sandy beaches, open dunes (early coloniser) and shingle. **Fl:** Jun–Sep. **Br Is dist:** Frequent around the coasts.

Sea-kale *Crambe maritima* Distinctive hairless bushy perennial to 50cm, greyish green or flushed purple. Leaves broad, succulent, wavy and variable in shape from oval to elliptical, often coarsely toothed and lobed. Flowers white in dense, flattish terminal heads. Fruit globular with 1–2 seeds. On sand, shingle coasts above drift-line. **Fl:** May–Aug. **Br Is dist:** Occasional to very locally abundant; possibly declining.

Wild Radish *Raphanus raphanistrum* ssp *raphanistrum* Annual to 1m, hairy below. Basal and lower stem leaves pinnate with up to 7 pairs of toothed lateral lobes; upper leaves lanceolate. Flowers white to yellow (sometimes purplish) with darker veins on petals; sepals erect. Fruit beaded with up to 10 segments, 2–5mm wide, often with narrow constrictions in between; terminal part conical and pointed. Common in arable and waste areas. **Fl:** Jun–Oct. **Br Is dist:** Common throughout.

Sea Radish *Raphanus raphanistrum* ssp *maritimus* Flowers almost always yellow and fruit with up to 5 strongly beaded segments, 5–10mm wide. On sand-dunes, sea-cliffs and coastal grassland. **Fl:** May–Jul. **Br Is dist:** Scattered around the coasts; locally abundant in S and W.

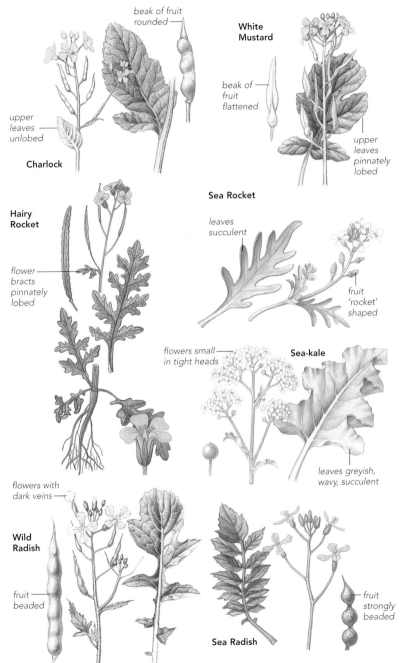

beak of fruit rounded

White Mustard

beak of fruit flattened

upper leaves unlobed

upper leaves pinnately lobed

Charlock

Sea Rocket

Hairy Rocket

flower bracts pinnately lobed

leaves succulent

fruit 'rocket' shaped

flowers small in tight heads

Sea-kale

leaves greyish, wavy, succulent

flowers with dark veins

Wild Radish

fruit beaded

fruit strongly beaded

Sea Radish

Wild Mignonette

White Mignonette

Round-leaved Sundew

Oblong-leaved Sundew

Great Sundew

MIGNONETTE FAMILY Resedaceae

Annuals or perennials with spirally arranged leaves and flowers in spikes or racemes. Petals 4–8, often deeply divided. Sepals 4–Aug.

Weld *Reseda luteola* Tall hairless biennial to 1.5m, with stiffly erect, ribbed, hollow stems. Basal rosette of narrow oblong leaves withering after 1st season; stem leaves unlobed with wavy margins. Flowers 4-petalled, yellowish-green in long slender racemes. Common in disturbed or stony ground, on calcareous soils. **Fl:** Jun–Sep. **Br Is dist:** Mostly common, local in N and W Britain.

Wild Mignonette *Reseda lutea* Similar to Weld but stems solid, to 75cm. Stem leaves pinnately lobed with 1–2 pairs of lobes, the margins slightly wavy. Flowers 6-petalled, greenish-yellow in more compact conical racemes. Common in disturbed areas on calcareous soils. **Fl:** Jun–Aug. **Br Is dist:** Locally common; absent N Scotland; probably not native Ireland.

White Mignonette *Reseda alba* Leaves with at least 5 pairs of lobes. Flowers white; fruit erect. In disturbed areas, stony places, on old walls and docks. **Fl:** Jun–Aug. **Br Is dist:** Casual, mainly in SW England.

Corn Mignonette *Reseda phyteuma* Leaves paddle-shaped usually with no lobes (occasionally 1–2). White flowers; fruit pendulous. Similar habitats to White Mignonette. **Fl:** Jun–Aug. **Br Is dist:** Rare casual in S England.

SUNDEW FAMILY Droseraceae

Perennial insectiverous herbs with leaves that have long glandular hairs adapted to trapping insects, and sepals united at the base. The leaves secrete enzymes which help to digest the insects.

Round-leaved Sundew *Drosera rotundifolia* Reddish plant to 25cm when in flower, with leaves in a basal rosette, rounded to 10mm in diameter, long-stalked and spreading. Flowers white (only opening in full sun) on long erect stalks, 2–4 times the length of leaves, arising from the centre of the rosette. Fruit a capsule. Locally frequent in wet peaty areas on moors and heaths. **Fl:** Jun–Aug. **Br Is dist:** Much decreased through habitat destruction, most frequent in N Britain and Ireland; increasingly local in S England.

Oblong-leaved Sundew *Drosera intermedia* Differs from Round-leaved Sundew in having narrow oblong leaves to 10mm, *tapering abruptly into the stalk*. Flower stalk arises below the rosette, and is usually not much longer than the leaves. Wet peaty places on heaths or moors, sometimes on sphagnum. More local than Round-leaved Sundew. **Fl:** Jun–Aug. **Br Is dist:** Decreasing, as Round-leafed Sundew, but least local in W Britain, Ireland and parts of S England.

Great Sundew *Drosera anglica* Long narrow leaves to 30mm, *gradually tapering into stalk*. Flower stalk arises from centre of rosette, up to twice the length of leaves. Wettest parts of peatbogs, decreasing in Europe through habitat destruction. **Fl:** Jun–Aug. **Br Is dist:** Locally frequent in N and W Scotland and W Ireland; rare in England and Wales.

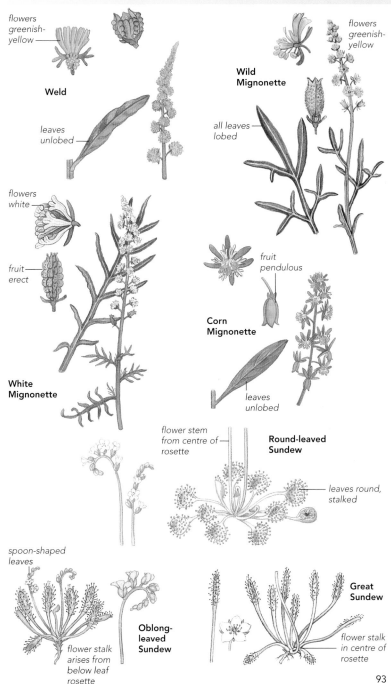

flowers greenish-yellow

Weld

leaves unlobed

flowers greenish-yellow

Wild Mignonette

all leaves lobed

flowers white

fruit erect

fruit pendulous

Corn Mignonette

White Mignonette

leaves unlobed

flower stem from centre of rosette

Round-leaved Sundew

leaves round, stalked

spoon-shaped leaves

Oblong-leaved Sundew

flower stalk arises from below leaf rosette

Great Sundew

flower stalk in centre of rosette

93

STONECROP FAMILY Crassulaceae

Succulent plants with fleshy undivided leaves and 5-petalled flowers; 3–20 sepals and petals, the stamens equalling or twice this number.

Mossy Stonecrop

Mossy Stonecrop *Crassula tillaea* Tiny, often reddish, annual with creeping and ascending stems to 50mm. Leaves opposite, fused, very crowded, blunt, 1–2mm long. Flowers whitish, minute (1–2mm) and numerous in leaf axils, with 3 petals and 3 longer sepals. Very local in bare, damp, sandy or gravelly ground. **Fl:** Jun–Sep. **Br Is dist:** Very local in S and E England.

Navelwort

Navelwort, Wall Pennywort *Umbilicus rupestris* Distinctive hairless perennial to 40cm, with stalked, rounded fleshy leaves, mostly basal, with a central navel-like depression and very broad blunt teeth. Flowers tubular, greenish-white and drooping in many-flowered spikes. Locally common on old walls, rocks, cliffs and hedge banks. **Fl:** Jun–Sep. **Br Is dist:** Common in the west; scarce elsewhere.

STONECROPS *Sedum* Leaves fleshy, alternate or whorled (occasionally opposite), flowers in cymes with petals free, usually 5 in number (can be 3–10) and stamens twice the number of petals. The shape and colour of the leaves plus the flower's colour help to separate species.

Roseroot

Roseroot *Sedum rosea* Greyish perennial to 30cm, with clustered erect stems bearing alternate, thick, overlapping, variably toothed leaves and terminal clusters of greenish-yellow, or dull yellow, 4-petalled flowers. Fruit orange. Locally frequent in mountain rocks, screes and sea-cliffs. **Fl:** May–Aug. **Br Is dist:** Locally common from Wales northwards and in N and W Ireland.

Reflexed Stonecrop

Reflexed Stonecrop *Sedum rupestre* Greyish mat-forming perennial to 30cm. Leaves rounded in cross-section, linear and evenly spread up stem. Flowers, many, in terminal cyme, drooping in bud, bright or pale yellow; usually petals 7. Locally common in stony or rocky places or on walls. **Fl:** Jun–Aug. **Br Is dist:** Introduced and naturalised on old walls.

Rock Stonecrop *Sedum forsterianum* Perennial with flowers very similar to Reflexed Stonecrop, but leaves flat on top and in distinctive terminal clusters on non-flowering shoots; dead leaves persist below. Local in rocky places and screes. **Fl:** Jun–Aug. **Br Is dist:** Very local in SW England and Wales; naturalised elsewhere.

Rock Stonecrop

Biting Stonecrop *Sedum acre* Hairless mat-forming evergreen to only 10cm. Leaves beak-shaped, broadest towards base, densely crowded and pressed to stem on non-flowering shoots; peppery taste. Flowers bright yellow, 10–12mm in diameter, in few-flowered terminal clusters. Frequent in dry places, sand-dunes and on old walls. **Fl:** May–Jul. **Br Is dist:** Frequent almost throughout.

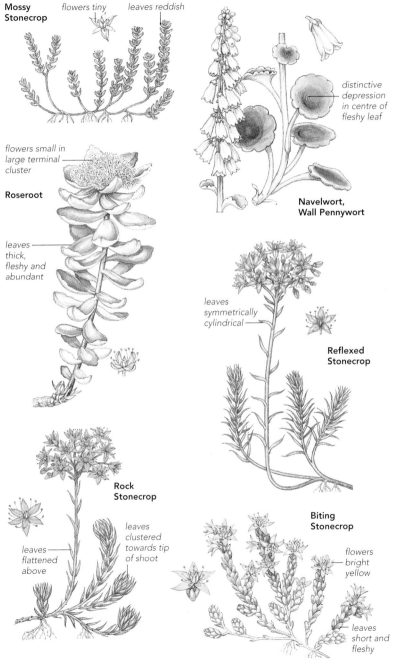

Mossy Stonecrop

flowers tiny

leaves reddish

distinctive depression in centre of fleshy leaf

Navelwort, Wall Pennywort

flowers small in large terminal cluster

Roseroot

leaves thick, fleshy and abundant

leaves symmetrically cylindrical

Reflexed Stonecrop

Rock Stonecrop

leaves clustered towards tip of shoot

leaves flattened above

Biting Stonecrop

flowers bright yellow

leaves short and fleshy

95

English Stonecrop *Sedum anglicum* Hairless, evergreen, mat-forming perennial to only 50mm. Leaves oblong, 3–6mm, alternate, greyish-green or red-tinged. Flowers almost unstalked, white (pink beneath), 12mm in diameter, in terminal clusters of 3–6. Locally common in a wide variety of dry, sandy or rocky places and shingle. **Fl:** Jun–Sep. **Br Is dist:** Most common in the west and Ireland; scattered localities near S and E coasts.

English Stonecrop

SAXIFRAGE FAMILY Saxifragaceae

Mainly perennial herbs with leaves simple; usually alternate or spiral, or entirely in basal rosette. Flowers with 5 petals and sepals (*Saxifraga*) or 4 sepals but no petals (*Chrysosplenium*), and twice the number of stamens. Carpels 2, united at the base but free above. Fruit a capsule with numerous seeds.

Alpine Saxifrage *Saxifraga nivalis* Perennial to 20cm, with glandular hairs on purplish stem and leaf margins. Leaves thick and spoon-shaped, *purplish beneath*, all in basal rosette. Flowers white or pink (without spots), *short-stalked* in dense terminal cluster. Sepals erect or spreading. In wet, often shady, rocks, screes and moraines; most frequent in Scandinavia. **Fl:** Jul–Aug. **Br Is dist:** Rare in N Wales, NW England, Scotland and W Ireland.

Alpine Saxifrage

Starry Saxifrage *Saxifraga stellaris* Perennial to 30cm, slightly hairy and often tufted. Leaves thick and oblong, toothed, *hardly stalked*, and all in basal rosettes. Inflorescence an open, loose panicle of up to 14 white flowers, the *petals having 2 yellow spots near the base but no red spots above*; sepals down-turned. Locally frequent in streamsides, mountain flushes and damp places. **Fl:** Jun–Aug. **Br Is dist:** Frequent in mountains.

Starry Saxifrage

Meadow Saxifrage *Saxifraga granulata* Hairy perennial to 50cm. Leaves mostly basal, rounded or kidney-shaped, with numerous shallow, *blunt teeth* all around the margin; at the base of the leaf stalks, below ground, are a number of bulbils by which the plant overwinters. Flowers white, 15–30mm in diameter, 2–12 in loose terminal clusters; petals twice the length of sepals. Widespread and locally frequent in grassland, usually on well-drained neutral or basic soils, but occasionally in damp or wet meadows. **Fl:** Apr–Jun. **Br Is dist:** Rather local, most common in the east; very local in E Ireland.

Meadow Saxifrage

Rue-leaved Saxifrage *Saxifraga tridactylites* Annual to 15cm, glandular hairy and usually reddish. *Lower leaves stalked* with 1–3 finger-like lobes; upper leaves simple. Flowers white, only 4–6mm in diameter, in loose clusters or solitary. Locally frequent on old walls and rocks, dry, sandy or calcareous ground. **Fl:** Jun–Sep. **Br Is dist:** Widespread but ranging from very local to locally frequent, rare in Scotland.

Mossy Saxifrage

Mossy Saxifrage *Saxifraga hypnoides* Mat-forming perennial to 20cm, characterised by having, in addition to the erect flowering shoots, *numerous procumbent non-flowering shoots bearing leafy bulbils in the axils of the leaves*. Leaves 3- to 5-lobed with narrow, pointed, linear lobes. Flowers white, 10–15mm in diameter, 1–5 in terminal cluster; buds nodding. Very local on rocks, screes and in grassy places; with a distinct northwest distribution. **Fl:** May–Jul. **Br Is dist:** Locally frequent from N England to N Scotland; rare in Mendips; very local in N and W Ireland.

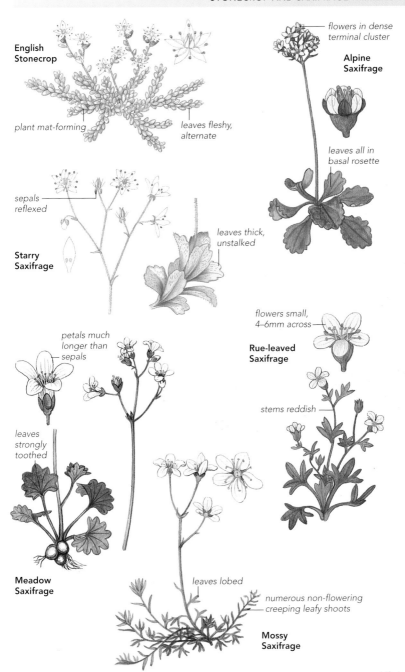

English Stonecrop

plant mat-forming

leaves fleshy, alternate

flowers in dense terminal cluster

Alpine Saxifrage

leaves all in basal rosette

sepals reflexed

Starry Saxifrage

leaves thick, unstalked

petals much longer than sepals

flowers small, 4–6mm across

Rue-leaved Saxifrage

stems reddish

leaves strongly toothed

Meadow Saxifrage

leaves lobed

numerous non-flowering creeping leafy shoots

Mossy Saxifrage

Drooping Saxifrage

Drooping Saxifrage *Saxifraga cernua* Slender perennial to 15cm. Basal leaves in a rosette, shallowly palmately lobed, with 3–5 lobes. Flowers white, 12–18mm in diameter, *solitary or often absent*, all or remaining flowers being replaced by *reproductive red bulbils in axils of bracts*. Local to very rare, in rocky, often shady places in mountains. **Fl:** Jun–Jul. **Br Is dist:** Very rare in Scottish Highlands.

Purple Saxifrage

Purple Saxifrage *Saxifraga oppositifolia* Low, mat-forming perennial with creeping stems. Distinctive in having *opposite leaves* and *purple flowers*. Leaves dark green, oblong and thick, 2–6mm long with a thick-ened tip bearing 1–5 lime-secreting pores, and bristly margins. Flowers solitary on a short stalk, rosy purple and 10–20mm in diameter. Local to locally frequent, on damp basic rocks in mountains, sea-cliffs and stony ground down to sea level. **Fl:** Mar–May (occasionally also Jul–Aug). **Br Is dist:** Local to rare in Wales and N England; locally frequent in Scottish Highlands, more local elsewhere in Scotland; very rare in NW Ireland.

Yellow Saxifrage

Yellow Saxifrage *Saxifraga aizoides* Perennial to 20cm, with leafy, slightly hairy, flowering stem. Leaves rather thick, lanceolate, *unstalked* and often toothed. Flowers bright yellow or orange-yellow, 7–15mm in diameter, *in a loose cluster of 1–10 flowers*; petals often bearing red dots near the base. Locally common, on wet stony ground and streamsides, usually in moun-tains but descending to sea level. **Fl:** Jun–Sep. **Br Is dist:** Locally common in N England, Scotland and N Ireland.

GOLDEN-SAXIFRAGES *Chrysosplenium* Perennials with stalked leaves and small apetalous 4-sepalled flowers in flat leafy clusters.

Alternate-leaved Golden-saxifrage

Opposite-leaved Golden-saxifrage *Chrysosplenium oppositifolium* Patch-forming perennial to 15cm, with creeping, rooting stems. Leaves in opposite pairs, slightly hairy, stalked and rounded with numerous blunt teeth, *the stalk usually no longer than the blade*. Flowers yellow, without petals and only 3–5mm in diameter, in dense flat clusters subtended by greenish-yellow bracts. Widespread and locally common in shady stream-sides, damp woodland flushes and mountain rocks; absent from most of Scandinavia and the far east of the region. **Fl:** Apr–Jul. **Br Is dist:** Locally common to common in most areas, but more local in E England.

Alternate-leaved Golden-saxifrage *Chrysosplenium alternifolium* Patch-forming and slightly hairy, as Opposite-leaved Golden-saxifrage, but has *creeping leafless stolons* instead of leafy stems, and *long-stalked, kidney-shaped leaves* with blunt teeth. Flowers very similar, but 5–6mm in diameter, with bracts deeply toothed. Local to very local, in damp, shady woodlands, usually on base-rich soils; also on mountain rocks. More fre-quent than Opposite-leaved Golden-saxifrage in Scandinavia and the east. **Fl:** Mar–Jun. **Br Is dist:** More local than Opposite-leaved Golden-saxifrage, absent from the extreme north, extreme west and Ireland.

Grass-of-Parnassus

Grass-of-Parnassus *Parnassia palustris* Hairless tufted perennial to 30cm. Basal leaves stalked and heart-shaped, often red-spotted beneath; stem leaf solitary and clasping. Flower solitary, white, 15–30mm in diameter; petals have conspicuous greenish veins. Locally frequent in marshes, moors and fens. **Fl:** Jun–Oct. **Br Is dist:** Widespread but varying from rare to locally frequent; most frequent in the north; rare in CS England; absent from extreme south.

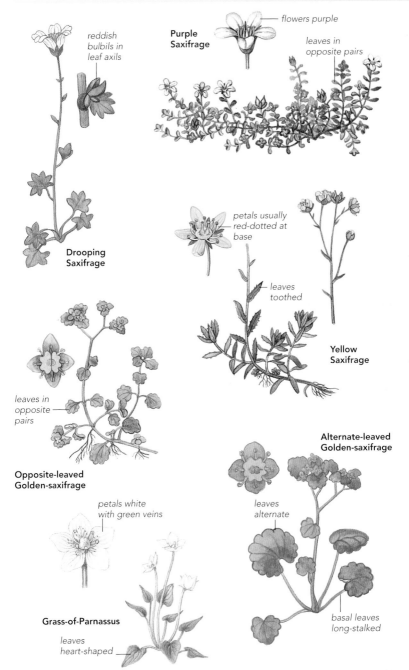

reddish
bulbils in
leaf axils

**Purple
Saxifrage**

flowers purple

leaves in
opposite pairs

**Drooping
Saxifrage**

petals usually
red-dotted at
base

leaves
toothed

**Yellow
Saxifrage**

leaves in
opposite
pairs

**Opposite-leaved
Golden-saxifrage**

**Alternate-leaved
Golden-saxifrage**

leaves
alternate

petals white
with green veins

Grass-of-Parnassus

leaves
heart-shaped

basal leaves
long-stalked

99

Dropwort

Cloudberry

Arctic Bramble

ROSE FAMILY Rosaceae

A very large and diverse family of trees, shrubs and herbs always possessing alternate, non-fleshy leaves (often lobed) and usually with stipules. A common feature is that the stamens and petals are attached to the sepals by their bases, so that when the sepals are removed the stamens and petals come with them. Flowers regular with parts usually in 5s, but sometimes 4s (lady's-mantles, burnets and cinquefoils), or rarely 6s. An epicalyx (outer ring of sepals below true sepals) is often present. Fruit very variable, ranging from capsule or collection of achenes to drupes (cherries and plums), drupelets (blackberries) or pomes (apples and pears).

Meadowsweet *Filipendula ulmaria* Perennial to 1.2m, with pinnate leaves bearing 2 types of leaflets: 2–5 pairs of larger sharply toothed leaflets, each 20–80mm, and between these a number of tiny leaflets, each 1–4mm; terminal leaflet 3- to 5-lobed. Inflorescence consisting of dense showy panicles of many creamy, fragrant flowers, each 4–8mm in diameter. Fruit a distinctive spirally twisting achene. Widespread and common in a variety of damp or wet habitats such as marshes, fens, streamsides, ditches and wet open woodland. **Fl:** Jun–Sep. **Br Is dist:** Common throughout.

Dropwort *Filipendula vulgaris* Perennial to 50cm, with similar features to Meadowsweet, the leaves bearing 2 types of leaflets, but differing in having 8–20 pairs of larger leaflets, each 5–15mm and *deeply pinnately cut into narrow lobes*. Inflorescence differs in being flat-topped, an inverted triangular shape and consisting of numerous, larger, creamy white flowers, reddish beneath and 10–20mm across. Rather local from S Sweden southwards; in dry calcareous grassland. **Fl:** May–Aug. **Br Is dist:** Local or sometimes locally abundant, north to Yorkshire and in Wales; very rare in E Scotland; very local in W Ireland.

BRAMBLES *Rubus* Perennials, often prickly and scrambling, and usually with compound leaves (except Cloudberry), the leaflets having stipules. Flowers with 5 sepals joined below, 5 (to 8) separate petals but no epicalyx; carpels on a conical receptacle (contrast with *Rosa* species, pp. 102–4). Fruit an aggregate of 1-seeded fleshy drupelets.

Cloudberry *Rubus chamaemorus* Low, downy creeping perennial to 20cm, without prickles and often forming patches. Leaves few, 1–3 per plant, rounded to 80mm in diameter, somewhat wrinkled and palmately lobed with 5–7 lobes. Flowers white (often absent), 15–25mm in diameter, solitary on a terminal stalk; usually dioecious. Fruit becoming red, then orange, a collection of about 20 drupelets. Locally abundant in mountain moors and bogs. **Fl:** Jun–Aug. **Br Is dist:** Locally abundant from N England to N Scotland; rare in N Wales; very rare in Ireland.

Arctic Bramble *Rubus arcticus* Creeping perennial to 40cm, without prickles. Leaves trifoliate with toothed leaflets. *Flowers solitary*, 15–20mm in diameter, *bright pink*. Fruit dark red, a collection of many drupelets. Locally frequent in moors and grassy places in mountains; Scandinavia only. **Fl:** Jun–Jul. **Br Is dist:** Apparently extinct, but formerly in Scottish Highlands.

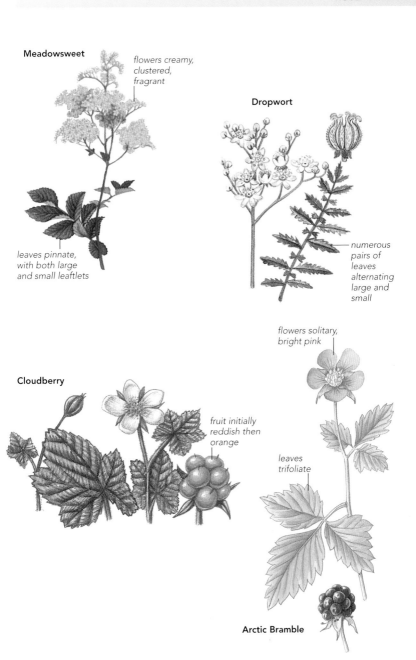

Meadowsweet

flowers creamy, clustered, fragrant

leaves pinnate, with both large and small leaftlets

Dropwort

numerous pairs of leaves alternating large and small

Cloudberry

fruit initially reddish then orange

flowers solitary, bright pink

leaves trifoliate

Arctic Bramble

Field-rose

Stone Bramble *Rubus saxatilis* Creeping perennial to 40cm, with either weak prickles or none. Leaves trifoliate, toothed, paler and slightly hairy beneath. Inflorescence consisting of *2–10 dull white flowers*, 5–10mm in diameter, and with 5 erect narrow petals equalling down-turned sepals. Fruit shiny red with 2–6 large drupelets. Mainly local to locally frequent on shaded rocks and in wooded areas, especially on limestone; most frequent in Scandinavia, and absent from the far west of mainland Europe. **Fl:** Jun–Aug. **Br Is dist:** Local from Wales to Scotland, local also in Ireland; very rare in S England.

Bramble, Blackberry *Rubus fruticosus* agg Very complex aggregate of hundreds of microspecies, too complex and difficult for this work, and separated by minute variations in structure. Generally, the aggregate comprises scrambling shrubs to 3m tall with biennial arching woody stems, variably prickled and angled. *Leaves with 3–5 (rarely 7), toothed leaflets, often prickly.* Flowers white or pink, 20–30mm in diameter, in loose panicles. Fruit changing from green to red, then shiny black or purplish red when ripe. Common in a variety of habitats ranging from damp woodland and scrub to dry open heaths and waste ground; most frequent in the west, and absent from much of the far north. **Fl:** May–Sep. **Br Is dist:** Very common throughout.

Wild Raspberry *Rubus idaeus* Tall erect perennial with arching biennial stems to 1.6m, bearing weak prickles. *Leaves pinnate with 3–7 toothed leaflets, markedly downy beneath.* Flowers white, about 10mm in diameter, in loose clusters of up to 10 flowers; petals narrow, erect and equalling sepals. Fruit red, not shiny, but downy with many drupelets. Widespread and common in woods, heaths and rocky places. **Fl:** Jun–Aug. **Br Is dist:** Common throughout.

Dewberry *Rubus caesius* Rather prostrate, sprawling perennial, with *very weak prickles* and weak biennial stems. *Leaves trifoliate*, toothed and rather wrinkled. Flowers always white, 20–25mm. Fruit bluish-black, *covered with a characteristic plum-like waxy bloom*; lateral fruits with 2–5 drupelets, terminal fruit with 14–20. Widespread and common in a variety of habitats ranging from dry grassland or scrub (often on calcareous soils) to fen carr; absent from the far north. **Fl:** Jun–Sep. **Br Is dist:** Generally common, but rare in N Scotland, and locally frequent in Ireland.

ROSES *Rosa* Shrubs with prickly stems, pinnate leaves, well-developed stipules, and flowers with 5 showy petals and 5 sepals, but no epicalyx. The genus differs from brambles in having a deep or concave receptacle, which ripens to the fleshy fruit, or hip, containing numerous achenes. Styles protrude through the orifice of a central disc, the character of which can help to separate species.

Field-rose *Rosa arvensis* Shrub to 1m, with *weak trailing or scrambling stems*, often purple-tinted. Prickles sparse and hooked, all about equal. Leaflets 5–7, to 35mm. Inflorescence of 1–6 white flowers, 30–50mm in diameter, with styles distinctively united into a *long column equalling the shortest stamens*. Outer 2 sepals have a few narrow, lateral, pinnate lobes. Fruit red, oblong or ovoid, the sepals not persisting. Widespread in woods, scrub and hedges. **Fl:** Jun–Aug. **Br Is dist:** Very common in S England, Wales and Ireland; becoming rare towards N England, and absent from Scotland.

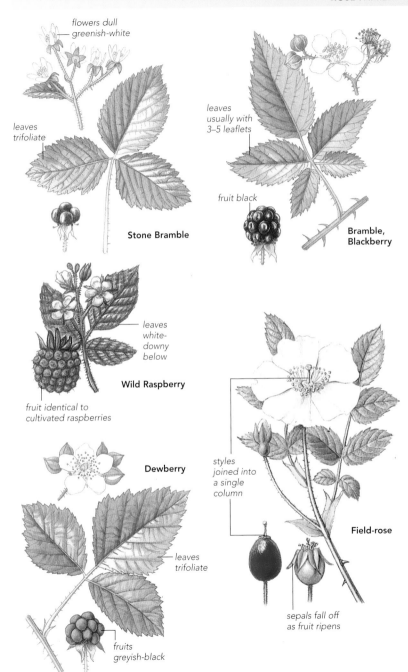

flowers dull greenish-white

leaves trifoliate

Stone Bramble

leaves usually with 3–5 leaflets

fruit black

Bramble, Blackberry

leaves white-downy below

Wild Raspberry

fruit identical to cultivated raspberries

Dewberry

styles joined into a single column

leaves trifoliate

Field-rose

fruits greyish-black

sepals fall off as fruit ripens

Short-styled Field-rose

Short-styled Field-rose *Rosa stylosa* Shrub to 4m, with *arching stems* and hooked prickles, often with stout bases. Leaflets 5–7, singly toothed and hairy beneath. Flowers 1–many, 30–60mm in diameter, white or pale pink; styles united into a column, *shorter than inner stamens* (compare with Field-rose, p. 102). Outer sepals with narrow side-lobes, not persisting in fruit. Widespread but local in the west of the region; in hedgerows, rough grassy areas and scrub. **Fl:** Jun–Jul. **Br Is dist:** Local north to Lancaster, N Wales in the west and Suffolk in the east.

Dog-rose

Rosa canina group Distinguished by having stout curved or hooked prickles (a) and leaflets usually either without glands or with glands only on main veins; not scented when bruised (compare with Sweet-briar). Outer sepals with narrow, projecting side-lobes.

Dog-rose *Rosa canina* Shrub to 4m with arching stems. Leaflets 5–7, to 40mm long, hairless. Flowers 1–4, pink or white, 30–50mm in diameter. Disc wide with narrow orifice, up to 1mm wide. Flower stalk 10–20mm, hairless and without glands. Fruit red, hairless, oval or rounded and without sepals when ripe. Widespread and common in hedges, scrub and woodland margins. **Fl:** Jun–Jul. **Br Is dist:** Throughout, but commonest in the south and becoming rare in N Scotland.

Sweet-briar

Sweet-briar *Rosa rubiginosa* Shrub to 3m, with erect stems, the prickles usually interspersed with bristles and glands. Leaflets 5–7, compound-toothed. Flowers 1–3, deep pink, 20–30mm in diameter. Sepals persistent in fruit. Widespread and often common in woods, hedges, scrub and rough grassy areas. **Fl:** Jun–Jul. **Br Is dist:** Locally common in England and Wales, but more scarce in Scotland and Ireland.

Burnet Rose

Burnet Rose *Rosa spinossima* Small patch-forming shrub to only 50cm, suckering freely. Prickles abundant and straight, long on main stems but shorter and less numerous on flowering stems. Leaflets 7–11, each oval, and up to 15mm long. Flowers solitary, creamy white (rarely pink), 20–30mm in diameter. Fruit spherical, small (about 6mm in diameter) and purplish-black when ripe. Widespread, but only locally frequent, on heaths, dunes, calcareous grassland, limestone pavement and mountain ledges. **Fl:** May–Jul. **Br Is dist:** Local throughout.

Harsh Downy-rose, Downy-rose

Harsh Downy-rose, Downy-rose *Rosa tomentosa* Rather compact shrub to 2m, with arching stems. Leaflets soft, densely tomentose, 20–40mm. Flowers 1–5, pink or white, 30–40mm in diameter. Sepals not persistent in fruit. Flower stalk about 20mm. Fruit rounded or pear-shaped, covered with glands. Locally common in woods, hedges, scrub and rough grassy margins. **Fl:** Jun–Jul. **Br Is dist:** Fairly common almost throughout, but rare in Scotland.

Agrimony *Agrimonia eupatoria* Softly hairy perennial to 60cm, often with reddish stems and slight sweet smell when bruised. Lower leaves pinnate with 3–6 pairs of larger, toothed leaflets, between which are 2–3 pairs of smaller ones; *undersurface of leaf covered with white or greyish tomentum.* Flowers yellow, 5–8mm in diameter, and numerous in dense narrow spikes. Fruit a bur-like achene with spreading (not backward-pointing) spines. Widespread and generally common in hedge banks, road-verges and rough grassy areas, but absent from the far north. **Fl:** Jun–Aug. **Br Is dist:** Common almost throughout, but rare in N Scotland and absent from Orkney and Shetland.

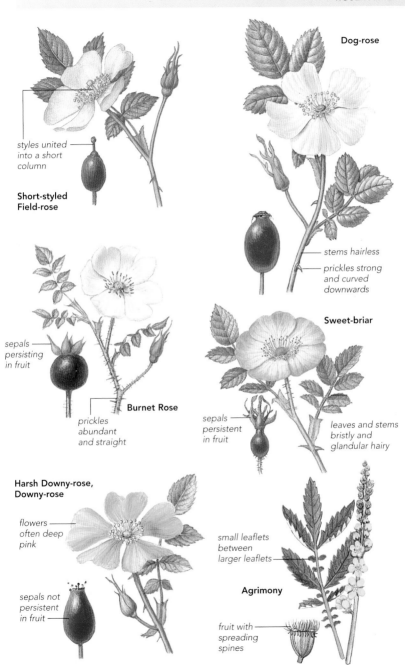

styles united into a short column

Short-styled Field-rose

Dog-rose

stems hairless

prickles strong and curved downwards

sepals persisting in fruit

Burnet Rose

prickles abundant and straight

Sweet-briar

sepals persistent in fruit

leaves and stems bristly and glandular hairy

Harsh Downy-rose, Downy-rose

flowers often deep pink

sepals not persistent in fruit

small leaflets between larger leaflets

Agrimony

fruit with spreading spines

Great Burnet

Pirri-pirri-bur

Mountain Avens

Salad Burnet *Sanguisorba minor* ssp *minor* Short perennial to 40cm, hairy below. Basal leaves in a rosette, pinnate with 4–12 pairs of toothed leaflets progressively larger to 20mm, towards apex. Flowers tiny, green and in compact rounded heads, dioecious with petalless male flowers below, and red-styled female flowers above. Fruit 4-angled and ridged. Widespread, and often common, in grassland, especially on calcareous soils, but absent from much of the far north. **Fl:** May–Aug. **Br Is dist:** Generally locally abundant but very local in Scotland, and absent from the north. Ssp *muricata* (Fodder Burnet) is more robust with deeply toothed leaflets. Introduced and naturalised in grassy places. **Br Is dist:** Scattered.

Great Burnet *Sanguisorba officinalis* Rather tall perennial to 1m. Leaves distinctive, pinnate with long-stalked toothed leaflets (to 40mm), progressively larger towards the apex and often with reddish stalks. Flowers tiny, dull crimson or purplish-red and in compact oblong heads on long stalks. Ranging from very local to locally frequent; in damp grassy places. **Fl:** Jun–Sep. **Br Is dist:** Local and decreasing due to agricultural improvement; absent from N Scotland and very local or rare in S England.

Pirri-pirri-bur *Acaena novae-zelandiae* Perennial undershrub to 15cm, rather similar to Salad Burnet, but creeping and much-branched with pinnate leaves having 3–4 pairs of toothed leaflets. Flowers white, in rounded compact heads, solitary on erect stalks. Fruit with soft reddish spines. Introduced from New Zealand, possibly with imported wool, and naturalised in Britain and Ireland. **Fl:** Jun–Jul. **Br Is dist:** Spreading in a number of places, usually dry and sandy, especially coastal.

Mountain Avens *Dryas octopetala* Creeping undershrub to only 80mm tall, with distinctive bluntly toothed, oblong evergreen leaves to 20mm, dark green above with deep veins and grey tomentose beneath. Flowers white with yellow stamens, to 40mm across and with 8 or more petals. Fruit a head of achenes made noticeable from a distance by the long feathery styles. Local to locally abundant on basic rocks, from sea level to 2,000m. **Br Is dist:** Local to locally frequent in Scotland and W Ireland; rare in N Wales and N England. Descends to sea level in W Ireland and N Scotland.

Geum Perennials distinctive for their combination of flowers with parts in 5s or 7s, an epicalyx and an erect terminal style persistent in fruit and often hooked for dispersal by animals.

Water Avens *Geum rivale* Tufted downy perennial to 60cm. Basal leaves pinnate with 3–6 pairs of side-leaflets and large, rounded, toothed terminal leaflet; stem leaves trifoliate. Flowers nodding, cup-shaped with orange-pink petals, and purple sepals and epicalyx. Fruit a collection of feathery achenes. Widespread and locally common in wet meadows, marshes, moist woods and on mountain ledges, usually in base-rich conditions. **Fl:** Apr–Sep. **Br Is dist:** Locally common but rare in SW England and absent from the south-east.

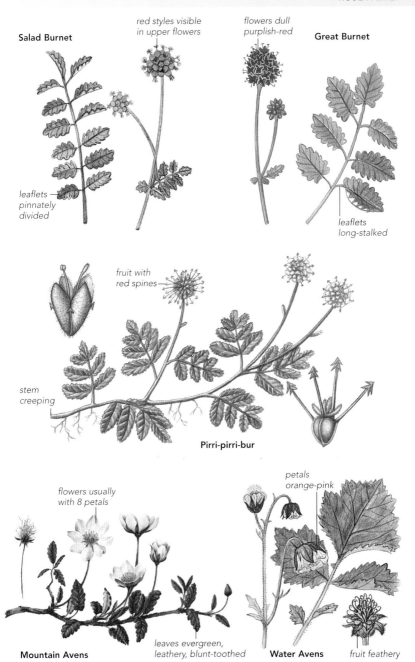

Salad Burnet

leaflets pinnately divided

red styles visible in upper flowers

flowers dull purplish-red

Great Burnet

leaflets long-stalked

fruit with red spines

stem creeping

Pirri-pirri-bur

flowers usually with 8 petals

petals orange-pink

leaves evergreen, leathery, blunt-toothed

Mountain Avens

Water Avens

fruit feathery

Shrubby Cinquefoil

Hoary Cinquefoil

Ternate-leaved Cinquefoil

Wood Avens *Geum urbanum* Hairy perennial to 60cm. Basal leaves pinnate with unequal toothed leaflets and large terminal leaflet usually 3-lobed; stipules large (often greater than 10mm) and leafy; stem leaves usually 3-lobed. Flowers yellow, 8–15mm with 5 rounded petals and sepals, erect at first but soon drooping. Fruit a rounded cluster of feathery achenes. Common in woods, hedge banks and shady places. **Fl:** May–Sep. **Br Is dist:** Common throughout. Hybridises with Water Avens (*see* p. 104) to produce *G.* x *intermedium*, which can have a range of characteristics from either parent.

CINQUEFOILS *Potentilla* Herbs or small shrubs, usually perennial. Leaves lobed, pinnate or digitate. Flowers with 4–6 petals, usually 5; epicalyx present; styles not persistent and feathery in fruit (a collection of achenes).

Marsh Cinquefoil *Potentilla palustris* Hairless perennial to 45cm. Leaves greyish-green, the lower ones pinnate with 5–7 leaflets and the upper ones trifoliate or palmate. Flowers distinctive, dull dark purple or red-wine coloured with 5 sharply pointed petals shorter than the (darker) purplish sepals. Widespread and locally frequent, in fens, marshes and pool margins. **Fl:** May–Jul. **Br Is dist:** Locally frequent in N Britain and Ireland; much more local in the south.

Shrubby Cinquefoil *Potentilla fruticosa* Deciduous downy *shrub* to 1m, distinctive *untoothed greyish-green leaves* with 3–7 lanceolate leaflets. Flowers yellow, 20mm in diameter, solitary or in loose clusters, dioecious. Rare in damp rocky places (usually basic) and riverbanks. **Fl:** May–Jul. **Br Is dist:** Rare in Teesdale and Lake District; very local in W Ireland.

Silverweed *Potentilla anserina* Creeping perennial with long stolons to 80cm. Basal leaves pinnate, *toothed and silvery,* either on both sides or underside only; *tiny leaflets alternate with larger ones.* Flowers yellow, 15–20mm, solitary with unnotched petals. Widespread and common, in a variety of damp places such as roadsides, dunes and grassland. **Fl:** May–Aug. **Br Is dist:** Common throughout.

Hoary Cinquefoil *Potentilla argentea* Downy perennial to 50cm, with spreading and ascending stems *covered with dense silvery hairs.* Leaves digitate, the 5 narrow leaflets with coarse forward-pointing teeth (basal leaves have 2–7 bluntish teeth; *undersurface silvery white with dense hairs all curled over.* Flowers yellow, 8–12mm, in loose branched clusters; *style conical.* In dry places, often sandy, gravelly or rocky. **Fl:** Jun–Sep. **Br Is dist:** North to mid-Scotland; local in the east and south-east but rare to the west; absent from Ireland.

Ternate-leaved Cinquefoil *Potentilla norvegica* Annual or short-lived hairy perennial to 70cm. Leaves trifoliate, green on both sides. Flowers bright yellow, 8–15mm in branched clusters; petals no longer than sepals. Locally frequent in rocky and waste places or roadsides; widely naturalised outside its native range **Fl:** Jun–Sep. **Br Is dist:** Introduced and naturalised, scattered.

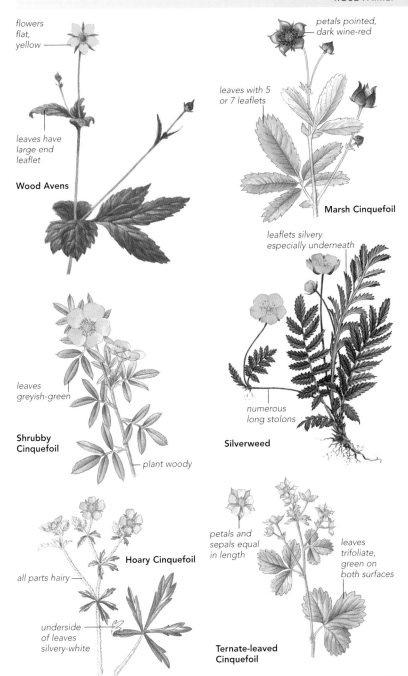

flowers flat, yellow

leaves have large end leaflet

Wood Avens

petals pointed, dark wine-red

leaves with 5 or 7 leaflets

Marsh Cinquefoil

leaflets silvery especially underneath

leaves greyish-green

Shrubby Cinquefoil

plant woody

numerous long stolons

Silverweed

Hoary Cinquefoil

all parts hairy

underside of leaves silvery-white

petals and sepals equal in length

leaves trifoliate, green on both surfaces

Ternate-leaved Cinquefoil

Alpine Cinquefoil

Sibbaldia

Alpine Cinquefoil *Potentilla crantzii* Hairy perennial to 25cm, not mat-forming. Leaves digitate with 5 wedge-shaped toothed leaflets, *the terminal tooth about equal to the adjacent lateral ones*. Stipules of basal leaves broadly ovate. Flowers yellow, 15–25mm in diameter, often with orange spot at base of each petal. Local to locally frequent in rocky and gravelly places, usually in mountains except in the extreme north. **Fl:** Jun–Jul. **Br Is dist:** Very local in N Wales, N England and the Scottish Highlands.

Tormentil *Potentilla erecta* Perennial with creeping and ascending stems to 30cm, but no rooting stolons. *Leaves unstalked*, almost entirely trifoliate, but often appearing digitate with 5 leaflets due to large stipules at leaf base; leaflets silky hairy on margins and veins beneath. Flowers yellow, 7–11mm, *with usually 4 petals*, on 20–40mm stalks. Common in a wide range of habitats from grassy places and woodland rides to heaths and moors. **Fl:** May–Sep. **Br Is dist:** Common throughout.

Creeping Cinquefoil *Potentilla reptans* Similar to Tormentil but has creeping flowering stems rooting at nodes, and *long-stalked hairless leaves* with 5–7 leaflets. Also, flowers are 17–25mm in diameter *with 5 petals*. Common in grassy places, waste areas and waysides. **Fl:** Jun–Sep. **Br Is dist:** Common throughout.

Barren Strawberry *Potentilla sterilis* Hairy perennial to 15cm *with long rooting stolons*. Leaves dull bluish-green, trifoliate and with terminal tooth of leaflet shorter than adjacent ones. Flowers white, 10–15mm in diameter, the petals widely separated. *Epicalyx segments shorter than sepals*. Fruit not fleshy. NB Wild Strawberry has shiny leaves with long terminal tooth and fleshy fruits. In open woodland, grassy places and waysides. Widespread and common in the west; very local or absent from the east and far north. **Fl:** Feb–May. **Br Is dist:** Common almost throughout; absent from N Scotland.

Sibbaldia *Sibbaldia procumbens* Dwarf, stiffly hairy, tufted perennial to 30mm. Leaves bluish-green and distinctive: trifoliate, ovate and rather wedge-shaped, broadening towards the tip which has 3 teeth, the central one often being narrower than the 2 lateral ones. Flowers small, about 5mm in diameter, pale yellow or greenish in dense clusters; petals often diminutive or absent. Local to locally frequent in short turf and rocky places in mountains. **Fl:** Jul–Aug. **Br Is dist:** Local in Scottish Highlands; very rare in N England.

STRAWBERRIES *Fragaria* Like *Potentilla* species but leaves always trifoliate in basal rosette and fruit fleshy and brightly coloured.

Wild Strawberry *Fragaria vesca* Perennial to 30cm, with long rooting stolons. Leaflets hairy, bright green above, toothed, the terminal tooth usually longer than the 2 immediately adjacent (compare with Barren Strawberry). Flowers white, 12–18mm, in loose stalked clusters hardly longer than leaves. Fruit (strawberry) 10–20mm long with projecting achenes. In dry grassy (often calcareous) places, woods and banks. **Fl:** Apr–Jul. **Br Is dist:** Common.

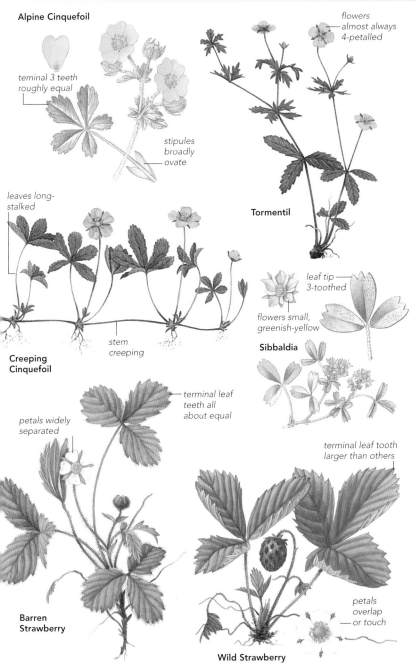

Alpine Cinquefoil

teminal 3 teeth roughly equal

stipules broadly ovate

flowers almost always 4-petalled

Tormentil

leaves long-stalked

Creeping Cinquefoil

stem creeping

leaf tip 3-toothed

flowers small, greenish-yellow

Sibbaldia

terminal leaf teeth all about equal

petals widely separated

Barren Strawberry

terminal leaf tooth larger than others

petals overlap or touch

Wild Strawberry

111

Alpine Lady's-mantle

LADY'S-MANTLES *Alchemilla* Tufted perennials with palmate or palmately lobed toothed leaves. Flowers tiny, greenish-yellow in characteristic rounded or flat-topped cymes.

Alpine Lady's-mantle *Alchemilla alpina* To 25cm. Leaf lobes 5–7, pointed (a), with terminal teeth, middle lobe free at base; leaflets hairless above, silky hairy beneath. Flower clusters dense, hardly overtopping leaves. In grassy and rocky places in mountains; upland areas throughout Europe. **Fl:** Jun–Aug. **Br Is dist:** Locally abundant on acid rocks in NW England and Scotland; very rare in Ireland.

Broom

Hairy Lady's-mantle *Alchemilla filicaulis* To 40cm. Leaves hairy (often only on folds above and veins beneath) with 7–9 lobes, the middle ones with 11–17 unequal teeth. Sinus widely open. Base of leaf stalk reddish. There are 2 subspecies: ssp *filicaulis* has upper part of stem, flower stalks and leaf stalks hairless. **Fl:** Jun–Sep. **Br Is dist:** Local in mountains from N Wales and Derbyshire northwards. Ssp *vestita* is hairy throughout. In grassland; locally frequent. **Fl:** Jun–Sep. **Br Is dist:** Almost throughout, and the most frequent species in S England.

Dyer's Greenweed

Parsley-piert *Aphanes arvensis* Rather inconspicuous *greyish* downy annual to 20cm (usually much smaller). Leaves 2–10mm, short-stalked and fan-shaped, divided into 3 segments, each of which has a number of finger-shaped lobes. Flowers minute, green, petalless and in unstalked dense clusters along stem, each cluster surrounded by a cup of leafy stipules with *triangular lobes*. Widespread and common in arable and dry bare soils. **Fl:** Apr–Oct. **Br Is dist:** Common throughout.

PEA FAMILY Fabaceae
A very distinctive and well-known family, variable in form, but with easily recognised pea-like flowers. Trees, shrubs or herbs, with leaves usually opposite, simple to twice pinnate. Flowers 5-petalled, with an erect standard at the top, 2 wing petals at the sides, and the lower 2 petals joined into the keel; 10 stamens and 1 style. Fruit usually an elongated pod.

Petty Whin

Broom *Cytisus scoparius* Much-branched, erect, spineless deciduous shrub to 2m, with long, green, straight, hairless, 5-angled stems. Leaves usually trifoliate, short-stalked. Flowers golden yellow, solitary or in pairs, up to 20mm long and short-stalked; pods oblong, becoming black. Common and widespread, mainly on acid soils, in scrub and grassy places; from S Sweden southwards. **Fl:** May–Jul. **Br Is dist:** Common throughout. Ssp *maritimus* is prostrate, with silky, hairy twigs. Occurs in coastal areas of W Britain and France.

a

Dyer's Greenweed *Genista tinctoria* Tufted erect or ascending small shrub to 1m or more. Leaves linear-lanceolate, simple, variable, to 30mm long, usually hairy on margins only and sometimes downy all over. Flowers in long usually terminal racemes, corolla yellow, about 15mm long, hairless; pods oblong, flat, hairless. Widespread and locally common throughout except N Scandinavia; in pastures and scrub on heavier soils. **Fl:** Jun–Jul. **Br Is dist:** Locally common in England, Wales and S Scotland.

Petty Whin *Genista anglica* Erect or spreading small shrub, to about 1m, hairless or hairy, but *with strong spines*. Leaves hairless, lanceolate to elliptical, to 10mm long and rather waxy. Flowers in short, leafy terminal racemes; corolla pale yellow, hairless, 6–8mm long; pods hairless, pointed, becoming swollen. Scattered on heaths and moors; from S Sweden southwards. **Fl:** Apr–Jun. **Br Is dist:** Scattered throughout, but local; absent from Ireland.

leaves divided to the base

Alpine Lady's-mantle

leaves silvery underneath

sinus

leaves hairy on folds and edges

divided to about ⅓ radius of leaf

Hairy Lady's-mantle

leaves tiny and fan-shaped

Parsley-piert

flowers surrounded by leafy stipules

pods black when ripe

leaves trifoliate

Broom

stem 5-angled

Dyer's Greenweed

flowers in long terminal racemes

leaves simple

corolla pale yellow

stems with long spines

Petty Whin

113

German Greenweed *Genista germanica* Erect branched shrub to 60cm, with branched spines (occasionally spineless). Leaves elliptical to lanceolate, with long hairs on under surface. Flowers yellow, about 10mm, in loose racemes, with *hairy petals and sepals*; bracts very small; pod pointed, curved, slightly inflated. Local on heaths and grassland; from S Sweden southwards. **Fl:** May–Jun. **Br Is dist:** Absent.

Winged Broom

Winged Broom *Chamaespartium sagittale* Spreading subshrub, mat-forming, with stems to 50cm. Distinguishable by its *strongly winged stems*, constricted at the nodes. Leaves elliptical, to 20mm long, downy below. Flowers yellow, 10–15mm, in short terminal clusters. In dry and rocky places; from SE Belgium and S Germany southwards. **Fl:** May–Jun. **Br Is dist:** Absent.

Gorse

Gorse *Ulex europaeus* Familiar spiny, dense, bushy, evergreen shrub to 2m. Twigs hairy or downy. Has trifoliate leaves only when young; *terminal spines 15–25mm long, straight*, stout, *deeply furrowed*, hairless (a). Flowers pale yellow, 20mm across, coconut-scented; little bracts at base at least 2mm wide and 3–5mm long; calyx with spreading hairs. Common and widespread on rough grasslands and heathy areas, usually on acid soils, from the Netherlands southwards; mainly western, introduced elsewhere. **Fl:** Jan–Dec, mainly in spring. **Br Is dist:** Common almost throughout.

Western Gorse

Dwarf Gorse *Ulex minor* Smaller shrub than above, to 1m but usually less, often spreading. *Spines about 10mm long*, not rigid, *weakly furrowed* or striped (b). *Flowers deep yellow*, 10–12mm long, with bracts at base only 0.5mm long; calyx teeth divergent. On heaths and moors in Britain and W France only. **Fl:** Jul–Sep. **Br Is dist:** Mainly southern and eastern, extending to S Scotland.

Western Gorse *Ulex gallii* Very similar to Dwarf Gorse, but usually slightly taller and more robust. Spines more rigid, *longer to 25mm* and *faintly ridged* (c). Calyx teeth convergent. On heaths and moors; strongly western in distribution, from Scotland and W France southwards. **Fl:** Jul–Sep. **Br Is dist:** Strongly western, barely overlapping with Dwarf Gorse, from S Scotland southwards.

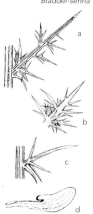

Bladder-senna

Bladder-senna *Colutea arborescens* Branched shrub to 6m. Leaves pinnate with 4–5 pairs of oval leaflets, silky-hairy below. Inflorescence has 3–8 flowers, corolla 15–20mm, yellow marked with red; *pods to 70mm long, strongly inflated*, becoming brown and papery-very distinctive. On dry slopes, rocky places and scrub, mainly on lime-rich soils; native from N-C France and S Germany southwards, naturalised elsewhere. **Fl:** May–Jul. **Br Is dist:** Locally naturalised, mainly SE England.

Astragalus Annual or perennial herbs, with pinnate leaves terminating in a single leaflet. Flowers in lateral clusters, often dense; keel blunt, with no small tooth-like point (d) (*see also* the very similar *Oxytropis* (pp. 116–18), in which the keel has a tooth at the tip).

Chick-pea Milk-vetch *Astragalus cicer* Ascending or almost erect perennial to 60cm. Leaves to 13cm long with 10–15 pairs of ovate, shortly hairy leaflets. Flowers pale yellow, in dense long-stalked inflorescences; standard 14–16mm long. Pods distinctive: *inflated*, ovoid-globose, *papery, covered with short black and white hairs*. Grassy places and woodland margins; southwards from Belgium and N France; occasionally naturalised elsewhere. **Fl:** Jun–Jul. **Br Is dist:** Absent.

114

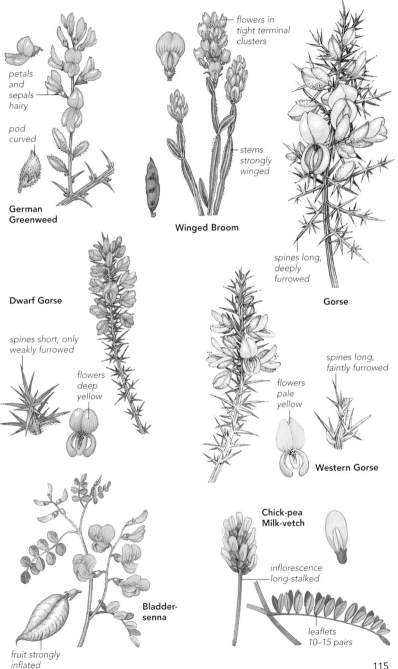

petals and sepals hairy

pod curved

German Greenweed

flowers in tight terminal clusters

stems strongly winged

Winged Broom

spines long, deeply furrowed

Gorse

Dwarf Gorse

spines short, only weakly furrowed

flowers deep yellow

flowers pale yellow

spines long, faintly furrowed

Western Gorse

Bladder-senna

fruit strongly inflated

Chick-pea Milk-vetch

inflorescence long-stalked

leaflets 10–15 pairs

115

Purple Milk-vetch

Purple Milk-vetch *Astragalus danicus* Slender spreading or ascending perennial herb to 35cm. Leaves hairy, 4–10cm long, with 6–13 pairs of leaflets; *stipules joined at base*. Flowers purplish-blue in clusters on stalks 1½–2 times as long as leaves; each flower 15–18mm long; fruit dark brown, *swollen*, with white hairs. From S Sweden southwards; on dry or calcareous grasslands, but very scattered and absent from large areas. **Fl:** May–Jul. **Br Is dist:** Scattered almost throughout but very local; very rare in Ireland.

Wild Liquorice

Yellow Alpine Milk-vetch *Astragalus frigidus* Stout erect perennial to 40cm, hairless, usually unbranched. Leaves with 3–8 pairs of leaflets. Flowers in narrow racemes, on stalks 1–1½-times as long as leaves; corolla pale yellowish-white, with standard 12–14mm long; calyx has densely black-hairy teeth. In mountain habitats; in Norway and Sweden (and the Alps). **Fl:** Jul–Aug. **Br Is dist:** Absent.

Alpine Milk-vetch *Astragalus alpinus* Slender spreading or ascending perennial, similar to Purple Milk-vetch. Leaflets 7–15 pairs, with *stipules usually not joined at base*. Flowers in inflorescences with stalks 1–2 times as long as leaves; corolla blue; calyx teeth lanceolate and pointed; *fruit not swollen*, black-hairy when young then smooth. Mountain habitats, mainly on calcareous soils; in Scandinavia, N Scotland, and mountains of C and S Europe. **Fl:** Jul–Aug. **Br Is dist:** Very rare in mountains of C Scotland only.

Yellow Oxytropis,
Yellow Milk-vetch

Norwegian Milk-vetch *Astragalus norvegicus* Rather similar to Alpine Milk-vetch, but differing in that there are usually only *6–7 pairs* of leaflets. *Corolla pale violet, calyx teeth triangular and blunt*. Open habitats, including roadsides; N Scandinavia only. **Fl:** Jul–Aug. **Br Is dist:** Absent.

Wild Liquorice *Astragalus glycyphyllos* Sprawling robust herb, with zigzagging stems to 1m long. Leaves to 20cm long, with 4–6 pairs of broadly ovate leaflets, sparsely hairy below; stipules large, to 20mm long. Flowers 10–15cm long, in racemes on stalks shorter than leaves; corolla dull greenish cream; pods to 40mm long, slightly curved. In grassy places and scrub; throughout except the far north. **Fl:** Jun–Aug. **Br Is dist:** Scattered through England to S Scotland, rare in the north.

Purple Oxytropis

Oxytropis Very similar to *Astragalus* (*see* p. 114 and above), differing mainly in the tooth-like point on the keel (a).

a

Yellow Oxytropis, Yellow Milk-vetch *Oxytropis campestris* Silky-hairy tufted perennial, with stems to 20cm and leaves up to 15cm long. Leaflets 10–15 pairs, lanceolate; stipules joined for about half their length. Inflorescence roughly *oval*, with 5–15 flowers; *corolla pale yellow* (occasionally pale violet); standard 15–20mm long; *fruit erect*, hairy. In calcareous mountain habitats; in N Scandinavia, Scotland and high mountains farther south. **Fl:** Jun–Jul. **Br Is dist:** Very rare in mountains of C Scotland only.

Purple Oxytropis *Oxytropis halleri* Similar in form and hairiness to Yellow Oxytropis, but with inflorescence of purple flowers on stout, erect, leafless stalks, which are *much longer* than leaves; corolla about 20mm long, keels tipped with dark purple. Fruit about 25mm long and downy. Mountains, mainly calcareous; in Scotland and C and S Europe. **Fl:** Jun–Jul. **Br Is dist:** Local in C and N Scotland only.

116

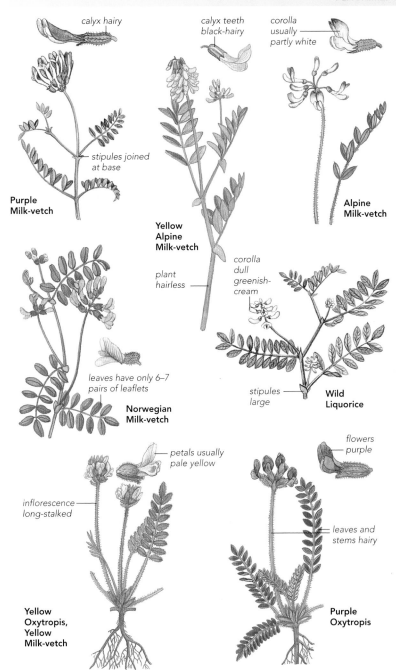

calyx hairy

calyx teeth black-hairy

corolla usually partly white

stipules joined at base

Purple Milk-vetch

Yellow Alpine Milk-vetch

plant hairless

Alpine Milk-vetch

corolla dull greenish-cream

leaves have only 6–7 pairs of leaflets

Norwegian Milk-vetch

stipules large

Wild Liquorice

petals usually pale yellow

inflorescence long-stalked

Yellow Oxytropis, Yellow Milk-vetch

flowers purple

leaves and stems hairy

Purple Oxytropis

117

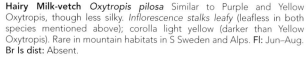

Hairy Milk-vetch *Oxytropis pilosa* Similar to Purple and Yellow Oxytropis, though less silky. *Inflorescence stalks leafy* (leafless in both species mentioned above); corolla light yellow (darker than Yellow Oxytropis). Rare in mountain habitats in S Sweden and Alps. **Fl:** Jun–Aug. **Br Is dist:** Absent.

VETCHES *Vicia* Climbing or scrambling annual or perennial herbs; stems rounded or ridged, not winged. Leaves pinnate, with 2 to many pairs of leaflets, ending in a tendril or a point, but not a leaflet. Flowers solitary or in axillary racemes.

Wood Bitter-vetch

Wood Bitter-vetch *Vicia orobus* Spreading or erect downy perennial to 60cm, with round stems. Leaves pinnate, ending at a point not a tendril; stipules toothed. Inflorescences short, rounded and long-stalked; flowers very pale lilac with purple veins, 12–15mm long; pod oblong, pointed and hairless, to 30mm long. In grassland and scrub in hilly districts; mainly western from Norway southwards, though local. **Fl:** May–Jul. **Br Is dist:** Scattered almost throughout, mainly western, but local and declining; rare in Ireland.

Tufted Vetch

Tufted Vetch *Vicia cracca* Downy or hairless perennial scrambling herb to 2m long. Leaves pinnate, with 6–12 (rarely 15) pairs of narrow-oblong leaflets, very short-stalked; stipules half-arrow shaped, untoothed; tendrils branched. Flowers in *long narrow raceme* to 10cm; *corolla bluish violet*, 8–12mm long, with limb of standard roughly equal to its claw. Generally common in grassy and bushy places; throughout the area. **Fl:** Jun–Aug. **Br Is dist:** Common and widespread throughout.

Wood Vetch

Wood Vetch *Vicia sylvatica* Straggling or climbing perennial, with hairless *rounded stems* to 2m long. Leaves with 5–12 pairs of oblong leaflets, tipped with points; tendrils much branched; stipules roughly semicircular with numerous fine teeth. Inflorescence loose, somewhat 1-sided, long-stalked, with 5–20 flowers; corolla 12–20mm long, whitish with purple veins; pods black and hairless. In woods, wood-margins and coastal cliffs; throughout, except the Netherlands and Belgium, though local. **Fl:** Jun–Aug. **Br Is dist:** Scattered throughout, but local; rare in Ireland.

Hairy Tare

Hairy Tare *Vicia hirsuta* Very slender trailing or scrambling downy annual to 70cm. Leaves with *4–10 pairs of leaflets*, often borne alternately, linear to ovate but usually truncated or notched. Inflorescences on slender stalks with *1–9 flowers*; corolla whitish-mauve, 2–4mm long, *calyx teeth roughly equal*, longer than tube (a); *pod oblong and downy*, usually 2-seeded. Throughout the area, widespread and common in grassy and rough places, especially on neutral or calcareous soils. **Fl:** May–Aug. **Br Is dist:** Throughout except the extreme north, rarer in Ireland.

Bush Vetch

Bush Vetch *Vicia sepium* Scrambling or spreading perennial to 1m, downy or almost hairless. Leaves with 3–9 pairs of ovate or almost round leaflets, with a bristle point at the tip; tendrils branched, stipules half-arrow shaped, usually untoothed, spotted. *Inflorescence 2–6-flowered*, short-stalked; corolla distinctive *dull bluish-purple* with darker veins 12–15mm long; calyx teeth unequal, shorter than tube; pods black and hairless, to 25mm. Throughout the area except the extreme north; in bushy and grassy places. **Fl:** May–Aug. **Br Is dist:** Common throughout.

a

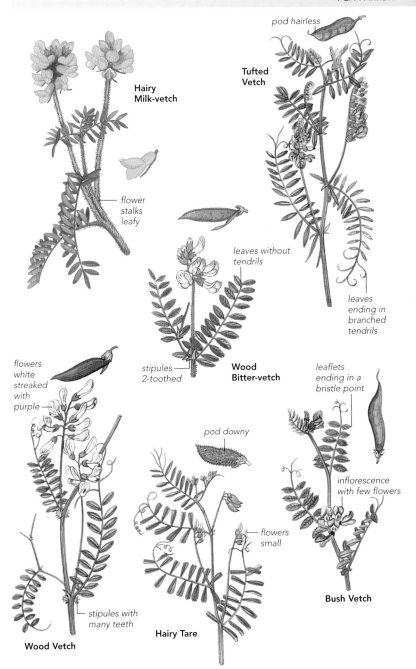

pod hairless

Tufted Vetch

Hairy Milk-vetch

flower stalks leafy

leaves without tendrils

leaves ending in branched tendrils

stipules 2-toothed

Wood Bitter-vetch

flowers white streaked with purple

leaflets ending in a bristle point

pod downy

inflorescence with few flowers

flowers small

Bush Vetch

stipules with many teeth

Wood Vetch

Hairy Tare

119

Common Vetch

Common Vetch *Vicia sativa* Downy scrambling, trailing or ascending annual to 80cm. Leaves with 3–8 pairs of linear to ovate leaflets which may be pointed, blunt or bristle-tipped; tendrils branched or simple; stipules half-arrow shaped, usually toothed, often with a dark blotch. *Flowers in groups of 1–2* (rarely more), corolla to 30mm, purplish-red; calyx teeth equal; pods very variable. The main wild form is ssp *nigra* which has narrow leaflets, corolla all reddish-purple, 10–18mm long. Ssp *sativa* is the cultivated and naturalised form from S Europe, which has broader leaflets, flowers to 30mm, usually with wings darker than remainder. Ssp *nigra* is widespread and common in grassy places throughout except the extreme north; ssp *sativa* is mainly southern, but widely cultivated and naturalised farther north. **Fl:** May–Sep. **Br Is dist:** Ssp *nigra* is common throughout; ssp *sativa* is locally naturalised.

Yellow-vetch

Yellow-vetch *Vicia lutea* Tufted prostrate hairless or hairy annual to 60cm. Leaves with 3–10 pairs of linear to oblong bristle-tipped leaflets; tendrils simple or branched; stipules small and triangular. Flowers in groups of 1–3, distinctively pale yellow, often tinged with purple, up to 35mm long; calyx teeth unequal, with lower ones longer than tube; pod yellowish-brown, hairy, to 40mm. On stabilised shingle and grassy coastal habitats; England and France southwards; naturalised in Germany. **Fl:** Jun–Sep. **Br Is dist:** Very local, mainly southern.

Lathyrus Similar to the vetches, differing mainly in the winged stems, and fewer leaflets, which are usually parallel-veined, though the differences between the 2 groups are small and inconsistent.

Spring Pea

Spring Pea *Lathyrus vernus* Erect or spreading tufted hairless or slightly hairy perennial to 40cm, with stems angled but not winged. Leaves with 2–4 pairs of ovate to lanceolate pointed leaflets, without tendrils; stipules similar, with arrow-shaped base. Flowers 3–10 together in a raceme, with reddish corolla ageing to blue, to 20mm long. Pods brown, hairless, to 60mm long. Almost throughout continental Europe, except the extreme north, and not native in Belgium and the Netherlands; in woods and rough grassy places. **Fl:** Apr–Jun. **Br Is dist:** Absent, except in cultivation.

Sea Pea

Sea Pea *Lathyrus japonicus* Prostrate grey-green more or less hairless perennial herb, with angled (but not winged) stems to 1m long. Leaves with 2–5 pairs of *oval, blunt and slightly fleshy leaflets*; tendrils present or absent; stipules broadly triangular, with arrow-shaped base. Inflorescence with 2–15 purple flowers, ageing to blue, to 20mm long; pod to 50mm long, swollen, hairless. On coastal shingle and sand, rarely inland; on the coasts of NW Europe, northwards from England. **Fl:** Jun–Aug. **Br Is dist:** Mainly on the coasts of S and E England, locally common, rare elsewhere.

Bitter-vetch

Bitter-vetch *Lathyrus linifolius* Erect, virtually hairless perennial with *winged stems* to 50cm. Leaves with 2–4 pairs of narrowly lanceolate to elliptical leaflets, usually pointed and without tendrils; stipules narrow with arrow-shaped base. Inflorescence with 2–6 flowers; corolla crimson-red, becoming bluish or greenish, to 16mm long; pod red-brown, hairless, to 40mm long. In woods, pastures and scrub, especially in hilly or acid regions; throughout except in the extreme north. **Fl:** Apr–Jul. **Br Is dist:** Widespread and locally common, though absent from a few areas.

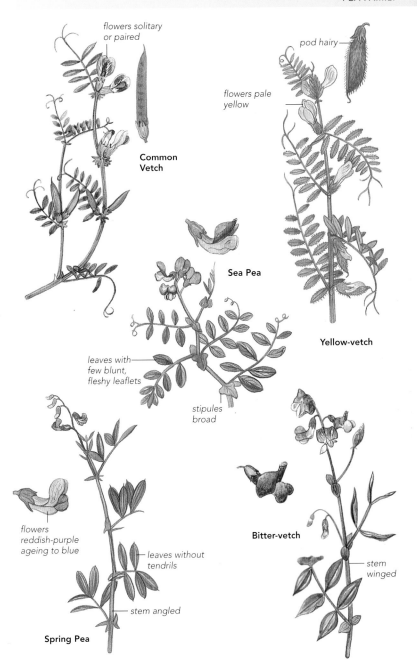

flowers solitary or paired

Common Vetch

pod hairy

flowers pale yellow

Sea Pea

leaves with few blunt, fleshy leaflets

stipules broad

Yellow-vetch

flowers reddish-purple ageing to blue

leaves without tendrils

stem angled

Spring Pea

Bitter-vetch

stem winged

Meadow Vetchling *Lathyrus pratensis* Scrambling hairless or downy perennial, with angled stems to 1.2m long. Leaves with 1 pair of grey-green narrowly lanceolate, parallel-veined pointed leaflets, with a tendril; stipules with arrow-shaped base, about the same size as leaflets. Inflorescence long-stalked, with 5–12 yellow flowers, each about 15–18mm long; pod to 35mm long, black when ripe. In grassy and bushy places; throughout the area. **Fl:** May–Aug. **Br Is dist:** Common throughout.

Marsh Pea

Marsh Pea *Lathyrus palustris* Erect climbing or scrambling slightly downy perennial herb, with winged stems to 1.2m. Leaves with 2–5 pairs of narrowly lanceolate leaflets, branched tendrils, and half-arrow shaped stipules. Inflorescences long-stalked, with 2–8 flowers; corolla pale purplish-blue, to 20mm long; pod flattened, to 50mm long, hairless. In damp or wet grassy places, usually calcareous; throughout though very local. **Fl:** May–Jul. **Br Is dist:** Scattered through England and Wales, local; rare in Ireland.

Tuberous Pea

Tuberous Pea or Fyfield Pea *Lathyrus tuberosus* Hairless scrambling perennial, with *angled, but unwinged, stems* to 1.2m. Leaves with 1 pair of roughly elliptical leaflets, and simple or branched tendrils; stipules narrowly half-arrow shaped. Inflorescence long-stalked, with 2–7 bright reddish-purple flowers, to 20mm long; pods brown, hairless, to 40mm long. In grassy places and waste ground; throughout, except Scandinavia and Britain, though naturalised locally there. **Fl:** Jun–Jul. **Br Is dist:** Very locally naturalised, mainly in England.

Narrow-leaved Everlasting-pea

Narrow-leaved Everlasting-pea *Lathyrus sylvestris* Climbing hairless or downy perennial herb, with *broadly winged stems* to 3m. Leaves with 1 pair of narrowly lanceolate leaflets, to 15cm long, with branched tendrils; *stipules lanceolate, less than half width of stem*, to 20mm long (a). Inflorescence long-stalked, with 3–12 flowers; corolla pinkish-purple flushed yellow, to 20mm long; calyx teeth shorter than tube; pods brown, hairless, to 70mm. In scrub, grassland and wood-margins; throughout except the far north. **Fl:** Jun–Aug. **Br Is dist:** Scattered throughout, local and mainly southern; also naturalised from gardens.

Grass Vetchling

Grass Vetchling *Lathyrus nissolia* Erect hairless or slightly downy annual, with unwinged stems to 90cm. Leaves reduced to grass-like midribs only, without leaflets or tendril – plant looks like grass when not in flower; stipules very small and narrow. Flowers solitary or paired, long-stalked, with crimson corolla to 18mm long; pods pale brown. A distinctive plant. In grassy places, especially on heavier soils; more common near the coast, from the Netherlands and Britain southwards. **Fl:** May–Jul. **Br Is dist:** Scattered and local through England, commoner in the south but declining.

Yellow Vetchling

Yellow Vetchling *Lathyrus aphaca* Hairless waxy grey-green scrambling annual with angled stems to 1m. Leaves reduced to a tendril only, but stipules very large and leaf-like, broad-triangular, paired, to 30mm long. Flowers solitary and erect on long stalks, with corolla yellow, to 12mm long; pod to 35mm, curved, hairless, brown. In dry grassy and disturbed places; from the Netherlands and Britain southwards, mainly western, and probably not native in north of range. **Fl:** Jun–Aug. **Br Is dist:** In S England and Wales, on sandy and chalky soil.

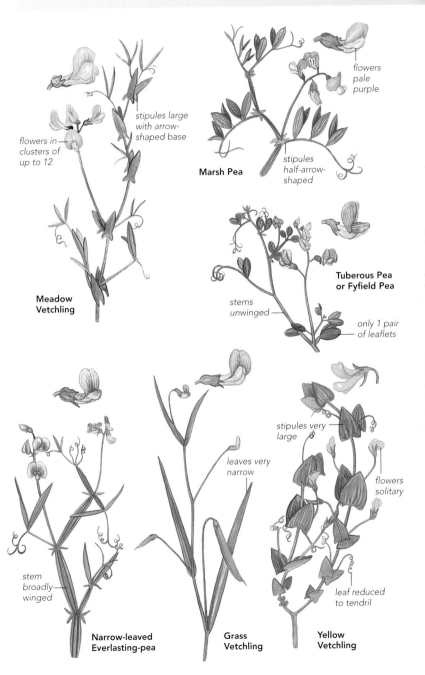

flowers in clusters of up to 12

stipules large with arrow-shaped base

Meadow Vetchling

flowers pale purple

stipules half-arrow-shaped

Marsh Pea

Tuberous Pea or Fyfield Pea

stems unwinged

only 1 pair of leaflets

stem broadly winged

Narrow-leaved Everlasting-pea

leaves very narrow

Grass Vetchling

stipules very large

flowers solitary

leaf reduced to tendril

Yellow Vetchling

123

Common Restharrow

RESTHARROWS *Ononis* Annual or perennial herbs or dwarf shrubs, usually sticky-hairy. Leaves trifoliate, usually toothed. Standard broad.

Yellow Restharrow *Ononis natrix* Small sticky-hairy subshrub to 60cm. Leaves trifoliate, with roughly ovate toothed leaflets. Flowers large, to 20mm, yellow with reddish veins, in loose leafy inflorescences: corolla twice as long as calyx. From N France and S Germany southwards; in dry grassy or rocky places, often calcareous. **Fl:** Jun–Aug. **Br Is dist:** Absent.

Spiny Restharrow

Common Restharrow *Ononis repens* Creeping, ascending or spreading perennial subshrub to 70cm; stems variably *hairy all round, usually spineless.* Leaves trifoliate or with a single leaflet (a), sticky-hairy. Flowers in loose irregular leafy inflorescences; corolla pink, 10–18mm long, with wings equal to keel, calyx very hairy; pods erect, to 7mm long, shorter than calyx. In grassland and on dunes, especially neutral to calcareous; widespread and generally common throughout except the far north. **Fl:** Jun–Sep. **Br Is dist:** Scattered throughout, locally common in calcareous areas, rare elsewhere.

Small Restharrow

Spiny Restharrow *Ononis spinosa* Similar to Common Restharrow, but differing in that: *stems hairy mainly on 2 opposite sides,* and *long spines usually present.* Leaflets narrower and more pointed (b); flowers deeper pink, with wings shorter than keel; pods longer than calyx. In grassland on heavy, often calcareous soils, from S Scandinavia southwards; commonest near the coast. **Fl:** Jun–Sep. **Br Is dist:** Local through England and Wales, through declining; rare in Scotland and absent from Ireland.

Small Restharrow *Ononis reclinata* Small spreading annual to 15cm, with hairy stems, spineless. Flowers small, to 10mm, pink, with corolla equalling calyx; pods pendent when ripe, 10–14mm. In dry grassy and rocky places, usually by the sea; from SW Britain and W France southwards; local. **Fl:** Jun–Jul. **Br Is dist:** Rare and local in SW England and S Wales only.

Tall Melilot

MELILOTS *Melilotus* Annuals or short-lived perennials. Similar to clovers, with trifoliate toothed leaves, but flowers in elongated inflorescences; pods oval, short and straight.

Tall Melilot *Melilotus altissimus* Tall branched biennial or short-lived perennial to 1.5m. Leaflets oblong-ovate, with upper ones almost parallel-sided, toothed; stipules bristle-like. Flowers yellow, 50–70mm long, in long racemes to 50mm; corolla has wings, standard and keel all equal; pods are oval, 5–6mm long, pointed, downy, black when ripe, with net-veined surface, style persistent in fruit. In damp places, saline habitats, open woods and waste ground; from S Scandinavia southwards, through naturalised elsewhere. **Fl:** Jun–Aug. **Br Is dist:** Local through England and Wales, absent from most of Scotland and very rare in Ireland.

Ribbed Melilot

Ribbed Melilot *Melilotus officinalis* Biennial to 2.5m, erect or spreading. Differs from Tall Melilot in that upper leaflets not parallel-sided; *wings and standard longer than keel;* pods hairless, 3–5mm long, wrinkled, blunt (with bristle-point), brown when ripe, *style not persisting.* In cultivated and disturbed ground, often on heavy or saline soils; throughout though not native in the north. **Fl:** Jun–Sep. **Br Is dist:** Locally common as naturalised plant, mainly in south and east; rare in Ireland.

124

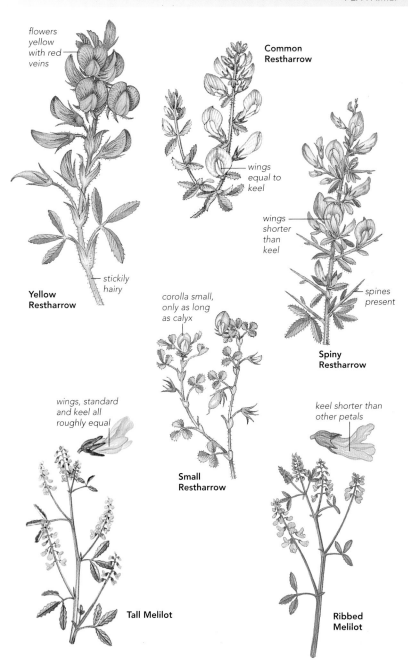

flowers yellow with red veins

Common Restharrow

wings equal to keel

wings shorter than keel

stickily hairy

Yellow Restharrow

corolla small, only as long as calyx

spines present

Spiny Restharrow

wings, standard and keel all roughly equal

keel shorter than other petals

Small Restharrow

Tall Melilot

Ribbed Melilot

White Melilot

White Melilot *Melilotus albus* The only Melilot in N Europe with white flowers. Very similar otherwise to Ribbed Melilot (*see* p. 124), with hairless brown fruits, but these are strongly net-veined, as in Tall Melilot (*see* p. 124). Throughout except the far north in disturbed habitats, but not native over much of north of range. **Fl:** Jun–Aug. **Br Is dist:** Naturalised locally in S and E Britain.

Star-fruited Fenugreek, Trigonella *Trigonella monspeliaca* Downy annual to 35cm. Leaves trifoliate. Flowers 3–4mm long, yellow in short-stalked umbel-like clusters of 4–14; pod narrow and pendent, to 20mm long. Found in waste and cultivated ground; from Belgium and N France southwards. **Fl:** Jun–Jul. **Br Is dist:** Absent.

Spotted Medick

Fenugreek *Trigonella foenum-graecum* Slightly downy annual to 50cm. Leaves trifoliate, with finely toothed ovate leaflets. Flowers solitary or paired, virtually unstalked; corolla creamy white, 10–15mm long, suffused with violet at base; pod erect, up to 10cm long. Cultivated and widely naturalised; from Belgium and Germany southwards. **Fl:** Apr–Jun. **Br Is dist:** Absent.

Sickle Medick

MEDICKS *Medicago* Similar to clovers (*see* pp. 128–30), with trifoliate leaves and compact heads of flowers, but differ in their sickle-shaped or spiral fruits, often spiny.

Black Medick *Medicago lupulina* Downy annual or short-lived perennial to 60cm. Leaves trifoliate, leaflets usually having a triangular tooth in the terminal notch. Inflorescence globular, up to 9mm in diameter, with 10–50 very small yellow flowers; pods coiled in a full turn, black when ripe, *not spiny*, hairless. Very common in grasslands and waste places throughout except the extreme north. **Fl:** Apr–Aug. **Br Is dist:** Common throughout.

Spotted Medick *Medicago arabica* Prostrate, *virtually hairless* annual to 50cm. Leaves trifoliate, with toothed heart-shaped leaflets, *each dark-spotted, stipules evenly toothed*. Flower heads with only 1–6 flowers, yellow, 5–7mm in diameter. Fruit tightly coiled (with 3–7 turns) becoming roughly globular, usually with hooked spines in a double row. In dry grasslands, especially coastal, from the Netherlands and Britain southwards. **Fl:** Apr–Sep. **Br Is dist:** Scattered, mainly S and E England, especially near coast.

Lucerne *Medicago sativa* ssp *sativa* Variable downy perennial to 80cm. Leaves trifoliate, with narrow leaflets, toothed towards tips. Flowers purple to lilac, in cylindrical heads of 5–40 flowers on stalks shorter than calyx tubes; *pod hairless, spiralled* 1½–3½ *times, not spiny*. Widely cultivated and often naturalised throughout, except the far north. **Fl:** Jun–Sep. **Br Is dist:** Naturalised locally almost throughout, except the far north.

Sickle Medick *Medicago sativa* ssp *falcata* Often distinguished as a separate species. Distinguished from Lucerne by the *yellow flowers*, with flower stalks longer than calyx tube; and *curved or sickle-shaped (not spiralled) pods*. Native in grassy places throughout except the far north, and locally naturalised. **Fl:** Jun–Aug. **Br Is dist:** Native in Brecklands; introduced elsewhere.

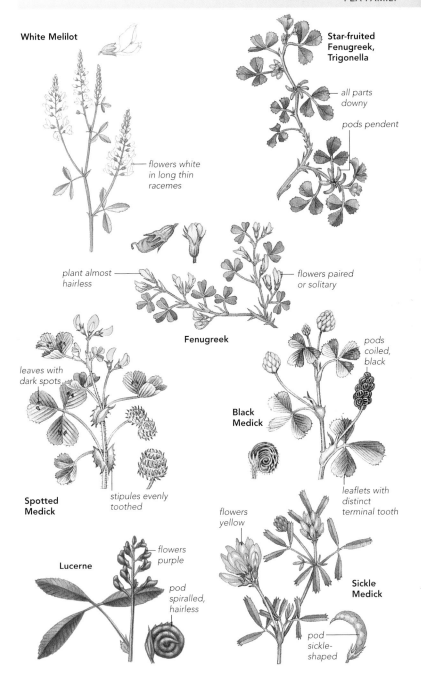

White Melilot

flowers white in long thin racemes

Star-fruited Fenugreek, Trigonella

all parts downy

pods pendent

plant almost hairless

flowers paired or solitary

Fenugreek

leaves with dark spots

pods coiled, black

Black Medick

Spotted Medick

stipules evenly toothed

leaflets with distinct terminal tooth

flowers yellow

Lucerne

flowers purple

pod spiralled, hairless

Sickle Medick

pod sickle-shaped

127

Bird's-foot Clover

Suffocated Clover

Strawberry Clover

Hare's-foot Clover

CLOVERS *Trifolium* Herbs with trifoliate leaves, flowers in heads (corolla persistent in fruit) and stipules different from leaflets (compare with trefoils (*see* p. 130) where stipules are very like leaflets).

Bird's-foot Clover *Trifolium ornithopodioides* Rather inconspicuous, prostrate, hairless annual with stems 2–20cm. Leaflets oval and toothed. Stipules lanceolate and long-pointed. Flowers 5–8mm, white or pink, in small heads of 1–5. Very local in open, dry, sandy or gravelly places, often coastal and damp in winter. **Fl:** May–Oct. **Br Is dist:** Very local, mainly south of a line from Anglesey to the Wash, and S and E Ireland.

White Clover *Trifolium repens* Creeping perennial to 50cm, *rooting at nodes. Leaflets oval often with whitish band and translucent lateral veins.* Stipules oblong and pointed. Flowers scented, white or pale pinkish in long-stalked rounded heads to 20mm in diameter, becoming light brown with age. Widespread throughout; often abundant in grassy places. **Fl:** May–Oct. **Br Is dist:** Common throughout.

Alsike Clover *Trifolium hybridum* Differs from White Clover in being erect, *not rooting at nodes* with *leaflets not having a whitish band* and flowers purple or white at first, then pink and brown. Widely cultivated and naturalised in meadows and roadsides. **Fl:** Jun–Oct. **Br Is dist:** Frequent throughout, more so in the south.

Suffocated Clover *Trifolium suffocatum* Very distinctive low, tufted, hairless annual to only 50mm. Leaves with oval leaflets overtopping the *unstalked* rounded 5mm heads of white flowers clustered at the base of the plant. Rare in dry sandy or gravelly ground, usually near coasts; W France and England only. **Fl:** Apr–May. **Br Is dist:** Rare in S and E England.

Strawberry Clover *Trifolium fragiferum* Creeping perennial with stems to 30cm, rooting at nodes. Leaflets oval, without whitish marks. Flowers pink or purplish in rounded heads 10–15mm in diameter. Calyx swells in fruit giving the flower head the appearance of a pinkish berry. Local to very locally common in short grassland on heavier soils. **Fl:** Jul–Sep. **Br Is dist:** Local but widely scattered; locally common near sea in the south.

Hare's-foot Clover *Trifolium arvense* Softly hairy annual to 30cm, with narrow leaflets, scarcely toothed. Flowers pale pink or white in *dense elongated oval or cylindrical stalked heads*, up to 25mm long, the flowers often shorter than the soft calyx teeth. Locally frequent in dry grassland, sandy or gravelly areas. **Fl:** May–Sep. **Br Is dist:** Locally common, but absent from N Scotland.

Red Clover *Trifolium pratense* Downy perennial to 45cm. Leaflets oval, usually with a crescent-shaped white mark. Stipules triangular towards tip and bristle-pointed. Flowers pinkish red, in rounded *unstalked heads* to 30mm in diameter. Common throughout in grassy places. **Fl:** May–Sep. **Br Is dist:** Widespread and common.

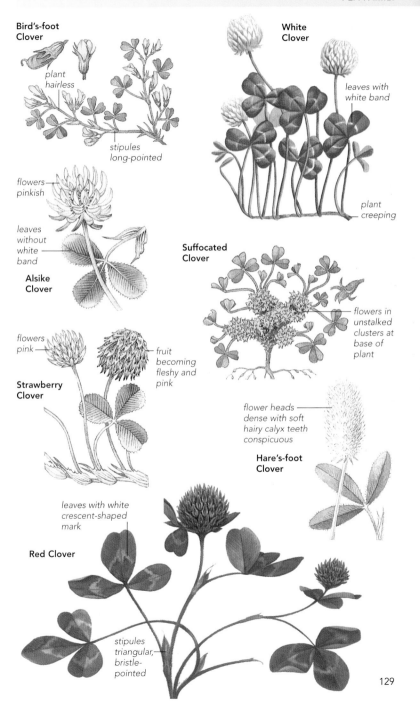

Bird's-foot Clover

plant hairless

stipules long-pointed

White Clover

leaves with white band

plant creeping

flowers pinkish

leaves without white band

Alsike Clover

Suffocated Clover

flowers in unstalked clusters at base of plant

flowers pink

Strawberry Clover

fruit becoming fleshy and pink

flower heads dense with soft hairy calyx teeth conspicuous

Hare's-foot Clover

leaves with white crescent-shaped mark

Red Clover

stipules triangular, bristle-pointed

129

Zigzag Clover *Trifolium medium* Downy perennial to 50cm, very similar to Red Clover (*see* p. 128) but with stems rather wavy, leaflets narrowly elliptical, stipules lanceolate but not bristle-pointed and *short-stalked flower heads*, reddish-purple, to 30mm in diameter. Common in old grassland. **Fl:** May–Jul. **Br Is dist:** Widespread, but local in the south, more common in the north.

Sulphur Clover

Sulphur Clover *Trifolium ochroleucon* Downy erect perennial to 50cm, similar to Red Clover (*see* p. 128) but with lemon-yellow flowers and unmarked leaflets. Very local in grassy places on clay. **Fl:** Jun–Jul. **Br Is dist:** Very local in E England.

Lesser Trefoil *Trifolium dubium* A slender annual, *almost hairless* with flowers up to 3.5mm long, 3–20 in *heads 8–9mm in diameter*. Differs from Black Medick (*see* p. 126) in not being downy and not having a tiny point in the terminal notch of each leaflet. Widespread and generally common, in dry grassy places, but absent from the far north. **Fl:** May–Oct. **Br Is dist:** Common.

Slender Trefoil

Slender Trefoil *Trifolium micranthum* Erect or ascending annual to 10cm, with short-stalked leaflets. Flowers yellow and tiny, 2–3mm, in loose heads of 2–6 stalked flowers. Local in dry grassland, sandy or gravelly places. **Fl:** Jun–Aug. **Br Is dist:** Widespread but generally local; rare in N England, Scotland and Ireland.

BIRD'S-FOOT-TREFOILS *Lotus* Low herbs with pinnate leaves that appear trifoliate because the lower pair is at the base of the stalk, looking like large stipules; actual stipules minute, brown. Flowers yellow, in small heads on long stalks from leaf axils. Pods, when ripe, spread out stiffly like a bird's foot.

Common Bird's-foot-trefoil

Common Bird's-foot-trefoil *Lotus corniculatus* Variable, often sprawling or creeping, perennial, usually almost hairless, occasionally hairy. Stems solid, to 40cm long. Leaflets ovate to lanceolate, occasionally nearly round. Heads 2–8 flowered, on stout stalks up to 80mm long; flowers yellow, about 15mm long, deep red in bud; calyx teeth (**a**) erect in bud, the 2 upper ones having an obtuse angle between them. Widespread and common in grasslands on all but the most acid soils; throughout the north, except the extreme north. **Fl:** Jun–Sep. **Br Is dist:** Very common throughout.

Greater Bird's-foot-trefoil

Greater Bird's-foot-trefoil *Lotus pedunculatus* Similar to Common Bird's-foot-trefoil, but usually more erect, taller (to 60cm), and very hairy; stem hollow. Leaflets broadly oval, blunt, rather bluish-green. Inflorescence stalks up to 15cm long; flowers usually without reddish tinge; upper calyx teeth separated by an acute angle (**b**). In damp grassy places and fens; throughout except most of Arctic Europe. **Fl:** Jun–Aug. **Br Is dist:** Locally common throughout, except the far north.

Dragon's-teeth

Dragon's-teeth *Tetragonolobus maritimus* Differs from bird's-foot-trefoils in having trifoliate leaves (with triangular stipules), and solitary flowers. Flowers on long stalks, with trifoliate bract below calyx; corolla pale yellow; pod up to 50mm long, 4-angled, winged on angles. Widespread on mainland Europe southwards from S Sweden; in grassy, usually calcareous places. **Fl:** May–Aug. **Br Is dist:** Probably introduced; very locally common in SE England.

Zigzag Clover

leaflets narrow, unmarked

flowers lemon-yellow

Sulphur Clover

up to 20 flowers in head

leaflets without point at tip

Lesser Trefoil

2–6 flowers in head

flowers tiny

Slender Trefoil

Common Bird's-foot-trefoil

flowers solitary, pale yellow

stem usually very hairy

separated leaflets appear stipule-like

pod winged

Dragon's-teeth

Greater Bird's-foot-trefoil

stem hollow

Kidney Vetch

Kidney Vetch *Anthyllis vulneraria* Prostrate or ascending, silky-hairy perennial up to 40cm. Leaves pinnate, lower ones with fewer leaflets; leaflets linear to oblong, silky-white below, green above, terminal leaflet much larger. Flowers in close-set paired heads, up to 40mm across, with numerous yellow flowers (rarely pink, white or purple) and conspicuous woolly, inflated calyces between; pods very short. In dry grasslands, often coastal or calcareous, and in rocky places; throughout the area except the far north. **Fl:** May–Sep. **Br Is dist:** Widespread and locally common in calcareous and coastal areas.

Bird's-foot

Bird's-foot *Ornithopus perpusillus* Prostrate, downy annual to 40cm, usually less. Leaves pinnate, with 4–13 pairs and a terminal leaflet. Flowers in heads of 3–8, with a pinnate bract just below head; corolla creamy and veined red (appearing orange at first sight), 3–5mm long; pods to 20mm long, curved, beaded, spreading out like a bird's foot. Found in dry sandy places; from S Sweden southwards, locally common. **Fl:** May–Aug. **Br Is dist:** Locally common in England and Wales, rarer farther north; very local in Ireland.

Crown Vetch

Goat's-rue *Galega officinalis* An erect, perennial, hairless or slightly downy herb to 1.5m. Leaves pinnate, with 9–17 oblong to ovate leaflets. Flowers white to bluish-mauve, in erect, long-stalked, cylindrical inflorescences; calyx teeth bristle-like; pods cylindrical, not angled or inflated, 20–30mm long. Widely naturalised (from S Europe) on waste ground as far north as Britain and Belgium. **Fl:** May–Aug. **Br Is dist:** Naturalised, mainly in S and C Britain.

Small Scorpion-vetch *Coronilla vaginalis* Small shrub to 50cm high. Leaves with 2–6 pairs of ovate to almost circular leaflets, with short stalks and rough margins; stipules 3–8mm long. Flowers in heads of 4–10, corolla yellow, 6–10mm long; pods up to 30mm long, beaded, 6-angled. Found in grassy places and scrub on calcareous soils and in mountain regions from France and Germany southwards. **Fl:** Jun–Aug. **Br Is dist:** Absent.

Horseshoe Vetch

Lesser Scorpion-vetch *Coronilla minima* Similar to Small Scorpion Vetch, with *unstalked leaflets, stipules only 1mm long*; corolla 5–8mm long, yellow. Dry open and grassy habitats, usually on calcareous soils; from NW France southwards. **Fl:** Jun–Sep. **Br Is dist:** Absent.

Crown Vetch *Securigera varia* Straggling or ascending hairless perennial herb to 1m. Leaves pinnate, with 7–12 pairs of oblong-ovate leaflets; stipules papery, up to 6mm long. Flowers in heads of 10–20, corolla white or pink (rarely purplish), 10–15mm long; pods 4-angled, to 60mm long. In grassy and bushy places, often on calcareous soils; probably native from the Netherlands and Germany southwards, but naturalised farther north. **Fl:** Jun–Aug. **Br Is dist:** Introduced; naturalised in scattered localities.

Horseshoe Vetch *Hippocrepis comosa* Spreading, almost hairless perennial herb with woody rootstock, to 40cm. *Leaves pinnate*, with 3–8 pairs of ovate to linear leaflets, almost hairless or downy below; stipules small and narrowly triangular. Heads with 5–12 flowers on long stalks; corolla pale yellow, 5–10mm long; pods in form of bird's foot, to 30mm long, strongly wavy, breaking up into small horseshoe-shaped segments. Widespread and locally common in short, dry turf on calcareous soils from the Netherlands and Britain southwards. **Fl:** May–Jul. **Br Is dist:** Local, to locally common in England, rarer in Wales and absent elsewhere.

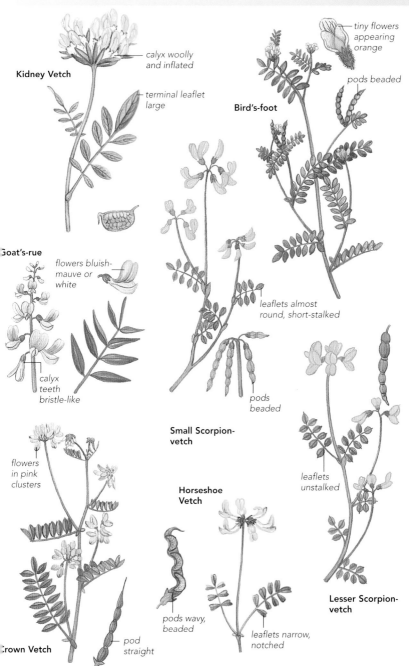

Kidney Vetch

calyx woolly and inflated

tiny flowers appearing orange

pods beaded

Bird's-foot

terminal leaflet large

Goat's-rue

flowers bluish-mauve or white

calyx teeth bristle-like

leaflets almost round, short-stalked

pods beaded

Small Scorpion-vetch

leaflets unstalked

flowers in pink clusters

Horseshoe Vetch

Lesser Scorpion-vetch

Crown Vetch

pods wavy, beaded

pod straight

leaflets narrow, notched

133

Sainfoin

Sainfoin *Onobrychis viciifolia* Erect or occasionally prostrate, downy to almost hairless perennial herb up to 80cm. Leaves pinnate, with 6–14 pairs of oblong to lanceolate leaflets; stipules triangular, papery and brown. Flowers in conical spikes, up to 90mm long, with numerous pink, red-veined flowers; calyx teeth much longer than downy tube; pods small, to 8mm, downy and oval, with toothed margins. In dry grassland, roadsides and disturbed ground, mainly on calcareous soils; throughout as far north as S Sweden, but probably not native through most of range. **Fl:** Jun–Aug. **Br Is dist:** Mainly introduced, widespread on roadsides and grassy places; possibly native in dwarfer form in SE England.

WOOD-SORREL FAMILY Oxalidaceae

Herbs with trifoliate untoothed leaves. Flowers solitary or in small clusters, in 5 parts. Only Wood Sorrel is native to the area – all other species are introduced.

Bloody Crane's-bill

Wood-sorrel *Oxalis acetosella* Creeping perennial herb, rarely more than 10cm. Leaves trifoliate and long-stalked, with drooping leaflets, yellowish-green above, purplish below. Flowers solitary on slender stalks to 10cm, bell-shaped, to 25mm in diameter, white or pale pink with lilac veins; fruit is a hairless capsule, 5-veined. In shady places, especially beech and oak woodland; throughout. **Fl:** Apr–Jun. **Br Is dist:** Locally common throughout, especially in ancient woodland.

Meadow Crane's-bill

Procumbent Yellow-sorrel *Oxalis corniculata* Creeping rooting downy perennial. *Leaves alternate*, with small, eared stipules. Flowers yellow, petals 4–7mm long, in umbels of 1–7, with stalks reflexed in fruit. In dry open habitats, northwards to S Norway, possibly native in south of range. **Fl:** May–Sep. **Br Is dist:** Introduced, locally naturalised.

CRANE'S-BILL FAMILY Geraniaceae

a

CRANE'S-BILLS *Geranium* Differ from the closely related Stork's-bills (*Erodium*) species (*see* p. 138) in having palmately lobed leaves (not pinnate), and fruits whose beaks roll up to release the seeds (rather than twisting spirally and retaining the seeds).

b

Bloody Crane's-bill *Geranium sanguineum* Low to medium perennial herb, much-branched and spreading. Leaves mainly basal, 30–50mm wide, deeply cut into 5–7 divided lobes (a). Flowers clear deep pink to reddish-purple, 20–30mm in diameter, usually solitary on long stalks, with a tiny pair of bracts half-way up. Widespread but local on light, often base-rich soils, usually in open habitats such as grassland, limestone pavement and stable dunes; from S Scandinavia southwards. **Fl:** Jun–Aug. **Br Is dist:** Local throughout; absent from SE England.

Meadow Crane's-bill *Geranium pratense* Medium to tall hairy perennial herb, often in clumps, up to 80cm. Leaves about 10cm wide, deeply divided, almost to the base, into 5–7 divided lobes (b). Flowers large, 25–35mm in diameter, *clear blue* with very little red in, borne in pairs on stalks 20–40mm long; petals rounded. Widespread and locally common, on roadsides and in meadows, usually on base-rich soils, but absent from the far north of Europe. **Fl:** Jun–Sep. **Br Is dist:** Locally common especially in the Midlands and the north.

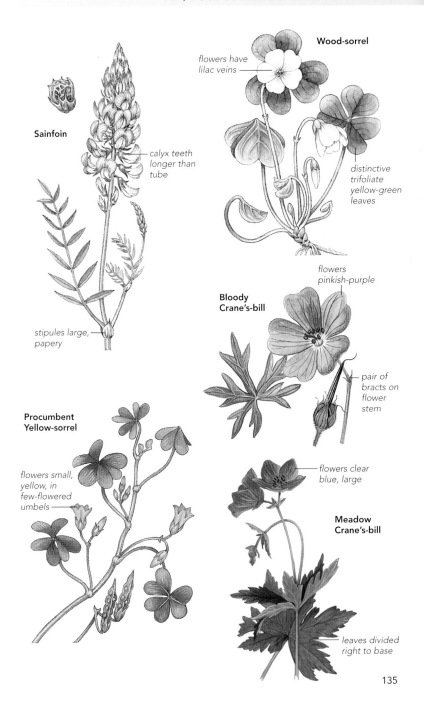

Wood-sorrel

flowers have lilac veins

distinctive trifoliate yellow-green leaves

Sainfoin

calyx teeth longer than tube

stipules large, papery

flowers pinkish-purple

Bloody Crane's-bill

pair of bracts on flower stem

Procumbent Yellow-sorrel

flowers small, yellow, in few-flowered umbels

flowers clear blue, large

Meadow Crane's-bill

leaves divided right to base

Dusky Crane's-bill

Wood Crane's-bill *Geranium sylvaticum* Medium, tufted perennial to 60cm. Similar to Meadow Crane's-bill (*see* p. 134), but leaves have broader, blunter lobes (**a**); flowers are slightly smaller, 20–25mm, more cupped, and usually *reddish-purple to pinkish-violet*, not clear blue. Centre often white. Widespread and locally common throughout, in damper grasslands, open woods, mountain pastures and hedge banks, usually on lime-rich soils. Fl: Jun–Aug. Br Is dist: Rare in the south, frequent from N England northwards.

Marsh Crane's-bill

Dusky Crane's-bill *Geranium phaeum* Medium, erect, tufted perennial to 70cm, usually hairy. Leaves divided just beyond half-way into 5–7 toothed lobes. Flowers distinctive – *deep blackish-purple* in colour, 15–20mm across, in pairs, petals somewhat reflexed, stamens in tight central cluster. Native from C France and S Germany southwards, but widely naturalised northwards to S Sweden. Occurs on woodland edges, roadsides, and damp semi-shaded places. Fl: May–Jul. Br Is dist: Locally naturalised, absent from the north.

Hedgerow Crane's-bill

Marsh Crane's-bill *Geranium palustre* Medium, tufted perennial to 60cm, erect or rather spreading, with short rhizomes. Leaves up to 10cm wide, divided just beyond the middle into 5 (or 7) lobes, each sharply toothed (**b**). Flowers purplish-red, 20–30mm in diameter, cup-shaped with rounded petals; produced in pairs in open inflorescences. Fruits hairy and erect, but with stalks reflexed. Local in mainland Europe in wet meadows and marshes, absent from the Netherlands and N Scandinavia. Fl: Jun–Aug. Br Is dist: Absent.

Round-leaved Crane's-bill

Hedgerow Crane's-bill *Geranium pyrenaicum* Short to medium hairy perennial, ascending or erect to 70cm, though often much shorter. Leaves rounded in outline, divided about half-way into 5–7 lobes and toothed only at the ends (**c**). Basal leaves long-stalked. Flowers pinkish to purple, 12–18mm in diameter, borne *in pairs, petals deeply notched*. Sepals bristle-tipped. Fruit and stalks hairy, reflexed. Local, in meadows and roadsides, rough ground; native to S areas of Europe. naturalised through much of C Europe. Fl: Jun–Aug. Br Is dist: Probably introduced. Frequent, but rare in W and N Britain.

Round-leaved Crane's-bill *Geranium rotundifolium* Rather similar to Hedgerow Crane's-bill, but an annual plant to 40cm; leaves scarcely cut (**d**). Flowers numerous in open groups, with stalks less than 15mm long, pink, 10–12mm in diameter, with *petals barely notched*, and sepals not bristle-tipped. In dry, sandy or calcareous places; from Germany and Belgium southwards. Fl: Jun–Jul. Br Is dist: Mainly southern, absent from Scotland and very rare in Ireland.

Dove's-foot Crane's-bill *Geranium molle* Low, very hairy annual to 40cm, branched and spreading. Stems have very long hairs. Leaves grey-green, hairy and rounded but divided beyond half-way into 5–7 lobes (**e**). Upper stem leaves more divided. Flowers pink, 5–10mm in diameter, in pairs, with notched petals barely longer than sepals. Fruit is hairless. Widespread and common throughout, except in the extreme north, in dry open habitats, including meadows, dunes, roadsides and cultivated areas. Fl: Apr–Sep. Br Is dist: Common and widespread, though rarer in the north.

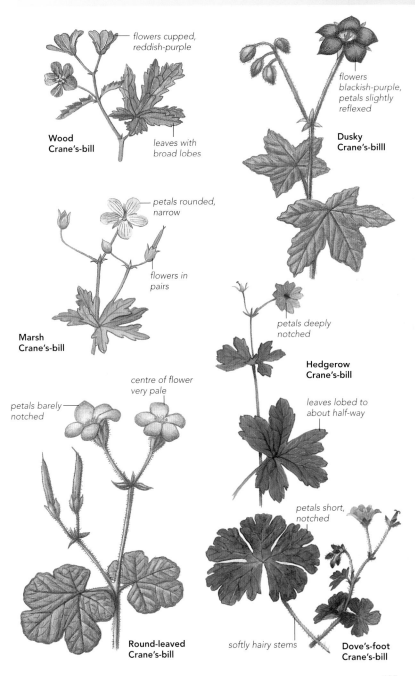

flowers cupped, reddish-purple

Wood Crane's-bill

leaves with broad lobes

flowers blackish-purple, petals slightly reflexed

Dusky Crane's-bill

petals rounded, narrow

flowers in pairs

Marsh Crane's-bill

petals deeply notched

Hedgerow Crane's-bill

leaves lobed to about half-way

centre of flower very pale

petals barely notched

petals short, notched

Round-leaved Crane's-bill

softly hairy stems

Dove's-foot Crane's-bill

Long-stalked Crane's-bill

Long-stalked Crane's-bill *Geranium columbinum* Short or medium, shortly hairy annual, erect or ascending to 60cm. Leaves divided almost to the base into narrow divided lobes (a); lower leaves long-stalked. Flowers pink-purple, 12–18mm in diameter, on *long slender stalks, standing clear of leaves*; petals not notched. Widespread in grassland and arable land, usually on base-rich soil, except in the far north. **Fl:** Jun–Aug. **Br Is dist:** Local in England and Wales; rare farther north.

Cut-leaved Crane's-bill *Geranium dissectum* Rather similar to Long-stalked Crane's-bill with leaves cut almost to base (b). Flowers on shorter stalks, less than 15mm; petals usually with small broad point at tip, not notched; fruit hairy. Widespread and common in cultivated and waste ground, grassy places, except in the extreme north. **Fl:** May–Aug. **Br Is dist:** Mostly common, though very local in N Scotland.

Shining Crane's-bill

Shining Crane's-bill *Geranium lucidum* Short, branched, ascending, almost hairless annual to 40cm. Leaves *shiny green*, often red-tinged, long-stalked; rounded in outline, divided about half-way into 5–7 lobes, each oval and bluntly toothed. Flowers pale pink, 10–15mm in diameter, petals unnotched and with a marked claw. Fruit hairless. Widespread in shady places, especially on rocks and walls, usually on lime-stone; not in the far north. **Fl:** Apr–Aug. **Br Is dist:** Widespread, mainly western or upland, though rare in N Scotland.

Herb-Robert

Herb-Robert *Geranium robertianum* Short-medium, hairy annual (though often overwintering), spreading or erect to 50cm, with strong unpleasant smell. Leaves divided to base into 5 pinnately divided lobes, hairy, and often red-tinged. Flowers bright pink, occasionally white, 12–16mm in diameter, petals unnotched, with a marked claw; pollen orange. Fruit hairy. Mainly shady places, woodland margins, hedges and walls, but also on shingle, where it is more prostrate. Throughout except in the far north. **Fl:** Apr–Sep. **Br Is dist:** Common throughout.

STORK'S-BILLS *Erodium* Closely related to Crane's-bills (*see* pp. 134–6), differing mainly in details of fruit and leaves).

Common Stork's-bill

Common Stork's-bill *Erodium cicutarium* Variable, spreading annual up to 60cm (usually less), normally sticky-hairy. Leaves pinnate, up to 15cm long, with lobes pinnately cut, with conspicuous whitish *pointed stipules*. Flowers in loose umbels of 1–12; petals 4–10mm long, rose-pink (occasionally white), usually unequal, and with dark spot at base of 2 upper larger petals. Widespread and common throughout, except in the extreme north; in dry sandy places and disturbed ground, especially near the coast. **Fl:** Jun–Sep. **Br Is dist:** Widespread and locally common throughout; mainly coastal.

a

b

Musk Stork's-bill *Erodium moschatum* Similar to Common Stork's-bill, but plant always sticky-hairy and smelling of musk. Leaves pinnate, with lobes toothed but not pinnately lobed; *stipules broad and blunt*. Flowers larger, with petals up to 15mm long. Found in cultivated and sandy ground, from the Netherlands southwards, mainly coastal, local. **Fl:** May–Jul. **Br Is dist:** Mainly coastal, on S and W coasts, and most of Ireland; introduced inland.

Sea Stork's-bill *Erodium maritimum* Prostrate annual, with simple leaves. Flowers solitary or paired, petals very small, to 3mm, absent or falling early. Dry coastal grasslands in Britain and France only (and farther south). **Fl:** May–Sep. **Br Is dist:** On S and W coasts, including Ireland, local.

flowers on long stalks, held above leaves

Long-stalked Crane's-bill

Cut-leaved Crane's-bill

leaves rounded and very deeply divided

flowers pale pink

Shining Crane's-bill

leaves shiny

Herb-Robert

plant with long hairs

flowers in loose umbel

petals tiny

stem and leaves sticky-hairy

Musk Stork's-bill

stipules broad, blunt

Common Stork's-bill

stipules narrow, pointed, white

leaves simple

Sea Stork's-bill

FLAX FAMILY Linaceae

A small family of erect hairless herbs, with narrow, untoothed, unstalked leaves. Flowers with 4 or 5 parts, petals contorted in bud; fruit a globose dry capsule.

Perennial Flax *Linum perenne* Erect or spreading hairless perennial, rather woody at base, to 60cm. Leaves linear, narrow to 2.5mm wide, 1-veined (or obscurely 3-veined), greyish-green. Flowers numerous in loose

Perennial Flax

inflorescence, individually 20–25mm in diameter, pale to mid-blue; outer sepals narrow and pointed, inner sepals broader and blunt. Ssp *anglicum* is more procumbent than type, with stems curved at base. Local in dry, often calcareous grasslands. Ssp *perenne* occurs in E France and S Germany only; ssp *anglicum* is confined to Britain. **Fl:** Jun–Jul. **Br Is dist:** In England only, mainly eastern, from Durham southwards.

Pale Flax *Linum bienne* Annual to perennial with slender erect or spreading stems, often branched, to 60cm. Leaves narrow and pointed, normally 3-veined. Flowers pale blue or lilac, *12–18mm in diameter; sepals all*

Pale Flax

ovate, pointed; inner ones with a rough, hairy margin. In dry grassland, often calcareous and most frequently near the coast; in Britain and W France only. **Fl:** May–Sep. **Br Is dist:** Local, almost entirely southern from Kent to SW Ireland; occasional farther north.

Fairy Flax *Linum catharticum* Slender erect annual (rarely biennial) herb to 15cm. Leaves narrow, ovate-lanceolate, blunt and 1-veined. Flowers in very open forked inflorescence; white, only 4–6mm in diameter, nodding in bud; sepals lanceolate and glandular-hairy. In a wide range of dry or damp habitats, usually calcareous or neutral; common throughout except

Fairy Flax

in the extreme north. **Fl:** Jun–Sep. **Br Is dist:** Locally common throughout.

Allseed *Radiola linoides* Very small bushy annual plant, rarely exceeding 80mm, often less, with branched stems. Leaves elliptical, in opposite pairs, 1-veined, to 3mm long (**a1**). Flowers numerous, in branched inflorescences; each is 1–2mm in diameter, with 4 tiny white petals, equal in length to the sepals (**a2**). Widespread but local on damp, sandy or peaty ground, usually acidic; throughout except in the north. **Fl:** Jun–Aug. **Br Is dist:** Widespread but very local; frequent only in SW England.

Annual Mercury

SPURGE FAMILY Euphorbiaceae

All herbaceous plants (in N Europe), usually with milky juice, with alternate simple leaves. Flowers regular, single-sex, (on the same, or separate, plants), without petals, in umbel-like terminal heads (*Euphorbia, see* pp. 142–4) or in spikes from leaf axils (*Mercurialis, see* below and p. 142).

Annual Mercury *Mercurialis annua* Erect annual to 50cm, often branched and virtually hairless. Leaves ovate to elliptical, shiny green, to 50mm long, with regular rounded teeth. Male flowers (usually on separate plants) in long erect spikes; female flowers few, almost stalkless; all yellowish-green, 2–4mm. Fruit bristly. In waste places and cultivated ground, widespread, though rare and probably not native in most of Scandinavia. **Fl:** Jul–Oct. **Br Is dist:** Locally common in S Britain, increasingly rare to the north.

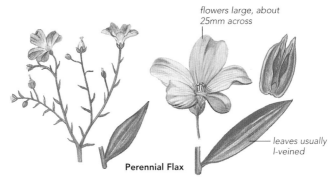

flowers large, about 25mm across

leaves usually l-veined

Perennial Flax

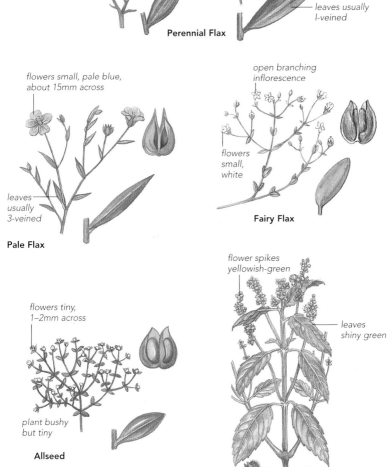

flowers small, pale blue, about 15mm across

leaves usually 3-veined

Pale Flax

open branching inflorescence

flowers small, white

Fairy Flax

flowers tiny, 1–2mm across

plant bushy but tiny

Allseed

flower spikes yellowish-green

leaves shiny green

Annual Mercury

Dog's Mercury *Mercurialis perenne* Perennial, rather similar to Annual Mercury (*see* p. 140), but with erect unbranched stems to 40cm, from creeping rhizomes, and *downy all over*. Leaves lanceolate-ovate (generally broader on female plants), to 80mm long, short-stalked, with rounded teeth. Male flowers 3–5mm in long spikes, female flowers 1–3 on short stalk, producing hairy fruits. Widespread throughout except in the far north, in woods, less commonly on rock ledges or limestone pavement. **Fl:** Feb–Apr. **Br Is dist:** Generally common except in N Scotland, very rare in Ireland.

Dog's Mercury

SPURGES *Euphorbia* Distinctive group of mainly erect plants with acrid milky juice, alternate (occasionally opposite) undivided leaves, and umbel-like flower heads. Flowers consist of cups with toothed rims, and 4–5 conspicuous rounded or crescent-shaped glands, with a single female flower and several 1-stamened male flowers in each.

Purple Spurge

Purple Spurge *Euphorbia peplis* Prostrate annual plant with *forked red-purple stems*, up to 40cm long. Leaves oblong, with single lobe at base, to 11mm long, short-stalked, greyish-green; stipules divided into narrow lobes. Flowers tiny with semicircular undivided glands. On sandy beaches, very local; from W France and possibly SW Britain southwards. **Fl:** Jul–Sep. **Br Is dist:** Formerly in SW England and Channel Islands, probably extinct.

Caper Spurge *Euphorbia lathyris* Tall erect grey-green biennial up to 1.5m. Leaves linear to oblong, to 15cm long, untoothed and unstalked, in opposite pairs appearing in 4 rows. Inflorescence has 2–6 main rays; upper bracts heart-shaped at base; glands crescent-shaped, with blunt horns; fruit large, to 17mm across. In waste and cultivated ground, less frequent in open woods; probably native only in S and E Europe, but widely naturalised as far north as the Netherlands. **Fl:** Jun–Jul. **Br Is dist:** Frequently naturalised in gardens, possibly native in a few S England woodland sites.

Sun Spurge

Sun Spurge *Euphorbia helioscopia* Erect, hairless annual, usually with a single stem, to 50cm. Leaves ovate, broadest towards tip, or almost spoon-shaped, up to 40mm long, toothed towards tip. Umbel usually 5-rayed, with 5 large distinctive yellow-green bracts at base; glands oval, green and untoothed; fruit 2.5–3.5mm in diameter, smooth. Generally common on disturbed, open and waste ground, almost throughout the region but rare and irregular in far north. **Fl:** May–Nov. **Br Is dist:** Common throughout.

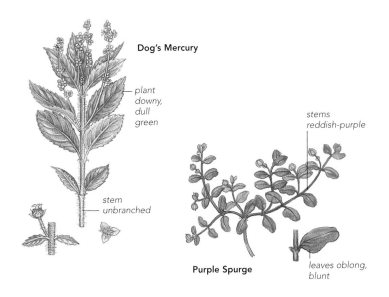

Dog's Mercury

plant
downy,
dull
green

stem
unbranched

stems
reddish-purple

Purple Spurge

leaves oblong,
blunt

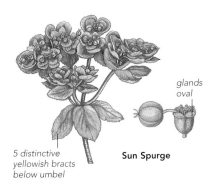

leaves
linear,
paired

glands
horned

Caper Spurge

5 distinctive
yellowish bracts
below umbel

Sun Spurge

glands
oval

Dwarf Spurge

Dwarf Spurge *Euphorbia exigua* Small *grey-green* annual to 35cm, usually much less, often branched from the base. Leaves differ from other species in being very narrow, lanceolate (to 25mm long x *2mm wide*), untoothed and unstalked. Rays 3–5, with narrowly triangular bracts; glands crescent-shaped. On cultivated ground; throughout except the far north. **Fl:** Jun–Oct. **Br Is dist:** Locally common in the south, much rarer to the north, mainly on calcareous soils.

Petty Spurge *Euphorbia peplus* Erect hairless annual to 40cm, with 2 or more branches from base and up to 3 side flowering branches. Leaves oval, blunt, to 25mm long, untoothed but stalked. *Umbels 3-rayed, with 3 unstalked spoon-shaped bracts at base*; glands crescent-shaped, with long slender horns. Fruit 2mm in diameter, smooth. Very common on arable and disturbed land; throughout except for Arctic areas. **Fl:** Apr–Nov. **Br Is dist:** Common throughout.

Portland Spurge

Portland Spurge *Euphorbia portlandica* Hairless perennial up to 40cm, usually branched from the base, ascending or prostrate. Leaves ovate to spoon-shaped, *broadest towards tip*, tapering to base, usually untoothed, grey-green and with midrib prominent below. Umbels 3- to 6-rayed, with oval lower but triangular to diamond-shaped upper bracts; glands yellow and *crescent-shaped with prominent horns* (g); seeds pitted. On coastal sands, rocks and grassland; from Britain and W France southwards. **Fl:** May–Sep. **Br Is dist:** S and W coasts from Sussex to S Scotland, common around Irish coasts.

Sea Spurge

Sea Spurge *Euphorbia paralias* Rather similar to Portland Spurge, found in similar habitats, but differing in that it is usually stiffly erect, with several branches, to 70cm. Leaves oval, thick and fleshy, grey-green, untoothed, closely set on stem, *broadest towards base*, midrib obscure below. *Glands roughly kidney-shaped, with horns* (h); seeds smooth. On sand-dunes and beaches; from the Netherlands southwards. **Fl:** Jun–Oct. **Br Is dist:** Round most of the coasts except NE England and much of Scotland.

Cypress Spurge

Cypress Spurge *Euphorbia cyparissias* Distinctive patch-forming hairless perennial herb, with numerous erect and sterile flowering stems, to 50cm high. Leaves numerous, linear, up to 40mm long x 3mm wide, untoothed and unstalked. Umbel with 9–15 rays, with lower axillary flower branches often present; upper bracts triangular, *yellow turning red*; glands crescent-shaped with 2 horns. In grassland, scrub and open woodland, often on calcareous soils; widespread except in the far north, but not considered native in Scandinavia. **Fl:** May–Jul. **Br Is dist:** Possibly native in a few S England localities, introduced elsewhere.

Wood Spurge

Wood Spurge *Euphorbia amygdaloides* Erect, tufted, downy perennial to 90cm. Rhizomes produce short overwintering stems with terminal rosettes, from which the following year's flower stems develop. Leaves of sterile shoots tapering into short stalk, strap-shaped, *dark green* and downy, up to 70mm long; leaves of flower shoots not tapering. Umbels with 5–10 rays, with *upper bracts joined in pairs, yellow*; glands crescent-shaped with 2 horns. Locally common in woodland and scrub, from the Netherlands and Germany southwards. **Fl:** Apr–Jun. **Br Is dist:** Absent from Scotland, rare in N England and Ireland, common in S England and Wales.

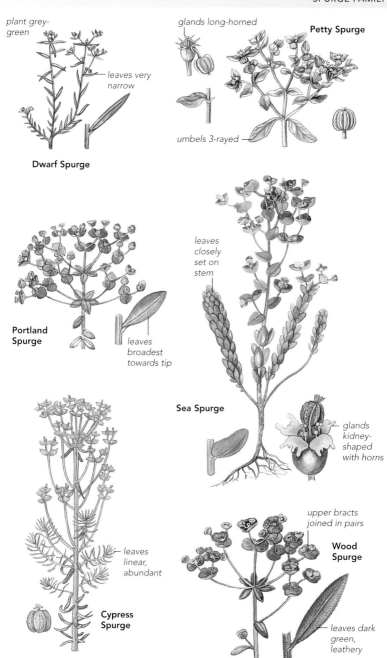

plant grey-green

leaves very narrow

Dwarf Spurge

glands long-horned

Petty Spurge

umbels 3-rayed

Portland Spurge

leaves broadest towards tip

leaves closely set on stem

Sea Spurge

glands kidney-shaped with horns

leaves linear, abundant

Cypress Spurge

upper bracts joined in pairs

Wood Spurge

leaves dark green, leathery

145

Heath Milkwort

Chalk Milkwort

MILKWORT FAMILY Polygalaceae

A small family of low herbaceous or shrubby perennials, with simple leaves. The flowers (of *Polygala*) are irregular and distinctive, with 3 tiny outer sepals, 2 large coloured petal-like inner ones (the 'wings') and 3 small petals joined into a whitish fringed tube with 8 stamens attached to it. The lower petal differs from the other 2, and is called the 'keel'.

Shrubby Milkwort *Polygala chamaebuxus* Low mat-forming shrubby perennial to 15cm. Leaves alternate, ovate to linear-lanceolate, leathery, to 30mm long. Flowers solitary or paired from leaf axils; wings large, may be white, yellow or purple; corolla 10–14mm, with keel bright yellow and remaining petals the same colour as the wings. In woods, mountain grassland and rocky slopes, mainly in hilly areas; from E France and S Germany southwards. **Fl:** May–Sep. **Br Is dist:** Absent.

Common Milkwort *Polygala vulgaris* Small ascending or erect plant, to 35cm (usually much less), hairless or slightly hairy, stems often branched. *Leaves all alternate*, pointed, widest at or below the middle, lowest ones shorter and broader, to 10mm long. Inflorescence with 10–40 flowers, which are blue, white or pink, and 6–8mm long; wings very small; wings ovate but with a small point, and with much-branched veins. Common throughout in neutral and base-rich grassy places, except Iceland and Spitzbergen. **Fl:** May–Sep. **Br Is dist:** Locally common throughout.

Heath Milkwort *Polygala serpyllifolia* Very similar to Common Milkwort, differing in that the plants are usually smaller and more spreading. *Lower leaves to some extent in opposite pairs.* Inflorescence with fewer flowers (3–10) that are most commonly dull blue and 5–6mm long. Widespread and common on more acid soils, from SW Norway southwards, mainly western. **Fl:** May–Sep. **Br Is dist:** Locally common throughout.

Chalk Milkwort *Polygala calcarea* Small perennial to 20cm, with a rosette of blunt leaves *slightly above ground level*; stem leaves alternate, widest above the middle. Inflorescences have 6–20 flowers, each 5–6mm long, most commonly bright blue, occasionally bluish-white; veins of wings much less branched than in Common Milkwort and Heath Milkwort. In calcareous grassland, from Belgium and S Britain southwards. **Fl:** May–Jun (not continuing through summer). **Br Is dist:** S and E England only.

BALSAM FAMILY Balsaminaceae

Herbs, with simple leaves. Flowers distinctive, with 5 parts, but only 3 sepals, of which the lowest is prolonged into a spur. Fruit is an explosive capsule.

Indian Balsam *Impatiens glandulifera* Tall annual to 2m, branched or unbranched, with reddish stem. Leaves lanceolate to elliptical, to 18cm long, opposite or in whorls of 3. Flowers purplish-pink or white, up to 40mm long, with short curved spur. Fruit club-shaped. Naturalised from the Himalayas; on riverbanks and damp or shady waste ground; widespread northwards to C Scandinavia. **Fl:** Jul–Oct. **Br Is dist:** Now widespread almost throughout.

wings white, yellow or purple

keel bright yellow

leaves leathery

Shrubby Milkwort

leaves all alternate

Common Milkwort

Heath Milkwort

at least some lower leaves in opposite pairs

Chalk Milkwort

small rosette of leaves just above ground level

Indian Balsam

flowers large and pink, with short spur

147

Touch-me-not Balsam

Musk-mallow

Common Mallow

Touch-me-not Balsam *Impatiens noli-tangere* Hairless erect annual plant to 1.8m, with branched or unbranched stems. Leaves alternate and roughly ovate, to 10cm long, with 7–16 usually pointed teeth on each side. Flowers in loose inflorescences of 3–6 from leaf axils; petals yellow with small brown spots, 20–35mm long including the curving, tapering spur; fruit linear in shape. In damp and shady places, widespread except in the far north. **Fl:** Jul–Sep. **Br Is dist:** Native and locally common in N Wales and NW England; introduced elsewhere.

Orange Balsam *Impatiens capensis* Similar to Touch-me-not Balsam, but differs in that its leaves are often wavy, with fewer than 10 teeth. Flowers orange, with reddish-brown blotches; spur contracts abruptly and is bent into a hook. A N American species, naturalised in Britain and France by rivers and canals. **Fl:** Jun–Aug. **Br Is dist:** Local, in England and Wales only.

MALLOW FAMILY Malvaceae

Herbs or shrubs, usually softly hairy or downy with star-like hairs. Leaves alternate, with stipules present. Flowers in 5 parts and often showy, with numerous stamens joined into a tube at the base; ovary superior, with numerous carpels joining into a flattened ring. An epicalyx is present below the true calyx, made up of 3 free segments in *Malva* (see below and p. 150), 3 joined segments in *Lavatera* (see p. 150) and 6–9 segments in *Althaea* (see p. 150).

Musk-mallow *Malva moschata* Erect, often-branched, perennial herb to 80cm, with scattered *simple hairs*. Basal leaves roughly kidney-shaped, 3-lobed, to 80mm long, long-stalked; stem leaves deeply cut palmately into narrow, further-divided segments. Flowers bright rose-pink, 30–60mm in diameter, 1–2 in leaf axils, and in loose terminal cluster; epicalyx segments linear-lanceolate and narrowed at both ends. In grassy and rocky places; from the Netherlands and N Germany southwards. **Fl:** Jun–Aug. **Br Is dist:** Throughout except the far north, local in Ireland.

Common Mallow *Malva sylvestris* Erect or spreading perennial herb up to 1.5m, woolly at base. Leaves variable, roughly kidney-shaped, 5–10cm across, palmately divided into 3–7 toothed lobes and long-stalked. Flowers pinky purple with darker veins, 25–40mm in diameter, stalked, in small clusters from leaf axils; *petals about 4 times as long as downy sepals. Fruit sharply angled*, not winged, netted. Widespread and common throughout, except in the north, in grassy and waste places. **Fl:** Jun–Sep. **Br Is dist:** Common in S Britain, rarer or absent farther north.

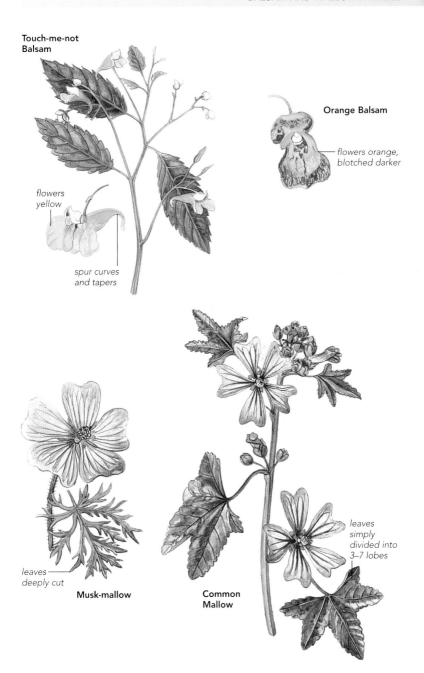

Touch-me-not Balsam

flowers yellow

spur curves and tapers

Orange Balsam

flowers orange, blotched darker

leaves deeply cut

Musk-mallow

Common Mallow

leaves simply divided into 3–7 lobes

149

Dwarf Mallow

Dwarf Mallow *Malva neglecta* Prostrate, downy annual. Leaves are similar to Common Mallow (*see* p. 148), though smaller (40–70mm across) and more shallowly lobed. Flowers in clusters of 3–6 along stem, 10–20mm in diameter, pale lilac with darker veins, with *petals 2–3 times length of sepals. Fruit smooth*, with blunt angles. Widespread almost throughout, except in the far north, on waste ground, roadsides and beaches. **Fl:** Jun–Sep. **Br Is dist:** Widespread and locally common in the south, much rarer farther north.

Tree-mallow

Tree-mallow *Lavatera arborea* Erect woody biennial to 3m tall, downy above with starry hairs. Leaves rounded, palmately 5- to 7-lobed, up to 20cm long and velvety. Flowers in clusters of 2–7 from leaf axils, forming a long terminal inflorescence; flowers are purplish-pink, veined darker, 30–50mm in diameter; epicalyx with 3 lobes joined into cup, *lobes longer than sepals*, greatly enlarged in fruit. In rocky places and waste ground, normally near the sea; from Britain and France southwards. **Fl:** Jun–Sep. **Br Is dist:** Around the S and W coasts of Britain northwards to S Scotland, and in S and W Ireland.

Marsh-mallow

Marsh-mallow *Althaea officinalis* Downy, velvety erect perennial to 2m, with all hairs star-like. Leaves triangular-ovate, slightly 3- to 5-lobed, often folded like a fan, 50–90mm across. Flowers 25–40mm in diameter, solitary or clustered, axillary and terminal, pale lilac-pink. Damp coastal habitats, especially upper salt-marshes; from Denmark southwards, local. **Fl:** Aug–Sep. **Br Is dist:** A plant of S coasts.

MEZEREON FAMILY Thymelaeaceae

Small shrubs or herbs with simple, untoothed, leaves. Flowers hermaphrodite in clusters, in 4 parts; petals absent; fruit is a berry or nut.

Mezereon

Mezereon *Daphne mezereum* Erect, bushy, deciduous shrub to 2m. Leaves oblong to lanceolate, up to 80mm long, thin, short-stalked, pale green, alternate and crowded towards tips of shoots. *Flowers rich rose-pink*, 8–12mm across, in long cylindrical inflorescence, usually appearing before or with leaves; individual flowers have 4 petal-like sepals on long tube (true petals absent); very fragrant. *Fruit is a red globular drupe.* Widespread, except in the far north, and parts of the west, in woods and scrub on calcareous soils. **Fl:** Feb–Apr. **Br Is dist:** Scattered in England, but rare; absent elsewhere, except as introduction.

Spurge-laurel

Spurge-laurel *Daphne laureola* Erect, evergreen hairless shrub to 1m tall, with greenish young shoots. Leaves leathery, lanceolate, alternate, dark shiny green, clustered towards tops of shoots. Flowers borne in short tight clusters on previous year's growth; *yellowish green*, 8–12mm across, slightly pendulous, with 4 petal-like sepal lobes, fragrant; *fruit is globose and black* when ripe. In woods, especially of beech, usually on calcareous soils; from Britain and S Germany southwards. **Fl:** Feb–Apr. **Br Is dist:** Local in England, rare in Wales, absent from Ireland and most of Scotland.

Annual Thymelaea *Thymelaea passerina* Erect, hairless (occasionally downy) annual up to 50cm. Leaves narrow, linear, to 15mm long x 2mm wide. Flowers tiny and greenish, arising from a tuft of silky hairs, with 2 narrow bracts. In dry places, from Belgium and S Germany southwards, local. **Fl:** Jul–Sep. **Br Is dist:** Absent.

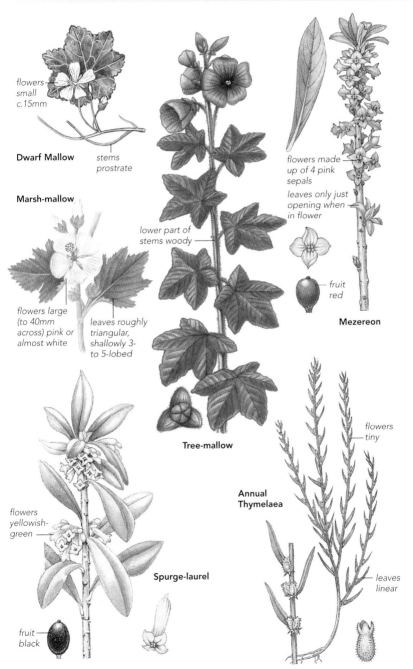

flowers small c.15mm

Dwarf Mallow

stems prostrate

Marsh-mallow

flowers large (to 40mm across) pink or almost white

leaves roughly triangular, shallowly 3- to 5-lobed

lower part of stems woody

Tree-mallow

flowers made up of 4 pink sepals

leaves only just opening when in flower

fruit red

Mezereon

flowers yellowish-green

Spurge-laurel

fruit black

Annual Thymelaea

flowers tiny

leaves linear

151

Tutsan

ST JOHN'S-WORT FAMILY Clusiaceae (Hypericaceae)

Shrubs or herbs, commonly with numerous translucent glands in the leaves, and scattered black or red glands; leaves simple, opposite or whorled. Flowers regular and yellow, usually with 5 free petals and sepals, and numerous stamens; ovary superior, with 3–5 styles.

Tutsan *Hypericum androsaemum* Spreading or ascending shrub to 70cm, with 2-edged stems. Leaves roughly oval, to 15cm, unstalked. Flowers relatively few, about 20mm in diameter, with yellow petals; sepals about as long as petals, broadly ovate, unequal, enlarging and turning back in fruit; fruit a fleshy ovoid berry (fruit is a dry capsule in all other native species), 6–8mm in diameter, red then black. In woods and shady places; from Belgium and Britain southwards, with a markedly western distribution. **Fl:** May–Aug. **Br Is dist:** Scattered throughout, but generally commonest in the south and west.

Hairy St John's-wort

Hairy St John's-wort *Hypericum hirsutum* Erect *downy* perennial to 1m, with *round stems*. Leaves oblong to elliptical, to 50mm long, downy, with strongly marked veins, and translucent dots. Flowers numerous, in roughly cylindrical inflorescence; pale yellow, about 15mm in diameter, with pointed sepals that have stalked black glands on margins. Widespread and generally common, except in the extreme north; in grassy places, scrub, and open woods, usually on calcareous soils. **Fl:** Jul–Aug. **Br Is dist:** Widespread, though local, and rare in the north and west.

Slender St John's-wort

Slender St John's-wort *Hypericum pulchrum* Hairless, stiffly erect plant to 90cm, usually less, with *round reddish stems*. Leaves oval, to 20mm long, blunt, with heart-shaped base and translucent dots. Inflorescence narrowly cylindrical or pyramidal; flowers about 15mm in diameter, orange-yellow, with red dots, and black dots on edges of petals and sepals. On heaths, dry grassland and open woods, avoiding lime-rich soils; from S Scandinavia southwards, local. **Fl:** Jun–Aug. **Br Is dist:** Widespread and locally common, except in calcareous areas.

Marsh St John's-wort

Marsh St John's-wort *Hypericum elodes* Distinctive, creeping, grey-hairy herb, with rounded stems. Leaves oval to almost circular, up to 30mm long, *grey-hairy*, slightly clasping the stem. Flowers in loose terminal clusters on erect stems, individually small, 10–15mm across, not opening widely, yellow, with *erect red-hairy sepals*. In wet acid and peaty places, from the Netherlands and Germany southwards. **Fl:** Jun–Aug. **Br Is dist:** Scattered throughout except in the far north, local, though more common in acid hilly districts.

Trailing St John's-wort

Trailing St John's-wort *Hypericum humifusum* Creeping hairless perennial, branching and rooting near the base; *stems with 2 ridges*. Leaves small, to 15mm, elliptical-oval, with translucent glands. Inflorescence few-flowered; flowers pale yellow, 8–10mm diameter, with petals equalling or up to 1½ times as long as sepals; sepals unequal, usually with scattered black glands. In open habitats, usually acidic, from S Sweden southwards. **Fl:** Jun–Sep. **Br Is dist:** Throughout.

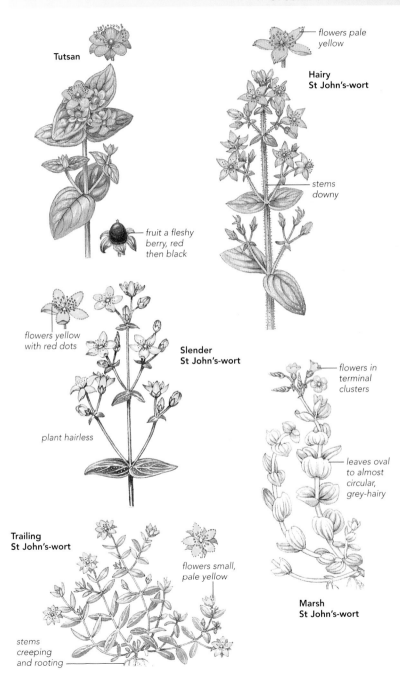

Tutsan

fruit a fleshy berry, red then black

flowers pale yellow

Hairy St John's-wort

stems downy

flowers yellow with red dots

Slender St John's-wort

plant hairless

flowers in terminal clusters

leaves oval to almost circular, grey-hairy

Marsh St John's-wort

Trailing St John's-wort

flowers small, pale yellow

stems creeping and rooting

153

Perforate St John's-wort *Hypericum perforatum* Erect herb to 1m (usually less), with a 2-lined stem – an easy way to distinguish it from the otherwise similar Imperforate St John's-wort (not shown). Leaves ovate to linear, to 30mm, barely stalked, hairless and blunt, with numerous translucent dots. Flowers rich yellow, 20mm in diameter, often with black dots on petal edges; sepals pointed, usually with a few black dots. Throughout, except in the extreme north, in scrub, grasslands, open woods and roadsides. **Fl:** Jun–Sep. **Br Is dist:** Common almost throughout, but rare in N Scotland.

Square-stalked St John's-wort

Square-stalked St John's-wort *Hypericum tetrapterum* Rather similar to Perforate St John's-wort, but *winged corners on a square stem*. Leaves oval, with small translucent dots. Flowers pale yellow, sepals narrow and pointed, without black dots. In wet marshy places, from S Sweden southwards. **Fl:** Jun–Sep. **Br Is dist:** Throughout, except N Scotland, though local in many areas.

Sweet Violet

VIOLET FAMILY Violaceae

Herbs, with alternate, stalked leaves with paired stipules at the base. Flowers with 5 sepals, each extended backwards into an appendage; and 5 petals, of which the lower lip has a spur. All species in N Europe are within the genus *Viola*, though this divides into Violets and Pansies.

Sweet Violet *Viola odorata* Small perennial herb to 15cm, with leaves and flowers arising directly from rootstock, closely downy, with long rooting runners. Leaves rounded and kidney-shaped, to 60mm long, heart-shaped at base, long-stalked, rather shiny, slightly hairy and becoming larger in summer; stipules usually fringed. Flowers fragrant, dark violet or white, 15mm long, sepals oblong with spreading appendages. In woods, scrub and hedgerows, usually on calcareous soils, throughout except the far north. **Fl:** Mar–May. **Br Is dist:** Widespread as far north as S Scotland, locally common.

Hairy Violet

Hairy Violet *Viola hirta* Similar to Sweet Violet, but hairier with spreading hairs on leaves and stalks; leaves narrower and runners completely absent. Flowers violet but not fragrant and paler than those of Sweet Violet. In grassland, scrub and rocky areas, usually calcareous, throughout except the far north. **Fl:** Mar–May. **Br Is dist:** Frequent through England and Wales, becoming rare then absent farther north.

Common Dog-violet

Common Dog-violet *Viola riviniana* Differs in form from Hairy and Sweet Violets, in having leafy, flower-bearing shoots around a central non-flower rosette; plant is virtually hairless. Leaves heart-shaped, up to 40mm, long-stalked; stipules over 10mm long, narrow, with short, wavy fringes. Flowers blue-violet, 15–25mm across, with dark purple lines on central area, especially on lower petal; *spur blunt, stout, paler than petals*, often whitish, *notched at tip*; sepals pointed, with large squared appendages (**a**). In grassland and open woods; throughout, generally common. **Fl:** Mar–Jun, and sometimes again in autumn. **Br Is dist:** Common throughout.

Early Dog-violet

Early Dog-violet *Viola reichenbachiana* Very similar to Common Dog-violet in general form, though leaves and stipules are slightly narrower. Flowers slightly paler violet, with narrower petals, 15–20mm across; spur straight, *pointed, not notched, darker than petals*; sepals with shorter appendages (**b**). In dry, often calcareous, woods; from S Sweden southwards. **Fl:** Mar–May. **Br Is dist:** Locally common in the south, rarer to the north, mainly in ancient woodland.

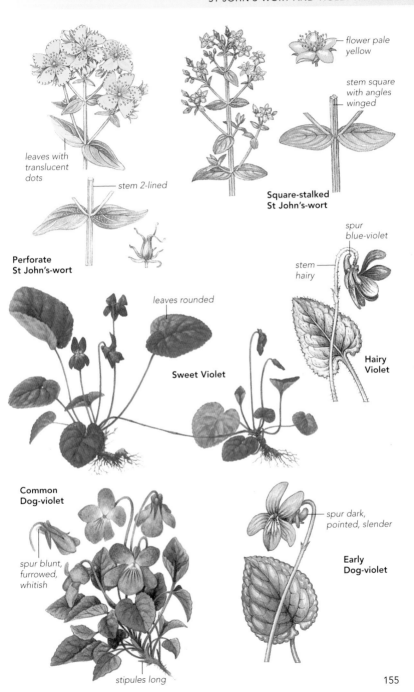

leaves with translucent dots

stem 2-lined

Perforate St John's-wort

flower pale yellow

stem square with angles winged

Square-stalked St John's-wort

leaves rounded

Sweet Violet

spur blue-violet

stem hairy

Hairy Violet

Common Dog-violet

spur blunt, furrowed, whitish

stipules long

spur dark, pointed, slender

Early Dog-violet

155

Teesdale Violet *Viola rupestris* Similar in form to Common Dog-violet (*see* p. 154), but finely downy all over (rarely hairless). Flowers 10–15mm across, pale blue to violet but lacking darker throat markings of Common Dog-violet; spur thick, pale violet, furrowed. Open, generally dry habitats, on limestone; very local, but scattered throughout N Europe. **Fl:** Apr–Jun. **Br Is dist:** Very rare, in Upper Teesdale and Cumbria only.

Teesdale Violet

Heath Dog-violet *Viola canina* Low perennial herb to 30cm, without basal rosette of leaves. *Leaves narrow* oval-lanceolate, *with rounded heart-shaped bases*; stipules third length of leaf stalk, barely toothed, or with broad teeth. Flowers slate-blue or white, 12–18mm across, with white or greenish straight spur. Widespread and locally common throughout, in heathy grasslands, heaths and fens. **Fl:** Apr–Jun. **Br Is dist:** Local throughout.

Fen Violet *Viola persicifolia* Low perennial herb to 20cm, but leaves have truncated to slightly heart-shaped bases. *Petals rounded* and bluish-white; *spur greenish and very short*, barely longer than calyx appendages. Widespread though local throughout, except the far north, in fens and marshy areas. **Fl:** May–Jun. **Br Is dist:** Local and rare, in EC England and W Ireland (locally common around seasonal lakes).

Fen Violet

Marsh Violet *Viola palustris* Distinctive low species, with few-leaved rosettes from creeping runners. Leaves long-stalked, *kidney-shaped*, 20–40mm long, rounded, hairless, wider than long; stipules ovate to lanceolate, untoothed or finely toothed. Flowers pale lilac with darker veins, very rounded petals, 10–15mm across; spur blunt and pale lilac. Widespread throughout; in bogs and acid wet places, rather local. **Fl:** Apr–Jul. **Br Is dist:** Local, throughout in suitable habitats.

Marsh Violet

Mountain Pansy *Viola lutea* Almost hairless, creeping perennial to 40cm. Leaves ovate to lanceolate, hairless or slightly downy; stipules palmately or pinnately divided into 3–5 segments. *Flowers 15–30mm*, on long stalks, may be bright yellow, blue-violet, or mixed, with lower petal having darker markings. In neutral or calcareous upland grassland, very local from Germany and Scotland southwards. **Fl:** May–Aug. **Br Is dist:** Locally common in mountains of N Wales, N England and Scotland.

Mountain Pansy

Wild Pansy, Heartsease *Viola tricolor* Variable plant, occurring both as an annual plant in cultivated ground (ssp *tricolor*) or as a tufted perennial in dry grassland (ssp *curtisii*). Stipules deeply pinnately lobed, with terminal lobe large, leaf-like and toothed. Flowers 15–25mm across, yellow, blue-violet or mixed, with *petals distinctly exceeding sepals*. Widespread throughout in cultivated or waste ground; ssp *curtisii* in dry, mainly coastal, grasslands. **Fl:** Apr–Sep. **Br Is dist:** Widespread and common. Ssp *curtisii* is mainly coastal in south and west, including Ireland.

Wild Pansy

Field Pansy *Viola arvensis* Rather similar to annual forms of Wild Pansy. Flowers smaller, to 15mm, with *sepals at least as long as petals*; petals variable, creamy yellow to bluish-violet; lowest petal cream or yellow; whole flower more or less flat. Common in arable and disturbed ground throughout, except in the extreme north and Iceland. **Fl:** Apr–Oct. **Br Is dist:** Common throughout.

Field Pansy

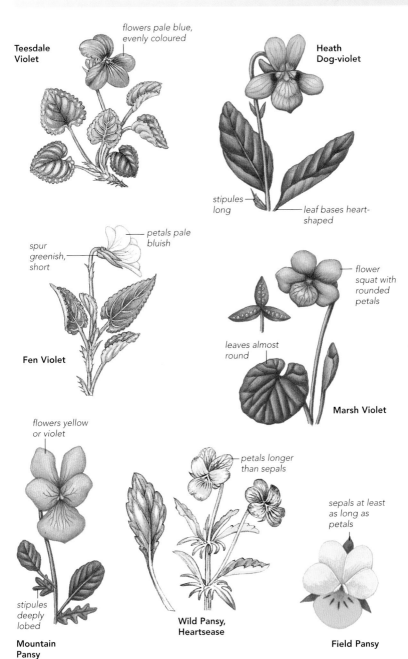

Teesdale Violet

flowers pale blue, evenly coloured

Heath Dog-violet

stipules long

leaf bases heart-shaped

spur greenish, short

petals pale bluish

Fen Violet

flower squat with rounded petals

leaves almost round

Marsh Violet

flowers yellow or violet

petals longer than sepals

sepals at least as long as petals

stipules deeply lobed

Mountain Pansy

Wild Pansy, Heartsease

Field Pansy

157

Spotted Rock-rose

Common Rock-rose

White Rock-rose

Common Fumana

Sea-heath

ROCK-ROSE FAMILY Cistaceae

Low, downy, usually perennial shrubby plants, with opposite undivided leaves (except Fumana). Flowers have 2 small outer and 3 large inner sepals, often striped; 5 equal petals, and numerous stamens. Fruit is a small 3- or 5-valved capsule.

Spotted Rock-rose *Tuberaria guttata* Erect, hairy annual to 30cm. Leaves in a basal rosette and in opposite pairs on stems, elliptical and hairy, to 15mm long. Flowers in terminal inflorescences, yellow, 10–20mm in diameter, often with *red spot at each petal base*, petals usually falling by midday, rendering the plants inconspicuous. In dry, often acid places, especially near the coast, from the Netherlands and N Wales southwards. **Fl:** Apr–Aug. **Br Is dist:** Very rare in Channel Islands, and as var. *breweri* in N Wales and W Ireland.

Common Rock-rose *Helianthemum nummularium* Spreading or ascending subshrub to 50cm, often much-branched from the base. Leaves oval-oblong, to 50mm long, *white woolly below*, usually with inrolled, untoothed margins; short-stalked, with narrow stipules longer than stalk. Flowers in loose inflorescences, bright yellow, to 25mm in diameter, with petals crumpled in bud. In dry grassland and rocky places, often calcareous; throughout, except in the north. **Fl:** Jun–Sep. **Br Is dist:** Widespread generally, though absent from parts of the north and west, and extremely rare in Ireland.

White Rock-rose *Helianthemum apenninum* Similar in form to Common Rock-rose, differing in that the leaves are *grey-downy above as well as below*, with strongly inrolled margins, and stipules no longer than leaf stalks. *Flowers white*. In dry limestone pastures and rocky areas, from S England and Belgium southwards, local. **Fl:** Apr–Jul. **Br Is dist:** Very local, in Devon and Somerset only.

Common Fumana *Fumana procumbens* Prostrate or spreading shrub to 40cm. *Leaves linear, very narrow* and finely pointed, without stipules, alternate. Flowers solitary in leaf axils (not forming terminal inflorescence); petals yellow, with squared ends. In dry rocky and grassy places; Öland and Gotland, and from Belgium southwards. **Fl:** May–Jul. **Br Is dist:** Absent.

SEA-HEATH FAMILY Frankeniaceae

Herbs with reduced heather-like leaves. Flowers hermaphrodite with 4–6 petals and usually 6 stamens.

Sea-heath *Frankenia laevis* Prostrate, branched, mat-forming, finely hairy woody perennial up to 40cm. Leaves linear and very small, with inrolled edges, opposite but densely crowded on short lateral shoots. Flowers regular, pink, 5mm in diameter, with 5 crinkly petals and 6 stamens. In drier parts of salt-marshes, or on shingle, from SE England and NW France southwards, local. **Fl:** Jun–Aug. **Br Is dist:** Local around S and E coasts of England, from Norfolk to Hampshire.

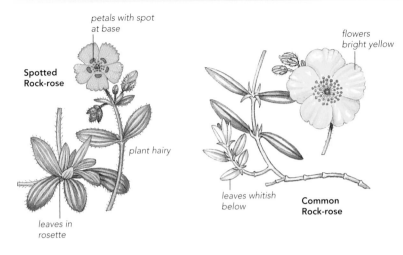

petals with spot at base

Spotted Rock-rose

plant hairy

leaves in rosette

flowers bright yellow

leaves whitish below

Common Rock-rose

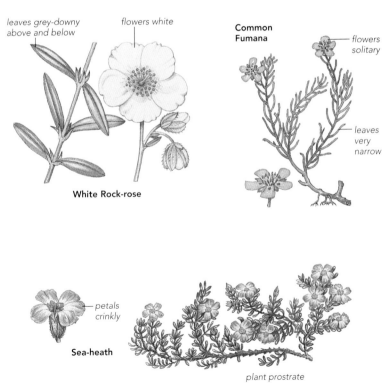

leaves grey-downy above and below

flowers white

White Rock-rose

Common Fumana

flowers solitary

leaves very narrow

petals crinkly

Sea-heath

plant prostrate

White Bryony

WHITE BRYONY FAMILY Cucurbitaceae

White Bryony *Bryonia dioica* Climbing perennial herb up to 4m, with bristly angled stems, and simple, unbranched, spirally coiled tendrils. Leaves palmately lobed, 40–80mm across, with curved stalks. Plants dioecious. Flowers pale green in short axillary inflorescences; male flowers 12–18mm in diameter, in 5 parts; female flowers smaller, with 3 forked stigmas. Fruit is a red berry, 6–10mm in diameter. In grassland, hedges and woodland margins; from Britain and the Netherlands southwards, naturalised farther north. **Fl:** May–Sep. **Br Is dist:** Common in most of England, rarer to west and north, absent from Scotland and Ireland, and all but the eastern fringes of Wales.

Grass-poly

PURPLE-LOOSESTRIFE FAMILY Lythraceae

Herbs, with simple untoothed leaves, opposite or whorled.

Purple-loosestrife *Lythrum salicaria* Downy, erect, perennial herb, to 1.5m, with stems bearing 4 or more raised lines. Leaves oval-lanceolate, 40–70mm long, unstalked, pointed and untoothed, in opposite pairs, or whorls of 3 below and alternate above. Flowers 10–15mm in diameter, in long terminal spike with leafy bracts; 6 red-purple petals and 12 stamens. In fens, damp grassland, and water-margins; throughout, except the extreme north. **Fl:** Jun–Aug. **Br Is dist:** Locally common throughout, except for parts of N Scotland.

Grass-poly *Lythrum hyssopifolium* Erect or spreading *hairless* annual to 25cm. Leaves narrow linear, alternate, usually less than 15mm long. Flowers pale pink, in 6 (occasionally 5) parts, 4–5mm in diameter, solitary in leaf axils. On seasonally flooded, bare or disturbed ground, often arable; widespread from N Germany southwards, but very local. **Fl:** Jun–Aug. **Br Is dist:** Very rare and local in Cambridgeshire and Dorset only, casual elsewhere.

Enchanter's-nightshade

WATER CHESTNUT FAMILY Trapaceae

Water Chestnut *Trapa natans* Aquatic annual, rooted in mud. Floating leaves diamond-shaped, in spreading rosette, stalks often swollen. Flowers white, 15mm in diameter, with 4 petals and sepals. Fruit distinctively horned and edible. In nutrient-rich neutral to slightly acid waters; from S Germany and C France southwards. **Fl:** Jun–Jul. **Br Is dist:** Absent.

WILLOWHERB FAMILY Onagraceae

Herbs or shrubs with opposite leaves (alternate in *Oenothera*, *see* p. 162). Flower parts in 4s, or 2s in *Circaea*; style solitary and ovary inferior.

ENCHANTER'S-NIGHTSHADES *Circaea* These plants have only 2 white petals, each deeply divided; 2 stamens; bristly fruit.

Enchanter's-nightshade *Circaea lutetiana* Perennial herb to 70cm, with creeping stolons, and erect sparsely downy stems, swollen at the nodes. Leaves opposite, oval, to 10cm, rounded or slightly heart-shaped at base, *with round stalks*. Flowers in a spike-like inflorescence, held well above leaves, *continuing to elongate as flowers open*; petals white, 2 stamens, stigma 2-lobed; fruit densely covered with stiff white bristles. Widespread throughout, except in the north, in woods, hedgerows, and on cultivated ground. **Fl:** Jun–Aug. **Br Is dist:** Common throughout except in the far north.

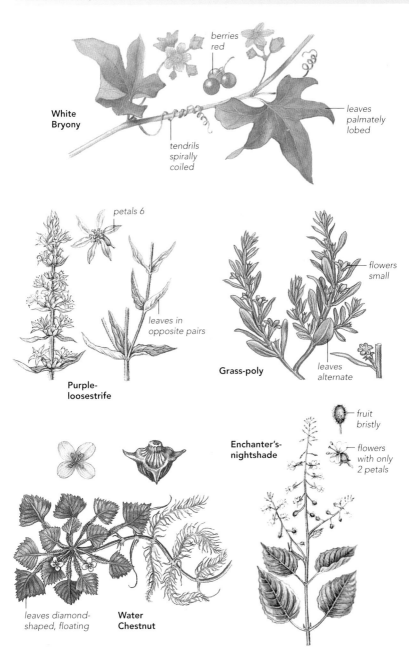

White Bryony

berries red

leaves palmately lobed

tendrils spirally coiled

petals 6

leaves in opposite pairs

Purple-loosestrife

flowers small

Grass-poly

leaves alternate

Enchanter's-nightshade

fruit bristly

flowers with only 2 petals

leaves diamond-shaped, floating

Water Chestnut

161

EVENING-PRIMROSES *Oenothera* These are all of American origin, becoming naturalised widely in Europe. All have 4 yellow, rarely pink, petals, a 4-lobed stigma, and alternate leaves. Only a few species are described here.

Large-flowered Evening-primrose *Oenothera erythrosepala* A tall biennial herb, with hairs on stem having swollen red bases; flowers 50–80mm in diameter, with sepals striped red or wholly red. On waste ground from Denmark southwards. **Fl:** Jun–Sep. **Br Is dist:** Local in England and Wales.

Hampshire-purslane

Hampshire-purslane *Ludwigia palustris* Creeping, hairless, reddish perennial, with stems to 50cm, rooting at the nodes. Leaves opposite, oval to elliptical, to 40mm long and short-stalked. Flowers inconspicuous, lacking petals, with 4 sepals and stamens, and 4-lobed stigma. In wet, muddy places, local, from the Netherlands and England southwards. **Fl:** Jun–Aug. **Br Is dist:** Very rare, almost confined to the New Forest.

Great Willowherb

WILLOWHERBS *Epilobium* and *Chamerion* A difficult group of perennial herbs, complicated by the occurrence of many hybrids. Flowers are pink or reddish, sepals and petals 4, stigma club-shaped (**a1**) or 4-lobed (**a2**), and fruit is a slender capsule splitting along its length to release plumed seeds. The *Chamerion* genus has all leaves alternate; *Epilobium* has at least the lower leaves opposite.

Hoary Willowherb

Rosebay Willowherb *Chamerion angustifolium* Familiar, showy, tall, erect perennial to 2m. Leaves lanceolate, alternate and spirally arranged up stem. Large flowers in a long terminal raceme, rose-purple, 20–30mm in diameter, spreading horizontally from stem; style sharply bent at first, becoming erect as anthers mature and bend down. Generally common throughout on waste ground, roadsides, in mountain areas, cleared woodland and riversides, on a variety of soils. **Fl:** Jul–Sep. **Br Is dist:** Common throughout.

Great Willowherb *Epilobium hirsutum* Tall perennial herb to 2m, with round stems, densely downy with spreading hairs. Leaves opposite, oblong-lanceolate, clasping, stalkless, with sharp teeth, to 12cm long. Large flowers strong purplish-pink, to 25mm in diameter, in loose, leafy terminal inflorescence; stigma with 4 arching lobes. In damp places, often among tall vegetation; widespread and common except in the far north. **Fl:** Jul–Aug. **Br Is dist:** Common throughout except in far NW Scotland.

a1

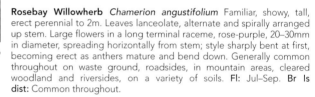

Hoary Willowherb *Epilobium parviflorum* Similar to Great Willowherb, but smaller, to 75cm at most; leaves not clasping; flowers paler pink, much smaller (to 12mm in diameter). Similar habitats, distribution and flowering time. **Fl:** Jul–Aug. **Br Is dist:** Common throughout the year except in NW Scotland.

a2

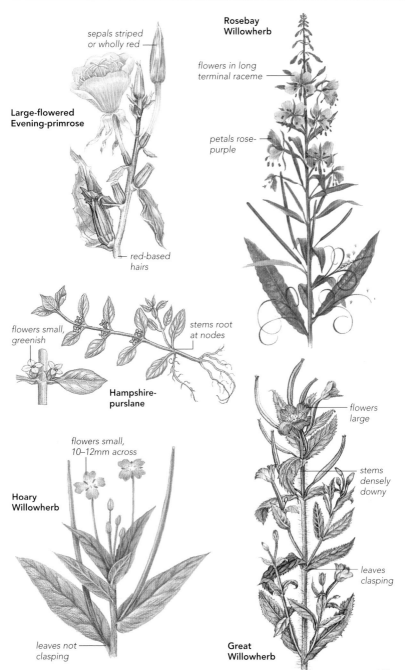

Large-flowered Evening-primrose

sepals striped or wholly red

red-based hairs

Rosebay Willowherb

flowers in long terminal raceme

petals rose-purple

flowers small, greenish

stems root at nodes

Hampshire-purslane

Hoary Willowherb

flowers small, 10–12mm across

leaves not clasping

flowers large

stems densely downy

leaves clasping

Great Willowherb

Alpine Willowherb

a

b

c

d

Broad-leaved Willowherb *Epilobium montanum* Similar in form to Hoary Willowherb (*see* p. 162), to 80cm tall, but *almost hairless*; leaves short-stalked with rounded bases, oval-lanceolate, up to 80mm long by 40mm wide (**a**); flowers 6–10mm in diameter, with pale pink petals; buds pointed. In woods, hedgerows, waste ground and rocky places, almost throughout. **Fl:** Jun–Aug. **Br Is dist:** Common and widespread.

Marsh Willowherb *Epilobium palustre* Erect slender plant to 60cm, with cylindrical, unridged stems. Leaves opposite, strap-shaped, less than 10mm wide and narrowed at each end, unstalked and untoothed (**b**). Flowers pale pink or white, only 4–7mm in diameter, held horizontally; stigma club-shaped. In bogs and other wet acid places, throughout. **Fl:** Jul–Aug. **Br Is dist:** Locally common throughout.

Alpine Willowherb *Epilobium anagallidifolium* Low, creeping, hairless perennial, with leafy stolons, stems up to 10cm, very slender (1–2mm in diameter). Leaves opposite, ovate to elliptical, to 25mm long, short-stalked and faintly toothed (**c**). Flowers small, 4–5mm in diameter, pale purplish, with the top of the inflorescence drooping in flower and young fruit; stigma club-shaped. In wet areas, especially flushes, in mountains, and more widespread in N Scandinavia. **Fl:** Jul–Aug. **Br Is dist:** Very local in mountain areas from N England northwards.

American Willowherb *Epilobium ciliatum* Perennial, with erect stems to 1m, with *4 raised lines*, and numerous *spreading glandular hairs*, especially above. Leaves opposite, oval-lanceolate, to 10cm, finely toothed, short-stalked and hairless (**d**). Flowers 8–10mm in diameter, purplish-pink or white, with deeply notched petals; stigma club-shaped; fruit glandular-hairy. Widespread almost throughout in waste ground, shady and rocky places; naturalised from N America. **Fl:** Jun–Aug. **Br Is dist:** Widespread in England and Wales, rarer in Scotland, but still spreading.

WATER-MILFOIL FAMILY Haloragaceae
Aquatic perennial hairless herbs, with finely divided leaves and spikes of flowers usually in 4 parts.

Whorled Water-milfoil *Myriophyllum verticillatum* Aquatic, with stems up to 3m long. Leaves in whorls of 5 (4 or 6 occasionally) finely pinnate with narrow bristle-like segments, up to 45mm long. Flowers in emergent spikes, with long *pinnately divided bracts* below each whorl of tiny red-dish flowers in 4 parts. Fruit is rounded and smooth. Widespread and locally common almost throughout, in still or slow-flowing base-rich waters. **Fl:** Jul–Aug. **Br Is dist:** Local in lowland areas, absent from the north and west; declining.

Spiked Water-milfoil *Myriophyllum spicatum* Similar to Whorled Water-milfoil, but leaves usually 4 in a whorl, rather shorter (to 30mm); tiny reddish flowers in whorls of 4 with *undivided bracts*, much shorter than the flowers. Fruit rounded, finely warty. In still and slow-flowing waters; common throughout. **Fl:** Jun–Aug. **Br Is dist:** Locally common throughout.

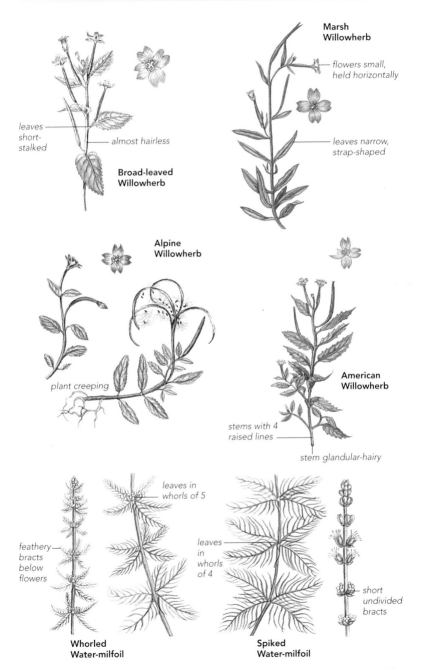

Marsh Willowherb

flowers small, held horizontally

leaves narrow, strap-shaped

leaves short-stalked

almost hairless

Broad-leaved Willowherb

Alpine Willowherb

plant creeping

American Willowherb

stems with 4 raised lines

stem glandular-hairy

feathery bracts below flowers

leaves in whorls of 5

leaves in whorls of 4

short undivided bracts

Whorled Water-milfoil

Spiked Water-milfoil

165

Dwarf Cornel

Ivy

Alternate Water-milfoil *Myriophyllum alterniflorum* More slender and smaller than Spiked Water-milfoil (*see* p. 164), with 3–4 leaves per whorl, less than 25mm long. Flowers whorled below, alternate above, *with tiny bracts*; petals are yellow with red streaks. Fruit warty and elongated. Throughout the area, most commonly in acid waters. **Fl:** May–Aug. **Br Is dist:** Widespread, though rather rare and declining, in lowland areas.

MARE'S-TAIL FAMILY Hippuridaceae
Aquatic herbs, with whorled linear leaves, and solitary flowers in the axils; single stamens.

Mare's-tail *Hippuris vulgaris* Aquatic perennial, with creeping rhizomes producing stout erect cylindrical spongy emergent stems. Leaves narrow strap-shaped, to 70mm long, in regular whorls of 6–12. Male and female flowers held separately, produced at base of leaves on emergent stems; both sexes greenish, tiny and without petals; male has one reddish anther. Widespread and common throughout; in neutral to base-rich still and flowing waters. **Fl:** Jun–Jul. **Br Is dist:** Locally common throughout.

DOGWOOD FAMILY Cornaceae
Shrubs with simple opposite leaves. Flowers, in 4 parts, in umbels.

Dwarf Cornel *Cornus suecica* Low creeping perennial herb, with flower stems to 25cm. Leaves broadly elliptical to ovate, rounded at unstalked base, untoothed with side veins curving round to tip of leaf. Flowers in a terminal umbel with 4 large conspicuous whitish bracts below it, resembling a single flower, 20mm across; individual flowers are tiny and blackish-purple, in a cluster of up to 25. Fruit is red, globular, to 5mm across. On moors, heaths and tundra, from the Netherlands and N England northwards, becoming locally abundant towards the Arctic. **Fl:** Jul–Sep. **Br Is dist:** From N England northwards, becoming locally common in C Scotland.

IVY FAMILY Araliaceae
Woody climbers (or trees or shrubs, outside Europe). Leaves alternate. Flowers small, often in umbel-like heads, usually in 5 parts. Fruit is a drupe or berry.

Ivy *Hedera helix* Familiar evergreen woody climber, reaching 30m, though also spreading widely at ground level in shade; stems covered with adhesive roots. Leaves glossy dark green above, paler below and hairless, 50–90mm long; palmately lobed on non-flowering stems, elliptical to ovate and unlobed on flowering stems. Flowers in dense spherical umbels at tops of stems in sunny conditions; flowers are in 4 parts and greenish-white; berry globular, black, 6–8mm in diameter. Widespread and generally common throughout, except in NE Europe, in woods, hedgerows and waste ground. **Fl:** Sep–Nov. **Br Is dist:** Common throughout.

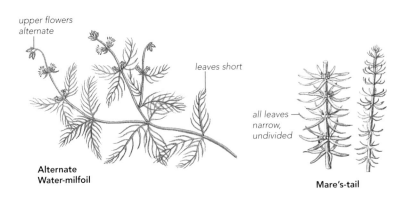

upper flowers alternate

leaves short

all leaves narrow, undivided

Alternate Water-milfoil

Mare's-tail

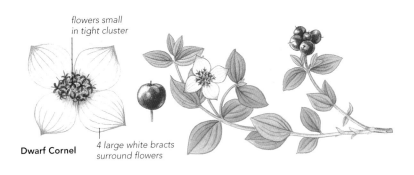

flowers small in tight cluster

Dwarf Cornel

4 large white bracts surround flowers

flowers in dense umbels

leathery evergreen leaves

Ivy

Marsh Pennywort

CARROT FAMILY Apiaceae (Umbelliferae)

A large family of annual to perennial herbs. Leaves alternate, without stipules, usually much-divided and often with sheathing bases. Flowers usually in compound umbels, i.e. the umbels themselves are in umbels; individual flowers have 5 free petals, 5 sepals (often absent), 5 stamens and 2 stigmas; ovary is inferior, enlarging to form a dry 2-part fruit of various shapes. A difficult family; key characters include: leaf shape, bracts to the main umbel and for the secondary umbels (called 'bracteoles'), as well as the shape of ripe fruit.

Sanicle

Marsh Pennywort *Hydrocotyle vulgaris* Low perennial plant with creeping stems rooting at the nodes. Leaves roughly circular, 20–50mm in diameter, with broad blunt teeth, often very long-stalked. Inflorescence small, 2–3mm across, consisting of whorls of tiny pinkish-green flowers, often partially hidden amongst the leaves; fruit rounded, 2mm wide and ridged. In damp or wet places, usually acidic, throughout except N Scandinavia. **Fl:** Jun–Aug. **Br Is dist:** Locally common throughout.

Sanicle *Sanicula europaea* Hairless erect perennial to 60cm. Basal leaves long-stalked and palmately lobed, with 3–7 toothed lobes; upper leaves smaller with shorter stalks. Umbels small with few rays; bracts 3–5mm long, simple or pinnately toothed; bracteoles undivided; flowers pink or white. Fruit oval, with hooked bristles. Throughout except the far north, in deciduous woodland, mainly on neutral to calcareous soils. **Fl:** May–Aug. **Br Is dist:** Locally common throughout in older woodland, though rarer in the north.

Astrantia, Great Masterwort

Astrantia, Great Masterwort *Astrantia major* Distinctive almost scabious-like umbellifer, with erect hairless stems to 1m. Basal leaves long-stalked and palmately lobed, to 15cm in diameter, strongly veined. Umbels simple, with *a conspicuous ruff of long narrow whitish bracts*, tinged with green and red, 20–30mm in diameter; flowers white or pink and very small. Fruit cylindrical, 6–8mm long. In woods and meadows; from France and Germany southwards, but naturalised farther north. **Fl:** May–Jul. **Br Is dist:** Introduced, very locally naturalised.

Sea-holly

Sea-holly *Eryngium maritimum* Branched hairless perennial to 60cm. Leaves waxy grey-green, 3- to 5-lobed, with thickened margins bearing long spines; basal leaves long-stalked, stem leaves unstalked. Umbels simple, oval, to 40mm long, with numerous densely packed small, blue flowers, surrounded by a ruff of spiny bracts. Fruit bristly, 5mm long. On coastal sand and shingle; from S Norway southwards. **Fl:** Jul–Sep. **Br Is dist:** Widespread around the coast.

Field Eryngo

Field Eryngo *Eryngium campestre* Similar in form to Sea-holly, but *greyish or yellowish-green*, with pinnate, lanceolate, spiny leaves, stalked at base, stalkless on stem. Flowers in numerous oval umbels, to 20mm long, with long narrow spiny bracts; *petals greenish-white*, with individual flower bracts longer than flowers. Fruit only 3mm long. In dry grasslands, from N Germany southwards, becoming common in the south. **Fl:** Jul–Aug. **Br Is dist:** Very rare in a few S England sites, and occasionally naturalised.

leaves circular

flowers tiny, often hidden

stems creeping and rooting

Marsh Pennywort

umbels small and rounded

plant hairless

Sanicle

conspicuous ruff of pinkish-white bracts

Astrantia, Great Masterwort

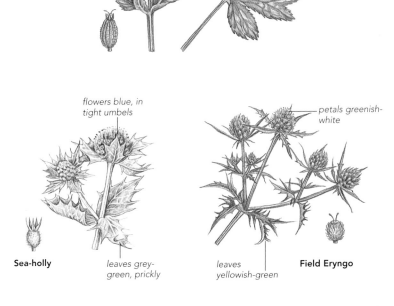

flowers blue, in tight umbels

Sea-holly

leaves grey-green, prickly

petals greenish-white

leaves yellowish-green

Field Eryngo

Chaerophyllum Biennials or perennials with twice to 3 times pinnate leaves, compound umbels with few or no bracts, but several bracteoles; sepals absent or insignificant; petals notched; fruit oblong-ovoid.

Rough Chervil

Rough Chervil *Chaerophyllum temulum* An erect biennial up to 1m, with ridged, *solid, purple-spotted* (or almost all purple), *bristly stems*. Leaves twice to 3 times pinnate, dull dark green and hairy, with rather blunt-pointed lobes. Flowers white, 2mm in diameter, in compound umbels up to 60mm in diameter, nodding in bud; bracts usually absent, bracteoles 5–8, hairy, reflexed in fruit. Fruit oblong-ovoid, narrowing upwards, 5–8mm. Rather similar to Cow Parsley, but flowering slightly later. Widespread and rather common on roadsides and hedge banks, through much of N Europe, but absent from N Scandinavia. **Fl:** Jun–Jul. **Br Is dist:** Widespread and common, except in N Scotland and W Ireland.

Anthriscus These are similar to *Chaerophyllum*, except that the stems are hollow.

Bur Chervil

Cow Parsley *Anthriscus sylvestris* Tall, downy, erect, perennial herb to 1.2m. Very similar to Rough Chervil, but *stems hollow and unspotted*; leaves fresher green, with more pointed segments (a). Flower and fruit very similar. Abundant throughout on roadsides, in meadows and woodland borders. **Fl:** Apr–Jun (earlier than Rough Chervil). **Br Is dist:** Common throughout, especially on roadsides.

Shepherd's-needle

Bur Chervil *Anthriscus caucalis* Wiry annual to 50cm (rarely more), with hairless stems, purplish towards the base. Leaflets very small and feathery. Umbels 20–40mm in diameter, with 2–6 hairless rays; bracts absent, bracteoles fringed and pointed; fruit distinctively bur-like, 3mm, ovoid, covered with thick spines (b). In sandy and waste ground, especially near the sea; from S Sweden southwards. **Fl:** May–Jun. **Br Is dist:** Widespread almost throughout, but local; most frequent in the south-east.

Sweet Cicely

Shepherd's-needle *Scandix pecten-veneris* Highly distinctive plant when in fruit. Annual, erect or spreading to 50cm. Leaves twice to 3 times pinnate, with segments widening towards tips. Umbels simple, or with 2–3 rays, and spiny-edged bracteoles; flowers small and white; *fruits elongating to 80mm long*, of which at least half is a distinctive slender flattened beak, the whole often forming a comb-like structure. In arable and disturbed land, northwards to S Sweden, but commoner in the south. **Fl:** May–Jul. **Br Is dist:** Widespread, mainly in S and E England, but increasingly local and declining.

Sweet Cicely *Myrrhis odorata* Bushy, downy, erect, strongly aromatic perennial to 2m, with hollow stems. Leaves twice to 3 times pinnate, fern-like, to 30cm long, with conspicuous basal sheaths. Umbels compound, with 4–20 rays; bracts usually absent, bracteoles narrow and pointed, usually 5; flowers white, heads up to 50mm in diameter; fruit linear to oblong, up to 25mm, beaked and strongly ridged, tasting of aniseed, becoming shiny dark brown when ripe. Native to mountains of C and S Europe, but widely naturalised northwards to S Sweden. **Fl:** May–Jun. **Br Is dist:** Common in N England and S Scotland; local or absent elsewhere.

b

a

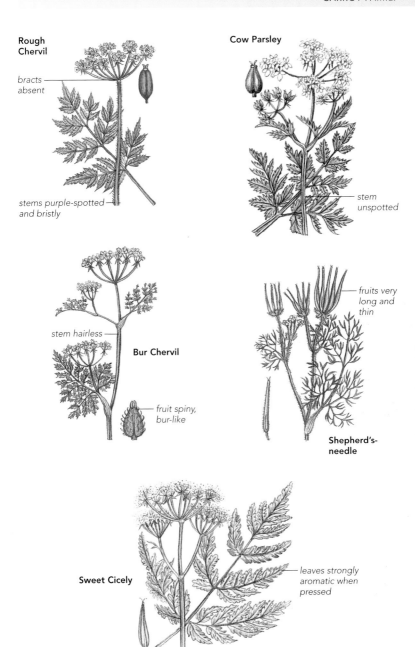

Rough Chervil

bracts absent

stems purple-spotted and bristly

Cow Parsley

stem unspotted

Bur Chervil

stem hairless

fruit spiny, bur-like

fruits very long and thin

Shepherd's-needle

Sweet Cicely

leaves strongly aromatic when pressed

Alexanders

Alexanders *Smyrnium olusatrum* Stout erect hairless biennial to 1.5m, with solid stems becoming hollow with age; whole plant rather celery-scented. Leaves shiny green, basal leaves 3-times trifoliate, triangular in outline, up to 30cm; upper leaves smaller, with short, inflated stalks, becoming yellower upwards. Umbels terminal and axillary, with 7–15 rays; bracts and bracteoles few or absent; flowers yellow, about 3mm in diameter, without sepals; fruit broadly ovoid, 7–8mm, black when ripe. In waste places, especially near the sea; native from NW France southwards, but widely naturalised in Britain and the Netherlands. **Fl:** Apr–Jun. **Br Is dist:** Common around the coasts of England, Wales and Ireland, rare in Scotland.

Pignut

Pignut *Conopodium majus* Slender erect perennial, with smooth stems (which become hollow after flowering), emerging from deeply buried brown globose tuber. Basal leaves twice to 3 times pinnate, to 15cm long, withering early; basal part of stem without leaves; upper leaves twice pinnate, with narrow segments. Flowers white in delicate umbels 30–70mm in diameter, with 6–12 rays; bracts usually absent, bracteoles 2 or more; fruit 3–4mm, oval, beaked, with short erect styles. In grassland and open woods, generally on dry, more acid soils; in British Isles, France and Norway. **Fl:** Apr–Jun. **Br Is dist:** Locally common throughout.

Great Pignut

Great Pignut *Bunium bulbocastanum* Similar to Pignut, but usually *larger*, to 1m; *stem remains solid after flowering*; umbels 30–80mm across, with 5–10 lanceolate bracts, and as many bracteoles; *styles bent* back on fruit, not straight. From S England and C Germany southwards, in rough calcareous grassland. **Fl:** Jun–Jul. **Br Is dist:** Rare and local, only in E-C England.

Greater Burnet-saxifrage

Burnet-saxifrage *Pimpinella saxifraga* Erect perennial to 60cm (occasionally 1m), with a round rough downy stem. Basal leaves usually once pinnate, with 3–7 pairs of ovate toothed leaflets, 10–15cm long; stem leaves are very different, twice pinnate, with very narrow segments. Umbels have 6–25 rays, usually without bracts, always without bracteoles; flowers 2mm in diameter, white or rarely pink, with short styles. Fruit oval, to 3mm, slightly ridged. Widespread and generally common, except in the far north, in dry, generally calcareous, grassy places. **Fl:** Jun–Sep. **Br Is dist:** Common , though rarer in the north, and absent in NW Scotland.

Ground-elder

Greater Burnet-saxifrage *Pimpinella major* Somewhat similar to Burnet-saxifrage, but generally larger, to 1.2m high. Stem hairless (very rarely downy), *deeply ridged* and hollow. Leaves usually once pinnate with deeply toothed, pointed lobes, but very variable, to 20cm long. Umbels 30–60mm in diameter, with 10–25 rays, lacking bracts, bracteoles normally absent; petals white or pink; styles long. Fruit ovoid, ridged, 4mm long. In grassy places and scrub, often on heavy soils; throughout except the far north. **Fl:** Jun–Sep. **Br Is dist:** Rather local, mainly in C England; rare or absent in most of the west and north.

Ground-elder *Aegopodium podagraria* Erect hairless perennial to 1m, with robust hollow stems arising from slender far-creeping rhizomes. Basal leaves triangular in outline, 10–20cm long, twice trifoliate, fresh green, with toothed, roughly oval leaflets. Umbels terminal, 20–60mm in diameter, with 10–20 rays; bracts and bracteoles usually absent; flowers white, 1mm in diameter. Fruit ovoid, 4mm long, with slender bent-back styles. In cultivated ground (often as a persistent weed), riversides and shady places; throughout except the far north, though natural limits uncertain. **Fl:** May–Jul. **Br Is dist:** Throughout in lowland areas.

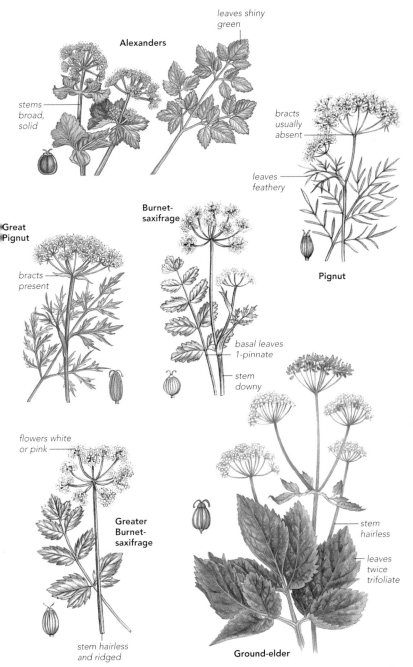

Alexanders

leaves shiny green

stems broad, solid

bracts usually absent

leaves feathery

Pignut

Great Pignut

bracts present

Burnet-saxifrage

basal leaves 1-pinnate

stem downy

flowers white or pink

Greater Burnet-saxifrage

stem hairless and ridged

stem hairless

leaves twice trifoliate

Ground-elder

173

Greater Water-parsnip

Greater Water-parsnip *Sium latifolium* Robust, erect, hairless perennial to 2m, with hollow, strongly ridged stems. Stem leaves once pinnate, to 30cm long, long-stalked, with 4–9 pairs of toothed pointed leaflets. Umbels terminal, flat-topped, 6–10cm in diameter, with 20–30 rays; bracts 2–6, often large and leafy, bracteoles lanceolate, variable; flowers white, about 4mm in diameter, with calyx teeth present; fruit oval and ridged. Throughout, except the far north and west, in shallow water and fens. **Fl:** Jul–Aug. **Br Is dist:** Scattered throughout to S Scotland, rare except in E Anglia.

Lesser Water-parsnip

Lesser Water-parsnip *Berula erecta* Rather similar to Greater Water-parsnip, but smaller in all respects, and more spreading. Leaves once pinnate, to 25cm long, with 7–14 pairs of unstalked, deeply toothed, roughly oval and bluish-green leaflets. Umbels 30–60mm in diameter, short-stalked, with 10–20 rays; bracts and bracteoles numerous, often leaf-like, sometimes pinnately divided. Fruit 2mm, broader than long. In fens and shallow water; throughout except the north. **Fl:** Jul–Sep. **Br Is dist:** Common through much of the lowlands, but rare in the north and in Ireland.

Rock Samphire

Rock Samphire *Crithmum maritimum* Bushy spreading perennial, branched from the base, with hairless, solid, ridged stems. Leaves fleshy, triangular in outline, but divided once or twice trifoliately into narrow pointed segments. Umbels 30–60mm in diameter, with 8–30 rays; bracts and bracteoles numerous, narrowly triangular, turning back as flowers mature; petals yellowish-green, sepals absent. Fruit to 6mm, oval and corky, becoming purple. Coastal habitats, usually on rock; from Scotland and the Netherlands southwards. **Fl:** Jun–Aug. **Br Is dist:** Frequent around most of the coast except NE England and E Scotland.

Moon Carrot

Moon Carrot *Seseli libanotis* Erect, stout, downy or almost hairless perennial to 1m, with solid ridged stems, and remains of old leaf bases persisting at base of stem as fibrous tuft. Lower leaves once to 3 times pinnate (usually twice pinnate), to 20cm long, with oblong pointed hairy lobes, spreading in different planes; some leaves opposite. Umbels terminal, 30–60mm in diameter, with 20–60 downy rays; bracts 8 or more, up to 15mm long, bracteoles 10–15, narrow; flowers white, or pink, 1–2mm in diameter, with long sepal lobes. Fruit oval, downy and ridged, with deflexed styles (**a**). Widespread, except in the north, on calcareous grassland, scrub and rocky areas. **Fl:** Jun–Aug. **Br Is dist:** Very rare; in a few SE England localities.

WATER-DROPWORTS *Oenanthe* Perennial hairless herbs of wet places. Leaves twice to 4 times pinnate, usually with sharply pointed lobes; stalk often tubular, sheathing the stem at its base. Bracts and bracteoles are both numerous; petals white, notched and unequal.

Tubular Water-dropwort

Tubular Water-dropwort *Oenanthe fistulosa* Erect perennial to 80cm (usually less), with slender hollow stems, inflated between leaf nodes. Leaves once pinnate (occasionally twice pinnate), with leaflets of lower leaves oval and stalked, and those of upper leaves narrowly linear and distant (**b1**); *leaf stalk inflated*, cylindrical and *longer* than blade. Umbels terminal, 20–40mm across, with 2–4 rays, bracts usually absent but bracteoles numerous; flowers white; secondary umbels form dense balls as the fruit ripens. Fruit 3mm, cylindrical, with styles as long as fruit (**b2**). In wet places and shallow water, from S Sweden southwards. **Fl:** Jul–Sep. **Br Is dist:** Local in England, but rare elsewhere, absent from N Scotland.

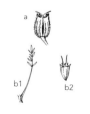

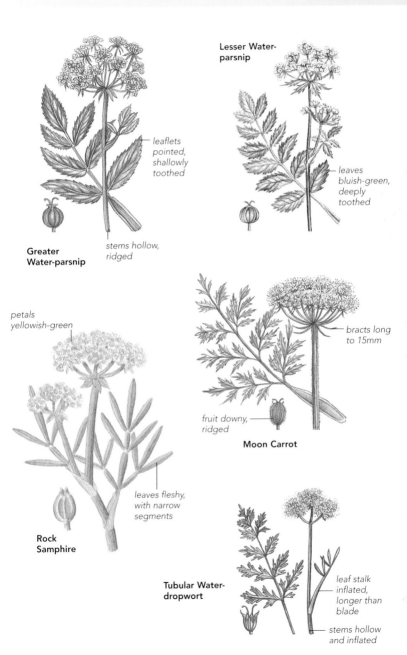

Greater Water-parsnip

leaflets pointed, shallowly toothed

stems hollow, ridged

Lesser Water-parsnip

leaves bluish-green, deeply toothed

petals yellowish-green

Rock Samphire

leaves fleshy, with narrow segments

bracts long to 15mm

fruit downy, ridged

Moon Carrot

Tubular Water-dropwort

leaf stalk inflated, longer than blade

stems hollow and inflated

175

Parsley Water-dropwort

Parsley Water-dropwort *Oenanthe lachenalii* Erect perennial to 1m. Stem solid. Basal leaves twice pinnate, with elliptical to spoon-shaped, blunt, toothless leaflets – *stalk shorter than blade*. Bracts present; rays not thickened in fruit; fruit oval, without corky base. In wet meadows and marshes, often coastal; from Denmark and S Sweden southwards. **Fl:** Jun–Sep. **Br Is dist:** Scattered throughout, mainly near the coast; absent from N Scotland.

Hemlock Water-dropwort

Hemlock Water-dropwort *Oenanthe crocata* The most distinctive water-dropwort. A robust, branched plant to 1.5m, with hollow, grooved stems; all parts highly poisonous. Basal leaves triangular in outline, 3 to 4 times pinnate, with oval to rounded leaflets, toothed above, tapering to base; stem leaves twice to 3 times pinnate, with narrower lobes. Umbels terminal and stalked, 5–10cm in diameter, with 10–40 rays, not thickening in fruit; bracts and bracteoles numerous, linear-lanceolate, soon falling. Flowers white, with unequal petals; fruit cylindrical, with erect styles. In shady or sunny wet places; from Belgium and Britain southwards. **Fl:** Jun–Jul. **Br Is dist:** Scattered throughout, but common only in the south and west.

Fine-leaved Water-dropwort

Fine-leaved Water-dropwort *Oenanthe aquatica* Erect bushy plant to 1.5m, from runners; stems hollow and grooved, with transverse joints, swollen near base. Submerged leaves are 3 to 4 times pinnate with very fine segments; aerial leaves 3 times pinnate with ovate, lobed, pointed segments. Umbels terminal and axillary, 20–50mm diameter, bracts absent, bracteoles bristle-like. Flowers white, with equal petals; fruit oval, 3–4mm long, with styles as long. Throughout, except the far north, in still or slow-flowing water. **Br Is dist:** Scattered as far north as SE Scotland, but very local.

Fennel

Fool's Parsley *Aethusa cynapium* Annual hairless herb to 1.2m, usually much less. Leaves twice pinnate. Bracts absent (occasionally 1); bracteoles are distinctive, long and narrow, hanging downwards conspicuously on outer side of secondary umbels; fruit oval and ridged, 3–4mm long. Widespread throughout as a weed of cultivated land; common. Ssp *cynapioides* is taller, with less-ridged stems and long bracteoles, occurring in woods in S Sweden, Germany and France. **Fl:** Jun–Aug. **Br Is dist:** Widespread and common in disturbed ground, except for N Scotland.

Pepper-saxifrage

Fennel *Foeniculum vulgare* Tall, stout, erect, hairless, grey-green perennial to 2.5m, with a faintly ridged solid stem, developing a small hollow when old. Leaves very finely divided into waxy, grey-green, thread-like, spreading leaflets, with toughened points, 4–6mm long. Umbels terminal and axillary, 40–80mm in diameter, with numerous rays; bracts and bracteoles usually absent; flowers yellow; fruit ovoid and ridged. In coastal habitats; from the Netherlands southwards, but probably native only in southern part of range. **Fl:** Jul–Oct. **Br Is dist:** Coastal, in England, Wales and Ireland.

Pepper-saxifrage *Silaum silaus* Hairless perennial to 1m, with solid ridged stems. Basal leaves triangular in outline, twice to 4 times pinnate, with linear, pointed leaflets, very finely toothed; stem leaves few and small. Umbels long-stalked, terminal and axillary, 20–60mm in diameter with 5–15 rays; bracts usually absent, or up to 3, bracteoles narrow; flowers bright yellow. Fruit ovoid to oblong, 5mm long. In grasslands, often on heavy soils; from S Sweden southwards, local. **Fl:** Jun–Aug. **Br Is dist:** Locally common in England, rare elsewhere, absent from Ireland.

Parsley Water-dropwort

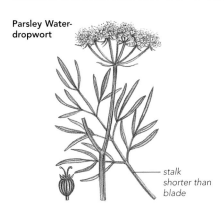

stalk shorter than blade

Hemlock Water-dropwort

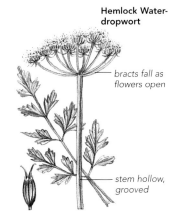

bracts fall as flowers open

stem hollow, grooved

Fine-leaved Water-dropwort

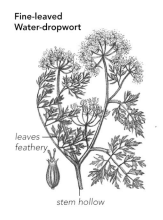

leaves feathery

stem hollow

bracteoles distinctive, long and pendulous

bracts absent

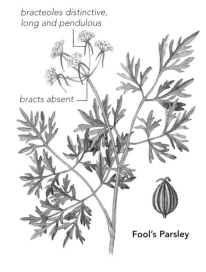

Fool's Parsley

Pepper-saxifrage

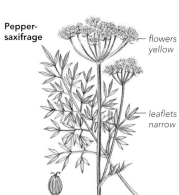

flowers yellow

leaflets narrow

flowers yellow

plant fragrant

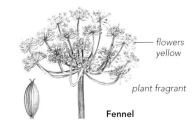

Fennel

Spignel

Spignel, Baldmoney *Meum athamanticum* Hairless, strongly aromatic perennial to 60cm, with rootstock crowned by fibrous remains of previous year's leaf stalks; stem hollow and striped. Leaves mainly basal, 3 to 4 times pinnate, with very fine bristle-like lobes, sometimes appearing to be in whorls. Umbels terminal or axillary, 30–60mm in diameter; bracts 0–2, bracteoles few, all bristle-like and small; fruit 6–10mm long, elliptical. In mountain areas in Belgium, France, Germany and Britain. **Fl:** Jun–Jul. **Br Is dist:** From N Wales and N England northwards.

Bladderseed

Bladderseed *Physospermum cornubiense* Almost hairless perennial, with erect, solid, striped stems to 1m. Basal leaves long-stalked, twice trifoliate, with long-stalked pinnately lobed segments, wedge-shaped at bases. Umbels 20–50mm in diameter, with narrow, pointed bracts and bracteoles; fruits smooth and rounded, 3–4mm long, like little bladders. In shaded places; S Britain and France southwards. **Fl:** Jul–Aug. **Br Is dist:** Rare, in Cornwall and Buckinghamshire.

Hemlock

Hemlock *Conium maculatum* Erect branched biennial or winter annual, almost hairless, with purple-spotted stems to 2.5m; strong-smelling and poisonous. Lower leaves large, up to 40cm, triangular in outline, but twice to 4 times pinnate with fine leaflets, soft but hairless. Umbels terminal and axillary, 20–50mm in diameter, with a few small turned-back bracts, and similar but smaller bracteoles; flowers white. Fruit almost spherical, with wavy ridges. Throughout, except the far north, in a wide variety of habitats, especially riversides, scrub and waste ground. **Fl:** Jun–Jul. **Br Is dist:** Throughout except the far north.

THOROW-WAX and HARE'S-EARS *Bupleurum* Hairless annual or perennial plants with distinctive simple undivided leaves. Flowers yellow, not notched; sepals usually missing.

Slender Hare's-ear

Slender Hare's-ear *Bupleurum tenuissimum* Slender spreading or erect annual, to 50cm, with wiry stems. Leaves linear-lanceolate to spoon-shaped, narrow, to 50mm long, pointed. *Inflore small, less than 5mm in diameter*, in leaf axils, very short-stalked. In grassy coastal habitats, upper salt-marshes; from Gotland (SE Sweden) southwards. **Fl:** Jul–Sep. **Br Is dist:** Coasts of S and E England only.

Honewort

Sickle-leaved Hare's-ear *Bupleurum falcatum* Erect hairless perennial, with hollow stems to 1.3m. *Leaves narrowly spoon-shaped*, 30–80mm long, *curved*, lower ones stalked, upper ones clasping the stem. Umbels stalked, to 40mm in diameter, with 3–15 rays; bracts 2–5, narrow and unequal; bracteoles 5, linear-lanceolate. Flowers are yellow, fruit is oblong and red-tipped. From Belgium and S England southwards, in grassy and waste places, often calcareous. **Fl:** Jul–Sep. **Br Is dist:** Very rare, in Essex only.

Honewort *Trinia glauca* Hairless, erect, waxy, grey-green perennial up to 50cm, though usually less and frequently branched from the base. Lower leaves twice to 3 times pinnate, with lobes to 30mm. Separate male and female plants; male plant umbels flat-topped, 10mm wide, with 4–7 equal rays; female plant umbels 30mm in diameter, with irregular rays; bracts absent or 1, 3-lobed; bracteoles 2–3, simple; fruit ovoid, ridged, about 2mm long. From S England and S Germany southwards, rare, in sunny limestone grassy and rocky areas. **Fl:** May–Jun. **Br Is dist:** Very rare, S Devon and N Somerset.

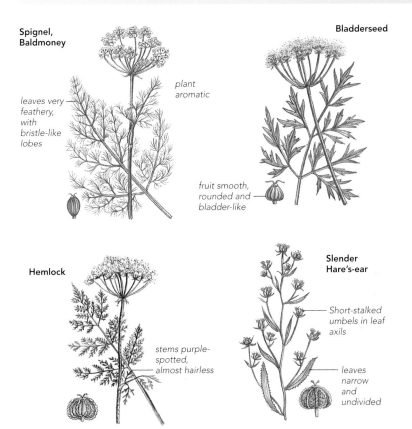

Spignel, Baldmoney

leaves very feathery, with bristle-like lobes

plant aromatic

Bladderseed

fruit smooth, rounded and bladder-like

Hemlock

stems purple-spotted, almost hairless

Slender Hare's-ear

Short-stalked umbels in leaf axils

leaves narrow and undivided

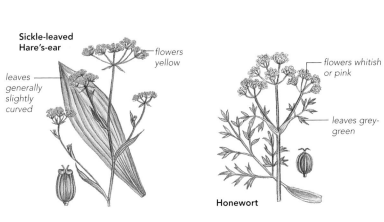

Sickle-leaved Hare's-ear

leaves generally slightly curved

flowers yellow

flowers whitish or pink

leaves grey-green

Honewort

Wild Celery

Fool's Water-cress

Corn Parsley

Stone Parsley

a

Apium Hairless perennial herbs, with once pinnate or ternate leaves; bracts and bracteoles few or absent; sepals minute or absent; flowers more or less white.

Wild Celery *Apium graveolens* Stout biennial up to 1m, with a strong characteristic celery smell; stems solid and grooved. Basal leaves once pinnate, with lobed and toothed diamond-shaped segments, occasionally almost twice pinnate; upper stem leaves ternate, stalked. Umbels terminal and axillary, 40–60mm across, short-stalked or unstalked; bracts and bracteoles absent; flowers greenish-white. Fruit broadly ovoid, to 2mm. From Denmark southwards; in damp, usually saline, habitats, mainly coastal. **Fl**: Jun–Aug. **Br Is dist**: Local around the coasts, occasionally inland, absent from N Scotland.

Fool's Water-cress *Apium nodiflorum* Creeping perennial, with ascending hollow stems, rooting at lower nodes. Leaves once pinnate, with 4–6 pairs of bright green leaflets (compare with Lesser Water-parsnip, *see* p. 174, which has more pairs of bluish leaflets). Umbels in leaf axils, with short stalks, 3–12 rays; bracts usually absent, 5 bracteoles, narrowly lanceolate; flowers white; fruit broadly oval. (Compare with Water-cress (*see* p. 78), which grows in similar places, but has very different flowers and rather different leaves). In wet places, from the Netherlands southwards, predominantly western. **Fl**: Jul–Aug. **Br Is dist**: Generally common, rarer in Scotland, absent from the far north.

Corn Parsley *Petroselinum segetum* Slender, hairless, rather *dark grey-green* parsley-scented annual or biennial, with round, solid stems up to 1m. Leaves once pinnate, with numerous ovate toothed or lobed segments, with hard forward-curving points. Umbels very irregular, up to 50mm in diameter, with only 2–5 rays of varying length; both bracts and bracteoles present and bristle-like; flowers white, few per umbel; fruit is ovoid, 2–4mm long (**a**). In hedgerows, fields and waste places, often near the coast, from the Netherlands southwards. **Fl**: Aug–Oct. **Br Is dist**: Local and decreasing in S and E England, rare in Wales, mainly coastal; absent elsewhere.

Stone Parsley *Sison amomum* Erect, much-branched slender biennial, with solid stems to 1m, with an unpleasant smell when crushed (described as a mixture of nutmeg and petrol!). Lower leaves simply pinnate, long-stalked, with 7–9 pairs of ovate, toothed lobes; upper leaves trifoliate, with narrower leaflets; all *leaves are bright green* (compare with Corn Parsley). Umbels terminal and axillary, 10–40mm across, with only 3–6 slender unequal rays; bracts and bracteoles present and bristle-like; flowers white; fruit almost spherical, 3mm long. From England and N France southwards, in hedgerows and grasslands, usually on heavy soil. **Fl**: Jul–Sep. **Br Is dist**: In England and Wales only, mainly in the south and east, local.

Cowbane *Cicuta virosa* Stout, erect perennial to 1.2m, with ridged, hollow stems. Highly poisonous. Leaves triangular in outline, up to 30cm long, twice to 3 times pinnate, with narrow, sharply toothed, pointed leaflets; stalks long and hollow. Umbels terminal, long-stalked, large, to 13cm across, rounded on top; bracts absent, bracteoles numerous and strap-shaped, long; flowers numerous, white; fruit globular, 2mm long. In fens, water-sides and shallow water, throughout. **Fl**: Jul–Aug. **Br Is dist**: Scattered almost throughout, but very local.

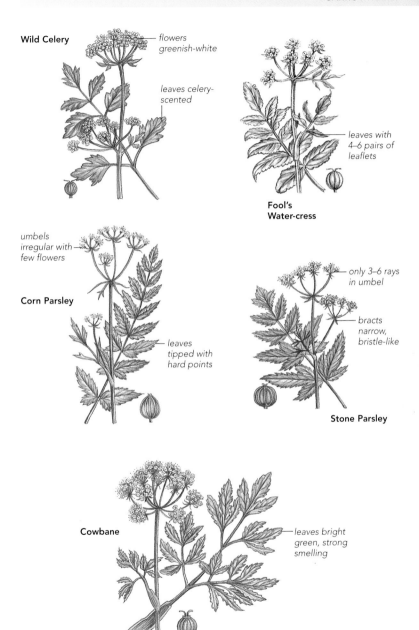

Wild Celery

flowers greenish-white

leaves celery-scented

Fool's Water-cress

leaves with 4–6 pairs of leaflets

umbels irregular with few flowers

Corn Parsley

leaves tipped with hard points

only 3–6 rays in umbel

bracts narrow, bristle-like

Stone Parsley

Cowbane

leaves bright green, strong smelling

Coriander *Coriandrum sativum* An erect perennial to about 50cm, with smooth or slightly ridged stems. Lower leaves pinnately lobed, upper leaves more divided, feathery and aromatic. Flowers white in small umbels with 3–5 rays; fruits spherical, 2–6mm diameter, aromatic when crushed. Widely naturalised in waste places in France and Germany. **Fl:** Jun–Aug. **Br Is Dist:** Uncommon, casual or occasionally naturalised in waste places.

Whorled Caraway

Caraway *Carum carvi* Erect, branched, hairless perennial, with a striped, hollow stem to 1.5m, usually less. Leaves twice to 3 times-pinnate, with linear lobes. Umbels long-stalked, 20–40mm in diameter and irregular; bracts and bracteoles usually absent, not bent back if present; flowers white or pink; fruit ovoid to 6mm long and aromatic if crushed – the caraway used in cooking. Native or naturalised in grassy areas and waste ground, throughout except the far north. **Fl:** Jun–Jul. **Br Is dist:** Possibly native in the south-east, rare, locally naturalised elsewhere.

Cambridge Milk-parsley

Whorled Caraway *Carum verticillatum* Erect hairless perennial to 1m, usually less, with solid, little-branched stem with few leaves. Basal leaves up to 25cm, narrowly oblong in outline, with at least 20 pairs of deeply divided segments, appearing as if in a whorl. Umbels 20–50mm in diameter, flat-topped, with numerous narrow, reflexed bracts and bracteoles; flowers white; fruit elliptical, about 2mm, with strong ridges. In damp acidic grasslands and marshy areas, from Scotland and the Netherlands southwards, predominantly western. **Fl:** Jun–Aug. **Br Is dist:** Local in SW England, Wales, Ireland and W Scotland.

Scots Lovage

Cambridge Milk-parsley *Selinum carvifolia* Tall, almost hairless perennial to 1m, with solid branched stems with winged angles. Leaves twice to 4 times-pinnate, with linear-lanceolate minutely toothed lobes with short spine-tips. Umbels terminal, long-stalked, 30–70mm in diameter, without bracts but with several linear bracteoles; flowers white; fruit oval, 3–4mm, flattened, with winged ridges. Throughout, in fens and damp meadows. **Fl:** Jul–Oct. **Br Is dist:** Rare, in E England only.

Scots Lovage *Ligusticum scoticum* Hairless, shiny, bright green perennial to 90cm, often purplish at base. Leaves twice-trifoliate, bright green, with oval leaflets, toothed towards tips; leaf stalks inflated, sheathing stem. Umbels terminal, dense and long-stalked, 40–60mm in diameter, with narrow linear bracts and bracteoles; flowers greenish-white; fruit oblong-ovoid, 5–8mm long, with persistent calyx teeth. On rocky or shingle coasts, from Britain to Norway, and isolated localities on the Baltic in Sweden. **Fl:** Jun–Aug. **Br Is dist:** Coasts of Scotland and N Ireland only, locally common.

Wild Angelica *Angelica sylvestris* Stout, almost hairless perennial with broad and hollow, purplish stems to 2m or more. Leaves large, to 60cm, triangular in outline, twice to 3 times-pinnate, with oblong-oval, unequal-based, toothed leaflets; stalk is very conspicuously broad, inflated, hollow and sheathing; uppermost leaves little more than sheaths. Umbels terminal and lateral, to 15cm in diameter, with numerous rays; bracts absent or very few, bracteoles few and very narrow; calyx teeth minute, petals white to pinkish; fruit oval, 5mm long, very flattened and winged. Damp or shaded places, throughout, common. **Fl:** Jun–Sep. **Br Is dist:** Widespread and generally common throughout.

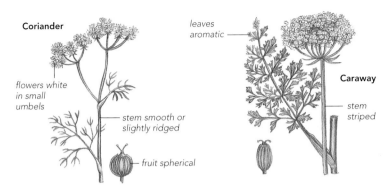

Coriander

flowers white in small umbels

stem smooth or slightly ridged

fruit spherical

leaves aromatic

Caraway

stem striped

Cambridge Milk-parsley

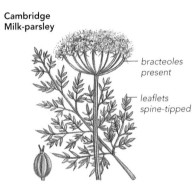

bracteoles present

leaflets spine-tipped

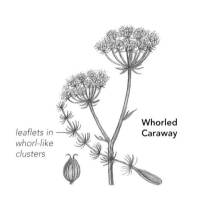

Whorled Caraway

leaflets in whorl-like clusters

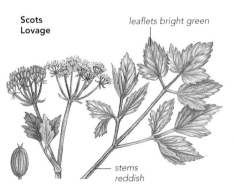

Scots Lovage

leaflets bright green

stems reddish

Wild Angelica

stems broad, hollow

conspicuously inflated leaf stalks

Garden Angelica *Angelica archangelica* Rather similar to Wild Angelica (*see* p. 182), but stems are usually green; leaf lobes more jaggedly cut and irregular, with terminal lobe deeply 3-lobed (**a1**); flowers are greenish-white to yellow; *fruit with thick corky* (not membranous) *wings* (**a2**). In pastures, riversides and damp places, northwards from the Netherlands and Denmark. Used in the making of confectionery, and a liqueur. **Fl:** Jun–Sep. **Br Is dist:** Locally naturalised.

Garden Angelica

Peucedanum Perennials or biennials Leaves pinnate or ternate. Flowers white, yellow or pinkish, with broadly ovate petals; calyx teeth small or absent; fruit compressed, ridged and winged.

Hog's Fennel *Peucedanum officinale* Robust, hairless perennial to 2m tall, with base of stem often very broad with abundant fibres; stem unridged or faintly ridged, solid. Leaves 4 to 6 times-trifoliate, with flat, linear, untoothed leaflets, 4–10cm long and narrowed at both ends. Umbels terminal and axillary, up to 20cm in diameter, with numerous rays, nodding in bud but erect later; bracts absent or up to 3, bracteoles several, all very narrow; flowers sulphur-yellow; fruit oblong-ovate, to 10mm long, ridged. Rough grassland on clay, usually near the sea, from N France and S Germany southwards. **Fl:** Jul–Sep. **Br Is dist:** Rare, though locally common, in SE England only, coastal.

Hog's Fennel

Milk-parsley *Peucedanum palustre* Virtually hairless biennial up to 1.6m, with ridged, hollow, often purplish stems. Leaves triangular in outline, twice to 4 times-pinnate (**b1**), with ultimate lobes linear-oblong and blunt; leaf stalks channelled and sometimes inflated. Umbels 30–80mm in diameter, with 20–40 rays; bracts and bracteoles 4 or more each, long and narrow, sometimes forked, bent back; petals white, sepals ovate; fruit oval, flattened and winged especially on edges (**b2**). In wet places, usually calcareous; throughout though local. **Fl:** Jul–Sep. **Br Is dist:** Very local, mainly in E Anglia, with scattered sites in England only.

Wild Parsnip

a1

a2

Wild Parsnip *Pastinaca sativa* Erect, downy, branched biennial, with hollow, ridged and angled (occasionally solid and unridged) stems to 1m. Basal leaves once pinnate, with ovate, lobed and toothed segments. Umbels 3–10cm in diameter, with 5–20 rays; bracts and bracteoles absent or very few, falling early; flowers yellow; fruit oval and flattened, with narrowly winged edges. In grassland, scrub and waste ground, especially on dry or calcareous soils; widespread except in parts of the north. **Fl:** Jun–Aug. **Br Is dist:** Widespread in S Britain, rare or absent from the north; not native in Ireland.

b1

b2

Hogweed *Heracleum sphondylium* Robust, erect, roughly hairy perennial to 2.5m, with hollow, ridged stems. Leaves large, to 60cm, usually once pinnate, but variable, with toothed or lobed ovate leaflets, hairy on both surfaces. Umbels large, up to 20cm in diameter, with up to 45 rays; bracts usually absent, bracteoles bristle-like and turned back; flowers white, up to 10mm in diameter, with notched petals, very uneven in size on outer flowers; fruit elliptical, flattened and hairless. Widespread and common, except in the extreme north, in grassland, roadsides, waste places and open woods. **Fl:** May–Aug. **Br Is dist:** Common throughout.

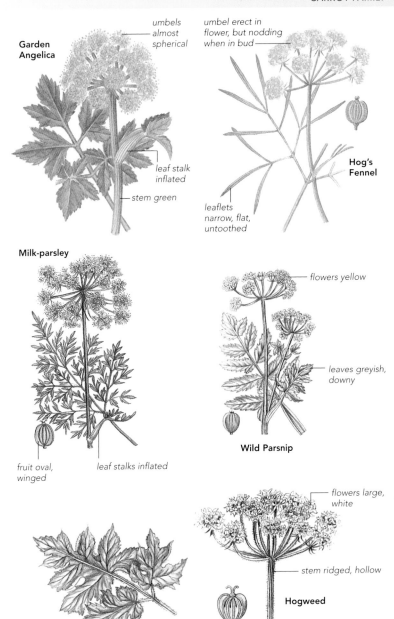

Garden Angelica

umbels almost spherical

leaf stalk inflated

stem green

umbel erect in flower, but nodding when in bud

Hog's Fennel

leaflets narrow, flat, untoothed

Milk-parsley

fruit oval, winged

leaf stalks inflated

flowers yellow

leaves greyish, downy

Wild Parsnip

flowers large, white

stem ridged, hollow

Hogweed

Giant Hogweed *Heracleum mantegazzianum* Huge herbaceous biennial or perennial up *to 5m tall*, with stems hollow, ridged and purple-spotted, up to 10cm in diameter. Leaves similar to Hogweed, but larger, to 1m, with more sharply pointed leaflets. Umbels up to 50cm in diameter, with larger flowers. Can cause blistering of skin if touched in sunlight. Introduced from Caucasus, now naturalised almost throughout, especially along riversides. **Fl:** Jun–Jul. **Br Is dist:** Widespread, though local.

Broad-leaved Sermountain

Broad-leaved Sermountain *Laserpitium latifolium* Robust, almost hairless, grey-green perennial, with rounded, striped, solid stems to 2m. Leaves triangular in outline, twice pinnate, with ovate, toothed leaflets, unequally heart-shaped at bases; stalks of upper leaves strongly inflated. Umbels large, with 25–40 rays; bracts numerous, narrow and drooping, bracteoles few, very narrow; flowers white; fruit oval, 5–10mm long, winged but not flattened. From C Sweden southwards, widespread though local, in scrub, open woodland and rocky places, usually on limestone, and mainly in the mountains. **Fl:** Jun–Aug. **Br Is dist:** Absent.

Knotted Hedge-parsley

Knotted Hedge-parsley *Torilis nodosa* Prostrate or ascending slender annual to 50cm, with solid ridged stems with few deflexed hairs. Leaves less than 10cm, once to twice pinnate, with deeply cut lobes. Umbels in leaf axils, small (less than 10mm in diameter) and virtually unstalked, with very short rays; bracts absent, bracteoles longer than flowers; petals pinkish-white, sepals very small; fruit 2–3mm long, covered with *warts and straight spines* (a). From the Netherlands southwards, on dry banks and in arable fields, local, probably not native in the north of range. **Fl:** May–Jul. **Br Is dist:** Scattered throughout, but mainly southern and eastern.

Upright Hedge-parsley *Torilis japonica* Erect, slender annual, with solid, unspotted rough stems to 1.25m, with straight appressed hairs. Leaves once to 3 times pinnate, dull green and hairy. Umbels terminal and axillary, stalked, to 40mm in diameter, with 5–12 rays; bracts and bracteoles present; flowers pinkish or purplish-white; fruit oval, to 4mm, with *hooked bristles* (b). Roadsides, hedgerows, wood margins and waste ground common throughout region except the far north. **Fl:** Jul–Aug (later than Cow Parsley, *see* p. 170). **Br Is dist:** Common throughout, except upland areas and N Scotland.

Spreading Hedge-parsley *Torilis arvensis* Rather similar to Upright Hedge-parsley but smaller, to 50cm, usually spreading, branched or unbranched. Umbels long-stalked, with 3–5 rays, bracts absent, bracteoles rough hairy; fruit with spines *curved, but not hooked*, thickened at tip; styles spreading in fruit (c). In arable fields and disturbed ground, from the Netherlands and S England southwards, local and declining. **Fl:** Jul–Sep. **Br Is dist:** Now SE England only, declining.

Small Bur-parsley *Caucalis platycarpos* Erect, slightly downy annual, with solid and somewhat angled stems to 40cm. Leaves twice to 3 times pinnate. Inflorescence similar to that of *Torilis* species, but has conspicuous green sepals, and fruit to 10mm, with single rows of spines on ridges (d). In arable fields and waste places, especially on calcareous soils, from the Netherlands and Germany southwards. **Fl:** Jun–Jul. **Br Is dist:** A casual introduction only, not persisting.

Giant Hogweed

leaves very large

stems very large, hollow

Broad-leaved Sermountain

leaflets ovate, toothed

stalks of upper leaves inflated

umbels in leaf axils

fruit warty and spiny

Knotted Hedge-parsley

stems rough with appressed hairs

fruit with hooked bristles

Upright Hedge-parsley

bracteoles rough hairy

spines curved, not hooked

Spreading Hedge-parsley

Small Bur-parsley

fruit with rows of spines

Diapensia

Common Wintergreen

a2

a1

b2

b1

Wild Carrot *Daucus carota* Variable erect or spreading annual or biennial to 1m, usually rough hairy; stems solid and ridged. Leaves twice to 3 times pinnate, with narrow linear segments. Umbels long-stalked, to 70mm in diameter, with numerous large pinnately divided leafy bracts forming a conspicuous ruff below each; flowers white and dense, with central flower often reddish; fruit oval, 2–4mm long, with 4 spiny ridges; umbel rays become stiffly erect after flowering, producing a concave fruit ball. Rough grassland, especially near the coast, throughout. **Fl:** Jun–Aug. **Br Is dist:** Throughout, except parts of the far north, and higher mountain areas. Ssp *gummifer* has more fleshy, blunter leaves, umbels flat or convex in fruit, and fruit spines pointing upwards, more webbed together. Confined to coasts of S Britain and France.

Diapensiaceae
Perennial herbs or low shrubs. Flowers regular, in 5 parts, with superior ovary and 3-lobed stigma.

Diapensia *Diapensia lapponica* Low-growing, dense, evergreen herb or subshrub, forming small cushions. Leaves small, to 10mm, leathery, deep green and shiny, roughly ovate and rounded at tip. Flowers with 5 parts, solitary but often numerous; petals creamy white, to 10mm long, rounded; stamens 5 alternating with petals, with wide filaments. Style single but 3-lobed; (compare with Saxifrage species, *see* pp. 96–8, which have 2 styles). Mountain habitats and tundra, especially exposed gravelly places, where it may be abundant. N Europe only. **Fl:** May–Jul. **Br Is dist:** Very rare, in 2 W Scotland sites, discovered in 1951.

WINTERGREEN FAMILY Pyrolaceae
Small perennial herbs with hermaphrodite flowes in 5 (occasionally 4) parts, petals separate, stamens usually 10.

Common Wintergreen *Pyrola minor* Low evergreen herb, with erect flowering stems to 25cm. Leaves roughly elliptical, to 40mm wide, with rounded teeth, stalk shorter than leaf blade (**a1**). Inflorescence terminal, with individual flowers bell-shaped, 5–7mm in diameter; petals white to pale pink; style straight, 1–2mm long and *not protruding beyond petals* (**a2**). Widespread throughout in open woods, moorland and mountain habitats, rarely on dunes but frequently on calcareous soils. **Fl:** Jun–Aug. **Br Is dist:** Uncommon and declining, and absent from many areas.

Yellow Wintergreen *Pyrola chlorantha* Low perennial, with yellowish-green oblong to rounded leaves, darker below, stalk longer than blade. Flowers 8–12mm in diameter, bell-shaped and *yellowish-green*; style about 7mm long, curved, protruding, with expanded disc below stigma. Widespread in continental Europe, mostly in coniferous woods, less often in open grassland. **Fl:** Jun–Jul. **Br Is dist:** Absent.

Round-leaved Wintergreen *Pyrola rotundifolia* Low perennial, with ovate to rounded leaves, with round teeth; stalk distinctly longer than blade (**b1**). Flowers 8–12mm in diameter, bell-shaped but *opening widely*; petals clear white, *style S-shaped*, up to 10mm long, (though 4–6mm long in ssp *maritima*), *distinctly protruding* (**b2**). Widespread throughout in fens, woodland and mountain pastures, often on base-rich soils. The commonest subspecies is ssp *rotundifolia*, but ssp *maritima*, which occurs in sand-dune slacks, is distinguished by shorter style, shorter flower stalks (less than 5mm), and 2–5 scales on the flowering stem, rather than 1–2. **Fl:** May–Aug. **Br Is dist:** Rare and local, scattered throughout; ssp *maritima* is confined to N Wales and NW England.

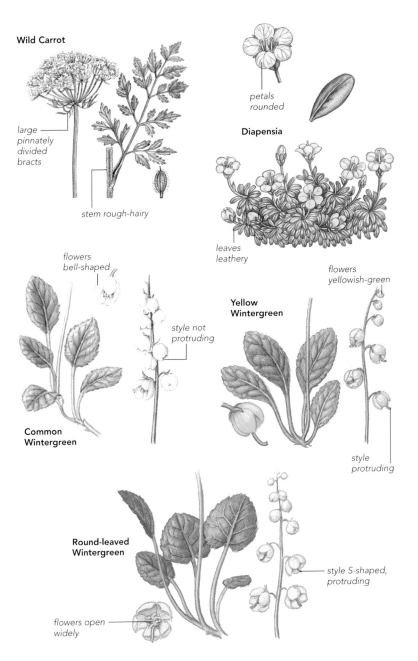

Wild Carrot

large pinnately divided bracts

stem rough-hairy

petals rounded

Diapensia

leaves leathery

flowers bell-shaped

Common Wintergreen

style not protruding

Yellow Wintergreen

flowers yellowish-green

style protruding

Round-leaved Wintergreen

flowers open widely

style S-shaped, protruding

Umbellate Wintergreen

Serrated, or Nodding, Wintergreen *Orthilia secunda* Generally similar in form to the *Pyrola* wintergreens (*see* p. 188). Leaves ovate to elliptical, 20–40mm long, distinctly toothed, light green, with stalk shorter than blade. Flower spikes differ in being strongly 1-sided, with individual flowers small, 5–6mm in diameter, greenish-white, with straight protruding style. Throughout as far as N Sweden; in coniferous and deciduous woodland, or open mountain habitats. **Fl:** Jun–Aug. **Br Is dist:** Local from Wales and N England northwards, mainly in mountainous areas.

One-flowered Wintergreen *Moneses uniflora* Similar in general appearance to *Pyrola* species (*see* p. 188), but leaves are opposite (not alternate) and *flowers are solitary*. Leaves ovate to almost circular, toothed, stalk shorter than blade. Flowers large, 15–20mm in diameter, opening widely, nodding, solitary and white; style 5–7mm, straight. Widespread throughout, but very local; in old woods, usually coniferous, on acid soils. **Fl:** Jun–Aug. **Br Is dist:** Rare, local and declining, confined to a few Scottish pinewoods, mainly eastern.

Umbellate Wintergreen *Chimaphila umbellata* Low subshrub, with opposite or almost whorled leaves, which are ovate, dark green and leathery. Flowers distinctive, in *umbel-like clusters* on short stem; individual flowers pink, globose, 8–12mm in diameter; style short, not protruding. Local in coniferous woods and damp rocky places in N and E Europe only. Absent from much of W Europe. **Fl:** Jun–Jul. **Br Is dist:** Absent.

Yellow Bird's-nest, Dutchman's Pipe *Monotropa hypopitys* Short herb, totally lacking chlorophyll, living saprophytically on leaf mould. Leaves all scale-like and alternate; whole plant yellow to creamy white, becoming browner with age. Stems erect. Flowers in terminal drooping spike, individually narrowly bell-shaped, 9–14mm long, partially obscured by bracts. Unlikely to be mistaken for anything else, except possibly young Bird's-nest Orchid. Widespread throughout except the far north, though local; in damp coniferous and beechwoods. **Fl:** Jun–Sep. **Br Is dist:** Scattered widely, but very local; usual habitat in beechwoods on chalk in S England, occasionally found in dune slacks.

HEATHER FAMILY Ericaceae

Shrubby plants, usually low-growing, but including a few trees. Leaves simple, without stipules. Flower parts usually in 4s or 5s, with petals normally joined together, at least partially, and often into a tube. Stamens usually twice as many as petals; ovary superior except in *Vaccinium*. Style simple, with an expanded head. A distinctive family, most often to be found in acid and frequently damp environments.

Heather, Ling *Calluna vulgaris* Spreading evergreen undershrub up to 50–60cm. Downy or hairless, but distinctive for its very small (1–2mm) unstalked leaves in 4 tight rows, and its small, pale pink-purple flowers (about 4mm long). Widespread throughout, often dominant, on heaths, moors, dunes, bogs and open woodland, wet or dry but usually acid. **Fl:** Jul–Sep. **Br Is dist:** Widespread and often abundant, especially in the north and west.

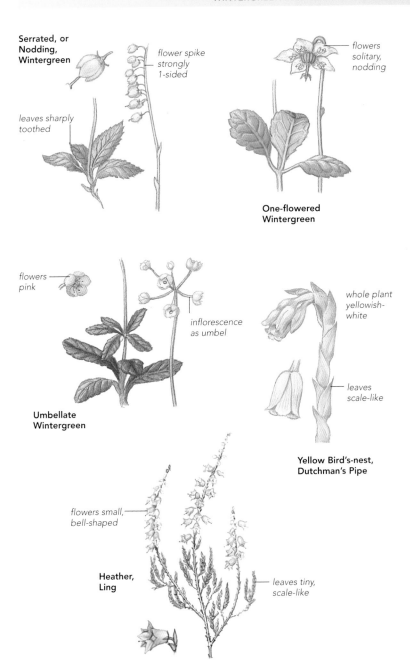

Serrated, or Nodding, Wintergreen

flower spike strongly 1-sided

leaves sharply toothed

flowers solitary, nodding

One-flowered Wintergreen

flowers pink

inflorescence as umbel

Umbellate Wintergreen

whole plant yellowish-white

leaves scale-like

Yellow Bird's-nest, Dutchman's Pipe

flowers small, bell-shaped

Heather, Ling

leaves tiny, scale-like

Dorset Heath

Cornish Heath

Irish Heath

Spring Heath

Cross-leaved Heath *Erica tetralix* Low, greyish, downy undershrub, shorter (to 30cm), and more erect, than most heathers. Little-branched, and distinctive for its large, (about 7mm long), pale pink bell-shaped flowers in tight 1-sided cluster, and its grey leaves in distinctive separate 4s (occasionally 5s) up the stem. Stamens hidden in corolla. *Fruits downy.* Widespread and locally frequent, always in wet or damp acid areas e.g. wet heaths, bogs. Fl: Jun–Sep. Br Is dist: Almost throughout, though rare in C and E England.

Bell Heather *Erica cinerea* Low hairless undershrub to 50cm, similar in habit to Cross-leaved Heath, but more spreading and with more flower spikes. Leaves in 3s, in less distinct whorls, dark green and hairless. Reddish-purple flowers, 5–6mm long, in scattered groups, not clustered at the top as in Cross-leaved Heath. Stamens hidden in corolla. Locally common on *drier* acid sites, often dominant. Widespread, but absent from the far north. Fl: Jun–Sep. Br Is dist: Locally abundant or dominant, commoner in the west.

Dorset Heath *Erica ciliaris* Usually taller than Cross-leaved Heath and Bell Heather, to 70cm, often in distinct clumps. Leaves in 3s, 2–3mm long, not downy but with glandular bristles on edges. Flowers large, 8–10mm long, in long, deep pink racemes, tapering towards top. *Fruit hairless.* Damp acidic areas, very local only in SW England, Ireland and W France. Fl: Jun–Sep. Br Is dist: Rare and local in England from Dorset westwards, and in W Ireland. Hybridises with Cross-leaved Heath.

Cornish Heath *Erica vagans* Bushy, medium-height shrub to 80–90cm. Leaves long, 8–10cm, linear, in 4s or 5s, edges recurved, whole plant hairless. Flowers small, 3–4mm long, on long stalks, pink, lilac or white, with brown anthers protruding, in long leafy racemes, usually with leafy tip. On drier heaths, rare but locally abundant only in SW England, NW Ireland and W France. Fl: Jul–Sep. Br Is dist: Only in Cornwall and Fermanagh, though very locally abundant.

Irish Heath *Erica erigena* Relatively tall hairless shrub to 2m high. Leaves in 4s, linear, 6–8mm long. Flowers 5–7mm, pale pink-purple, in long, leafy racemes, like Cornish Heath in form. Reddish anthers protruding half-way. Drier parts of bogs, very locally frequent in W Ireland and W France only Fl: Early (Feb) Mar–May. Br Is dist: W Ireland only, very local.

Spring Heath *Erica herbacea* Dwarf spreading shrub to 30cm only. Leaves densely set in whorls of 4. Flowers red or pink, in 1-sided racemes, with protruding purple anthers. Stony places and open woods; Germany only. Fl: Mar–Jun. Br Is dist: Absent.

Rhododendron *Rhododendron ponticum* Erect, strong-growing, evergreen shrub, with spreading branches. Leaves elliptical, untoothed, leathery, dark shiny green above and paler below, 10–25cm long. Flowers in clusters, bell-shaped, 40–60mm long, violet-purple, pinkish or mauve. Introduced from E Europe/W Asia, but now widely naturalised on acid and damp soil, through much of W Europe. Fl: May–Jul. Br Is dist: Widely naturalised, locally abundant, often becoming a problem through its invasive nature.

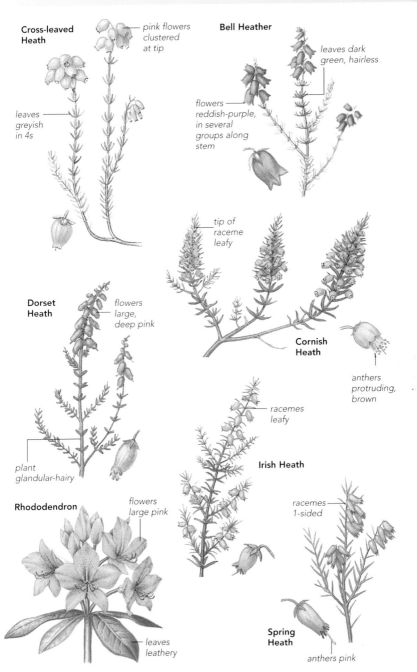

Cross-leaved Heath

pink flowers clustered at tip

leaves greyish in 4s

Bell Heather

leaves dark green, hairless

flowers reddish-purple, in several groups along stem

tip of raceme leafy

Dorset Heath

flowers large, deep pink

Cornish Heath

anthers protruding, brown

plant glandular-hairy

racemes leafy

Irish Heath

Rhododendron

flowers large pink

racemes 1-sided

leaves leathery

Spring Heath

anthers pink

193

Labrador-tea

Labrador-tea *Ledum palustre* Evergreen, spreading or erect, small shrub, commonly to 1m, occasionally taller. Young twigs covered with rusty down. Leaves linear to oblong, 20–50mm long, rusty below with margins in-rolled. Flowers in umbels, creamy white, 10–15mm long, numerous, upright in flower, then reflexed in fruit. Widespread through N Europe from Germany northwards in bogs, damp woodland and heaths. **Fl:** May–Jul. **Br Is dist:** Absent.

Trailing Azalea

Trailing Azalea *Loiseleuria procumbens* Very small, prostrate, mat-forming, evergreen dwarf shrub. Leaves opposite, oblong, only 5–6mm long, not adpressed to stem, with margins rolled under. Flowers very small, about 5mm in diameter, pale to dark pink, bell-shaped, but deeply lobed – like a miniature rhododendron; petals soon falling, solitary or in small terminal clusters. Widespread and often common in mountain regions, on dry, stony or peaty acid situations. **Fl:** May–Jul. **Br Is dist:** Local in the Scottish Highlands and northwards; most frequent in the Cairngorms.

Blue, or Mountain, Heath

Blue, or Mountain, Heath *Phyllodoce caerulea* Dwarf, evergreen heather-like shrub, spreading, but producing erect flowering shoots. Leaves small, to 12mm long, linear, rolled, alternate and leathery dark green. Flowers terminal on long reddish sticky stems, in clusters of most commonly 2; bell-shaped, 7–12mm long, pendulous and pink to purple. Stamens and style not protruding. Locally frequent on dry, usually acidic mountains and moorlands, in Iceland and Scandinavia north of S Norway, and in Scotland. **Fl:** Jun–Aug. **Br Is dist:** Very rare, in a few Scottish Highland localities.

St Dabeoc's Heath

St Dabeoc's Heath *Daboecia cantabrica* Dwarf evergreen, heath-like straggling shrub, reaching 70cm if supported. Leaves variable in size, to 14mm, ovate to lanceolate, dark green and hairy above, white below, with rolled-under margins. Flowers in loose terminal spikes, urn-shaped, 10–14mm long, with 4 petal lobes, reddish-purple and hairy. Differs from *Erica* species (see pp. 190–92 and above) in the broader leaves, and the corolla that falls before the fruit ripens. Local on dry heaths and in open woods on acid soil, in W France and Ireland only. **Fl:** Jun–Oct. **Br Is dist:** Locally common in CW Ireland.

Bearberry

Bearberry *Arctostaphylos uva-ursi* Prostrate mat-forming evergreen shrub producing long creeping shoots. Leaves oval, broadest towards tip, untoothed, leathery, dark shiny green above, paler below, with conspicuous net-veining and flat margins. Flowers in dense terminal clusters, individually urn-shaped, with 5 short spreading lobes, white to pink, 5–6mm long. Berry shiny red, 7–9mm in diameter. (Cowberry, see p. 196, is similar, but distinguishable by less creeping habit, leaves not so net-veined, with in-rolled margins and more open flowers). Widespread and frequent in much of N Europe, especially in N and mountain areas; on heaths, moors and open woods. **Fl:** May–Aug. **Br Is dist:** Rare in N England, commoner in Scotland.

Alpine Bearberry

Alpine Bearberry *Arctostaphylos alpinus* Similar to Bearberry, but less far-creeping, *leaves toothed*, not leathery, withering by autumn (though persisting); berry often larger, to 10mm in diameter, *black* when ripe. Widespread in Scandinavia and mountains farther south, on acid moors and tundra. **Fl:** May–Jul. **Br Is dist:** Very local in N Scotland.

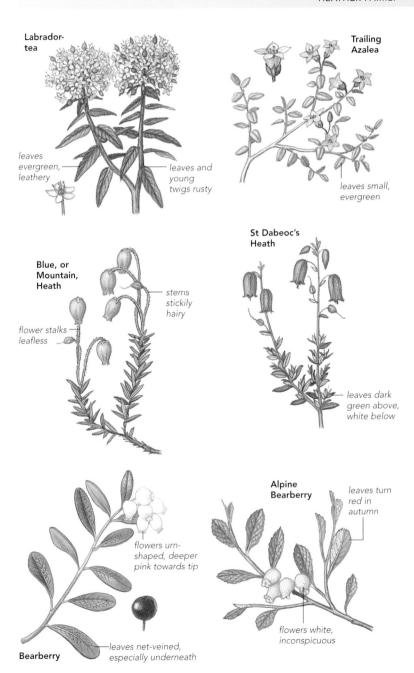

Labrador-tea

leaves evergreen, leathery

leaves and young twigs rusty

Trailing Azalea

leaves small, evergreen

Blue, or Mountain, Heath

flower stalks leafless

stems stickily hairy

St Dabeoc's Heath

leaves dark green above, white below

Bearberry

flowers urn-shaped, deeper pink towards tip

leaves net-veined, especially underneath

Alpine Bearberry

leaves turn red in autumn

flowers white, inconspicuous

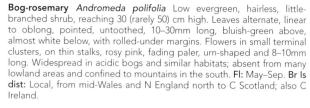

Bog-rosemary *Andromeda polifolia* Low evergreen, hairless, little-branched shrub, reaching 30 (rarely 50) cm high. Leaves alternate, linear to oblong, pointed, untoothed, 10–30mm long, bluish-green above, almost white below, with rolled-under margins. Flowers in small terminal clusters, on thin stalks, rosy pink, fading paler, urn-shaped and 8–10mm long. Widespread in acidic bogs and similar habitats; absent from many lowland areas and confined to mountains in the south. **Fl:** May–Sep. **Br Is dist:** Local, from mid-Wales and N England north to C Scotland; also C Ireland.

Bog-rosemary

Leatherleaf *Chamaedaphne calyculata* Evergreen shrub, with alternate elliptical leaves which are scaly brown below. Flowers white, pendulous, in leafy racemes. In marshes and wet woods in NE Europe, south to Poland. **Fl:** Jun–Jul. **Br Is dist:** Absent.

Cranberry *Vaccinium oxycoccos* Distinctive, tiny, creeping evergreen shrub, with alternate widely spaced oblong leaves on long thread-like stems. Leaves dark green above, waxy-greyish below, with in-rolled margins. Flowers (1–2) on long downy stalks; petals rosy pink, with 4 strongly reflexed lobes, exposing central cluster of stamens. Nothing else resembles it except Small Cranberry (not shown). Fruit globose, red or brownish. Throughout, except the extreme north, in wet peatbogs. **Fl:** May–Jul. **Br Is dist:** Widespread but local, and absent from many lowland areas.

Cranberry

Cowberry *Vaccinium vitis-idaea* Prostrate or scrambling evergreen dwarf shrub, with some erect stems. Leaves elliptical-oblong, leathery, untoothed, dark green above, paler dotted with glands below, with margins down-turned (a). Flowers in short dense clusters, bell-shaped, 5–8mm long, white or pink, with 4 or 5 lobes and with a protruding style. Berry globose, shiny red, to 10mm in diameter. Most easily confused with Bearberry (see p. 194). Widespread on moors, heaths, montane pastures and in coniferous woods, on acid soils. **Fl:** Jun–Aug. **Br Is dist:** In hilly or mountain areas, from N England northwards.

Cowberry

Bog, or Northern, Bilberry *Vaccinium uliginosum* Small, deciduous shrub, with erect stems from a creeping rhizome; twigs round and brown. Leaves ovate, bluish-green, hairless and untoothed. Flowers white or pinkish, urn-shaped, to 6mm long, in small clusters of 1–3; style does not protrude. Fruit a globose blue-black berry, 7–10mm in diameter, edible. Widespread and locally frequent in boggy areas, damp moors, heaths and open woods. **Fl:** May–Jun. **Br Is dist:** Local from N England northwards, commonest in N Scotland.

Bog, or Northern, Bilberry

Bilberry, Whortleberry *Vaccinium myrtillus* Closely related to Bog Bilberry, though more familiar and easily distinguished. Differs in the 3-angled green stems, the small bright green, finely toothed, deciduous leaves, and the lantern-shaped green to reddish flowers which are solitary or in 2s; berries similar to those of Bog Bilberry, though bilberries are often smaller and more ovoid. Throughout the area in woods, on heaths and moors, on acid soils. Well known for its edible fruit. **Fl:** Apr–Jun. **Br Is dist:** Widespread and common, except in drier, more cultivated lowland areas.

flowers urn-shaped

leaves bluish-green above, almost white below

Bog-rosemary

Leatherleaf

flowers in leafy racemes

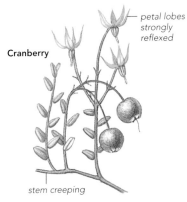

Cranberry

petal lobes strongly reflexed

stem creeping

flowers bell-shaped

Cowberry

leathery leaves, gland-dotted underneath

Bog, or Northern, Bilberry

flowers white or pinkish

twigs brown, round

Bilberry, Whortleberry

leaves bright green, deciduous

twigs green, 3-angled

Crowberry

Primrose

Oxlip

CROWBERRY FAMILY Empetraceae

A small family of evergreen heath-like shrubs. Leaves alternate, with flowers in leaf axils. 4–6 perianth segments in 2 similar whorls; 3 stamens.

Crowberry *Empetrum nigrum* ssp *nigrum* Prostrate heather-like, mat-forming shrub. Stems reddish when young. Leaves linear, crowded, to 7mm long, shiny green, with rolled margins. Flowers tiny at base of leaves, with 6 separate pinkish petals; male and female flowers separate. Fruit a black globose berry, 5–7mm in diameter, and much more visible than flowers. In acid, often damp, habitats including heaths, moors, tundra, and open woods. **Fl:** May–Jun. **Br Is dist:** Frequent in N Britain, with outposts on southern uplands. Ssp *hermaphroditum* (sometimes treated as a separate species) has hermaphrodite flowers with stamens persisting on the fruit, and greenish stems, not rooting; slightly broader leaves, grooved beneath. Generally more northern, and the commonest subspecies in the Arctic. Very local in Scottish mountains.

PRIMROSE FAMILY Primulaceae

Herbs with leaves without stipules, often in a basal rosette, usually simple. Flowers regular, usually with 5 parts, with the petals often joined at the base to form a tube.

Primrose *Primula vulgaris* Familiar low, herbaceous perennial, with a rosette of wrinkled, hairy, spoon-shaped leaves, to 15cm long, unstalked but tapering gradually to the base (a). *Flowers solitary* on long hairy stalks from rosette centre, often numerous; pale yellow, often with orange markings in centre, to 40mm in diameter, 5-lobed. Widespread, often abundant in damp shady places, or in pastures; absent over much of Scandinavia. **Fl:** Feb–May, normally. **Br Is dist:** Widespread and common in many areas, least frequent in the south-east.

Oxlip *Primula elatior* Similar plant to Primrose. *Leaves abruptly contracted* into long winged stalk, about as long as blade (b), less wrinkled than Primrose or Cowslip. Flowers in a 1-sided drooping umbel, with 10–20 pale yellow flowers, 15–25mm in diameter, very like smaller primroses; throat of corolla tube open, without folds. Widespread but local as far north as S Scandinavia, in woods, meadows and streamsides, usually on heavy soil. In mountain pastures farther south. **Fl:** Mar–May. **Br Is dist:** Locally common in a small area of E Anglia and adjacent counties, mainly in coppiced woodland.

Cowslip *Primula veris* Rather similar to Oxlip, but leaves more wrinkled (c). Flowers 10–30 in an umbel, less strongly 1-sided than Oxlip; *flowers deeper yellow-orange*, with orange markings in centre, 8–15mm in diameter, with distinct folds at the mouth of the tube. Widespread and locally common throughout, except in the far north, in meadows, pastures and open woods, usually on drier sites than Primrose or Oxlip. **Fl:** Apr–May. **Br Is dist:** Widespread, sometimes frequent, as far north as C Scotland, usually on lime-rich soils. Decreasing through agricultural changes.

False Oxlip *Primula vulgaris x veris = P. x polyantha* Common, naturally occurring hybrid, superficially similar to Oxlip, but differing in the less 1-sided umbels, and the folds in the throat of the corolla, though it is variable. Occurs where both parents grow. **Fl:** Apr–May. **Br Is dist:** Widespread but local.

a

b

c

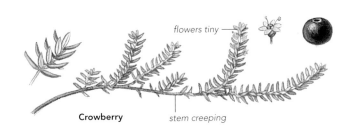

flowers tiny

Crowberry

stem creeping

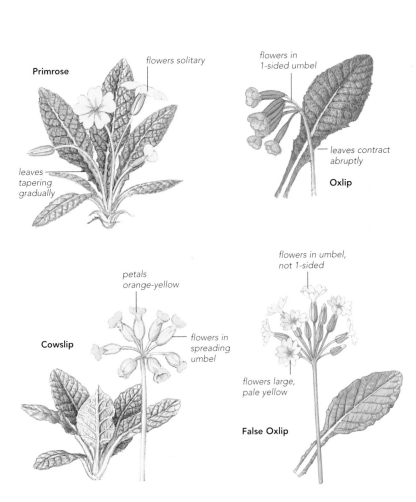

Primrose

flowers solitary

leaves tapering gradually

flowers in 1-sided umbel

leaves contract abruptly

Oxlip

petals orange-yellow

Cowslip

flowers in spreading umbel

flowers in umbel, not 1-sided

flowers large, pale yellow

False Oxlip

199

Bird's-eye Primrose

Annual Androsace

Water-violet

Yellow Pimpernel

Bear's-ear *Primula auricula* Small perennial, with a rosette of mealy leaves, and a leafless stem to 16cm. Leaves spoon-shaped, toothed. Flowers yellow, with a white centre, in terminal clusters of 2–20. In damp, rocky and grassy places, usually at high altitudes, from S Germany southwards. **Fl:** May–Jul. **Br Is dist:** Absent.

Bird's-eye Primrose *Primula farinosa* Small perennial herb, with rosette of spoon-shaped leaves, mealy white below and shallowly toothed. Flowers in umbels on long mealy stalks, pale pink to rosy violet, 10–16mm across, with yellow 'eye', and distinct gaps between petals. Calyx mealy, often tinged dark purple. In fens and damp meadows, usually in mountain areas, most often on base-rich soil, from S Sweden southwards. **Fl:** May–Jul. **Br Is dist:** Local on calcareous soils in N England only.

Scottish Primrose *Primula scotica* Similar to Bird's-eye Primrose, differing in untoothed leaves, widest at middle. Flowers smaller, 5–8mm across, purplish with large yellow eye, on shorter stalks, petals broader, without gaps, stigma 5-lobed. In damp pastures and dunes near the sea; N Scotland only. **Fl:** Mainly May–Jun, some Jul–Sep. **Br Is dist:** As above.

Scandinavian Primrose *Primula scandinavica* Very similar to Scottish Primrose, but taller, with more flowers, and stigma globose, not 5-lobed, as in Scottish Primrose. Calcareous mountain areas in N Scandinavia only. **Fl:** Jun–Aug. **Br Is dist:** Absent.

Annual Androsace *Androsace maxima* Has tiny pink or white flowers, dwarfed by much larger sepals. In dry, open, mainly calcareous sites, from C Germany and France southwards. **Fl:** Apr–Jun. **Br Is dist:** Absent.

Water-violet *Hottonia palustris* Aquatic perennial herb, with pale green, submerged and floating leaves. Leaves finely divided, once or twice pinnate, with narrow flattened leaflets. Flowers emergent on erect robust hairless stems, with several whorls of flowers, individually pale lilac with central yellow eye, and 5 petals, 20–25mm across. Widespread and not uncommon as far north as S Sweden in shallow, still or slow-flowing fresh water. **Fl:** May–Jul. **Br Is dist:** Local, mainly in S and E England; very rare in Wales; absent from Scotland.

Yellow Pimpernel *Lysimachia nemorum* Evergreen, prostrate, hairless perennial herb, reaching 45cm long. Leaves oval, 20–30mm long, *pointed*, short-stalked, and in opposite pairs. Flowers solitary from leaf axils on *slender stalks, longer than leaves*, bright yellow, star-like, 10–15mm in diameter, with 5 petals; calyx very narrow, bristle-like. Widespread as far north as S Sweden; in damp and shady places. **Fl:** May–Aug. **Br Is dist:** Widespread, often common almost throughout; rarest in dry and highly cultivated areas.

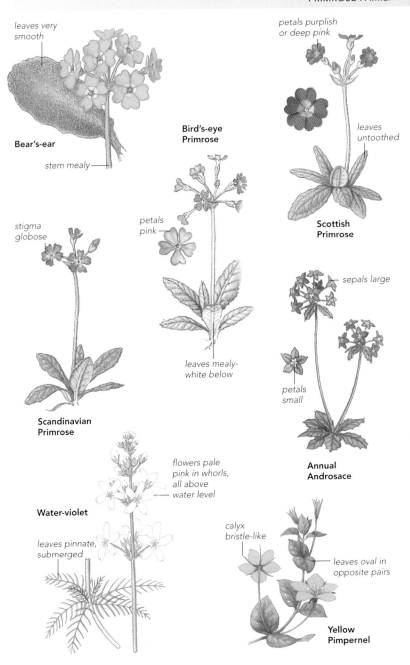

leaves very smooth

Bear's-ear

stem mealy

petals purplish or deep pink

leaves untoothed

Scottish Primrose

Bird's-eye Primrose

stigma globose

petals pink

Scandinavian Primrose

leaves mealy-white below

sepals large

petals small

Annual Androsace

flowers pale pink in whorls, all above water level

Water-violet

leaves pinnate, submerged

calyx bristle-like

leaves oval in opposite pairs

Yellow Pimpernel

Tufted-loosestrife

Creeping-jenny *Lysimachia nummularia* Creeping hairless perennial, rooting at the nodes. Similar to Yellow Pimpernel (*see* p. 200), but leaves 10–20mm long, wider to almost round, blunt at tip; flowers larger, 15–25mm in diameter, on *stout stalks, shorter than leaves*, solitary or in pairs; calyx teeth ovate not bristle-like. Widespread and locally common in damp grassy habitats, throughout except the extreme north. **Fl:** Jun–Aug. **Br Is dist:** Locally common through most of England, but rare to the north and south-west.

Chickweed-wintergreen

Yellow-loosestrife *Lysimachia vulgaris* Medium or tall, softly hairy perennial, erect from creeping stems and reaching 1m or more. Leaves ovate, in pairs or whorls of 3–4, up to 10cm long, dotted with glands. Inflorescence forms a terminal panicle, made up of clusters of flowers from the upper nodes; flowers bright yellow, star-like, 5-pointed, 15–20mm in diameter; sepals with red-orange margins. Widespread and frequent virtually throughout in wet habitats – fens, carr woodland, meadows and streamsides. **Fl:** Jun–Aug. **Br Is dist:** Locally common through most of Britain except the far north.

Bog Pimpernel

Tufted-loosestrife *Lysimachia thyrsiflora* Usually hairless perennial, with erect stems to 70cm from a creeping stem. Leaves in opposite pairs, unstalked, lanceolate, with numerous black glands. Flowers in dense, stalked clusters from nodes at centre of stem; individual flowers small, 5mm across, with 7 petals, dark yellow, stamens protruding. Wet habitats, often with standing water, from C France northwards, commonest in the north. **Fl:** Jun–Jul. **Br Is dist:** Rare and local only in N England and C Scotland.

Chickweed-wintergreen *Trientalis europaea* Low perennial, with slender stalks to 25cm arising from creeping rootstock. Leaves mostly in a whorl near top of stem, lanceolate to ovate, with a few small leaves below. Flowers arise from rosette, 1–2 together, on long stalks, starry, white, 12–18mm in diameter and with 5–9 (usually 7) petal lobes. A distinctive combination. Fruit a globular capsule. Widespread in N Europe in coniferous woods and mossy habitats; commoner in the north of range, confined to mountains in the south. **Fl:** Jun–Jul. **Br Is dist:** Mainly in Scotland, where it is locally common, but extending into N England; rare in E Anglia.

Sea-milkwort *Glaux maritima* Low, fleshy, partly procumbent herb, rooting at some nodes, with erect stems to 20cm. Leaves opposite below, alternate above, fleshy, elliptical, unstalked, up to 12mm long. Flowers on erect shoots, solitary at bases of leaves, pink or white, 5mm in diameter, without petals. Frequent in damp coastal habitats throughout N Europe and occasionally inland on saline soils. **Fl:** May–Aug. **Br Is dist:** Common all around the coast; also inland in W Midlands (rare).

Bog Pimpernel *Anagallis tenella* Low, hairless, creeping, rooting perennial, with slender stems up to 15cm long. Leaves in pairs, elliptical to almost round, short-stalked, to 9mm long. Flowers pink (white, finely veined red), funnel-shaped, 5-lobed, to 10mm long, on long slender stalks. Petals 2–3 times longer than calyx. Numerous overlapping stems can often produce a dense mass of flowers. On damp open ground, especially near the coast, usually on acid soil. Frequent in W Europe, not in the north, and becoming rarer eastwards. **Fl:** Jun–Aug. **Br Is dist:** Widespread, commonest in the west, rarest in the north and east; local or absent in many areas.

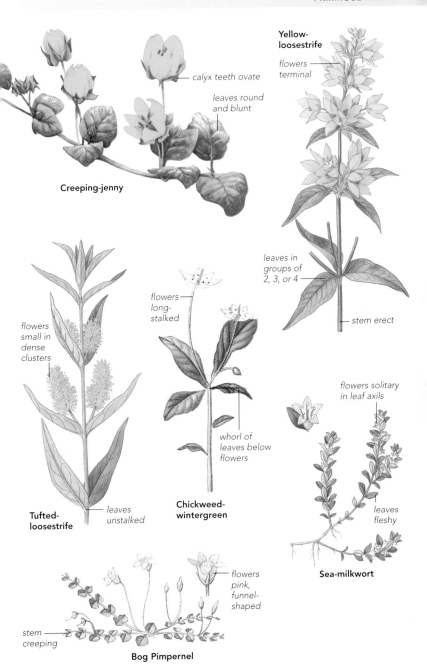

Creeping-jenny
— calyx teeth ovate
leaves round and blunt

Yellow-loosestrife
flowers terminal
leaves in groups of 2, 3, or 4
stem erect

Tufted-loosestrife
flowers small in dense clusters
leaves unstalked

Chickweed-wintergreen
flowers long-stalked
whorl of leaves below flowers

Sea-milkwort
flowers solitary in leaf axils
leaves fleshy

Bog Pimpernel
flowers pink, funnel-shaped
stem creeping

203

Brookweed

Thrift

a

Scarlet Pimpernel *Anagallis arvensis* ssp *arvensis* Prostrate to ascending, low, hairless annual (occasionally biennial or longer-lived), with squarish stems. Leaves opposite in pairs, occasionally whorls, ovate, pointed, unstalked, up to 20mm long, both surfaces covered with minute glands (a). Flowers scarlet or orange-pink, occasionally blue or pink, borne singly on long stalks from leaf axils; calyx teeth narrow, almost as long as petals; corolla flat (opening most widely in sunshine), 10–15mm, petals fringed with hairs. Throughout, except Iceland, in bare sites, such as cultivated ground, sand-dunes, etc. **Fl:** May–Oct. **Br Is dist:** Throughout, though rare and mainly coastal in Scotland.

Brookweed *Samolus valerandi* Perennial hairless herb with a basal rosette and erect, flowering stems. Leaves spoon-shaped, rather shiny, short-stalked in rosette, becoming stalkless and alternate up stems. Flowers small, cup-shaped, 2–3mm across, white, 5-petalled, borne in long, lax raceme; calyx fused into hemisphere with ovary, with 5 small free teeth. Damp, flushed habitats, most frequently saline or calcareous, usually open, occasionally shaded. Widespread as far north as S Finland. **Fl:** Jun–Aug. **Br Is dist:** Local, but widespread; mainly coastal except in E Anglia.

Alpine Snowbell *Soldanella alpina* Distinctive creeping herb to 25cm. Leaves all basal, evergreen, leathery, long-stalked and kidney-shaped, to 40mm wide. Flowers bell-shaped with fringed edges, blue-violet, in terminal clusters of 2–4. Wet pastures and rocks in mountains, often flowering as the snow melts, from SW Germany southwards. **Fl:** Apr–Aug. **Br Is dist:** Absent.

THRIFT FAMILY Plumbaginaceae

Perennial herbs, with basal rosettes of leaves. Flowers in 5 parts, in tight heads or loose branched inflorescences.

Thrift *Armeria maritima* ssp *maritima* Low, cushion-forming perennial, becoming woody at base. Leaves linear or thinly spoon-shaped, flattened, dark green, to 10cm long, 1-veined and in loose rosettes. Inflorescences borne on tall, leafless, slightly hairy stalks, 5–30cm long; beneath the globular head of flowers is a papery, brown bract, extending 20–30mm down stem; flowers pink or white, fragrant, 8–9mm in diameter. Throughout; mainly in coastal habitats, less frequent in mountains. **Fl:** Apr–Oct, mainly May–Jun. **Br Is dist:** Common around the coasts, uncommon on mountains in N England and Scotland. A highly variable plant, for which a number of subspecies are recognised: Ssp *elongata* is taller, with pale pink flowers, and leaves with shortly hairy edges. On dry grassland and sandy heaths; in Lincolnshire, and scattered localities in N Europe. Ssp *halleri* has smaller flower heads (10–15mm in diameter), bright pink to red. In pastures and dry areas, especially on serpentine soils; in the Netherlands, Denmark and Germany.

Jersey Thrift *Armeria arenaria* Similar to Thrift, but leaves fewer, wider, 3- to 7-veined; calyx teeth spine-like; flowers often paler, on taller stems. Dry grassland, mainly in mountains, occasionally coastal. **Br Is dist:** Dunes in Jersey.

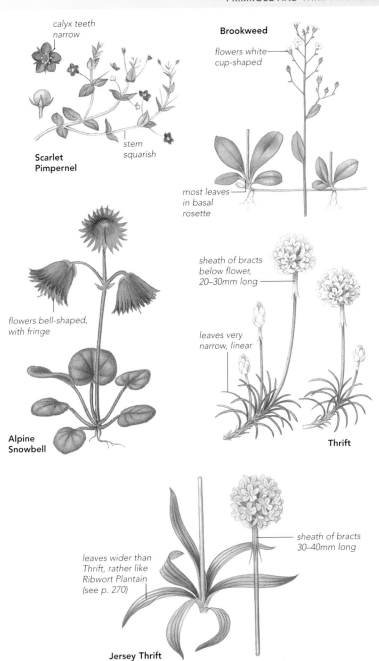

calyx teeth narrow

Scarlet Pimpernel

stem squarish

Brookweed

flowers white cup-shaped

most leaves in basal rosette

flowers bell-shaped, with fringe

Alpine Snowbell

sheath of bracts below flower, 20–30mm long

leaves very narrow, linear

Thrift

leaves wider than Thrift, rather like Ribwort Plantain (see p. 270)

sheath of bracts 30–40mm long

Jersey Thrift

205

SEA-LAVENDERS *Limonium* This is a difficult group, with many superficially similar species, distinguishable only on close examination. All are broadly similar to Common Sea-lavender, differing in the points described.

Common Sea-lavender *Limonium vulgare* Short to medium, hairless perennial with a woody rootstock and rosette of ascending leaves. Leaves elliptical to spoon-shaped, 10–15cm long, with stalk as long as to half the length of blade, veins pinnately branched, tip of leaf with tiny spine. Inflorescence branched only above the middle, up to 40cm tall (usually less), with dense, arching spikes of flowers in small clusters; each cluster has green bracts, with outer one rounded on back. Flowers small, 6–8mm, reddish to purple-blue; calyx papery, pale lilac, with 5 sharp teeth and 5 smaller teeth between. In coastal salt-marshes; from S Sweden southwards, locally frequent. **Fl:** Jul–Aug. **Br Is dist:** Widespread, common in the south, rare in the north.

Common Sea-lavender

Rock Sea-lavender *Limonium binervosum* Low plant to 30cm, hairless. Leaves 3-veined (occasionally only 1 visible), spoon-shaped with winged stalk. Inflorescence branches low down, but spreads little, with no sterile shoots; flower clusters do not overlap. On sea-cliffs, shingle and drier salt-marshes; in Britain and W France, commoner towards the south. **Br Is dist:** Local in the south, extending northwards to S Scotland.

Rock Sea-lavender

GENTIAN FAMILY Gentianaceae

Usually hairless herbs, with opposite, untoothed and often unstalked leaves. Flowers regular, with 4–5 (occasionally more) lobes. Petals twisted together in bud. Ovary superior.

Yellow Centaury

Yellow Centaury *Cicendia filiformis* Slender, annual herb 2–14cm tall, with erect simple or branched stems. Leaves linear, in widely spaced pairs, 2–6mm long. Flowers yellow, tiny, 3–6mm in diameter, corolla 4-lobed, opening only in sun, solitary on long stalks. Local, on damp sandy or peaty open ground, especially near the sea; from the Netherlands and Germany southwards. **Fl:** Jun–Oct. **Br Is dist:** Local, only in SW Britain.

Yellow-wort

Yellow-wort *Blackstonia perfoliata* Erect annual to 40cm high, waxy grey-green, with a basal rosette of leaves. Leaves ovate and spoon-shaped in rosette, stem leaves fused around the stem forming a distinctive feature. Flowers in loose, branching inflorescence, individually yellow, 10–15mm in diameter, with 6–8 petal lobes. Britain and continental Europe as far north as the Netherlands and S Germany; in calcareous grassland and dunes, or lime-rich damp areas. **Fl:** Jun–Sep. **Br Is dist:** Locally common in England, Wales and Ireland except the north.

Common Centaury *Centaurium erythraea* Variable, hairless, erect annual, with a basal rosette and 1 or more stems. Rosette leaves elliptical to oval, greyish-green, with 3–7 veins, blunt, 10–20mm wide; stem leaves narrower, 3-veined, *never parallel-sided*. Flowers pink, 10–15mm in diameter, in lax, branching inflorescence towards top of stem, often with scattered flowers lower down; petal lobes flat and spreading. Common throughout, though absent from NW Scandinavia; in drier grassy habitats, scrub and dunes. **Fl:** Jun–Sep. **Br Is dist:** Common throughout, except NE Scotland.

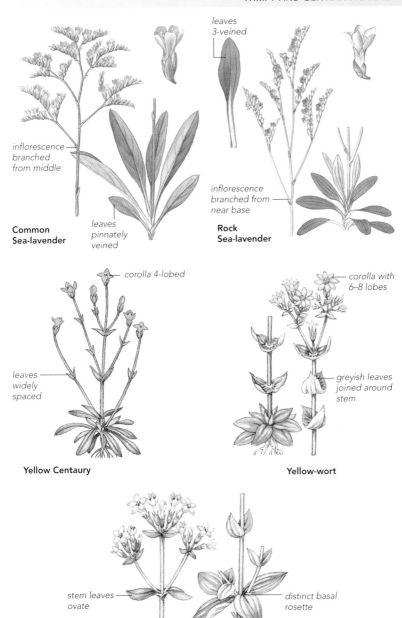

leaves
3-veined

inflorescence
branched
from middle

**Common
Sea-lavender**

leaves
pinnately
veined

inflorescence
branched from
near base

**Rock
Sea-lavender**

corolla 4-lobed

leaves
widely
spaced

Yellow Centaury

corolla with
6–8 lobes

greyish leaves
joined around
stem

Yellow-wort

stem leaves
ovate

distinct basal
rosette

Common Centaury

Seaside Centaury

Seaside Centaury *Centaurium littorale* Similar to Common Centaury (*see* p. 206), but usually shorter; basal leaves narrow, to 5mm wide; *stem leaves parallel-sided*, strap-shaped, blunt with 1–3 veins. Flowers pink, 12–14mm in diameter, corolla more concave, in dense, umbel-like, flat-topped clusters. Locally common on dunes and other grassy habitats; mainly coastal from N France to S Scandinavia, more inland farther north. **Fl:** Jun–Aug. **Br Is dist:** Locally frequent on coasts of N and W Britain; very rare in the south.

Marsh Gentian *Gentiana pneumonanthe* Procumbent or erect hairless perennial to 40cm, without basal rosette. Leaves on stem linear-oblong, blunt, 1-veined and rather fleshy. Flowers large, 25–45mm long, blue, in tight terminal cluster of 1–7 flowers; outside of corolla tube has 5 green stripes; calyx with 5 narrow, pointed teeth. Wet acidic sites, such as bogs and wet heaths; throughout except the far north. **Fl:** Jul–Oct. **Br Is dist:** Scattered through England and Wales, very locally frequent in S England.

Marsh Gentian

Cross Gentian *Gentiana cruciata* Rather similar to Marsh Gentian, but leaves elliptical, much wider, longer than flowers; flowers smaller, 20–25mm long, with *4 petal lobes* in a cross, corolla green-speckled outside. In dry grassy habitats or open woods; Europe as far north as the Netherlands. **Fl:** Jul–Oct. **Br Is dist:** Absent.

Cross Gentian

Spring Gentian *Gentiana verna* Low, hairless, short-lived perennial, with basal leaf rosettes. Often forms loose clumps. Leaves lanceolate to ovate, 10–20mm long, bright green, mainly in rosette, with few opposite pairs on stem. Flowers bright blue, usually solitary terminal, but occasionally produced lower on stem on robust plants; corolla 5-lobed, spreading at 90° to corolla tube, 15–20mm in diameter. Calyx winged on angles. In limestone grassland, wet calcareous flushes, mountain habitats; in W Ireland, N England, and mountains in south of area only; oddly absent from Arctic Europe. **Fl:** Apr–Jun. **Br Is dist:** Very locally frequent in Upper Teesdale and the Burren.

Spring Gentian

Alpine, or Snow, Gentian *Gentiana nivalis* Very small slender annual, rather similar to Spring Gentian, but smaller in all respects. Leaves 6–10mm long. Flowers bright blue, but only 5–8mm in diameter, solitary or few together. Calyx angled but not winged. Throughout area, locally common in Arctic Europe, confined to mountains farther south; in grassy, occasionally heathy habitats, and rock ledges. **Fl:** Jun–Sep. **Br Is dist:** Very rare, on a few Scottish mountains only.

Alpine, or Snow, Gentian

Great Yellow Gentian *Gentiana lutea* Highly distinctive plant, in N Europe. Stout, erect plant to 1m or more, with broad, strongly veined leaves, and whorls of yellow flowers with deeply separated petal lobes. Mainly southern, reaching into the region in the Vosges and S German mountains. **Fl:** Jun–Aug. **Br Is dist:** Absent.

Purple Gentian *Gentiana purpurea* Erect perennial to 60cm, with terminal cluster of trumpet-shaped, dull purple flowers, 20–25mm long, and a few in whorls below. Very local in mountains of C Europe, and S Norway; in grassy and rocky places. **Fl:** Jul–Oct. **Br Is dist:** Absent.

Purple Gentian

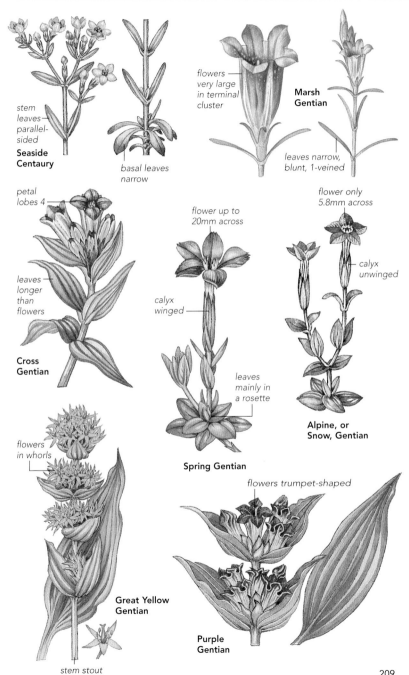

stem leaves parallel-sided
Seaside Centaury

basal leaves narrow

flowers very large in terminal cluster
Marsh Gentian

leaves narrow, blunt, 1-veined

petal lobes 4

leaves longer than flowers

Cross Gentian

flower up to 20mm across

calyx winged

leaves mainly in a rosette

Spring Gentian

flower only 5.8mm across

calyx unwinged

Alpine, or Snow, Gentian

flowers in whorls

Great Yellow Gentian

stem stout

flowers trumpet-shaped

Purple Gentian

209

Slender Gentian

Gentianella This genus differs from *Gentiana* in having no secondary lobes between the petals, and in having a fringe of hairs in the throat of the corolla (usually).

Slender Gentian *Gentianella tenella* Tiny annual 2–10cm, with a basal rosette and several erect, flowering stems. Similar to Alpine Gentian (*see* p. 208), differing in the genus differences described above, and in the 4-petalled flowers, usually blue, occasionally violet or yellowish. Local on acid often gravelly habitats in Arctic Europe, and mountains farther south. **Fl:** Jul–Sep. **Br Is dist:** Absent.

Fringed Gentian

Fringed Gentian *Gentianella ciliata* Low, unbranched biennial to 30cm. Very like a *Gentiana* species (*see* p. 208). There is no basal leaf rosette, lower leaves spoon-shaped, upper ones narrow. The flowers are large, 25–50mm, blue, with 4 triangular lobes, fringed with fine blue hairs. Very distinctive in flower. Dry grassy and rocky habitats throughout mainland Europe except the far north, but very local. **Fl:** Aug–Oct. **Br Is dist:** Very rare; recently rediscovered in the Chilterns.

Field Gentian

Autumn Gentian, Felwort *Gentianella amarella* Erect, simple or branched biennial to 30cm; 1st-year rosette dies before flowering. Stem leaves oval-lanceolate, pointed and 10–20mm long. Flowers in dense terminal and axillary clusters; individual flowers reddish-purple, bluish or creamy, 4- or 5-lobed, 10mm in diameter; corolla tube 14–22mm long, less than twice as long as calyx. Calyx has 4 or 5 equal lobes. Widespread and locally common throughout; in dry often calcareous grassland, dunes, mountain habitats. Ssp *septentrionalis* has corolla tube creamy white inside, reddish outside, and petal lobes erect; in Iceland and N Scotland only. **Fl:** Jul–Oct. **Br Is dist:** Widespread and fairly common; replaced by ssp *septentrionalis* in NW Scotland.

Marsh Felwort

Field Gentian *Gentianella campestris* The commonest form, ssp *baltica*, is similar in form to Autumn Gentian, but differing mainly in that the flowers are usually more bluish, occasionally creamy, always with 4 petal lobes, and the calyx is distinctly separated into 2 large outer lobes over-lapping the 2 smaller inner lobes. Grassland, dunes, heaths and montane habitats on acid-neutral soils; throughout the area except the extreme north, and rare towards the south. Ssp *baltica* is an annual, with corolla tube barely longer than calyx; found in a restricted area from S Sweden to N France. **Fl:** Jul–Oct. **Br Is dist:** Rare in S England and Wales, commoner farther north (ssp *campestris* only).

Northern Gentian *Gentianella aurea* Broadly similar to Autumn Gentian, only 7–10mm long, but with pale yellow (rarely blue) flowers, which are smaller. Coasts and lake shores; Arctic Europe only. **Fl:** Aug–Oct. **Br Is dist:** Absent.

Marsh Felwort *Swertia perennis* Medium-height perennial to 60cm, with 4-angled stems. Differs from *Gentianella* species in the deeply divided petals, and the fringed nectaries. Leaves roughly ovate, upper ones slightly clasping the stem. Flowers large, 15–30mm in diameter, star-shaped with 4–5 lobes, dull blue-violet, occasionally yellow-green or white, in branched clusters. Primarily a mountain species of S and C Europe, extending as far as S Germany and NC France; in marshy places and riversides. **Fl:** Jun–Aug. **Br Is dist:** Absent.

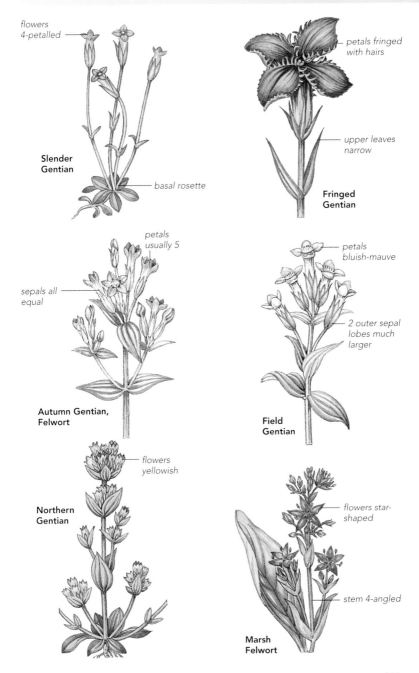

flowers
4-petalled

Slender
Gentian

basal rosette

petals fringed
with hairs

upper leaves
narrow

Fringed
Gentian

petals
usually 5

sepals all
equal

Autumn Gentian,
Felwort

petals
bluish-mauve

2 outer sepal
lobes much
larger

Field
Gentian

flowers
yellowish

Northern
Gentian

flowers star-
shaped

stem 4-angled

Marsh
Felwort

Fringed Water-lily

Lesser Periwinkle

Swallow-wort,
Vincetoxicum

BOGBEAN FAMILY Menyanthaceae

Similar to Gentian family, but always aquatic or bog plants. Lower leaves alternate.

Bogbean *Menyanthes trifoliata* Hairless perennial with stout creeping rhizome, bearing erect leaves and flower stems. Mainly aquatic. Leaves all trifoliate, held above water level, reminiscent of broad-bean leaves in texture. Flowers in dense, erect spikes to 30cm, individual flowers with 5 petal lobes, star-shaped, 15mm across, pinkish-white and with conspicuous fringing of thick white hairs. No other N European plant is similar. In shallower water, or wet peaty areas; throughout, often common, though rare in Arctic. Fl: Apr–Jun. **Br Is dist:** Widespread and common almost throughout, but local in C England.

Fringed Water-lily *Nymphoides peltata* Floating aquatic, with creeping stems, resembling water-lilies in habit, but flowers very different. Leaves round to kidney-shaped, floating, 3–10cm in diameter. Flowers solitary or in small groups, orange-yellow, 30–40mm in diameter, with 5 strongly fringed petal lobes. Widespread and common as far north as S Sweden; in still and slow-flowing water; sometimes dominant. Also cultivated in garden ponds. Fl: Jun–Sep. **Br Is dist:** Mainly S England, though becoming naturalised elsewhere.

PERIWINKLE FAMILY Apocynaceae

Woody plants, often climbing, with milky poisonous juice. Leaves opposite. Flowers in 5 parts, usually solitary.

Lesser Periwinkle *Vinca minor* Prostrate, trailing, evergreen perennial, forming mounded mats. Leaves shiny, dark green, leathery, in opposite pairs, elliptical-ovate, 20–40mm long, short-stalked. Flowers solitary from leaf axils and long-stalked; corolla blue-violet, flat, 25–30mm in diameter, with 5 lobes obliquely truncated. *Calyx lobes narrowly triangular and hairless* (**a**). Widespread through Europe as far north as Denmark, but probably naturalised only in the N part of range; occurs in hedgerows, woods, and shady places. Fl: Feb–May. **Br Is dist:** Possibly native in S England, certainly introduced elsewhere.

Greater Periwinkle *Vinca major* Similar to Lesser Periwinkle, but has larger, wider, longer-stalked leaves; flowers larger (40–50cm in diameter), *calyx lobes very narrow with densely hairy margins* (**b**). Similar habitats, but only as naturalised plant from S Europe. Fl: Mar–May. **Br Is dist:** Naturalised as far north as C Scotland, commonest in the south.

SWALLOW-WORT FAMILY Asclepiadaceae

Perennial shrubs or herbs, with opposite leaves. Flowers in 5 parts, with lobes contorted in bud. Anthers joined in a ring, usually with the stigma.

Swallow-wort, Vincetoxicum *Vincetoxicum hirundinaria* Perennial almost hairless herb, with erect stems to 1m tall. Leaves heart-shaped or narrower, 6–10cm long, opposite, pointed and stalked. Flowers greenish-yellow to almost white, starry, 5-lobed, 4–10mm in diameter, in lax clusters from the bases of the upper leaves. Fruits are long pods to 50mm containing silky seeds. Highly poisonous. Widespread and locally frequent in mainland Europe as far north as S Scandinavia; in grasslands, scrub and roadsides, often on calcareous soils. Fl: May–Sep. **Br Is dist:** Absent.

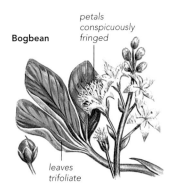

Bogbean

petals
conspicuously
fringed

leaves
trifoliate

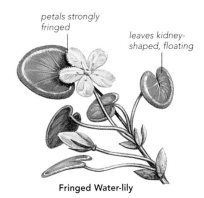

petals strongly
fringed

leaves kidney-
shaped, floating

Fringed Water-lily

calyx lobes
(under petals)
hairless

leaves leathery

**Lesser
Periwinkle**

calyx lobes
narrow, hairy

**Greater
Periwinkle**

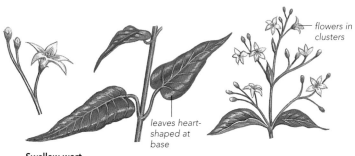

flowers in
clusters

leaves heart-
shaped at
base

**Swallow-wort,
Vincetoxicum**

213

Squinancywort

Northern Bedstraw

Hedge Bedstraw

BEDSTRAW FAMILY Rubiaceae

Herbs (in N Europe) with opposite, or often apparently whorled, leaves (in fact, the intermediate leaves of the whorl are technically stipules not leaves), which are usually simple and untoothed. Flowers funnel-shaped, usually in open branching inflorescences, sometimes tight heads. Corolla 4- or 5-lobed; calyx very small. Ovary inferior. A mainly tropical, woody family.

Field Madder *Sherardia arvensis* Procumbent, annual plant up to 40cm long, with leaves in whorls of 4–6. Upper leaves 5–20mm long, pointed, elliptical, with backward-pointing prickles on edges. Inflorescence with 4–8 flowers in terminal heads, with a conspicuous ruff of leafy bracts below them; flowers pink to purple, 4–6mm in diameter; calyx 6-toothed, enlarging in fruit. Throughout, except the far north; in open disturbed habitats. **Fl:** May–Oct. **Br Is dist:** Widespread and common, becoming rarer towards the north.

Squinancywort *Asperula cynanchica* Perennial prostrate herb, with 4-angled ascending stems, reaching 20cm. Leaves whorled in 4s, narrowly linear, often uneven in length. Inflorescence consists of long-stalked, branched clusters of pink flowers (whiter inside tube), 3–4mm in diameter and 4-lobed; calyx tiny. Fruit finely warty. Dry calcareous pastures and dunes; in continental Europe and UK as far north as N England and the Netherlands. **Fl:** Jun–Sep. **Br Is dist:** England and Wales only, locally common in S England, rare in the north.

Blue, or Field, Woodruff *Asperula arvensis* Annual to 50cm, with leaves in whorls of 6–8. Flowers 3–5mm across, bluish-violet in groups, surrounded by ruff of leafy bracts. Corolla 4-lobed. In fields and waste ground; possibly native in S parts of region. **Fl:** Apr–Jul. **Br Is dist:** A rare casual; England only.

BEDSTRAWS *Galium* This is a difficult group, comprising almost 30 often similar species in this area. Detailed examination is required for many species to be identified accurately.

Northern Bedstraw *Galium boreale* Stoloniferous perennial with ascending or erect, 4-angled stems to 60cm. Leaves dark green, 20–40mm long, in 4s, slightly leathery, widest at the middle, 3-veined and blunt. Flowers white, 4mm in diameter, in branched terminal inflorescences with numerous leafy bracts. Fruit brownish, 2–3mm across, with hooked bristles. Throughout, but local; in grassy and rocky places, and mountain habitats. One of the most easily recognised bedstraws. **Fl:** Jun–Aug. **Br Is dist:** From N Wales and N England northwards.

Hedge Bedstraw *Galium mollugo* Variable scrambling perennial, sometimes climbing to 1–2m in hedges, etc. Stems 4-angled, smooth and solid. Leaves 10–25mm long, oblong to elliptical, 1-veined, pale green, bristle-tipped, with forward-pointing prickles on margins. Flowers white, 3mm in diameter, with 4 pointed lobes, in large loose branched inflorescences. Fruit hairless, wrinkled, 1–2mm across. In hedges, rough grassy places and scrub; throughout except the far north, generally common. **Fl:** Jun–Sep. **Br Is dist:** Common in the south, rarer farther north.

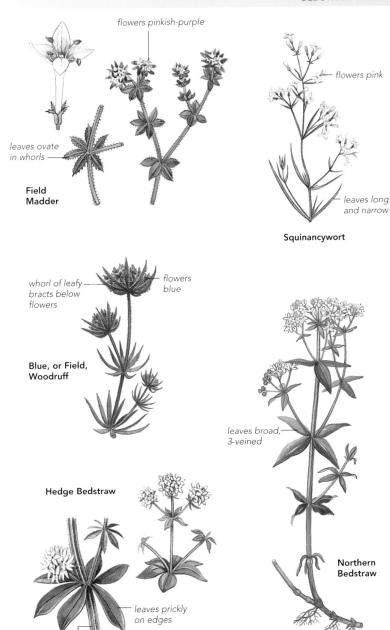

flowers pinkish-purple

leaves ovate in whorls

Field Madder

flowers pink

leaves long and narrow

Squinancywort

whorl of leafy bracts below flowers

flowers blue

Blue, or Field, Woodruff

leaves broad, 3-veined

Hedge Bedstraw

leaves prickly on edges

stem 4-angled, smooth

Northern Bedstraw

215

Slender Bedstraw

Fen Bedstraw

Lady's Bedstraw

a

b

Slender Bedstraw *Galium pumilum* Slender ascending plant to 30cm high, with smooth 4-angled stems. Leaves linear-lanceolate, often distinctly *sickle-shaped*, bristle-pointed, with few *backward-pointing prickles* on edges, in whorls of 6–9. Flowers white-cream, 2–3mm in diameter, in long loose inflorescences. Fruit about 1.5mm across, hairless, sometimes with blunt warts. Uncommon in grassland, scrub and open woodlands, usually on calcareous soil; in lowland areas, as far north as Denmark. **Fl:** Jun–Jul. **Br Is dist:** S England only, local. Four species are very similar to Slender Bedstraw, but are very local and difficult to distinguish. *Galium fleurotii* occurs on limestone cliffs and screes in NW France and possibly Somerset; *Galium valdepilosum* occurs in dry grassland in Denmark and Germany; and *Galium suecicum* is local in dry grassland in N Germany and S Sweden. *Galium oelandicum* occurs on limestone in Oland, Sweden only.

Fen Bedstraw *Galium uliginosum* Slender, straggling-ascending herb, with thin stems reaching 80–90cm, rough on the 4 angles, with backward-pointing prickles. Leaves 10–20mm long, narrowly lanceolate, with *spine at tip*, 1-veined, *in whorls of 6–8*, with backward-pointing prickles on margins (**a**). Flowers white, 2.5–3mm across, in a narrow inflorescence; anthers yellow. Fruit 1mm across, wrinkled, brown, on deflexed stalks. Widespread and locally common throughout except the extreme north; in mainly calcareous marshes and fens. **Fl:** Jun–Aug. **Br Is dist:** Throughout except N Scotland; frequent.

Common Marsh-bedstraw *Galium palustre* Rather similar in habit and habitat to Fen Bedstraw. Usually rather more robust; leaves 5–20mm long, *4–6 in a whorl*, broadest towards the tip, *blunt or slightly pointed*, but *never with spine at tip* (**b**). Flowers white, 35–45mm in diameter, in wide-spreading branching inflorescence; anthers red. Widespread and common; in wet places throughout. **Fl:** Jun–Aug. **Br Is dist:** Common throughout. Robust forms of Common Marsh-bedstraw, with leaves at least 20mm long, are sometimes distinguished as Great Marsh-bedstraw *G. elongatum*, or as subspecies of Common Marsh-bedstraw, though intermediate forms also occur.

Lady's Bedstraw *Galium verum* Distinctive as the only bedstraw with bright yellow flowers (but *see* Hedge Bedstraw, p. 214). Stem creeping with erect flower stems to 80cm, faintly 4-angled, with 4 lines. Leaves linear, spine-tipped, 15–30mm long, dark green above, downy below, with rolled margins; 8–12 in a whorl. Flowers golden yellow, 2–3mm in diameter, in a dense, oval terminal inflorescence and fragrant. Fruit 1.5mm across, smooth and black when ripe. Widespread and common throughout, except in the extreme north; in grasslands, hedge banks and dunes. **Fl:** Jun–Sep. **Br Is dist:** Common throughout.

False Cleavers *Galium spurium* Very similar to Cleavers (*see* p. 218), but a more prostrate plant; nodes less hairy, leaves narrower and shorter. *Only 2–3 bracts below flowers* (4–8 in Cleavers). Fruit smaller, 1.5–3mm across, turning blackish when ripe, the hooked hairs without swollen bases. In cultivated land, hedgerows and waste ground; widespread in Europe except in the far north. **Br Is dist:** Very rare in S England only

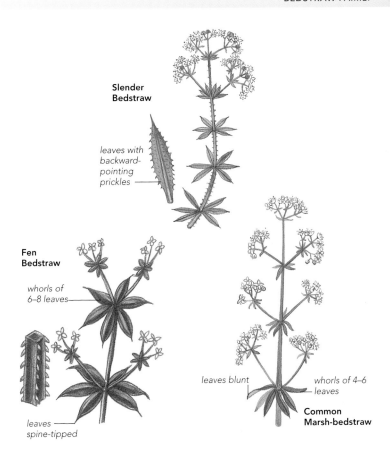

Slender Bedstraw

leaves with backward-pointing prickles

Fen Bedstraw

whorls of 6–8 leaves

leaves spine-tipped

leaves blunt

whorls of 4–6 leaves

Common Marsh-bedstraw

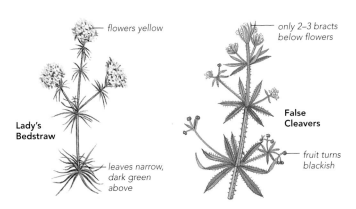

flowers yellow

only 2–3 bracts below flowers

False Cleavers

fruit turns blackish

Lady's Bedstraw

leaves narrow, dark green above

Cleavers, Goosegrass

Cleavers, Goosegrass *Galium aparine* Familiar sprawling, scrambling plant, reaching 1.8m long; stems very rough and square, with large backward-pointing prickles, hairy around the nodes. Whole plant very sticky, like velcro. Leaves robust, elliptical, abruptly contracted towards the tip with backward-pointing prickles on the margins, 6–8 in a whorl. Flowers greenish white, 2mm in diameter, in few-flowered axillary clusters *longer than the subtending leaves*. Fruit 3–6mm across, green becoming purplish, covered with dense hooked bristles with swollen bases. Widespread and common throughout, except in the far north of Europe; in cultivated land, hedgerows, woods, scrub and waste ground. **Fl:** May–Sep. **Br Is dist:** Widespread and common.

Woodruff

Woodruff *Galium odoratum* Erect, virtually hairless perennial, with 4-angled stems to 30cm. Whole plant hay-scented. Leaves lanceolate-elliptical, to 40mm, in distant whorls of 6–8; leaf margins with forward-pointing prickles. Flowers white, in dense umbel-like terminal inflorescences, funnel-shaped, 4-lobed to roughly half-way, 6mm in diameter. Fruit 2–3mm across, with hooked, black-tipped bristles. Frequent and widespread in base-rich, often damp, woods; throughout except the far north. **Fl:** May–Jun. **Br Is dist:** Throughout, though rare in N Scotland.

Crosswort

Crosswort *Cruciata laevipes* Creeping perennial, with erect, *hairy*, 4-angled stems up to 60cm tall. Leaves in distinctive whorls of 4 (the 'cross' of the name), oval-elliptical, 3-veined, to 20mm long, yellow-green and hairy. Flowers yellow-green, 2–3mm in diameter, in dense axillary clusters which do not exceed the leaves. Fruit 2–3mm across, almost globose, blackening when ripe, smooth. Common in pastures, roadsides, woodland edges and scrub, often on calcareous soils; as far north as the Netherlands and Germany (introduced in Denmark). **Fl:** Apr–Jun. **Br Is dist:** Common and widespread, becoming rarer to the north and west.

Wild Madder

Wild Madder *Rubia peregrina* Scrambling, trailing perennial, with long hairless 4-angled stems, prickly on the angles, reaching 1.5m. Leaves dark green, leathery, rigid, ovate-elliptical, to 60mm long, 1-veined, with curved prickles on the margins and midrib below. Flowers yellow-green, 4–6mm in diameter, in spreading axillary and terminal inflorescences, exceeding the leaves. Fruit a globular black berry, 4–6mm in diameter. Local in S Britain, Ireland and W France; in hedges, woods, coastal habitats, much rarer inland. **Fl:** Jun–Aug. **Br Is dist:** S and W parts of England, Wales and Ireland, rarer inland.

JACOB'S-LADDER FAMILY Polemoniaceae

Herbs or shrubs. Leaves without stipules. Flowers in 5 parts, with lower parts of petals fused into a tube. Ovary superior.

Jacob's-ladder

Jacob's-ladder *Polemonium caeruleum* Erect perennial herb up to 90cm high. Stems hollow, angled and downy above. Leaves pinnate, with 6–12 pairs of leaflets, 10–40cm long, alternate, hairless. Flowers in terminal heads, dense at first, petals blue (occasionally white), with a short tube and 5 spreading lobes, 20–30mm in diameter; stamens golden, style 3-lobed, both protruding. Local throughout except the far north and many lowland areas; commonest in hilly limestone areas, in grassland, scrub, rock ledges and screes. **Fl:** Jun–Jul. **Br Is dist:** N England only as a native, naturalised elsewhere. Two similar species occur in Arctic Europe. *P. acutifolium* has less than 8 pairs of leaflets per leaf; flowers smaller, more bell-shaped, with tiny hairs on petals. *P. boreale* has only 1 stem leaf at most, flowers bell-shaped, without tiny hairs.

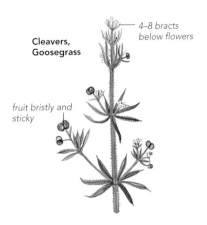

Cleavers, Goosegrass

4–8 bracts below flowers

fruit bristly and sticky

flowers clear white

leaves long and narrow, in whorls

Woodruff

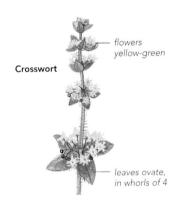

Crosswort

flowers yellow-green

leaves ovate, in whorls of 4

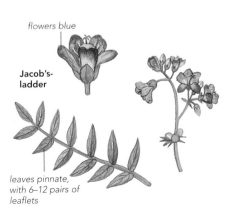

flowers blue

Jacob's-ladder

leaves pinnate, with 6–12 pairs of leaflets

Wild Madder

fruit a black berry

leaves leathery with strong marginal prickles

Greater Dodder

Sea Bindweed

BINDWEED FAMILY Convolvulaceae

A family of mainly climbing plants, with alternate leaves and twining stems. *Convolvulus* flowers (see p. 222) are regular, with 5 sepals and 5 petals, 5-lobed or joined and 5-angled. The dodders, *Cuscuta* species, are wholly parasitic plants, lacking green colouring and with scale-like leaves, often separated into the family *Cuscutaceae*.

Greater Dodder *Cuscuta europaea* Reddish parasitic climbing plant, twining anticlockwise around its host plant; stems up to 1mm in diameter, frequently branching. Leaves scale-like. Flowers pinkish, 4–5mm in diameter, in dense pinkish heads 10–15mm in diameter, with bracts, stamens not protruding, corolla lobes blunt. Parasitic mainly on nettles and hops, occasionally other plants. Widespread in continental Europe except in the far north; usually on roadsides and in hedges. **Fl:** Jul–Oct. **Br Is dist:** Rare and local; only in S England.

Dodder *Cuscuta epithymum* Similar generally to Greater Dodder, with a mass of trailing, branched, very slender, red stems. Flowers pinkish, 3–4mm across, in dense clusters 6–10mm across; petals pointed, stamens protruding. Parasitic on gorse, heather, clover and other shrubs and herbs. Widespread and locally common throughout area except the extreme north; especially on heaths, moors and rough grasslands. **Fl:** Jul–Sep. **Br Is dist:** Locally common in England, decreasing northwards; absent from N Scotland.

Sea Bindweed *Calystegia soldanella* Procumbent hairless perennial, with stems not, or barely, twisting. Leaves fleshy, kidney-shaped, 10–40mm long, broader than long and long-stalked. Flowers trumpet-shaped, 30–50mm, pink with white stripes, epicalyx shorter than sepals. Mainly on coastal dunes, occasionally shingle; on coast of W Europe from Denmark southwards. **Fl:** May–Aug. **Br Is dist:** All around the coasts, though rare in N Scotland, mainly on acid sands.

a

b

Hedge Bindweed *Calystegia sepium* Strong-growing climbing plant, often reaching 2–3m high on other plants or supports, with strongly twisting stems. Leaves arrow-shaped, to 15cm long. Flowers white (or very rarely pink), 30–40mm in diameter, 30–50mm in length; 2 epicalyx bracts, longer than sepals, surrounding them but not overlapping each other (a). Widespread and common throughout, except in the far north; in waste places, hedge-rows, riversides and woodland edges. **Fl:** Jun–Sep. **Br Is dist:** Very common throughout, less so in the far north. Ssp *roseata* is pubescent, more procumbent, with bright pink flowers. In salt-marshes and coastal areas from Denmark southwards. **Br Is dist:** Local, coastal.

Large, or Great, Bindweed *Calystegia silvatica* Similar to Hedge Bindweed, and formerly treated as a subspecies of it. Differs in that the flowers are larger (60–75mm in diameter), white rarely striped pink; 2 epicalyx bracts strongly inflated and overlapping each other, concealing the sepals (b). Similar habitats. Locally naturalised, especially in France and Britain. **Fl:** Jun–Sep. **Br Is dist:** Widespread and frequent, especially in England, but only in cultivated and waste habitats.

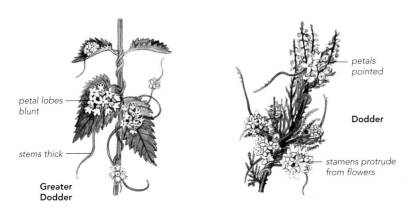

petal lobes blunt

stems thick

Greater Dodder

petals pointed

Dodder

stamens protrude from flowers

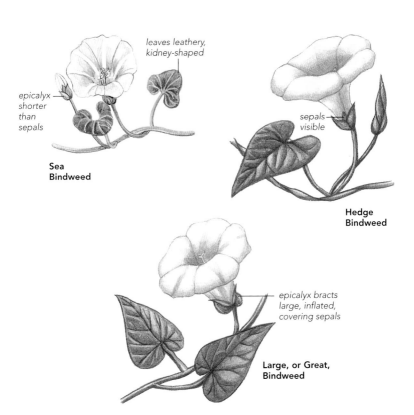

leaves leathery, kidney-shaped

epicalyx shorter than sepals

Sea Bindweed

sepals visible

Hedge Bindweed

epicalyx bracts large, inflated, covering sepals

Large, or Great, Bindweed

Common Gromwell

Purple Gromwell

Field Gromwell

Field Bindweed *Convolvulus arvensis* Creeping or climbing perennial, with stems up to 2m arising from fleshy rhizomes. Leaves arrow-shaped, 20–50mm long, stalk shorter than blade, often rather greyish. Flowers trumpet-shaped, white, or pink with white stripes, smaller than *Calystegia* species (*see* p. 220) species (about 20mm in diameter); sepals 5-lobed, without epicalyx bracts. Very common throughout, except the extreme north; in disturbed habitats and coastal grasslands. A persistent weed. **Fl:** Jun–Sep. **Br Is dist:** Very common throughout, except N Scotland where it is rarer.

BORAGE FAMILY Boraginaceae

Herbs or dwarf shrubs, frequently bristly-hairy. Leaves alternate, undivided and without stipules. Flowers usually in curved clusters (scorpioid cymes). Petals and sepals 5. Fruit 4 (occasionally 2) separate 1-seeded nutlets.

Common Gromwell *Lithospermum officinale* Erect, downy perennial to 60cm, often in clusters. Leaves lanceolate, pointed, unstalked, to 10cm long, with strongly marked veins. Flowers greenish-white, funnel-shaped, 3–4mm in diameter, in short dense clusters, elongating in fruit. Fruit consists of 4 shiny white porcelain-like nutlets, 3–4mm long, that persist well into winter. Widespread and common throughout, becoming rarer to the north and west; in scrub, grassland and wood margins, often on calcareous soils. **Fl:** Jun–Jul. **Br Is dist:** Local in England and Wales; much rarer farther north.

Purple Gromwell *Lithospermum purpurocaeruleum* Creeping, downy, woody perennial, from which arise erect or arching stems. Leaves lanceolate, narrow, long-pointed, dark green and stalkless. Flowers reddish at first, becoming bright deep blue; corolla funnel-shaped, 12–15mm in diameter, tube twice as long as sepals; in terminal forked leafy inflorescences. Fruit white, smooth, shiny, 4–5mm long. Local from Belgium and Germany southwards; in woods, roadsides and scrub, on calcareous soils. **Fl:** Apr–Jun. **Br Is dist:** Uncommon and local in S England and Wales only, in limestone areas.

Field Gromwell *Lithospermum arvense* Erect, downy annual, with barely branched stem to 50cm. Leaves oblong to strap-shaped, not sharp-pointed, upper ones unstalked, lower short-stalked, without marked side-veins. Flowers 3–4mm in diameter, white or bluish, with a violet corolla tube, in short clusters at tip of stem. Nutlets grey-brown and warty, 2.5–4mm long. Cultivated ground and dry open habitats; throughout most of Europe, except the far north. **Fl:** May–Aug. **Br Is dist:** Local, most frequent in S and E England.

Viper's-bugloss *Echium vulgare* Erect, roughly bristly biennial, with scattered red-based bristles, to 90cm tall, very variable in form. Root leaves stalked and 1-veined; stem leaves unstalked with rounded bases. Flowers usually bright blue or blue-violet, funnel-shaped, with 5 somewhat unequal petal lobes, 15–20mm long, in short, curved axillary clusters. Stamens, 5, of which 4 protrude. Fruit rough nutlets. In open grassy places, often near the coast, frequently on light or calcareous soils; throughout area except the far north. **Fl:** Jun–Sep. **Br Is dist:** Common through most of England, Wales and E Ireland; rarer elsewhere, or absent.

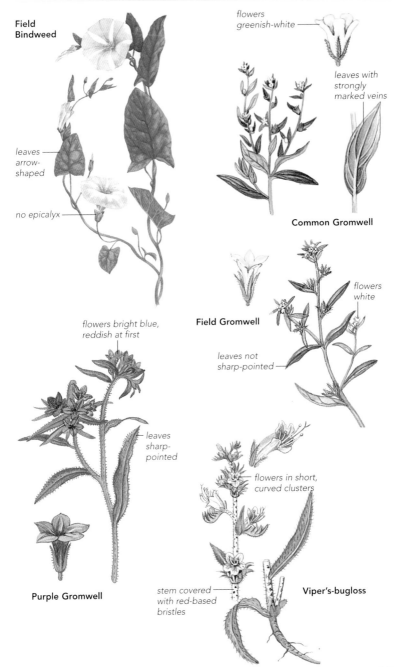

Field Bindweed

leaves arrow-shaped

no epicalyx

flowers greenish-white

leaves with strongly marked veins

Common Gromwell

Field Gromwell

flowers white

leaves not sharp-pointed

flowers bright blue, reddish at first

leaves sharp-pointed

Purple Gromwell

flowers in short, curved clusters

stem covered with red-based bristles

Viper's-bugloss

223

Lungwort

Lungwort *Pulmonaria officinalis* Low perennial herb, tufted and very rough-hairy. Basal leaves roughly ovate, sometimes heart-shaped at base, abruptly narrowed into long, winged stalk (**a**), normally white-spotted. Stem leaves ovate, unstalked, partly clasping the stem. Flowers pink in bud, becoming red-violet to blue, 10mm in diameter; calyx teeth between a third and a quarter the length of the cylindrical calyx tube. Fruit rounded oval nutlets. In shady or partially shaded places on chalk and clay soils; from the Netherlands and S Sweden southwards. **Fl:** Mar–May. **Br Is dist:** Introduced, locally naturalised.

Common Comfrey

Common Comfrey *Symphytum officinale* Erect bristly perennial, to 1.2m; stem strongly winged. Root leaves large, 15–25cm long, stalked, oval-lanceolate, softly hairy and untoothed; stem leaves smaller, unstalked, clasping stem, with bases running down stem. Flowers in branched, coiled inflorescences; corolla tubular to bell-shaped, 12–18mm long, with short reflexed petal lobes, white, pink or purple-violet. On riverbanks and in damp grassland; through much of N Europe, but rarer and mainly naturalised farther north. **Fl:** Jun–Jul. **Br Is dist:** Common throughout southern half of Britain, rare in N Scotland and Ireland.

Tuberous Comfrey

Tuberous Comfrey *Symphytum tuberosum* Similar in habit to other comfreys, but has tuberous roots; stems simple or slightly branched, unwinged or slightly winged; middle leaves of stem longest, basal leaves disappearing by flowering time. Flowers yellow, 13–19mm long, corolla lobes turned back at the tip. Woods and damp shady places; from England and Germany southwards. **Fl:** Jun–Jul. **Br Is dist:** Widespread, most frequent in Scotland, but rarely common.

Alkanet

Alkanet *Anchusa officinalis* Bristly, erect perennial to 80cm, rarely more. Leaves long-lanceolate to oval-lanceolate, only lower ones stalked. Flowers bluish red or violet, rarely white or yellow, 10mm in diameter, with straight corolla tube, in long curling inflorescences. Bracts not wavy-edged. From S Scandinavia southwards; in scattered localities in grassy, rocky and disturbed places, often over limestone. **Fl:** Jun–Sep. **Br Is dist:** Naturalised or casual in scattered localities, mainly S England.

Bugloss *Anchusa arvensis* Erect or ascending very bristly annual to 60cm. Bristles mostly have swollen bases. Leaves linear-lanceolate or broader, wavy-edged and somewhat toothed, lower ones stalked, upper ones clasping stem. Flowers bright blue or rarely pale, with a curved corolla tube 4–7mm long, in branched leafy inflorescences; throat of corolla closed by 5 hairy scales. Fruit 3–4mm wide, irregularly ovoid, with net pattern on surface. Common and widespread on sandy and light soils, in grassland, dunes and waste ground. **Fl:** Jun–Sep. **Br Is dist:** Locally common throughout much of Britain, rarer in the north, tending to be coastal.

Green Alkanet *Pentaglottis sempervirens* Erect bristly perennial up to 80cm. Basal leaves ovate, narrowed into long stem, stem leaves unstalked and untoothed. Flowers bright blue with whitish centre, 8–10mm in diameter, in stalked, bristly clusters from the axils of the upper leaves; corolla throat closed by 5 hairy scales. Nutlets rough, netted on surface. Widely naturalised, originally from SW Europe; in hedges, roadsides and shaded areas, often close to habitation. **Fl:** Apr–Jun. **Br Is dist:** Scattered, commonest in the south-west.

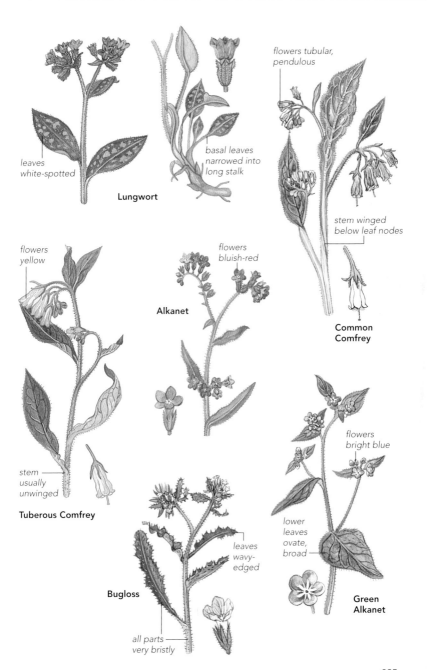

leaves
white-spotted

Lungwort

basal leaves
narrowed into
long stalk

flowers tubular,
pendulous

stem winged
below leaf nodes

**Common
Comfrey**

flowers
yellow

flowers
bluish-red

Alkanet

stem
usually
unwinged

Tuberous Comfrey

flowers
bright blue

lower
leaves
ovate,
broad

Bugloss

leaves
wavy-
edged

all parts
very bristly

**Green
Alkanet**

Oysterplant

Oysterplant *Mertensia maritima* Distinctive, prostrate, hairless, fleshy, blue-grey plant, with stems to 60cm, sometimes forming mats. Leaves oval to spoon-shaped, lower ones stalked, upper unstalked. Flowers long-stalked, about 6mm across, bell-shaped, pink in bud becoming pink and blue, in branched leafy inflorescences; flower stalks become recurved as fruit ripens. On sandy or shingly shores, often amongst high-tide debris; from N England, N Ireland and Denmark northwards, frequent in the far north. **Fl:** Jun–Aug. **Br Is dist:** From NW England northwards, locally frequent farther north.

Madwort

Madwort *Asperugo procumbens* Bristly procumbent or climbing annual herb. Leaves lanceolate. Flowers purplish becoming blue, with white tube, about 3mm in diameter, solitary or paired in leaf axils, becoming surrounded by greatly enlarged leaf-like toothed sepals (**a**). In cultivated places and disturbed ground, usually rich in nitrogen; throughout much of N Europe, but often not native. **Fl:** May–Sep. **Br Is dist:** Casual, occasionally naturalised, in scattered sites, mainly near ports.

Green Hound's-tongue

Hound's-tongue *Cynoglossum officinale* Erect, softly *grey-downy* biennial to 80cm. Basal leaves lanceolate-ovate, stalked and pointed, to 30cm; stem leaves smaller, unstalked and narrower. Flowers dull purplish-red, funnel-shaped, 5–7mm in diameter, with 5 equal lobes; calyx lobes spreading in fruit; inflorescence long and often branched. Fruit consists of 4 flattened oval nutlets covered with hooked bristles, and with a raised border. Widespread and locally common throughout, except the far north; in dry open habitats especially near the coast. **Fl:** May–Aug. **Br Is dist:** Commonest in the east, rarer in the west.

Green Hound's-tongue *Cynoglossum germanicum* Similar to Hound's-tongue in form, but differs in that the *leaves are green,* bristly and barely hairy; flowers smaller, 5–6mm in diameter, and the nutlets have no thickened border. C Europe extending north-west to England and Belgium; in woods and hedgerows, usually on basic soil. **Fl:** May–Jul. **Br Is dist:** Very rare in S England.

FORGET-ME-NOTS *Myosotis* Readily recognised group of small annual or perennial herbs, usually with pale blue flowers. Many species need close examination for certain identification; important features include the degree of hairiness and type of hairs on the sepals, length of the flower stalks and presence or absence of leafy bracts in the inflorescence.

Field Forget-me-not *Myosotis arvensis* Variable, erect, pubescent annual, occasionally perennial, stem branching, with spreading hairs. Lower leaves forming a loose rosette, roughly elliptical, broadest above the middle and barely stalked; stem leaves lanceolate and unstalked, with spreading hairs on both surfaces. Flowers pale to bright blue, with 5 concave lobes, up to 5mm in diameter, corolla tube shorter than calyx. Calyx bell-shaped, with hooked hairs on tube (**b**), lobes spreading when in fruit. Inflorescence without bracts. Flower stalks remain erect in fruit, and are roughly twice as long as calyx. Very common throughout; in dry grasslands, scrub, open woods and arable land. **Fl:** Apr–Oct. **Br Is dist:** Common throughout except the far north.

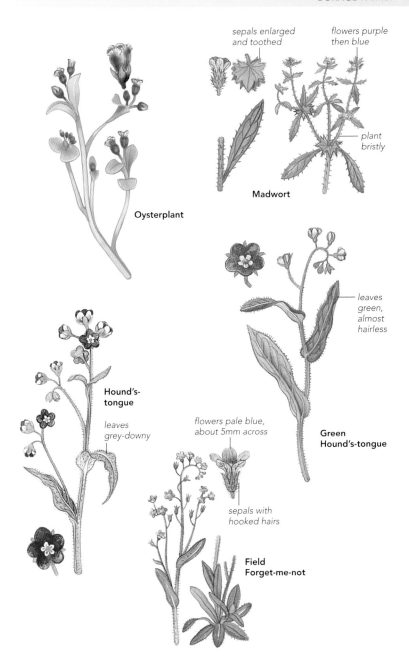

sepals enlarged
and toothed

flowers purple
then blue

plant
bristly

Madwort

Oysterplant

leaves
green,
almost
hairless

**Hound's-
tongue**

leaves
grey-downy

flowers pale blue,
about 5mm across

sepals with
hooked hairs

**Green
Hound's-tongue**

**Field
Forget-me-not**

Wood Forget-me-not

Early Forget-me-not *Myosotis ramossissima* Low bristly annual, only to 15cm. Similar characteristics to Field Forget-me-not (*see* p. 226), but stem with spreading hairs below, appressed hairs above; calyx teeth spreading in fruit, flowers only 2–3mm in diameter, inflorescence longer than leafy part of stem when in fruit. Flower stalks roughly equal to calyx when in fruit. Common in dry open habitats, especially on sand; throughout except the far north. **Fl:** Apr–Jun. **Br Is dist:** Widespread and common, rarer in west and north.

Creeping Forget-me-not

Wood Forget-me-not *Myosotis sylvatica* More robust, hairy perennial to 50cm, often much-branched and leafy, with spreading hairs on stem. Leaves with spreading hairs. Corolla pale blue, flat and *6–10mm in diameter*; calyx with stiffly hooked hairs (**a**); fruit stalks 1–2 times the length of calyx, spreading when ripe. Inflorescence not leafy, not longer than leafy part of stem when in fruit. Nutlets brown when ripe. In woods and shady or damp grassland; widespread and locally common, except in the north. **Fl:** Apr–Aug. **Br Is dist:** Locally common, but rare in W and N Britain.

Water Forget-me-not

Creeping Forget-me-not *Myosotis secunda* Creeping, rhizomatous perennial producing erect hairy branches. Flowers blue, 6–8mm in diameter, with slightly notched lobes; calyx divided half-way into pointed teeth, half the length of calyx (**b**), with straight hairs; *fruit stalks 3–5 times the length of calyx, reflexed when mature*. Lower part of inflorescence has leafy bracts. Nutlets dark brown and shiny. In acid marshes, bogs and wet places in Britain, France (local) and mountains farther south. **Fl:** Jun–Aug. **Br Is dist:** Common in W and N Britain, increasingly rare to the east.

Bur Forget-me-not

Water Forget-me-not *Myosotis scorpioides* Rather similar to Creeping Forget-me-not, but hairless or with appressed hairs on stem; fruit stalks only *1–2 times the length of calyx; calyx teeth short and triangular*, not more than a third of the length of calyx; corolla larger, 8–10mm in diameter; no leafy bracts on inflorescence. Wet habitats, often on neutral-basic soils; throughout, often common. **Fl:** May–Sep. **Br Is dist:** Common and widespread.

Bur Forget-me-not *Lappula squarrosa* Very similar to above, differing mainly in the bell-shaped flowers and spiny erect fruits. In dry habitats, disturbed, and waste ground; widespread in mainland Europe except in the far north, but often only casual or naturalised. **Br Is dist:** Casual only.

Vervain

VERVAIN FAMILY Verbenaceae

Herbs or shrubs with opposite leaves. Flowers in 5 (or 4) parts; corolla with flat petal lobes and short tube.

Vervain *Verbena officinalis* Medium-tall erect perennial, with 4-angled stems, rough on corners. Lower leaves roughly diamond-shaped, but deeply cut, almost to the midrib, with the lobes often divided again. Upper leaves smaller, unstalked, barely divided. Flowers bluish-pink, 4–5mm across, 5-lobed divided roughly into 2 lips, corolla tube twice the length of calyx; in long narrow, often branched, leafless spikes, 8–12cm long. Fruit separates into 4 ribbed nutlets. Widespread northwards to N Germany (and naturalised beyond that); in dry grasslands, woodland edges, roadsides and scrub. **Fl:** Jun–Sep. **Br Is dist:** Common and widespread through most of England and Wales, becoming increasingly rare northwards.

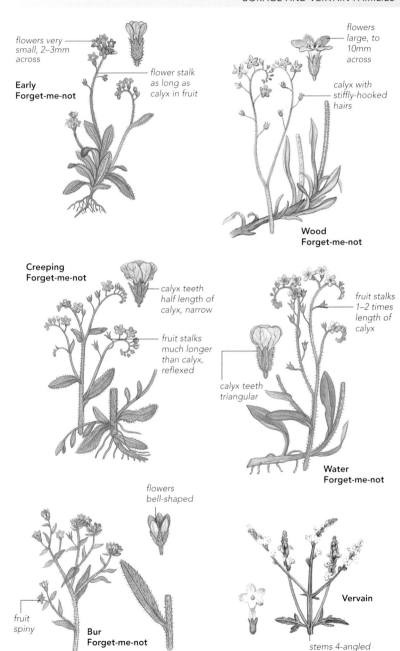

Early Forget-me-not

flowers very small, 2–3mm across

flower stalk as long as calyx in fruit

Wood Forget-me-not

flowers large, to 10mm across

calyx with stiffly-hooked hairs

Creeping Forget-me-not

calyx teeth half length of calyx, narrow

fruit stalks much longer than calyx, reflexed

Water Forget-me-not

fruit stalks 1–2 times length of calyx

calyx teeth triangular

flowers bell-shaped

Bur Forget-me-not

fruit spiny

Vervain

stems 4-angled

Cornish, or Blue Bugle

Ground-pine

WATER-STARWORT FAMILY Callitrichaceae

The water-starworts are a difficult group of small aquatic or mud-dwelling plants. Most species can vary considerably in form according to conditions, and all except 2 produce different water and land forms. For reliable identification, close examination of ripe fruit is required.

Common Water-starwort *Callitriche stagnalis* Has no parallel-sided leaves, all leaves elliptical to oval, not (or barely) notched; upper leaves, often 6, forming a rosette; leaves commonly 5-veined. Flowers from rosette leaves only, solitary or paired; stigmas 2–3mm, becoming recurved; *fruit has all 4 lobes broadly winged.* Very common and widespread throughout; in still and slow-moving water, or on mud. **Fl:** May–Sep. **Br Is dist:** Common throughout.

DEAD-NETTLE FAMILY Lamiaceae (Labiatae)

Herbs or subshrubs, with square stems, and opposite leaves without stipules. Frequently aromatic, the source of many volatile oils. Flowers irregular, usually clearly 2-lipped, in apparent whorls in the axils of opposite leaf-like bracts. Calyx with 5 teeth.

Bugle *Ajuga reptans* Small perennial herb, with long, leafy rooting runners. Erect flower stems, up to 40cm, shortly hairy on 2 opposite faces only. Basal leaves between ovate and spoon-shaped, 40–70mm long, stalked, sometimes shallowly toothed; stem leaves in pairs, unstalked. Inflorescence made up of whorls of flowers from bracts, uppermost bracts shorter than flowers; corolla blue to blue-violet, 14–17mm long, lower lip often with white lines. Widespread and frequently common in woods and grasslands, often on heavy soils; as far north as S Norway. **Fl:** Apr–Jun. **Br Is dist:** Very common, less so in the north.

Cornish, or Blue Bugle *Ajuga genevensis* Similar in form to Bugle, differing in that there are no above-ground runners and the stem is normally *hairy on all 4 faces*; the leaves are toothed, with the lower ones withering by flowering time. Flowers similar, but *brighter*, richer blue. Stamens markedly protruding from tube. Locally common on mainland Europe northwards to Belgium and Germany; in woods, roadsides and dry rocky places, often on lime-rich soils. **Fl:** Apr–Jul. **Br Is dist:** Absent as native, occasionally naturalised.

Ground-pine *Ajuga chamaepitys* Hairy, ascending, low annual to 20cm, quite different to other *Ajuga* species. Basal leaves withering early, stem leaves divided into 3 narrow linear lobes, smelling of pine when crushed. Flowers 7–15mm long, yellow with red-purple markings (rarely all purple), 2 (to 4) at each node, much shorter than bracts. Widespread from the Netherlands and Germany southwards, very local except to the south; in open calcareous habitats including arable fields. **Fl:** May–Sep. **Br Is dist:** Rare and local, decreasing, in S England only.

Mountain Germander *Teucrium montanum* Dwarf spreading shrub, 10–25cm, with spreading hairs. Leaves linear-lanceolate, untoothed, grey-green above and *white-hairy below* with edges rolled under. Flowers in dense rounded heads of *creamy yellow flowers*, 12–15mm long, with leaf-like bracts. On dry or rocky calcareous soils, including chalk downland; from the Netherlands and Germany southwards. **Fl:** May–Aug. **Br Is dist:** Absent.

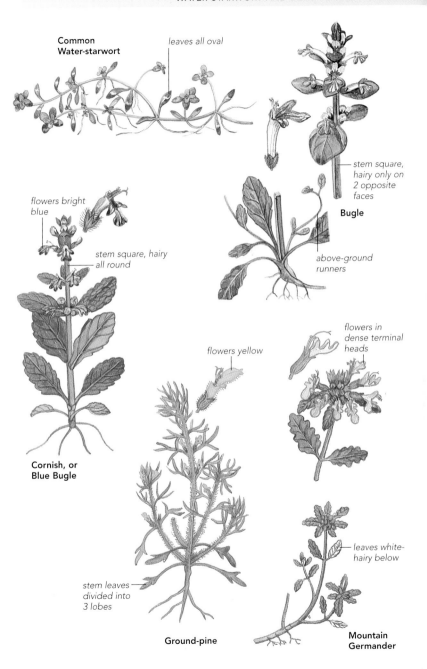

Common Water-starwort

leaves all oval

stem square, hairy only on 2 opposite faces

Bugle

above-ground runners

flowers bright blue

stem square, hairy all round

Cornish, or Blue Bugle

flowers yellow

flowers in dense terminal heads

stem leaves divided into 3 lobes

Ground-pine

leaves white-hairy below

Mountain Germander

231

Water Germander

Water Germander *Teucrium scordium* Softly hairy perennial, with creeping rhizomes or leafy runners, and erect flower stems to 40cm. Leaves oblong, coarsely toothed, rounded at base, more or less unstalked, grey-green and with garlic smell when crushed. Flowers typical *Teucrium* shape, pink-purple, lip to 10mm long, in whorls of 2–6 forming a loose terminal inflorescence. Wet, often calcareous damp places, including dune-slacks; local or rare, as far north as S Scandinavia. **Fl:** Jun–Oct. **Br Is dist:** Very rare in a few sites in SW and E England and W Ireland only.

Cut-leaved Germander

Cut-leaved Germander *Teucrium botrys* Short, erect, downy annual or biennial, often with branched stems up to 30cm. Leaves stalked, *deeply pinnately lobed*, with lobes often cut farther; bracts similar but smaller, longer than flowers. Flowers bright pink, lip about 8mm long, in whorls of 2–6 up stem. Dry grassland, disturbed sites, and rocky areas on calcareous soils; local or rare from Belgium and the Netherlands southwards. **Fl:** Jun–Sep. **Br Is dist:** Rare and local in S England only, from Cotswolds eastwards.

Wood Sage

Wall Germander *Teucrium chamaedrys* Tufted, hairy perennial, woody at the base, without creeping rhizomes. Stems erect or ascending, to 40cm. Leaves oval-oblong, about twice as long as wide, blunt, short-stalked, shiny dark green above and varying from untoothed to deeply toothed. Flowers pink-purple, corolla lip 8–10mm long, in whorls, upper bracts shorter than flowers. From Belgium and the Netherlands southwards; on calcareous rocks, in grassland and on walls; often naturalised. **Fl:** Jun–Sep. **Br Is dist:** In chalk grassland in Sussex, possibly native; rarely naturalised on walls elsewhere.

Skullcap

Wood Sage *Teucrium scorodonia* Medium, erect, downy, perennial herb to 60cm, usually less. Leaves oval, heart-shaped at base, to 70mm, stalked, wrinkled, with rounded teeth, aromatic. Flowers in pairs in bract axils, pale greenish-yellow, with typical *Teucrium* shape (a single, 5-lobed, lower lip, 5–6mm long); stamens red, distinctly protruding. Inflorescence terminal, without true leaves. Widespread and common outside Scandinavia, local or naturalised in S Scandinavia; in dry grassy and wooded areas, heaths, usually on acid soils. **Fl:** Jul–Sep. **Br Is dist:** Common throughout.

Lesser Skullcap

Skullcap *Scutellaria galericulata* Medium, creeping, downy or hairless perennial, with erect flower stems to 50cm. Leaves oval-lanceolate, 20–50mm long, slightly toothed, variably heart-shaped at base, stalked. Flowers blue-violet, much longer than calyx, 10–20mm long, tube curved slightly; in loose erratic inflorescence towards top of stem. Common and widespread throughout N Europe except in the far north; in marshes, riversides and wet woods. **Fl:** Jun–Sep. **Br Is dist:** Common and widespread, though scarce in Ireland and NE Scotland.

Lesser Skullcap *Scutellaria minor* Similar to Skullcap in form, but smaller, to 15cm tall and almost hairless. Leaves 10–30mm long, ovate to lanceolate, untoothed, though sometimes lobed near base. Flowers in pairs in axils of leaf-like bracts, pink and 2-lipped with lower lip purple-spotted; corolla tube 6–10mm long, 2–4 times length of calyx, straight. In damp, often acid, habitats; from the Netherlands and Germany southwards (and very rare in Sweden). **Fl:** Jul–Oct. **Br Is dist:** Widespread and local as far north as C Scotland, rarer farther north.

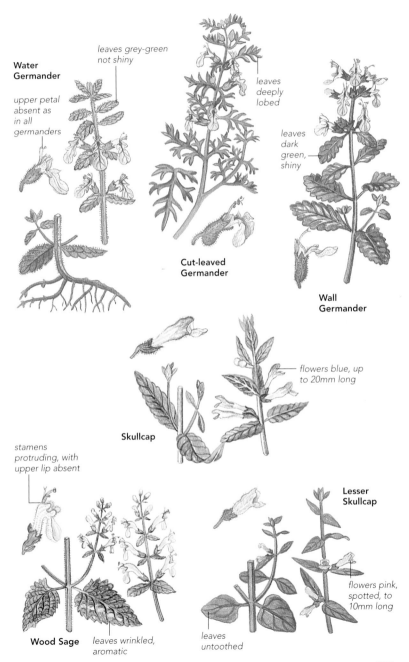

Water Germander

leaves grey-green not shiny

upper petal absent as in all germanders

leaves deeply lobed

Cut-leaved Germander

leaves dark green, shiny

Wall Germander

flowers blue, up to 20mm long

Skullcap

stamens protruding, with upper lip absent

Lesser Skullcap

Wood Sage *leaves wrinkled, aromatic*

leaves untoothed

flowers pink, spotted, to 10mm long

233

White Horehound

White Horehound *Marrubium vulgare* Erect, white-downy perennial to 45cm, often with numerous non-flowering branches. Leaves rounded-oval, to 40mm long, wrinkled and greyish-downy above, felted white below. Flowers white, 12–15mm long, in many-flowered separated whorls. Scattered localities northwards to S Sweden; on dry grasslands and waste places, especially near the coast. **Fl:** Jun–Oct. **Br Is dist:** Occasional on the S coast in calcareous grassy sites; very rare elsewhere.

Bastard Balm

Bastard Balm *Melittis melissophyllum* Perennial herb, with erect often clustered stems to 70cm, hairy and strong-smelling. Leaves ovate to 80mm long, pointed, with rounded teeth and stalked. Flowers very large, 25–40mm long, white, pink, purple or a mixture of these, greatly exceeding the sepals, fragrant, in clusters of 2–6 from the upper leaf-like bract axils. Woodland edges and rides, hedge banks, shady areas; as far north as Belgium and S Britain. Common in the south of area. **Fl:** May–Jul. **Br Is dist:** Rare in S Britain, W Sussex; decreasing.

Red, or Narrow-leaved, Hemp-nettle

Common Hemp-nettle *Galeopsis tetrahit* Erect branched annual, with bristly-hairy, slightly sticky, stems up to 60cm, *swollen at the nodes*. Leaves ovate to lanceolate, pointed, toothed, 3–10cm long, and stalked. Flowers pink-purple, rarely white, with darker markings, 15–20mm long, *corolla tube roughly equal to calyx*, middle lobe of lower corolla lip not notched; calyx bristly, with long pointed teeth. Inflorescence consists of leafy dense whorls in upper part of stem. Throughout; in disturbed habitats, tracksides and heaths. **Fl:** Jul–Sep. **Br Is dist:** Common throughout.

Red, or Narrow-leaved, Hemp-nettle *Galeopsis angustifolia* Similar in form to Common Hemp-nettle. *Stem not swollen at the nodes.* Leaves narrower, less than 10mm wide, with few small teeth, silkily hairy. Flowers deep reddish-pink, to purplish, with yellow markings, 15–25mm long, *tube much longer than calyx teeth.* In arable land, on shingle, and other open habitats; local from Germany southwards, naturalised farther north. **Fl:** Jul–Oct. **Br Is dist:** Local and erratic in appearance, mainly in SE England, rare elsewhere.

Spotted Dead-nettle

Large-flowered Hemp-nettle *Galeopsis speciosa* Resembles other hemp-nettles in form, but very distinctive. Stem stout, uniformly bristly-hairy, with additional yellow-tipped glandular hairs. Corolla 27–34mm long, yellow and violet, corolla tube twice the length of calyx. In arable land on acid and peaty soils, frequently with potatoes; throughout except the far north. **Fl:** Jul–Sep. **Br Is dist:** Rather common in the north, much less frequent in the south.

Spotted Dead-nettle *Lamium maculatum* Very variable, hairy, aromatic perennial, often forming patches with rhizomes, with erect flower stems to 60cm. Leaves triangular to ovate, pointed, toothed and stalked, often (but not always) with a large white to pale green blotch in the centre. Flowers pinkish purple, 20–35mm, with curved corolla tube, lateral lobes of corolla with a single tooth. Woodlands, hedge banks and shady habitats; from the Netherlands southwards on mainland Europe, naturalised elsewhere. **Fl:** Apr–Oct. **Br Is dist:** Introduced, locally naturalised, most commonly as form with silver-blotched leaves.

flowers white —

leaves wrinkled, greyish

White Horehound

flowers large

Bastard Balm

calyx bristly

stem swollen at nodes

Common Hemp-nettle

flowers reddish-pink

leaves narrow

Red, or Narrow-leaved, Hemp-nettle

lip yellow and violet

stem glandular-hairy

Large-flowered Hemp-nettle

corolla tube curved —

leaf often with pale blotch

Spotted Dead-nettle

Yellow Archangel

Motherwort

Black Horehound

White Dead-nettle *Lamium album* Similar in form to Spotted Dead-nettle (*see* p. 236). Leaves ovate, heart-shaped at the base, coarsely toothed, roughly Common nettle shape (*see* p. 26), but not stinging (hence the name). Flowers white, 20–25mm, with corolla tube curved near base, upper lip hairy, lower lip with 2–3 teeth on each side lobe. A familiar, common and widespread species, in grassy, disturbed and semi-shaded habitats almost throughout, except the far north. **Fl:** Apr–Dec. **Br Is dist:** Common almost throughout, except N Scotland.

Red Dead-nettle *Lamium purpureum* More or less erect, downy annual to 40cm, usually much less, often branched near base, and purplish. Leaves oval to heart-shaped, 10–50mm long, all stalked, coarsely round-toothed. Inflorescence dense and leafy; flowers pink-purple, corolla 10–18mm, tube longer than calyx, straight; calyx downy, with teeth equal to tube length, becoming spreading as fruit ripens. In cultivated ground and waste places; throughout N Europe. **Fl:** Mar–Oct. **Br Is dist:** Common throughout.

Henbit Dead-nettle *Lamium amplexicaule* Rather similar to Red Dead-nettle. Lower leaves rounded to ovate, blunt-toothed and long-stalked; bracts quite different in appearance (stalkless, *rounded, clasping the stem in pairs*, sometimes appearing like a ruff below the flowers). Flowers pink-purple, mostly 15–20mm long, but some remaining small and closed; calyx tube with dense, white, spreading hairs, teeth shorter than tube, not spreading in fruit. Widespread throughout except the extreme north; in cultivated and disturbed ground. **Fl:** Mar–Nov. **Br Is dist:** Throughout, but much rarer in the north, mainly on dry soils.

Yellow Archangel *Lamiastrum galeobdolon* Hairy perennial, with long leafy runners, especially after flowering time; flower stems more or less erect, to 45cm. Very similar to dead-nettles, but with yellow flowers, 17–20mm long, streaked reddish, with lip of corolla divided into 3 equal lobes, with the middle lobe triangular and untoothed. In woods and hedgerows; as far north as S Scandinavia, most commonly on heavier base-rich soils. **Fl:** Apr–Jun. **Br Is dist:** Frequent throughout most of England and Wales, much rarer farther north and in Ireland.

Motherwort *Leonurus cardiaca* Tall, variably hairy perennial, usually about 1m, occasionally more. Lower leaves palmately 3- to 7-lobed, with the lobes further toothed or lobed; upper leaves 3-lobed. Flowers pink or white, in whorls with conspicuous 3-lobed bracts; corolla 8–12mm, distinctly exceeding calyx, upper lip very hairy on back; calyx prominently 5-veined, with teeth almost as long as tube. In hedge banks, woodland edges and shady waste places; widespread in mainland Europe except in the far north. **Fl:** Jul–Sep. **Br Is dist:** Rarely naturalised.

Black Horehound *Ballota nigra* Straggling to erect, roughly hairy perennial, to 80cm, with an unpleasant smell. Leaves ovate to heart-shaped, stalked, coarsely toothed, 30–80mm long. Flowers dull purple to pink, 12–18mm long, hairy, with concave upper lip; calyx funnel-shaped with 5 triangular long-pointed lobes; in dense leafy whorls. Widespread on roadsides and hedge banks; from S Sweden southwards, probably not native in north of range. **Fl:** Jun–Oct. **Br Is dist:** Common throughout England and Wales, rarer farther north and in Ireland.

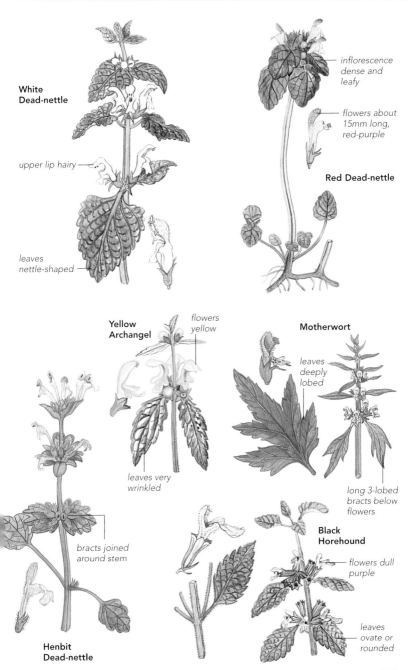

White Dead-nettle

upper lip hairy

leaves nettle-shaped

inflorescence dense and leafy

flowers about 15mm long, red-purple

Red Dead-nettle

Yellow Archangel

flowers yellow

leaves very wrinkled

Motherwort

leaves deeply lobed

long 3-lobed bracts below flowers

bracts joined around stem

Henbit Dead-nettle

Black Horehound

flowers dull purple

leaves ovate or rounded

Betony

Betony *Stachys officinalis* Erect, hairy or hairless perennial to 60cm. Basal leaves roughly oblong, heart-shaped at base, on long petioles; stem leaves narrower, with decreasing length stalks up the stem; all leaves with even rounded teeth. Inflorescence a short, cylindrical, dense terminal spike, sometimes with looser whorls below; *corolla red-purple*, 12–18mm, tube exceeding calyx; calyx has 5 bristle-pointed teeth. In open woods, pastures, hedge banks, heaths, usually on lighter soils; from S Sweden and Scotland southwards; common. **Fl**: Jun–Sep. **Br Is dist**: Common in England and Wales, rarer farther north and in Ireland.

Downy Woundwort

Downy Woundwort *Stachys germanica* Patch-forming biennial or perennial, with erect or ascending stems, wholly *densely felted with white hairs*. Leaves ovate, white-hairy especially underneath. Flowers rosy pink, hairy, in dense spikes. Rare in calcareous grassland and disturbed areas; from S England, Belgium and Germany southwards. **Fl**: Jul–Aug. **Br Is dist**: Very rare, declining, in Oxfordshire only.

Perennial Yellow-woundwort

Hedge Woundwort *Stachys sylvatica* Unpleasant-smelling bristly perennial, with erect stems to 90cm from a creeping rhizome. Leaves ovate, coarsely toothed, pointed, heart-shaped at base, blade 40–90mm long, with stalks to 70mm. Flowers 12–18mm long, *claret-red* with white markings, in whorls forming a long terminal spike; flower bracteoles minute; calyx with 5 rigid triangular teeth, more than the length of the tube. In shaded places and disturbed ground, almost throughout the area. **Fl**: Jul–Sep. **Br Is dist**: Common almost throughout.

Marsh Woundwort *Stachys palustris* Unscented bristly perennial, with erect stems to 1m or more from creeping rhizomes. Leaves narrow oblong to lanceolate, rounded or heart-shaped at base, lower ones short-stalked, upper stalkless, all coarsely toothed. *Flowers dull pink-purple*, with white markings, hairy outside, 12–15mm; calyx with narrowly triangular teeth, more than half as long as tube and hairy. In damp habitats such as ditchsides, lake margins, marshes, occasionally in arable land; throughout. **Fl**: Jun–Sep. **Br Is dist**: Throughout, frequent. Marsh and Hedge Woundworts readily hybridise to produce *Stachys* x *ambigua*, intermediate between the parents, often in large clumps.

Perennial Yellow-woundwort *Stachys recta* Variable, usually erect, aromatic perennial to 1m, slightly hairy but not glandular. Lower leaves oblong to ovate, rounded at base, wrinkled, dark green, usually downy; upper leaves narrower, unstalked. *Flowers in whorls of 6–16*, crowded towards the top; corolla pale yellow with red-purple streaks on lower lip, 15–20mm long. Calyx teeth broad, triangular, hairless, shorter than tube. In dry grassland and scrub; northwards to Belgium and Germany. **Fl**: Jun–Aug. **Br Is dist**: Absent as native, rarely naturalised.

Field Woundwort *Stachys arvensis* A low-growing hairy annual herb with rounded leaves and with *pink, purple-streaked flowers*. Almost throughout on sandy and disturbed acid ground. **Fl**: Apr–Nov. **Br Is dist**: Locally common in the south and west, rarer in the north.

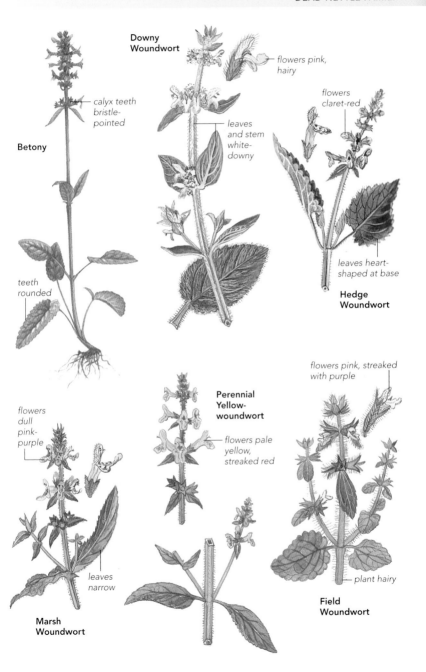

Betony

calyx teeth bristle-pointed

teeth rounded

Downy Woundwort

flowers pink, hairy

leaves and stem white-downy

flowers claret-red

leaves heart-shaped at base

Hedge Woundwort

flowers dull pink-purple

Perennial Yellow-woundwort

flowers pale yellow, streaked red

flowers pink, streaked with purple

leaves narrow

Marsh Woundwort

plant hairy

Field Woundwort

239

Cat-mint

Cat-mint *Nepeta cataria* Perennial mint-scented herb with grey-downy erect stems up to 80cm. Leaves ovate to heart-shaped, stalked, coarsely toothed, grey-woolly below and downy but green above. Inflorescence cylindrical and spike-like, sometimes with separate lower whorls; flowers white with purple spots, 7–12mm, corolla tube curved, upper lip flat and rounded; calyx downy, with straight teeth. On dry banks, grassland and rocky areas, normally calcareous; native as far north as the Netherlands, naturalised northwards into S Scandinavia. **Fl:** Jul–Sep. **Br Is dist:** Only frequent in S and E England and Wales; very rare elsewhere.

Cut-leaved Selfheal

Ground-ivy *Glechoma hederacea* Softly hairy, creeping perennial, rooting at the nodes, flowering stems erect, to 20cm. Leaves rounded, kidney-shaped, toothed, blunt at the tip, long-stalked, to 40mm long. Flowers in whorls of 2–4 with leaf-like bracts; corolla violet-blue, 15–20mm long, with purplish spots on lower lip, tube straight; calyx 2-lipped. Common throughout; in woods, grassland and waste ground. **Fl:** Mar–Jun. **Br Is dist:** Common throughout.

Northern Dragonhead *Dracocephalum ruyschiana* Hairless or slightly hairy perennial, with erect stems to 60cm. Leaves linear-lanceolate, untoothed. Flowers large (20–28mm) blue-violet, held erect in whorls forming a terminal spike. In mountain grassland and open woods; Scandinavia and Germany, local. **Fl:** Jul–Sep. **Br Is dist:** Absent.

Selfheal *Prunella vulgaris* More or less downy creeping herb, with erect flower stems to 20cm. Leaves oval to diamond-shaped, 10–30mm long, untoothed or slightly toothed, pointed and wedge-shaped at base. Flowers violet-blue, 10–15mm, with concave upper lip, in dense, cylindrical, terminal head; bracts purplish and hairy; calyx with 3 short bristle-pointed teeth and 2 long narrow teeth. Widespread and common throughout; in grassy places and open woods, on neutral-calcareous soils. **Fl:** Jun–Oct. **Br Is dist:** Common throughout.

Cut-leaved Selfheal *Prunella laciniata* Similar to Selfheal, but leaves and bracts normally *pinnately lobed*, very downy, and *flowers white*. In grass-lands on calcareous soils; north to Belgium and C Germany. **Fl:** Jun–Oct. **Br Is dist:** Rare in S England only.

Wild Basil *Clinopodium vulgare* Erect, hairy, aromatic herb to 40cm, rarely to 80cm, simple or branched. Leaves ovate, 20–50mm, stalked, rounded or wedge-shaped at base, blunt at tip and shallowly toothed: Flowers bright pinkish-purple, corolla 12–22mm, in dense whorls; calyx tubular, somewhat 2-lipped, curved, hairy and 13-veined; flower bracts linear, about as long as calyx. Widespread and common throughout N Europe except the far north; in dry, often calcareous, habitats. **Fl:** Jun–Sep. **Br Is dist:** Common in the south and east, rarer to the north, absent in the far north.

Wild Marjoram *Origanum vulgare* Erect, sparsely hairy, perennial herb to 70cm. Leaves oval, to 40mm long, stalked, untoothed or slightly toothed, aromatic. Flowers in dense terminal heads, with lower whorls; corolla pinky-purple, 2-lipped, 6–8mm, with tube longer than calyx; stamens protruding; calyx 2-lipped but with 5 equal teeth. Widespread through-out, except the extreme north; in dry grassy usually calcareous habitats. **Fl:** Jul–Sep. **Br Is dist:** Widespread and generally common, but increasingly rare to the north.

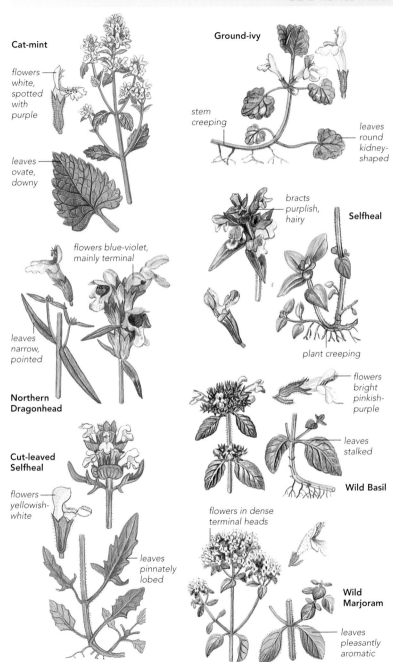

Cat-mint

flowers white, spotted with purple

leaves ovate, downy

Ground-ivy

stem creeping

leaves round kidney-shaped

bracts purplish, hairy

Selfheal

plant creeping

flowers blue-violet, mainly terminal

leaves narrow, pointed

Northern Dragonhead

Cut-leaved Selfheal

flowers yellowish-white

leaves pinnately lobed

flowers bright pinkish-purple

leaves stalked

Wild Basil

flowers in dense terminal heads

Wild Marjoram

leaves pleasantly aromatic

Wild Thyme

Wild Thyme *Thymus polytrichus* Familiar, mat-forming, creeping, slightly aromatic perennial with a woody base. Flower stems ascending, rarely more than 70mm, bluntly 4-angled and *very hairy on opposite faces*, virtually hairless on the other 2 (**a**). Leaves 4–8mm long, rounded to elliptical, short-stalked, flat. Flowers in dense terminal heads, petals rose-purple or pink, 3–4mm; calyx 2-lipped. In a wide range of habitats, usually dry, including short grassland, rocky areas, banks and cliffs; western, locally from Norway southwards. **Fl**: May–Aug. **Br Is dist**: Common throughout.

Large Thyme

Large Thyme *Thymus pulegioides* Generally similar in appearance to Wild Thyme, though larger in most respects, and more strongly thyme-scented. Flower stems *with long hairs on the angles, 2 faces hairless, and 2 shortly hairy* (**b**). Flowers in more or less interrupted spikes of whorls, or in tighter heads in short-grazed grass, up to 20cm tall. Widespread and common in N Europe except in the far north; in dry acid or calcareous banks, grasslands and roadsides. **Fl**: Jun–Aug. **Br Is dist**: Common only in the south, much rarer northwards.

Breckland Thyme *Thymus serpyllum* Very similar to Wild Thyme, differing in that the *flower stems are almost round, with short white hairs all round*; and the leaves are held more erect. On dry, often acid or sandy sites such as dunes, heaths and grasslands; northwards from N France to N Scandinavia. **Fl**: May–Sep. **Br Is dist**: In E Anglia only, in Breckland area.

Gypsywort

Gypsywort *Lycopus europaeus* Variable, erect, rather hairy perennial, sometimes single-stemmed, less often a large, branched plant to 1m. Leaves ovate, but deeply pinnately lobed with narrow lobes, except at tip. Flowers small, 3mm in diameter, with 4 roughly equal corolla lobes, white and in dense whorls well spaced out up stem, each with a pair of lobed bracts. Common in wet habitats such as carr woodlands, pond margins and ditchsides; throughout except the far north. **Fl**: Jun–Sep. **Br Is dist**: Common almost throughout, rarer to the north-east.

MINTS *Mentha* Herbs with flowers divided into 4 nearly equal lobes, with 4 stamens. There are many hybrids involving both native and introduced species.

Water Mint

Corn Mint *Mentha arvensis* Variable perennial, more or less hairy, erect to ascending, to 40cm, pleasantly mint-scented. Leaves oval to elliptical, to 60mm long, short-stalked, blunt, toothed, hairy on both sides. Flowers lilac, 3–4mm long, corolla hairy outside, stamens protruding; calyx bell-shaped, very hairy, with short triangular teeth; in dense well-separated whorls, with bracts much longer than flowers, and *no terminal head*. Common throughout; on paths, arable land, waste ground and damp habitats. **Fl**: May–Oct. **Br Is dist**: Common throughout, though less so in the north.

a

b

Water Mint *Mentha aquatica* Similar in form to Corn Mint, usually taller, to 60cm. Strongly mint-scented. *Flowers in rounded terminal heads*, about 20mm long, with separate whorls below; flowers mauve, stamens projecting, calyx hairy. Very common in wet places or standing water; throughout, except the far north. **Fl**: Jul–Oct. **Br Is dist**: Common throughout.

Wild Thyme *stems squarish, hairy on 2 opposite faces*

erect taller flowering stems **Large Thyme** *stems squarish, with long hairs on angles*

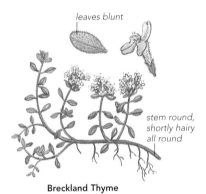

leaves blunt

stem round, shortly hairy all round

Breckland Thyme

Gypsywort

leaves pinnately lobed

flowers very small, white, in axils

spikes without terminal flowers

Corn Mint *bracts much longer than flowers*

terminal heads present

Water Mint

Wild Clary

Deadly Nightshade

Henbane

Spearmint *Mentha spicata* An erect perennial herb, to 90cm with leaves usually green, barely hairy with *a few branched hairs below;* scent of mint sauce. Flower stalks and *calyx tube hairless* (calyx teeth sometimes shortly hairy). Naturalised widely in damp places from its use as a pot herb; almost throughout. **Fl:** Aug–Sep. **Br Is dist:** Naturalised locally.

Meadow Clary *Salvia pratensis* Erect, perennial herb, with stems to 1m, downy at the base, glandular higher up. Basal leaves in a rosette, oval to oblong, heart-shaped at base, long-stalked, wrinkled and toothed. Stem leaves becoming stalkless higher up. Flowers with violet-blue corolla, *20–30mm,* with upper lip strongly curved, in a series of whorls of 4–6 forming a long spike; *calyx downy, without long white hairs;* style long-projecting. North to the Netherlands and C Germany only; in dry grasslands, roadsides and rocky areas; commonest in the south of the area. **Fl:** May–Jul. **Br Is dist:** A rare native in a few S England areas only.

Wild Clary *Salvia verbenaca* Erect, downy perennial to 80cm, little-branched. Rosette leaves with deep irregular jagged teeth or lobes; upper stem leaves, bracts and calyces purplish blue. Flowers in whorled spikes, smaller than Meadow Clary, blue to violet, *8–15mm long, or much smaller* and unopened; *calyx sticky and downy, with long white hairs.* In dry grassy habitats, especially on lime-rich soils, frequent near the coast; in Britain and France only. **Fl:** May–Aug. **Br Is dist:** Locally frequent in S and E England; rare elsewhere.

NIGHTSHADE or POTATO FAMILY Solanaceae

A family of herbs or shrubs, with alternate leaves lacking stipules. Flowers normally regular, with 5 parts and 5 stamens, projecting in a tube in some genera. Ovary superior, forming a capsule or berry. Many members of the family are poisonous, whilst many are food plants.

Deadly Nightshade *Atropa belladonna* Stout, much-branched perennial up to 1.5m, hairless or downy glandular. Leaves oval, pointed, to 20cm long, alternate or opposite. Flowers 1–2, in leaf or branch axils, bell-shaped, hanging, dull purplish-brown or green, 25–30mm long, stalked. Fruit a black, fleshy, glossy, globose berry, 15–20mm in diameter, surrounded by the persistent calyx; highly poisonous, as is the rest of the plant. In scrub, semi-shaded areas and damp places, most commonly on calcareous soils or in mountain areas; widespread as far north as N England and the Netherlands, naturalised elsewhere. **Fl:** Jun–Sep. **Br Is dist:** Locally common, mainly on chalky soils, in S and E England, rarer to the north and west.

Henbane *Hyoscamus niger* Erect, branched or simple, stickily hairy annual or biennial to 80cm. Leaves oval to oblong, roughly toothed or lobed, 10–20cm long and strong-smelling, lower ones stalked, upper ones clasping the stem. Flowers unequally funnel-shaped, 20–30mm across, dull yellowish with purple veins and centre, stalkless in 2 rows in a forked curving inflorescence. Fruit a capsule, 12–20mm in diameter, opening at top. Whole plant poisonous. Widespread and locally common throughout most of N Europe except the far north, on bare, sandy and disturbed ground, most frequently near the sea. **Fl:** Jun–Aug. **Br Is dist:** Local in S and E England, rare elsewhere.

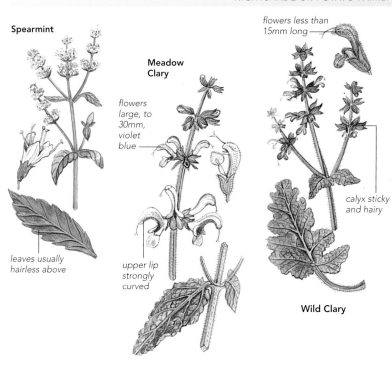

Spearmint

leaves usually hairless above

Meadow Clary

flowers large, to 30mm, violet blue

upper lip strongly curved

flowers less than 15mm long

calyx sticky and hairy

Wild Clary

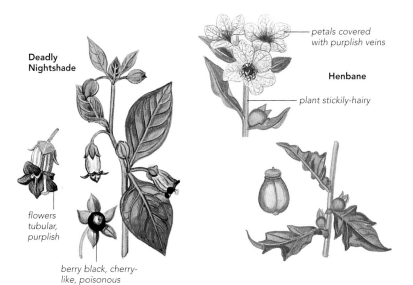

Deadly Nightshade

flowers tubular, purplish

berry black, cherry-like, poisonous

petals covered with purplish veins

Henbane

plant stickily-hairy

Gratiole

a

Black Nightshade *Solanum nigrum* Hairless or downy annual, erect or straggling, to 70cm. Leaves ovate, 30–60mm long, pointed, untoothed or wavy-toothed, not lobed at base and short-stalked. Flowers white with a cone of yellow anthers, 7–10mm in diameter, in stalked clusters of 5–10. Fruit globose, 7–9mm in diameter, becoming black. Common in cultivated and disturbed ground, including gardens; throughout most of N Europe, though probably not native to the north. **Fl:** Jul–Oct. **Br Is dist:** Common in England and Wales; rare in Scotland and Ireland.

Bittersweet, Woody Nightshade *Solanum dulcamara* Woody, rather downy, scrambling perennial, reaching 2m. Leaves ovate, up to 80mm long, usually with distinct spreading lobes at base. Flowers have purple corolla, 10–15mm across, with 5 reflexed lobes and a cone of yellow stamens, in loose clusters of 10–25; fruit an ovoid berry, about 10mm long, green becoming red. Common in various grassy, wooded and semi-shaded habitats, often near water, and occasionally on shingle beaches; throughout except the far north. **Fl:** Jun–Sep. **Br Is dist:** Common throughout except for N Scotland and Ireland where it is rare.

Thorn-apple *Datura stramonium* Stout, erect, branched annual herb up to 1m. Leaves variable, ovate, up to 20cm long, toothed or lobed and long-stalked. Flowers large and trumpet-shaped, up to 10cm in diameter, usually white but occasionally purple, with long tube and 5 petal lobes. Fruit distinctive: large, ovoid, green, robustly spiny capsules, up to 50mm long. All parts highly poisonous. Naturalised on waste and cultivated ground; through much of N Europe except the far north, originally from C and S America. **Fl:** Jun–Oct. **Br Is dist:** An occasional weed, varying in abundance with the weather.

FIGWORT FAMILY Scrophulariaceae
Herbaceous plants, with leaves without stipules. Corolla irregular, usually 5-lobed.

Gratiole *Gratiola officinalis* Perennial hairless herb, with erect 4-angled stems, to 50cm from a creeping base. Leaves linear-lanceolate, finely toothed or untoothed, 20–50mm long, unstalked. Flowers trumpet-shaped, white tinged with purplish-red, 10–18mm long, in pairs from leaf axils. In wet grassy places; northwards to the Netherlands and Germany. **Fl:** May–Sep. **Br Is dist:** Absent.

Mudwort *Limosella aquatica* Hairless annual, creeping by runners that produce rosettes of leaves. Upper leaves with stalks much longer than blade (**a**), lower ones spoon-shaped or linear, up to 12cm long. Flowers small, long-stalked from leaf axils, white or pink with bell-shaped corolla and 5 pointed lobes, 2–5mm in diameter; calyx longer than corolla tube. On muddy pond margins, or areas where water has stood; rare or local but widespread throughout. **Fl:** Jun–Oct. **Br Is dist:** Now very rare, and declining; mainly southern.

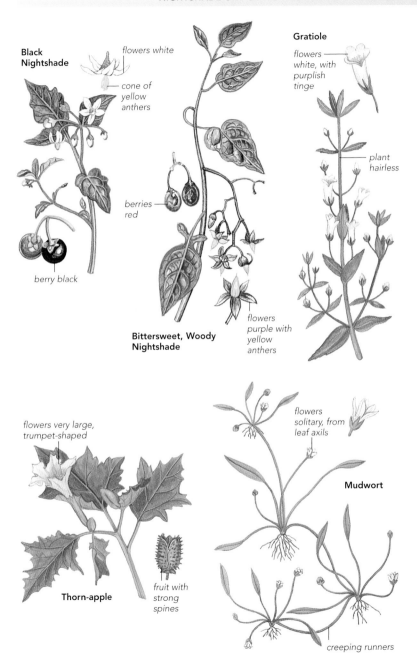

Black Nightshade

flowers white

cone of yellow anthers

berries red

berry black

Gratiole

flowers white, with purplish tinge

plant hairless

Bittersweet, Woody Nightshade

flowers purple with yellow anthers

flowers very large, trumpet-shaped

Thorn-apple

fruit with strong spines

flowers solitary, from leaf axils

Mudwort

creeping runners

Water Figwort

Monkeyflower *Mimulus guttatus* Erect perennial to 50cm, hairless on lower parts, usually glandular-downy above. Leaves opposite, ovate to oblong, to 70mm long, irregularly toothed, lower ones stalked and upper ones clasping. Flowers in loose, leafy inflorescences, large (25–45mm), yellow *corolla dotted with small red spots in the throat*, almost closed by 2 hairy ridges; calyx and flower stalks downy. Introduced from N America, now naturalised, especially along streams, over most of N Europe. **Fl:** Jun–Sep. **Br Is dist:** Widespread and locally common almost throughout.

MULLEINS *Verbascum* Tall, stout, white- or yellow-flowered herbs.

Great Mullein, Aaron's Rod *Verbascum thapsus* Erect, stout, white-woolly biennial up to 2m, with a round, usually unbranched stem. Basal leaves broadly ovate to spoon-shaped, with winged leaf stalks; *stem leaves unstalked, running down stem to next leaf*. Flowers in long thin terminal spikes, occasionally with side branches; petals bright yellow, with 5 roughly equal lobes, 15–35mm in diameter; stamens 5, with the upper 3 having stalks covered with yellow-white hairs, *lower 2 almost hairless*. Common throughout except the extreme north; in dry grassy areas, waste ground and roadsides. **Fl:** Jun–Aug. **Br Is dist:** Common throughout, except N and W Scotland.

Dark Mullein *Verbascum nigrum* Tall, thin plant, not mealy, stems angled. Leaves dark green above, paler below, slightly hairy; lower leaves long-stalked, with heart-shaped bases, upper ones wedge-shaped at base, short-stalked to unstalked. Flowers yellow, 12–20mm in diameter, with dense purple hairs on stalks of all stamens, in long simple or branched spikes. In grassy places, waste ground and roadsides, often on calcareous or sandy soil; north to S Scandinavia. **Fl:** Jun–Sep. **Br Is dist:** Locally common in S and E England, much rarer to the north and west.

Common Figwort *Scrophularia nodosa* Erect perennial to 80cm, from short rhizomes, with *square, unwinged stems* which are hairless below the flowers. Leaves oval, pointed, coarsely toothed, truncated at base and short-stalked. Flowers 10mm long, with greenish tube, and purplish-red upper lip; stamens 4, plus 1 without an anther; calyx 5-lobed, with very *narrow white border*. Common in damp woods, grassland, riverbanks and waste places; through-out, except the far north. **Fl:** Jun–Sep. **Br Is dist:** Common throughout except N Scotland where it is rare.

Water Figwort *Scrophularia auriculata* Similar in character to Common Figwort, but differing mainly in the *markedly 4-winged stems*, the blunt-tipped, round-toothed leaves and the *broad white borders* to the sepal lobes. In wetter habitats, north to the Netherlands, Scotland and Germany. **Fl:** Jun–Sep. **Br Is dist:** Common in England, Wales and Ireland, rarer in Scotland.

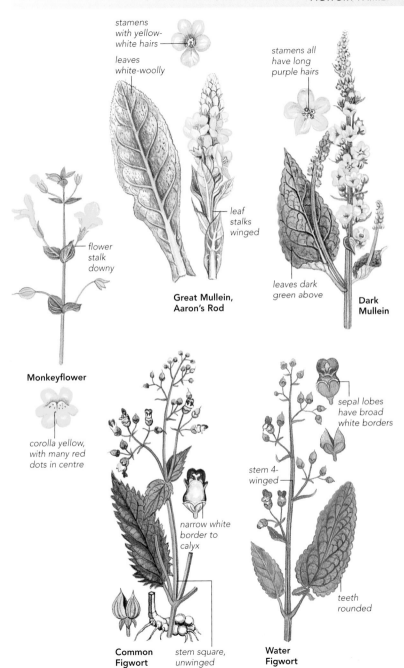

stamens with yellow-white hairs

leaves white-woolly

stamens all have long purple hairs

flower stalk downy

leaf stalks winged

Great Mullein, Aaron's Rod

leaves dark green above

Dark Mullein

Monkeyflower

corolla yellow, with many red dots in centre

sepal lobes have broad white borders

stem 4-winged

narrow white border to calyx

Common Figwort

stem square, unwinged

Water Figwort

teeth rounded

249

Small Toadflax

Pale Toadflax

Balm-leaved Figwort *Scrophularia scorodonia* Similar to Common Figwort (*see* p. 248), but whole plant greyish-downy. Leaves downy on both surfaces, *wrinkled*, double-toothed, with hair-points. Flowers purple, 8–12mm long, sterile, stamen rounded, calyx lobes with broad membranous margins. Very local in open woods, wet places and cliffs; in SW Britain and W France, occasionally abundant. **Fl:** May–Aug. **Br Is dist:** Locally common in SW England and the Channel Islands.

Anarrhinum, Daisy-leaved Toadflax *Anarrhinum bellidifolium* Hairless, erect, biennial or perennial herb to 70cm. Basal leaves variable, spoon-shaped to elliptical, up to 80mm, stalked and blunt; stem leaves numerous, crowded, divided into 3–5 narrow lobes. Flowers blue to pale lilac, 4–5mm, in long slender terminal spikes. On dry banks, walls, and open woodland; very local in N France, commoner in S Europe. **Fl:** May–Jul. **Br Is dist:** Absent.

Snapdragon *Antirrhinum majus* The familiar garden plant. Erect or ascending and bushy, with linear to ovate leaves to 70mm. Flowers large, 30–45mm, unspurred, usually pink or purple, sometimes yellow. Widespread on old walls, and in waste places; only as a naturalised garden escape. **Fl:** Jun–Sep. **Br Is dist:** Local, scattered.

Small Toadflax *Chaenorhinum minus* Erect sticky-downy annual, reaching 25cm, occasionally more. Leaves linear-lanceolate to oblong, to 30mm, alternate, blunt, untoothed, narrowed to short stalk. Flowers 6–8mm, with pale purple corolla, with yellow patch, short-spurred, solitary on long stalks from upper leaf axils. Arable, disturbed and waste ground including roadsides and railways; throughout except the far north. **Fl:** May–Oct. **Br Is dist:** Common throughout except N Scotland.

Pale Toadflax *Linaria repens* Erect, grey-green, hairless perennial to 1m, with creeping rhizome and, often, numerous stems. Leaves linear, to 50mm, whorled on lower part of stem. Flowers with corolla pale lilac or white, 7–14mm, with violet stripes, and an orange spot on the lower lip; *spur straight, about a quarter of the length of corolla*. In dry places, rocky banks, grassland and cultivated soil, often on calcareous soils; from S Sweden southwards, though uncertainly native in northern parts. **Fl:** Jun–Sep. **Br Is dist:** Throughout England and Wales, locally, possibly native.

Common Toadflax *Linaria vulgaris* Erect, almost hairless, grey-green perennial, with erect tufted stems to 80cm from a creeping rhizome. Leaves linear-lanceolate, 30–80mm, mostly alternate, but whorled lower down. Flowers in dense cylindrical terminal inflorescences; corolla yellow with orange central palate, 20–30mm long, with straight, stout long spur; sepals oval and pointed. Common throughout except the extreme north, in grassy places, waste ground, and cultivated land. **Fl:** Jul–Oct. **Br Is dist:** Common almost throughout, though rare in N Scotland, local in Ireland.

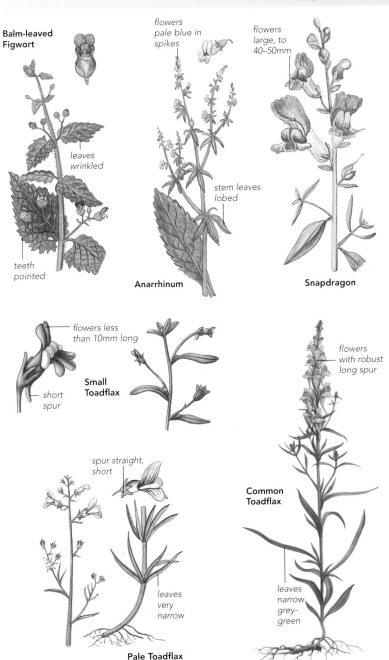

Balm-leaved Figwort

leaves wrinkled

teeth pointed

flowers pale blue in spikes

stem leaves lobed

Anarrhinum

flowers large, to 40–50mm

Snapdragon

flowers less than 10mm long

short spur

Small Toadflax

spur straight, short

leaves very narrow

Pale Toadflax

flowers with robust long spur

Common Toadflax

leaves narrow grey-green

Ivy-leaved Toadflax

Ivy-leaved Toadflax *Cymbalaria muralis* Trailing, hairless, or slightly downy, perennial with purplish stems to 80cm. Leaves roughly ivy-shaped to rounded, fleshy, 20–40mm long, long-stalked, alternate. Flowers solitary from leaf axils, long-stalked, corolla 10–15mm, violet to lilac (occasionally white), with white and yellow palate, spur curved and less than length of corolla. Flower stalks becoming recurved in fruit. Very widely naturalised on rocks and walls; as far north as S Scandinavia; native of S Europe. **Fl:** May–Sep. **Br Is dist:** Commonly naturalised throughout, rare in N∞Scotland.

Sharp-leaved Fluellen

Sharp-leaved Fluellen *Kickxia elatine* Prostrate, hairy, slightly glandular annual, with stems branching from base. Leaves usually *triangular, arrow-shaped*, pointed and stalked (**a**). Flowers solitary, long-stalked from leaf axils, with hairless stalks; corolla yellow with purple upper lip, *spur straight*. In cultivated and waste ground; as far north as S Scandinavia, though only native in the south of area; locally common. **Fl:** Jul–Oct. **Br Is dist:** Local or common in S England; rare or absent elsewhere. Declining.

Round-leaved Fluellen

Round-leaved Fluellen *Kickxia spuria* Very similar to Sharp-leaved Fluellen, but hairier and stickier; *leaves oval* (**b**); flowers with deeper purple upper lip, *spur curved*, flower stalks woolly. Similar habitats and distribution. **Fl:** Jul–Oct. **Br Is dist:** Frequent in S and E England, becoming rare then absent to west and north.

Foxglove

Foxglove *Digitalis purpurea* Erect, unbranched, greyish-downy biennial or perennial reaching 1.8m. Leaves ovate-lanceolate, to 30cm long, downy above, with rounded teeth and winged stalk. Flowers familiar, in long terminal erect racemes; flowers tubular, 40–50mm long, pale purple, reddish pink or white, usually spotted inside; calyx much shorter. Widespread as far north as S Scandinavia; rarer or naturalised to north of range; in open woods, clearings and rocky areas, usually on acid soils. **Fl:** May–Aug. **Br Is dist:** Very common throughout in suitable habitats.

Yellow Foxglove *Digitalis grandiflora* Similar in form to Foxglove, but generally shorter, to 1m. Leaves hairless, to 20cm, and shiny green above. Flowers tubular, 40–50mm long, pale yellow with faint red-brown markings inside, in long terminal racemes. In woods, rocky areas and scrub; from Belgium southwards. **Fl:** Jun–Aug. **Br Is dist:** Absent.

Fairy Foxglove *Erinus alpinus* Tufted perennial, with many erect shoots up to 30cm. Leaves oblong-lanceolate, toothed, in basal rosette. Flowers pinkish-purple, 10–15mm across, with 5 roughly equal lobes, in terminal clusters elongating into spikes. Stony places and mountains; S Germany and C France southwards, naturalised to north. **Fl:** May–Sep. **Br Is dist:** Naturalised in N England and Scotland.

a

b

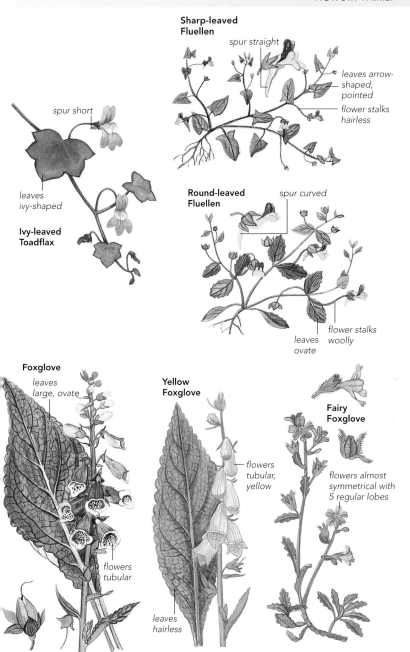

Sharp-leaved Fluellen

spur straight

leaves arrow-shaped, pointed

flower stalks hairless

spur short

leaves ivy-shaped

Ivy-leaved Toadflax

Round-leaved Fluellen

spur curved

flower stalks woolly

leaves ovate

Foxglove

leaves large, ovate

flowers tubular

Yellow Foxglove

flowers tubular, yellow

leaves hairless

Fairy Foxglove

flowers almost symmetrical with 5 regular lobes

253

Rock Speedwell

Spiked Speedwell

Spring Speedwell

SPEEDWELLS *Veronica* Large genus, with some 25 species in N Europe, many of which look superficially similar. Herbaceous annuals or perennials, with opposite leaves. Corolla 4-lobed, flat or cup-shaped; calyx 4-lobed. Fruit flattened and heart-shaped.

Thyme-leaved Speedwell *Veronica serpyllifolia* Perennial herb, with creeping rooting stems to 30cm, more or less hairless; flower stems erect or ascending. Leaves oval, rounded at both ends, 10–20mm long, untoothed or faintly toothed and hairless. Flowers in loose, more or less erect terminal spikes, with oblong bracts longer than flower stalks. Corolla pale blue to white, with darker lines, 6–8mm in diameter; flower stalks longer than calyx; capsule broader than long and roughly equal to calyx (**a**). Common throughout; on bare, cultivated and sparsely grassy habitats, heaths and open woods. **Fl:** Mar–Oct. **Br Is dist:** Common throughout. A mountain form, ssp *humifusa*, has larger flowers (7–10mm), brighter blue, in fewer-flowered inflorescences.

Rock Speedwell *Veronica fruticans* Perennial, with stem woody at base, and numerous ascending, often branching, shoots. Leaves oblong, to 10mm, untoothed or slightly toothed, wedge-shaped at base and almost stalkless. Flowers deep blue, with red-purple centre, 10–15mm in diameter, in rather loose few-flowered terminal clusters. Fruit oval, with a slight notch at tip (**b**). Rocky and grassy habitats, usually in mountains; local from the Alps northwards in suitable habitats. **Fl:** Jul– Sep. **Br Is dist:** Very local in the Scottish Highlands.

Spiked Speedwell *Veronica spicata* Distinctive, erect, downy perennial to 60cm, with several stems arising from a mat. Leaves oval at base of stem, stalked, shallowly toothed, becoming narrower and unstalked farther up. Flowers in conspicuous, dense, long, leafless, many-flowered terminal inflorescences; corolla bright blue, 4–8mm in diameter, with a longish tube and narrow lobes. Fruit rounded (**c**). In dry grassland and rocky outcrops, frequently calcareous; from Scandinavia southwards, though often very local. **Fl:** Jul–Sep. **Br Is dist:** Rare, in grassland in E Anglia and limestone rocks in W England and Wales.

Wall Speedwell *Veronica arvensis* Erect, downy, annual plant, to 25cm but very variable, often much smaller. Leaves triangular to ovate, coarsely round-toothed, to 15mm, lower ones stalked, upper ones unstalked. Flowers in terminal racemes, with upper bracts longer than flowers, flower stalks very short; corolla blue, 2–4mm in diameter. Fruit hairy, *heart-shaped, as long as broad* (**d**). Common in dry open habitats, on old walls, rocky banks and heaths; throughout the area. **Fl:** March–Oct. **Br Is dist:** Common throughout.

Spring Speedwell *Veronica verna* Similar to Wall Speedwell, differing in that it has deeply pinnate 3- to 7-lobed upper leaves, denser more glandular inflorescence, and *capsule broader than long* (**e**). In dry, bare areas; local, throughout except the far north. **Fl:** Apr–Jun. **Br Is dist:** Rare, in Breckland, in E Anglia only.

a

b

c

d

e

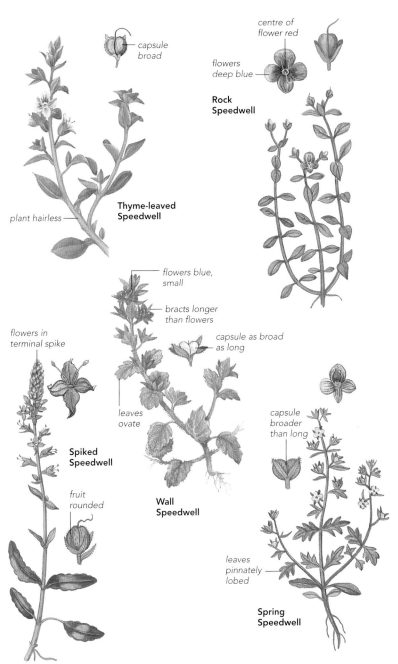

capsule broad

centre of flower red

flowers deep blue

Rock Speedwell

Thyme-leaved Speedwell

plant hairless

flowers blue, small

bracts longer than flowers

capsule as broad as long

flowers in terminal spike

leaves ovate

Spiked Speedwell

fruit rounded

Wall Speedwell

capsule broader than long

leaves pinnately lobed

Spring Speedwell

255

Germander Speedwell

Heath, or Common, Speedwell *Veronica officinalis* Mat-forming, perennial herb, with creeping rooting stems and erect flower spikes; stems hairy all round. Leaves oblong to ovate, 20–30mm, shallowly toothed, hairy on both sides, unstalked. Flowers in long-stalked cylindrical to pyramidal inflorescences from leaf axils; *corolla lilac-blue*, with darker veins, 6–8mm in diameter; flower stalks short, 2mm. Capsule heart-shaped, longer than calyx. Throughout N Europe, except Spitzbergen; common in grassy and heathy places. **Fl**: May–Aug. **Br Is dist**: Common throughout in suitable habitats.

Wood Speedwell

Germander Speedwell *Veronica chamaedrys* Perennial herb with prostrate stems rooting at the nodes, and ascending flower stems; *stems with 2 opposite lines of long white hairs*, otherwise hairless. Leaves oval-triangular, to 30mm, very short-stalked, toothed, hairy. Flowers in loose, long-stalked inflorescences from leaf axils, usually only 1 spike per leaf pair. *Corolla bright blue* with white eye, about 10mm across. Fruit heart-shaped, hairy on margin, shorter than calyx. Common throughout, except the far north; in grassland, scrub and open woods, often on damper ground. **Fl**: Mar–Jul. **Br Is dist**: Common throughout.

Wood Speedwell *Veronica montana* Similar to Germander Speedwell, but differing in that the s*tem is hairy all round;* leaves are distinctly stalked (5–15mm long), light green in colour; *flowers lilac,* smaller (7–9mm); fruit heart-shaped to almost round, and longer than calyx lobes. Common northwards to Denmark and S Sweden; in woods, often on damp or less acid soils. **Fl**: Apr–Jul. **Br Is dist**: Widespread and locally common, normally in ancient woodland; rare in N Scotland.

Marsh Speedwell *Veronica scutellata* Hairless or slightly downy perennial, with creeping and ascending stems. *Leaves linear-lanceolate*, 20–40mm long, unstalked, *often reddish-brown*, few-toothed, pointed. Flowers borne in long-stalked, lax, alternate inflorescences from leaf axils; flower stalks 7–10mm, much longer than bracts; *corolla pale pink-lilac*, or white, often with purplish lines, 6–7mm in diameter. Fruit flat, broader than long, much longer than calyx. Locally common throughout, except the extreme north; in bogs, marshy areas and pondsides. **Fl**: Jun–Aug. **Br Is dist**: Locally common throughout.

Brooklime *Veronica beccabunga* Hairless perennial, with creeping rooting stems, then ascending, rather fleshy. *Leaves oval-oblong*, rounded at base, blunt, 30–60mm long, thick, shallowly toothed and short-stalked. Flowers in paired racemes from leaf axils; flower bracts narrow, roughly equal to flower stalks; *corolla blue*, sometimes with red centre, 7–8mm in diameter; fruit rounded and shorter than calyx. In wet places and standing water; common throughout, except in Arctic region. **Fl**: May–Sep. **Br Is dist**: Common throughout.

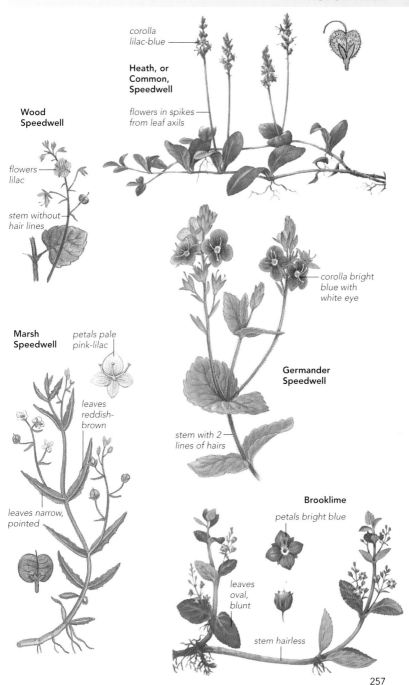

corolla
lilac-blue

**Heath, or
Common,
Speedwell**

**Wood
Speedwell**

flowers in spikes
from leaf axils

flowers
lilac

stem without
hair lines

corolla bright
blue with
white eye

**Marsh
Speedwell**

petals pale
pink-lilac

leaves
reddish-
brown

**Germander
Speedwell**

stem with 2
lines of hairs

leaves narrow,
pointed

Brooklime

petals bright blue

leaves
oval,
blunt

stem hairless

257

Cornish Moneywort

Blue Water-speedwell *Veronica anagallis-aquatica* Hairless perennial (sometimes glandular-hairy amongst flowers), with short-creeping rhizome and ascending stems to 30cm. *Leaves lanceolate-slightly oval and pointed, to 12cm long,* slightly toothed and unstalked. Flowers in paired, long racemes from leaf axils; flower stalk at least as long as bract, becoming erect after flowering; *corolla pale blue,* 5–6mm in diameter. Fruit almost round, slightly notched, slightly longer than broad. In wet places, water and damp woods; throughout except the far north, common. **Fl:** Jun–Aug. **Br Is dist:** Locally common throughout in suitable habitats.

Crested Cow-wheat

Common Field-speedwell *Veronica persica* Procumbent, hairy, branched annual to 60cm long. Leaves triangular to ovate, 10–30mm long, short-stalked, light green, coarsely toothed and hairy below. Flowers solitary in leaf axils, stalks longer than leaves; corolla blue, *with white lower lip,* 8–12mm in diameter; calyx lobes oval, pointed and hairy, spreading when in fruit. Fruit hairy and twice as wide as long, with 2 divergent sharp-edged lobes (a). Common throughout, except in the extreme north, though almost certainly not native anywhere in area; in cultivated and bare ground. **Fl:** All year. **Br Is dist:** Common throughout.

Ivy-leaved Speedwell *Veronica hederifolia* Hairy, spreading annual, branched from the base. Leaves kidney-shaped, palmately lobed like ivy leaf, to 15mm long. Flowers in leaf axils on stalks shorter than leaves; corolla pale blue or lilac, shorter than calyx and 4–5mm in diameter; calyx lobes oval and heart-shaped at base. Fruit broader than long, barely flattened and hairless. Widespread and common throughout N Europe, except Arctic regions; in cultivated land, waste ground and woodlands. **Fl:** March–Aug. **Br Is dist:** Common and widespread, though much rarer in the north.

Crested Cow-wheat *Melampyrum cristatum* Erect, finely hairy annual to 50cm, usually unbranched. Leaves lanceolate, to 10cm, unstalked, toothed or untoothed, in opposite pairs. *Flowers in dense 4-angled spikes,* with conspicuous narrowly heart-shaped bracts, curved back. Bracts have short, 2mm-long teeth on the lower half and are often pinky purple, but untoothed and green on the other half; corolla yellow suffused with purple, 12–16mm long. Widespread in N Europe except in the far north; on roadsides, rough grass and wood-borders. **Fl:** Jun– Sep. **Br Is dist:** Rare, in C E England only.

Cornish Moneywort *Sibthorpia europaea* Slender, creeping perennial, with stems rooting at the nodes, hairy. Leaves alternate, kidney-shaped, to 20mm diameter, 5- to 7-lobed and long-stalked. Flowers solitary and short-stalked, 2 corolla lobes yellow and 3 pink, 1–2mm in diameter; 4 stamens. Very local, though occasionally common, in damp shady habitats in W France and S Britain only. **Fl:** Jul–Oct. **Br Is dist:** Very local in S and SW Britain only.

Slender Speedwell *Veronica filiformis* Downy perennial plant, with numerous creeping stems, often forming mats. Leaves small, 5–10mm, short-stalked, rounded to kidney-shaped, with rounded teeth, opposite on non-flower stems, alternate on flower stems. Flowers blue with white lip, 8–10mm in diameter, stalks 2–3 times length of leaves. Fruit rarely produced. Native of Caucasus area, but now widespread in N Europe as far north as S Sweden; in lawns, pastures and waste places. **Fl:** Apr–Jul. **Br Is dist:** Widespread, locally common in S Britain.

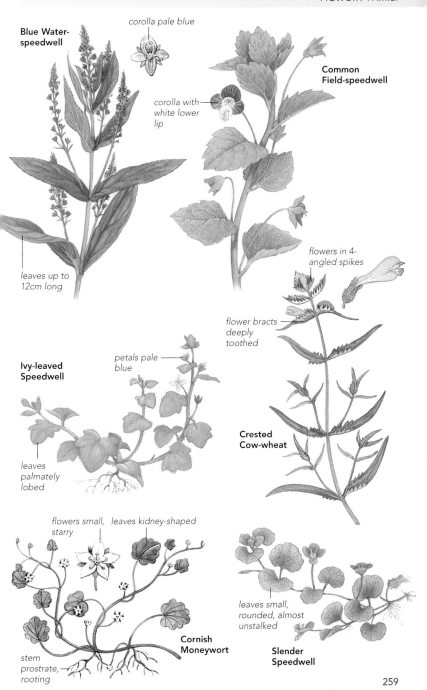

Blue Water-speedwell

corolla pale blue

corolla with white lower lip

Common Field-speedwell

leaves up to 12cm long

flowers in 4-angled spikes

flower bracts deeply toothed

Ivy-leaved Speedwell

petals pale blue

leaves palmately lobed

Crested Cow-wheat

flowers small, starry *leaves kidney-shaped*

leaves small, rounded, almost unstalked

Cornish Moneywort

stem prostrate, rooting

Slender Speedwell

259

Field Cow-wheat

Melampyrum nemorosum

Small Cow-wheat

Field Cow-wheat *Melampyrum arvense* Similar to Crested Cow-wheat (*see* p. 258), but *spikes cylindrical* not 4-sided, and slightly looser; bracts more or less erect, with long teeth (to 8mm), *not heart-shaped at base*, bright rosy red. Corolla yellow and pink, 20–25mm long. In arable fields, grassland and roadsides; local, from S Finland southwards. **Fl:** May–Oct. **Br Is dist:** Rare and local in scattered S England localities.

Melampyrum nemorosum Beautiful and distinctive species, rather similar to Field Cow-wheat, but with wider leaves, *violet bracts* and *yellow and violet flowers.* In woods, grassland and scrub; mainly Scandinavian extending south into Germany. **Fl:** Jun–Sep. **Br Is dist:** Absent.

Common Cow-wheat *Melampyrum pratense* Very variable, hairless or slightly bristly annual, single or branched, erect or ascending, to 40cm high. Leaves oval-lanceolate, to 80mm, short-stalked or unstalked untoothed; bracts leaf-like, but usually toothed at base. Flowers paired in axils, turned to the same side; corolla pale yellowish-white, 10–18mm, much longer than calyx; with *corolla mouth virtually closed;* calyx teeth erect. Common and widespread throughout, except in the extreme north; in woods, scrub and heaths. **Fl:** May–Sep. **Br Is dist:** Locally common throughout, usually on acid soils.

Small Cow-wheat *Melampyrum sylvaticum* Similar to Common Cow-wheat, but smaller; *corolla golden yellow,* only 8–10mm long, *mouth of tube open,* with the lower lip bent back, tube roughly equal to calyx; calyx teeth spreading. In birchwoods and pinewoods, moorlands and grassy areas; common in Scandinavia, but rarer and mainly in mountains farther south. **Fl:** Jun–Sep. **Br Is dist:** Rare and local, in N England and Scotland only; very rare in Ireland.

Red Bartsia *Odontites vernus* Erect, branching, downy annual to 50cm, often purple-tinged. Leaves oblong-lanceolate, 10–30mm long, usually few-toothed and unstalked. Flowers in long, branched, leafy terminal inflorescences; corolla reddish-pink, 8–10mm, 2-lipped, tube about equalling calyx; anthers slightly protruding. Capsule downy and more or less equalling calyx. In meadows, pastures, tracks, roadsides and disturbed ground; throughout except the extreme north, generally common. **Fl:** Jun–Sep. **Br Is dist:** Common throughout.

Yellow Odontites *Odontites luteus* Generally similar to Red Bartsia, with untoothed or slightly toothed linear leaves; flowers bright yellow, anthers markedly protruding. Dry grassland and scrub; extending into N France from S Europe. **Fl:** Jul–Sep. **Br Is dist:** Absent.

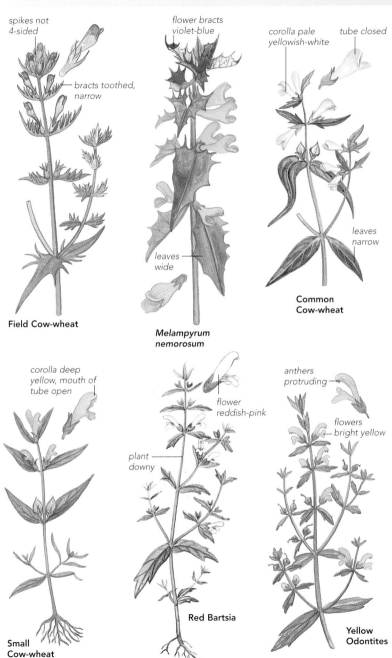

spikes not 4-sided

bracts toothed, narrow

Field Cow-wheat

flower bracts violet-blue

leaves wide

Melampyrum nemorosum

corolla pale yellowish-white

tube closed

leaves narrow

Common Cow-wheat

corolla deep yellow, mouth of tube open

Small Cow-wheat

flower reddish-pink

plant downy

Red Bartsia

anthers protruding

flowers bright yellow

Yellow Odontites

261

Alpine Bartsia *Bartsia alpina* Erect, downy, unbranched perennial to 30cm, from a short rhizome. Leaves opposite, unstalked, oval, 10–20mm long and blunt, with rounded teeth; bracts similar, purplish and decreasing in size up stem, but longer than calyx. Flowers in short few-flowered terminal inflorescence; corolla dull dark purple, 15–20mm long, upper lip longer than lower. In damp base-rich habitats, frequently in mountains; in Scandinavia, then confined to mountains farther south. Fl: Jun–Aug. **Br Is dist:** Rare, in N England and parts of Scotland only.

Yellow Bartsia *Parentucellia viscosa* Erect, very *sticky-hairy*, unbranched annual to 50cm, usually less. Leaves lanceolate, to 40mm, toothed, pointed and unstalked. Flowers in long, loose terminal inflorescence with leaf-like bracts; corolla yellow, 16–24mm long, with 3-lobed lower lip much longer than upper; calyx tubular with 4 triangular teeth. Local in W Europe from France and Scotland southwards; often near the coast, in grassy and sandy habitats. Fl: Jun–Oct. **Br Is dist:** Local, mainly in SW Britain, extending to SW Scotland.

LOUSEWORTS *Pedicularis* Perennial or occasionally annual herbs, semi-parasitic on other herbs. Leaves alternate or whorled, usually deeply divided pinnately. Flowers in dense terminal, often leafy, spikes. Corolla 2-lipped, upper lip compressed and hooded, lower lip 3-lobed and flatter. 4 stamens.

Moor-king *Pedicularis sceptrum-carolinae* Large and distinctive species, with erect stems to 80cm, often reddish. Basal leaves in a rosette, lanceolate in shape but pinnately lobed with oval segments; stem leaves few. Flowers most often in whorls of 3 in a long, lax spike; corolla large, to 32mm, erect, pale dirty yellow with orange-red margins to lower lip; corolla mouth usually closed with lower lip wrapped around upper. In boggy areas, marshes and wet woodlands; in the lowlands of Scandinavia, extending south into Germany. Fl: Jun–Aug. **Br Is dist:** Absent.

Leafy Lousewort *Pedicularis foliosa* Distinctive species with long, finely divided leaves, and leafy conical spikes of large (to 25mm) pale yellow flowers. In meadows and damp areas in mountains only; from the Vosges southwards. Fl: Jun–Aug. **Br Is dist:** Absent.

Marsh Lousewort, Red Rattle *Pedicularis palustris* Virtually hairless erect *annual*, reaching *60cm*, with a single branching stem. Leaves oblong in outline, to 60mm long, but deeply lobed pinnately, with toothed lobes. Flowers in loose leafy spikes; corolla pinky purple, 20–25mm, 2-lipped, *upper lip with 4 teeth* (a); calyx tubular, inflated at base, with 2 leafy lobes. Common and widespread in marshes, bogs and wet heaths and fens, though usually on slightly acid soils; throughout except the far north. Fl: May–Sep. **Br Is dist:** Locally common and widespread, though decreasing through drainage. Much more scarce in C and S England.

a

Lousewort *Pedicularis sylvatica* Rather similar to Marsh Lousewort, but perennial, *shorter, to 20cm*, with many branches spreading from the base. Inflorescence fewer flowered; corolla paler pink, with *upper lip 2-toothed* (b); calyx 5-angled with 4 small leafy lobes. In bogs, heaths, moors, damp grassland and open woods, usually acid; frequent in N to C Sweden. Fl: Apr–Jul. **Br Is dist:** Locally common almost throughout, especially in the west and north; scarce in C England.

b

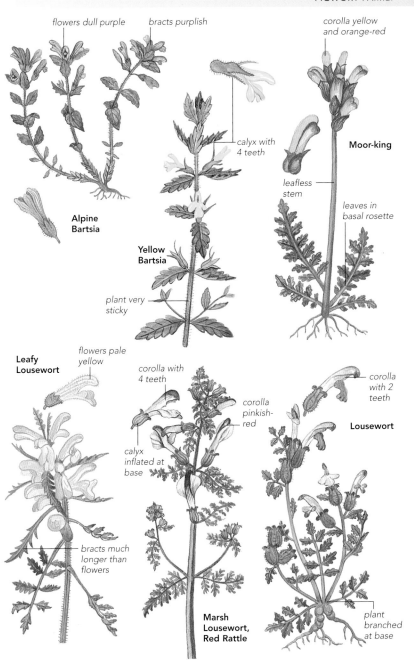

flowers dull purple

bracts purplish

corolla yellow
and orange-red

calyx with
4 teeth

Moor-king

**Alpine
Bartsia**

leafless
stem

leaves in
basal rosette

**Yellow
Bartsia**

plant very
sticky

**Leafy
Lousewort**

flowers pale
yellow

corolla with
4 teeth

corolla
pinkish-
red

corolla
with 2
teeth

Lousewort

calyx
inflated at
base

bracts much
longer than
flowers

**Marsh
Lousewort,
Red Rattle**

plant
branched
at base

263

Toothwort

EYEBRIGHTS *Euphrasia* Annual, short, branched or simple, semi-parasitic herbs. Leaves opposite or alternate in upper part of stem. Flowers in leafy terminal inflorescences; corolla white, often with yellow and purple, 4–11mm, 2-lipped, with upper lip 2-lobed and lower lip 3-lobed. The eyebrights are a distinctive but very difficult group. Some 30 species occur in this area, but they are not readily identifiable by normal means, and samples from a population are often required, combined with extremely close examination.

Eyebright *Euphrasia nemorosa* Erect plant to 35cm, with 1 to 9 pairs of ascending branches, often purplish. Leaves oval-triangular, 2–12mm, hairy below, sharply toothed; bracts (with flowers) oval, sharp-toothed and rounded at base. Flowers white to lilac, 5–7. 5mm long, lower lip longer than upper. Fruit more than twice as long as wide and hairy. In grassy places and open woods; throughout N Europe. **Fl:** Jul–Sep. **Br Is dist:** Common in England and Wales, uncommon in Scotland and Ireland.

YELLOW-RATTLES *Rhinanthus* Small, but difficult group of annual semi-parasitic herbs, with opposite leaves, and leafy spikes of flowers. Corolla usually yellow, 2-lipped, with a long tube. Stamens 4 included in the upper lip.

Yellow-rattle *Rhinanthus minor* Erect, almost hairless annual to 50cm, often with black-spotted stem. Leaves oblong to linear-lanceolate, 5–15mm wide, with rounded or pointed teeth, directed towards the leaf tip; bracts similar but more triangular, strongly toothed at base and pointed. Flowers in long, leafy terminal inflorescences; corolla yellow, 2-lipped, 13–15mm long, upper lip with 2 short violet teeth (about 1mm); calyx flattened, becoming inflated when in fruit, hairless except for the margins. Common almost throughout; in grasslands, especially meadows and dunes. **Fl:** May–Sep. **Br Is dist:** Common and widespread.

Although formerly regarded as part of the Scrophulariaceae, the genus *Lathraea* is now normally placed in the Broomrape family, Orobanchaceae.

Toothwort *Lathraea squamaria* Distinctive plant, wholly parasitic on the roots of Hazel, Maple and other woody plants. Stout and erect, with white or pink stems to 30cm. Leaves scale-like, alternate, clasping and untoothed. Flowers 15–17mm long, in a 1-sided spike with scale-like bracts; corolla pinky white, tubular and exceeding calyx; calyx with 4 equal lobes (compare with broomrapes, *see* pp. 266–8, which have a 2-lipped calyx). Widespread and locally common, though absent from the far north; mainly in woods on base-rich soils. **Fl:** March–May. **Br Is dist:** Widespread but local, northwards to mid-Scotland. Often included in the Broomrape family, but now thought to be closer to the Figwort family.

GLOBULARIA FAMILY Globulariaceae
A small family of low herbs, with alternate untoothed leaves. Flowers with 5 parts, in dense heads; stamens 4; ovary superior (compare with inferior in similar Scabious species, pp. 276–8, or Sheep's-bit, p. 282.)

Common Globularia *Globularia vulgaris* Hairless perennial evergreen herb, with a rosette of stalked, oval to spoon-shaped leaves, notched or 3-toothed at tip, lateral veins barely visible on top surface; stems erect and unbranched, to 20cm. Stem leaves alternate, stalkless, lanceolate. Flowers in dense, rounded terminal heads, 20–25mm in diameter; corolla blue, tubular, 2-lipped. In S Sweden only. **Fl:** Apr–Jul. **Br Is dist:** Absent.

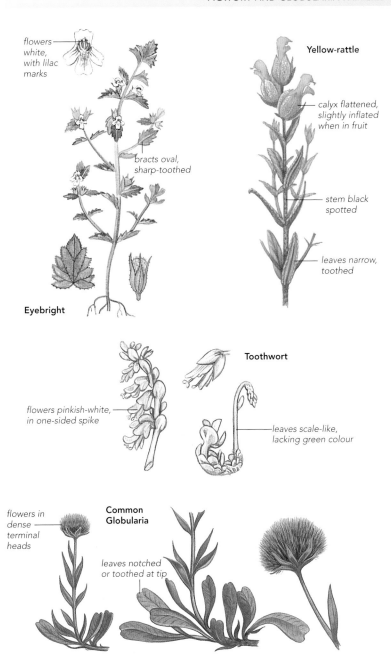

flowers white, with lilac marks

Yellow-rattle

calyx flattened, slightly inflated when in fruit

stem black spotted

bracts oval, sharp-toothed

leaves narrow, toothed

Eyebright

flowers pinkish-white, in one-sided spike

Toothwort

leaves scale-like, lacking green colour

flowers in dense terminal heads

Common Globularia

leaves notched or toothed at tip

Yarrow Broomrape

BROOMRAPE FAMILY Orobanchaceae

Annual or perennial herbs, parasitic on a variety of other plants by means of root tubers. Plants totally lacking chlorophyll. Flower stems erect, with spikes of tubular 2-lipped flowers; stamens 4. The host plant, where known, can be a useful but not diagnostic aid to identification.

Yarrow Broomrape *Orobanche purpurea* Erect, unbranched stems to 60cm, minutely hairy and bluish. Flowers bluish-violet, with deeper violet veins, 18–25mm; stigma white or pale blue. Parasitic on Yarrow, occasionally other composites. Local N to SE Sweden; in rough grassy areas. **Fl:** Jun–Jul. **Br Is dist:** Rare and local in scattered localities south of a line from Lincolnshire to SW Wales, only on Yarrow.

Thistle Broomrape *Orobanche reticulata* Similar in form to Common Broomrape, though generally larger, to 70cm. Flowers barely fragrant; corolla 15–25mm, yellow with purple margins, lower lip with 3 equal lobes; filaments slightly hairy or hairless; stigma lobes touching, *dark purple*. On thistles, Scabious and relatives, in grasslands; as far north as S Scandinavia. **Fl:** Jun–Aug. **Br Is dist:** Very rare, only in Yorkshire.

Common Broomrape

Common Broomrape *Orobanche minor* Spikes to 50cm, usually yellowish flushed purple. Corolla usually pale yellow-tinged or veined with purple, 10–18mm long, with *back of tube arched in a smooth curve;* upper lip notched to 2-lobed, lower lip with 3 roughly equal lobes. Filaments hairy below (**a1**); stigmas purple (occasionally yellow, in pale yellow corolla), with separated lobes (**a2**). Most commonly parasitic on a variety of legumes, especially clovers, but also on many other herbaceous species. From the Netherlands and Germany southwards. **Fl:** Jun–Sep. **Br Is dist:** Common to the south and east, but rare or absent farther west and north. Spp *maritima* Similar to Common Broomrape, but corolla white or cream, tinged with violet; *bracts longer* (12–22mm rather than 7–15mm), stamens inserted 3–5mm above base of corolla (not 2–3mm). On Sea Holly, Wild Carrot, and various other herbs; from N France and S Britain southwards, local. **Fl:** Jun–Aug. **Br Is dist:** Isle of Wight and Channel Islands only.

Knapweed Broomrape

a1 a2

Knapweed Broomrape *Orobanche elatior* Relatively tall plant to 70cm, slightly glandular hairy, stem slightly swollen at base, yellowish or reddish. Bracts as long as flowers. Flowers numerous in dense long spike; corolla yellow, usually purple-tinged, 18–25mm, *evenly curved on the back;* corolla-lobes finely toothed, not hairy; filaments hairy below (**b1**), attached half-way up corolla tube; stigma-lobes (**b2**) yellow. Scattered in grassy areas; from Denmark and S Sweden southwards, parasitic on *Centaurea* species and other composites. **Fl:** Jun–Jul. **Br Is dist:** Locally common in parts of S and E England, usually on shallow calcareous soils; rarer to the north and west, absent from Scotland.

b1 b2

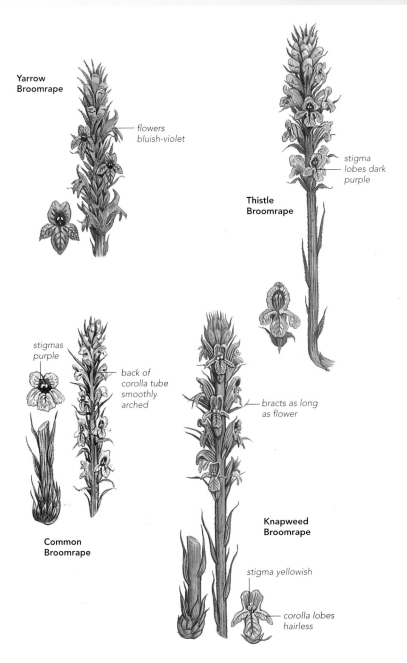

Yarrow Broomrape

flowers bluish-violet

stigma lobes dark purple

Thistle Broomrape

stigmas purple

back of corolla tube smoothly arched

bracts as long as flower

Common Broomrape

Knapweed Broomrape

stigma yellowish

corolla lobes hairless

Greater Broomrape

Greater Broomrape *Orobanche rapum-genistae* Large, often clumped plant to 80cm tall, with stout yellowish stems, *strongly swollen at bases;* flower spike long and dense. Bracts longer than flowers. Corolla 20–25mm, yellowish, tinged purple, with back curved evenly; upper lip barely lobed and untoothed; *filaments hairless at base,* with a few glands at top (**a1**), stamens attached at base of corolla tube; stigma lobes separated (**a2**), yellow. Parasitic on Broom, Gorse and related shrubs, in dry grassy areas. Generally rare and declining, from the Netherlands and C Germany southwards. **Fl:** May–Jul. **Br Is dist:** Widespread to S Scotland, but local and rare, decreasing.

Pale Butterwort

BLADDERWORT FAMILY Lentibulariaceae

A distinctive family of small carnivorous herbs. Corolla 2-lipped, 5-lobed; calyx 5-lobed; stamens 2, attached to corolla. Fruit a many-seeded capsule. All species grow in wet places, often nutrient-poor, and have the ability to digest insects.

Pale Butterwort *Pinguicula lusitanica* Small plant, with an overwintering rosette of 5–12 *pale grey-green*, oblong, blunt leaves, 10–20mm long, with rolled-up margins. Flowers on stalks up to 12cm long, downy, slender, 1–8 together; *corolla pale lilac-pink,* 7–9mm, yellow in throat; lobes of upper lip rounded, spur short (2–4mm), blunt and cylindrical. Locally frequent in bogs and wet heaths; in W Britain and W France only. **Fl:** Jun–Oct. **Br Is dist:** Strongly western in distribution, from Hampshire to NW Scotland, and throughout Ireland.

Alpine Butterwort

Hairy Butterwort *Pinguicula villosa* Similar to Pale Butterwort, but overwintering as bud; leaves more rounded; *flower stalks very glandular-hairy;* corolla pale violet. Only in bogs; from C Sweden northwards. **Fl:** Jun–Aug. **Br Is dist:** Absent.

Alpine Butterwort *Pinguicula alpina* Easily recognised species. Leaves yellowish-green, overwintering as bud. *Flowers white with yellow spot at mouth,* 8–16mm. In bogs and other wet places; throughout Arctic Europe, and in mountains farther south. **Fl:** Jun–Aug. **Br Is dist:** Extinct, formerly in N Scotland.

Large-flowered Butterwort

Large-flowered Butterwort *Pinguicula grandiflora* Overwinters as bud. Leaves in rosettes of 5–8, ovate to oblong, to 60mm long, bright yellow-green. Flower stalks to 18cm; corolla violet or paler, *25–30mm wide,* with long white purple-streaked patch at throat; *lobes of lower lip partially overlapping,* rounded and wavy. Spur 10–12mm, straight and backwardly directed, occasionally notched at tip. In bogs, wet rocks, flushed areas; in SW Ireland and mountains from Jura southwards. **Fl:** May–Jul. **Br Is dist:** SW Ireland, locally common; introduced in Cornwall.

Common Butterwort

Common Butterwort *Pinguicula vulgaris* Rather similar to Large-flowered Butterwort, but smaller; flower stalks to 15cm; *corolla violet, 11–13mm wide,* with broad clear white patch at throat; *lobes of lower lip well separated and flat.* Spur 4–7mm, tapering to a point, slender. In bogs, fens and flushes, often calcareous; throughout the area, though absent from many southern lowland areas. **Fl:** May–Jul. **Br Is dist:** Common in the north and west, but rare or absent in much of SE England.

a1   a2

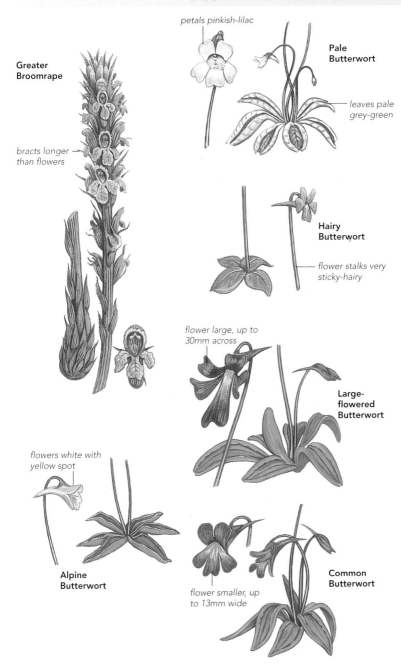

Greater Broomrape

bracts longer than flowers

petals pinkish-lilac

Pale Butterwort

leaves pale grey-green

Hairy Butterwort

flower stalks very sticky-hairy

flower large, up to 30mm across

Large-flowered Butterwort

flowers white with yellow spot

Alpine Butterwort

flower smaller, up to 13mm wide

Common Butterwort

BLADDERWORTS *Utricularia* Loosely rooted aquatic plants, with erect emergent flower spikes and horizontal submerged stems with finely divided leaves; small, flask-shaped bladders which trap minute invertebrates.

Lesser Bladderwort *Utricularia minor* Main leaves finely divided into thread-like untoothed segments, only 3–10mm long, without bristles. Inflorescences 4–15cm tall, with 2–6 flowers; *corolla pale yellow, small* (6–8mm), with short blunt spur. In pools in bogs and other acid waters; throughout though local. **Fl:** Jun–Sep. **Br Is dist:** Throughout, but local; mainly in NW Britain, though frequent in bogs in C and S England.

Lesser Bladderwort

Greater Bladderwort *Utricularia vulgaris* Stems up to 1m long bearing pinnately divided leaves, to 30mm long, toothed with *1 or more bristles on teeth.* Inflorescence to 30cm tall, 4–10 flowers; *corolla deep yellow,* 12–18mm long, *upper lip same length as central palate,* lower lip with vertically turned-back margin; spur conical and pointed. In still waters, up to about 1m deep; almost throughout, but local. **Fl:** Jul–Aug. **Br Is dist:** Widespread but mainly eastern, most frequently in calcareous waters.

Greater Bladderwort

PLANTAIN FAMILY Plantaginaceae

Herbs, usually with leaves in basal rosettes. Flowers usually in terminal inflorescences; very small, with reduced 4-lobed calyx and corolla, and 4 long conspicuous stamens. Normally hermaphrodite, but unisexual in *Littorella* (see p. 272).

Greater Plantain *Plantago major* Perennial herb with basal rosette. Leaves broadly ovate to elliptical, up to 25cm long, 3- to 9-veined, usually hairless, narrowing abruptly into a petiole about as long as blade (**a**). Flower heads on unfurrowed hairy stalks, 10–15cm long, carrying long thin dense spike of flowers; corolla yellowish white, 3mm in diameter, anthers lilac then yellowish. Widespread throughout, and very common, in open cultivated and disturbed habitats. **Fl:** Jun–Oct. **Br Is dist:** Common throughout. Ssp *winteri* has leaves 3- to 5-veined, gradually narrowing into stalk; blade thin; yellowish-green. Widespread in saline habitats. Br Absent.

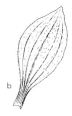

Hoary Plantain *Plantago media* Similar to Greater Plantain, but differs in that the leaves are elliptical (**b**), greyish-downy, *gradually narrowing into a short stalk,* forming a flat rosette. Inflorescence cylindrical on long unfurrowed stalk (up to 30cm long), much longer than leaves. Flowers whitish, 2mm in diameter, scented; *filaments purple, anthers lilac.* In dry, grassy places, often on calcareous soils; widespread and frequent almost throughout. **Fl:** May–Aug. **Br Is dist:** Common in England, but rare elsewhere.

Ribwort Plantain *Plantago lanceolata* Basal leaves in a spreading rosette; *leaves lanceolate,* up to 20cm long (occasionally 30cm), with 3–5 strongly marked almost parallel veins, usually short-stalked. Inflorescence on long deeply furrowed stalks, up to 45cm, much longer than leaves; inflorescence short, usually less than 20mm; *corolla brownish,* 4mm in diameter; *stamens long and white.* In cultivated and waste land, grassy places and roadsides; almost throughout, very common. **Fl:** Apr–Oct. **Br Is dist:** Common and widespread.

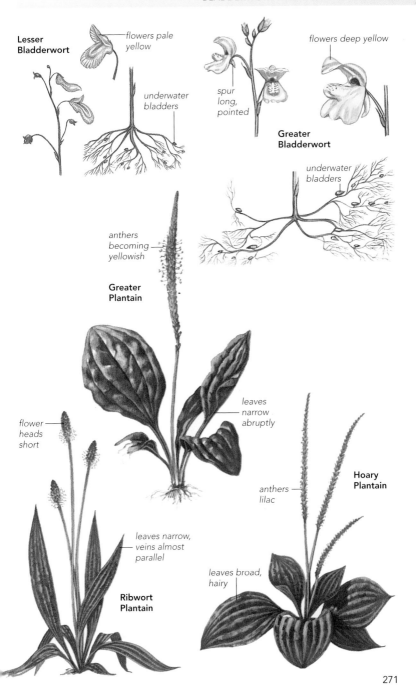

Lesser Bladderwort

flowers pale yellow

underwater bladders

flowers deep yellow

spur long, pointed

Greater Bladderwort

underwater bladders

anthers becoming yellowish

Greater Plantain

leaves narrow abruptly

flower heads short

leaves narrow, veins almost parallel

Ribwort Plantain

Hoary Plantain

anthers lilac

leaves broad, hairy

271

Buck's-horn Plantain *Plantago coronopus* Distinctive plantain, with flat rosette of deeply pinnately divided leaves, to 20cm, 1-veined, with linear segments (though occasionally just toothed). Flower spikes numerous, with arching stems exceeding the leaves; spikes 20–40mm long; corolla brownish, lobes without a midrib, stamens yellow; bracts of flower spike with long spreading points. Common and widespread; in coastal habitats, less common on disturbed ground and grassland inland, mainly on sand or gravel soils. **Fl:** May–Jul. **Br Is dist:** Common around the coasts, and inland in the south and east.

Buck's-horn Plantain

Sea Plantain *Plantago maritima* Plant with woody rootstock and erect, loose rosette of linear, fleshy, faintly 3- to 5-veined, *untoothed leaves*. Flower stalks numerous, stout, unfurrowed, bearing cylindrical inflorescence 20–60mm long. Flowers about 3mm in diameter, corolla brownish with darker midrib, stamens pale yellow; flower bracts oval and appressed. Widespread and locally common throughout; mainly coastal but also on saline soils inland, and some mountains. **Fl:** Jun–Aug. **Br Is dist:** Widespread around coasts, most frequently in salt-marshes, and local in mountains.

Sea Plantain

Branched Plantain *Plantago arenaria* Differs from other plantains in its branched inflorescence, with many egg-shaped flower clusters; leaves linear, not fleshy. Annual. An uncommon casual, occasionally naturalised, in dry sandy places; north to the Netherlands. Native to S Europe. **Fl:** May–Aug. **Br Is dist:** Occasional.

Shoreweed *Littorella uniflora* Dwarf, hairless perennial; aquatic, with slender rooting stolons. Leaves in erect basal rosettes, narrowly linear to 10cm, semi-circular in section, spongy, with sheathing bases. Flowers unisexual: male flowers solitary on slender flower stalks 50–80mm long, with 4 tiny, whitish petals, and 4 long-stalked, white stamens; female flowers short-stalked, several at base of male stalk, with 10mm long style. Margins of lakes and ponds, usually acidic, to a depth of 4m. Local, but widespread almost throughout, except the far north. **Fl:** Jun–Aug. **Br Is dist:** Locally common in Ireland and N Britain, rarer in the south and east.

Shoreweed

HONEYSUCKLE FAMILY Caprifoliaceae
Woody perennial shrubs, occasionally herbs, with opposite, paired leaves. Flowers usually in 5 parts, often tubular; calyx small. Ovary inferior, fruit usually fleshy.

Twinflower

Twinflower *Linnaea borealis* Low, creeping, evergreen subshrub, with long trailing stems. Leaves oval to almost round, 10–15mm long, bluntly toothed, in rather distant opposite pairs. Flowers usually paired, on erect glandular-downy stalks to 80mm, with flowers often hanging 1 to each side; corolla bell-shaped, 5-lobed, pink, 5–9mm long and fragrant. A very distinctive plant when in flower. Widespread and common in Arctic Europe, becoming much rarer and increasingly confined to mountains southwards; mainly in coniferous woods and moorlands. **Fl:** Jun–Aug. **Br Is dist:** Rare and declining in native pinewoods, NE Scotland only.

Honeysuckle, Woodbine

Honeysuckle, Woodbine *Lonicera periclymenum* Vigorous, twining climbing shrub, reaching 6m on a support, though also low and spreading in shady places. Leaves grey-green, opposite pairs, oval-elliptical, to 90mm long, untoothed and pointed, lower ones short-stalked. Flowers familiar, in whorled terminal heads of creamy white or yellow, tinged red, trumpet-shaped flowers, 30–50mm long, 2-lipped; very fragrant, especially at night. Fruit red, globose and fleshy. From S Sweden southwards; in scrub, hedgerows and woods, widespread and common, mainly on acid soils. **Fl:** Jun–Sep. **Br Is dist:** Common throughout.

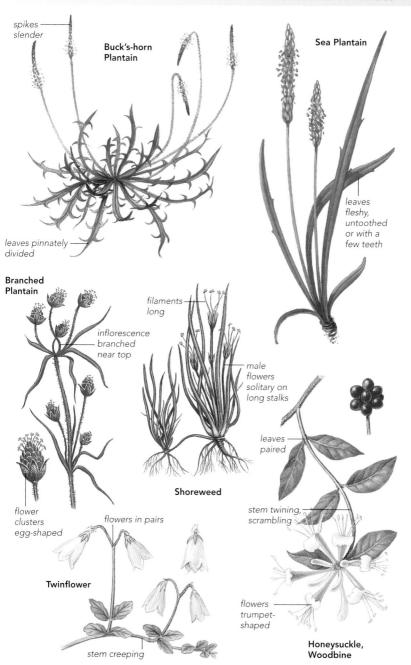

spikes slender

Buck's-horn Plantain

Sea Plantain

leaves pinnately divided

leaves fleshy, untoothed or with a few teeth

Branched Plantain

filaments long

inflorescence branched near top

male flowers solitary on long stalks

leaves paired

flower clusters egg-shaped

Shoreweed

stem twining, scrambling

flowers in pairs

Twinflower

flowers trumpet-shaped

stem creeping

Honeysuckle, Woodbine

273

MOSCHATEL FAMILY Adoxaceae

A family with only the one species. Family characteristics as for species.

Moschatel, Townhall Clock *Adoxa moschatellina* Perennial herb, with creeping rhizomes, and short erect stems to 10cm. Basal leaves long-stalked, twice 3-lobed, with spine-tipped lobes; stem leaves only 1 opposite pair of stalked 3-lobed leaves, smaller than basal ones; all leaves fleshy, pale green. Flowers in long-stalked terminal head, 6–8mm in diameter, made up of 5 flowers, 4 in square facing outwards, 5th facing upwards; corolla green, 5-lobed (4-lobed in top flower), with 10 stamens (8 in top flower). Easily recognised when in flower. In woods, shady places and rock ledges; through most of Europe, mainly on damp or heavy soils. **Fl:** Apr–May. **Br Is dist:** Locally common, becoming rarer northwards.

Moschatel,
Townhall Clock

VALERIAN FAMILY Valerianaceae

Family of herbaceous plants with opposite leaves, without stipules. Flowers in dense umbel-like heads, or cylindrical. Calyx very small, toothed or not; corolla funnel-shaped, sometimes spurred, 5-lobed; ovary inferior.

Common Cornsalad,
Lamb's Lettuce

CORNSALADS *Valerianella* Small annual plants with symmetrical branching; flowers small in clusters in axils of branches and in terminal heads. The species are difficult to distinguish, and ripe fruit is required for certain identification.

Common Cornsalad, Lamb's Lettuce *Valerianella locusta* Variable hairless annual, to 40cm, very forked in favourable conditions. Lower leaves spoon-shaped, to 70mm, blunt, sometimes toothed, upper ones oblong. Flowers in dense terminal heads, 10–20mm in diameter; corolla pale lilac-mauve, 1–2mm in diameter, 5-lobed; calyx very small, 1-toothed. Fruit 2.5 x 2mm, compressed laterally, with a corky bulge on the fertile seed-bearing cell. In dry grasslands, waste places, walls and dunes; throughout, though much rarer in the north. The commonest species in most areas. **Fl:** Apr–Jun. **Br Is dist:** Widespread though local.

Common Valerian

Common Valerian *Valeriana officinalis* Tall erect perennial herb to 1.5m, singly or clustered. Leaves pinnate, to 20cm long, in opposite pairs, lower ones stalked, upper ones short-stalked; leaflets lanceolate and toothed. Flowers in terminal head, often with a few separate lower clusters; hermaphrodite; corolla funnel-shaped, pink, tube swollen at base, 2.5–5mm long and 5-lobed, with 3 protruding stamens. Fruit oblong, with a white, feathery pappus. Widespread and common almost throughout; in fens, riversides, wet woods and occasionally in dwarfer form in dry grasslands. **Fl:** Jun–Aug. **Br Is dist:** Common throughout.

Marsh Valerian

Marsh Valerian *Valeriana dioica* Perennial, with creeping runners and erect stems to 30cm. *Root leaves long-stalked, roughly ovate,* blade 20–30mm long, untoothed and blunt; upper leaves virtually unstalked and pinnately divided. Male and female flowers produced on separate plants; flowers in terminal heads, pink: male heads larger, 40mm in diameter, with 5mm-diameter flowers; females 10–20mm in diameter, with 2mm-diameter flowers. Fruit similar to Common Valerian, but smaller. In fens and wet meadows; from SE Norway southwards, local. **Fl:** May–Jun. **Br Is dist:** Local throughout England, Wales and S Scotland; absent from N Scotland and Ireland.

flowers in 5s, one on each face, one on top

lower leaves 3-lobed

Moschatel, Townhall Clock

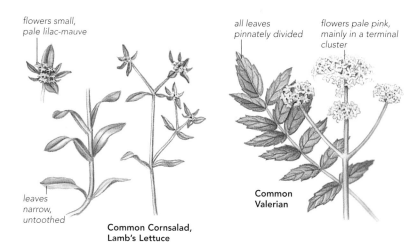

flowers small, pale lilac-mauve

leaves narrow, untoothed

Common Cornsalad, Lamb's Lettuce

all leaves pinnately divided

flowers pale pink, mainly in a terminal cluster

Common Valerian

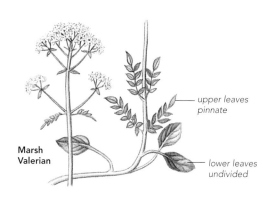

Marsh Valerian

upper leaves pinnate

lower leaves undivided

Wild Teasel

Red Valerian *Centranthus ruber* Branched ascending perennial to 80cm. Leaves *grey-green*, opposite, *ovate*, 5–10cm long and usually *untoothed*; lower ones narrowed into stalk, upper ones stalkless. Flowers in terminal inflorescence; *corolla red, pink or white*, tubular, 8–10mm long, with a pointed 3–4mm spur; 1 stamen, protruding. Fruit with hairy pappus. Native to S Europe, but widely naturalised on walls and rocky places, especially coastal; from the Netherlands southwards. **Fl:** Jun–Aug. **Br Is dist:** Widespread, commonest in the west, absent from the far north.

Small Teasel

TEASEL FAMILY Dipsacaceae

Comprises the teasels and scabiouses. Annual or perennial herbs, with opposite leaves, erect stems, and dense clearly defined heads of flowers surrounded by a whorl of bracts. Corolla tubular, 4- to 5-lobed, or 2-lipped; stamens 2 or 4, long-protruding, not joined together, style long, ovary inferior. The rather similar rampions and Sheep's-bit (*see* pp. 280–82) differ in their lack of protruding stamens, and short calyx teeth. (*See also* Asteraceae p. 284 ff).

Wild Teasel *Dipsacus fullonum* Stout erect biennial herb to 2m, with angled stems, prickly on angles; in 1st year, produces a rosette of short-stalked, roughly oblong, untoothed leaves with swollen-based prickles; in 2nd year, these die, and tall flower stem is produced bearing opposite leaves joined at base to form a cup. Flowers in dense egg-shaped heads, to 80mm, surrounded by a whorl of long thin spiny bracts, to 90mm long; corolla pink-purple, not all opening at once. Widespread and common, but absent from Scandinavia; in grassy places, woods and damp places, especially on heavy soils. **Fl:** Jul–Aug. **Br Is dist:** Locally common in S Britain, absent from N Scotland, rare in Ireland.

Small Teasel *Dipsacus pilosus* Erect, slender, branched plant to 1.2m, sparsely prickly. Basal rosette leaves ovate, long-stalked, hairy and prickly on midrib below; stem leaves roughly oval, sometimes with 2 basal lobes, not joined around stem. Flowers in globose heads, 15–20mm, surrounded by narrowly triangular bracts, shorter than head; corolla white or pinkish. Local in damp or shady places; from Denmark southwards. **Fl:** Jul–Sep. **Br Is dist:** Local through England and Wales, absent elsewhere.

Devil's-bit Scabious *Succisa pratensis* Erect perennial to 1m (usually less), with hairy or hairless stems. Basal leaves oval to spoon-shaped, to 30cm, usually untoothed, short-stalked and firm in texture; stem leaves narrower. Flower heads long-stalked and hemispherical, 15–25mm in diameter, with all florets the same size; corolla mauve to dark violet-blue, with 4 roughly equal lobes, calyx with 5 bristle teeth; heads either hermaphrodite (with conspicuously protruding anthers) or female only, with shorter anthers. Widespread and common, except for the extreme north; in meadows, fens, damp woods and downlands. **Fl:** Jun–Oct. **Br Is dist:** Common throughout.

Field Scabious *Knautia arvensis* Stout biennial or perennial plant, with roughly hairy stems to 75cm. Basal leaves roughly spoon-shaped, roughly hairy, undivided, toothed or lobed; *stem leaves pinnately divided* with ovate-lanceolate terminal leaflet, all roughly hairy. Flowers in hemispherical heads, 30–40mm in diameter, on long hairy stalks; corolla blue-violet to lilac, marginal flowers larger than central ones; bracts below heads ovate, calyx with 8 bristle teeth. In meadows, pastures and open woods; throughout except the far north, common. **Fl:** Jul–Sep. **Br Is dist:** Common and widespread except in N and W Scotland.

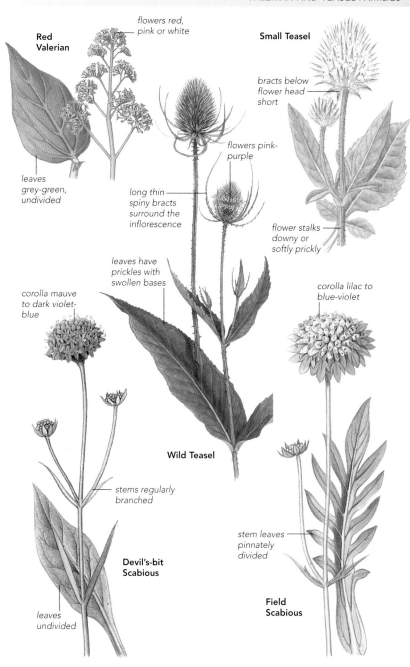

Red Valerian

flowers red, pink or white

leaves grey-green, undivided

Small Teasel

bracts below flower head short

flowers pink-purple

long thin spiny bracts surround the inflorescence

flower stalks downy or softly prickly

leaves have prickles with swollen bases

corolla mauve to dark violet-blue

corolla lilac to blue-violet

Wild Teasel

stems regularly branched

Devil's-bit Scabious

stem leaves pinnately divided

leaves undivided

Field Scabious

277

Wood Scabious

Wood Scabious *Knautia dipsacifolia* Similar to Field Scabious (*see* p. 276), but less hairy; upper stem leaves toothed, heart-shaped to clasping at base, but not divided or deeply lobed. In shady habitats; Belgium and C Germany southwards. **Fl:** Jul–Sep. **Br Is dist:** Absent.

Small Scabious

Small Scabious *Scabiosa columbaria* Slender erect perennial, with branching stems to 70cm. Rosette leaves long-stalked, spoon-shaped but toothed or roughly pinnately lobed, with large end-leaflet; stem leaves pinnate, with narrow lobes. Flower heads 20–30mm in diameter on long, rather slender downy stalks. Involucral bracts narrow, about 10 in 1 row, shorter than flowers; outer flowers larger than inner; corolla bluish-violet with 5 lobes, calyx with 5 long blackish bristle teeth. In calcareous grassy areas; from Denmark and S Sweden southwards; locally common. **Fl:** Jun–Sep. **Br Is dist:** Locally common in much of England and Wales, rarer to the north, absent from much of Scotland and all of Ireland.

BELLFLOWER FAMILY Campanulaceae

Herbs, with alternate undivided leaves without stipules. Corolla regular with 5 equal lobes.

Spreading Bellflower

Spreading Bellflower *Campanula patula* Slender erect perennial herb to 70cm, with rough stem and leaves. Basal leaves spoon-shaped, stalked, to 40mm, round-toothed; stem leaves smaller, narrower and unstalked. Inflorescence branched, open, with flowers erect on slender stalks; corolla bell-shaped, 20–25mm long, but usually much more open than other species, with lobes as long as tube, rosy purple to blue. In grassy places, through much of area, but largely absent from Scandinavia. **Fl:** Jul–Sep. **Br Is dist:** Very local, mainly on the England-Wales border; declining.

Bearded Bellflower *Campanula barbata* Has erect, simple, hairy stems to 30cm, with flowering and non-flowering leaf rosettes. Basal leaves lanceolate-oblong, roughly hairy; inflorescence few-flowered, pendent, hairy, blue, bell-shaped flowers, 20–30mm long. Acid grassland rare in S Norway; common in Alps. **Fl:** Jun–Aug. **Br Is dist:** Absent.

Giant Bellflower

Clustered Bellflower *Campanula glomerata* Erect, downy perennial to 30cm, occasionally more. Basal leaves ovate, rounded or heart-shaped at base, long-stalked, with blunt teeth; upper stem leaves ovate-lanceolate, clasping. *Flowers mainly in dense terminal cluster*, with a few others lower down stem, erect and virtually unstalked; *corolla violet-blue*, narrowly bell-shaped, 15–20mm long, with lobes about equal to tube; calyx teeth narrowly triangular. Downs, meadows and other grassy habitats, on calcareous soils; throughout except the far north. **Fl:** Jun–Oct. **Br Is dist:** Locally common in S and E England, rarer to the north; absent from Ireland.

a

Giant Bellflower *Campanula latifolia* Tall, erect, *hairless or downy herb* to 1m, with unbranched, *bluntly angled stems*. Basal leaves to 20cm long, ovate, narrowed gradually into stalk, which is often winged, margins shallowly and irregularly toothed (a). Flowers in a leafy, usually unbranched, spike, individually on 20mm stalks, semi-erect; corolla blue (rarely white), bell-shaped, 40–55mm long, lobes slightly shorter than tube; calyx lobes narrowly triangular, to 25mm long. Semi-shaded habitats; widespread except far north, local in many lowland areas. **Fl:** Jul–Aug. **Br Is dist:** Widespread, but very local in the south, commoner to the north.

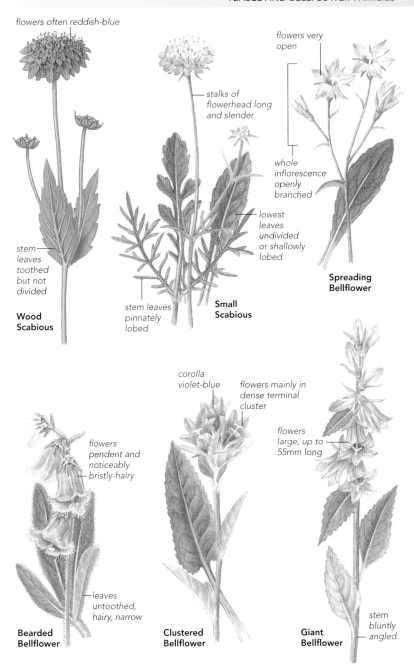

flowers often reddish-blue

stalks of flowerhead long and slender

flowers very open

whole inflorescence openly branched

Spreading Bellflower

stem leaves toothed but not divided

lowest leaves undivided or shallowly lobed

stem leaves pinnately lobed

Small Scabious

Wood Scabious

corolla violet-blue

flowers mainly in dense terminal cluster

flowers large, up to 55mm long

flowers pendent and noticeably bristly-hairy

leaves untoothed, hairy, narrow

Bearded Bellflower

Clustered Bellflower

stem bluntly angled

Giant Bellflower

279

Nettle-leaved Bellflower

Creeping Bellflower

Venus's-looking-glass

Spiked Rampion

Nettle-leaved Bellflower *Campanula trachelium* Similar to Giant Bellflower (*see* p. 278), *but more bristly-hairy*, with *sharply angled stems*. Basal leaves to 10cm, narrowed abruptly to the stalk, stem leaves short-stalked, coarsely toothed and rather *nettle-like* (**a**). Flowers darker blue, 30–40mm on 10mm stalks; calyx lobes triangular, to 10mm long. In woods, hedgerows and scrub; north to S Sweden, locally common. **Fl:** Jun–Sep. **Br Is dist:** South and east, very local elsewhere.

Creeping Bellflower *Campanula rapunculoides* Erect downy or hairless perennial to 1m, often forming clumps from creeping rootstock. Root leaves ovate, to 80mm, long-stalked, heart-shaped at base and toothed; stem leaves narrower and unstalked. Flowers in long racemes, *all drooping to one side*, on 5mm stalks; corolla bell- or funnel-shaped, blue-violet, 20–30mm long; calyx teeth narrowly triangular, *bent back at flower time*. Meadows, roadsides and wood-margins; native in most of N Europe except the Arctic. **Fl:** Jun–Sep. **Br Is dist:** Locally naturalised, widespread.

Harebell *Campanula rotundifolia* Slender erect or ascending herb to 40cm. Basal leaves long-stalked, rounded to ovate, heart-shaped at base, 5–15mm long and toothed; stem leaves narrowly linear, upper ones unstalked. Flowers few, drooping, on slender stalks, in loose, branched inflorescences; corolla pale blue and bell-shaped with short triangular teeth; calyx teeth very narrow and spreading. In dry grassy places, on acid or calcareous soils, common and widespread. **Fl:** Jul–Sep. **Br Is dist:** Common and widespread, though rare in SW Britain.

Venus's-looking-glass *Legousia hybrida* Erect or straggling bristly annual to 40cm. Leaves oblong, to 30mm long, wavy, lower ones short-stalked, upper ones unstalked. Flowers rather few, erect and mainly in terminal cluster; corolla lilac to dull purple, 5–10mm in diameter, flat not bell-shaped, 5-lobed, with *lobes only as long as calyx teeth, opening in sunshine*. Differs from bellflowers in the long ovary, about 3 times as long as wide. In arable land, on free-draining soils; from the Netherlands and Germany southwards, local and declining. **Fl:** May–Aug. **Br Is dist:** Locally common only in S and E England; virtually absent elsewhere.

Large Venus's-looking-glass *Legousia speculum-veneris* Rather similar to Venus's-looking-glass, but usually much-branched and spreading. Corolla red-purple to violet, *to 20mm in diameter, lobes at least as long as calyx teeth*, opening to star shape, *remaining open in dull weather*. In cultivated land, generally on dry soils; from the Netherlands southwards; rare. **Fl:** May–Jul. **Br Is dist:** Absent, except as rare introduction.

Spiked Rampion *Phyteuma spicatum* Erect hairless perennial herb to 80cm. Basal and lower stem leaves oval, to 70mm long, with heart-shaped base, long-stalked and blunt-toothed; upper stem leaves narrower and unstalked. Flowers in a dense spike, ovoid but becoming cylindrical and longer (to 80mm); corolla creamy yellow, curved in bud, about 10mm long, lobes joined at tip at first, then eventually separating almost to base; stigmas 2. In meadows, woods and shady roadsides; from S Norway southwards, local, becoming commoner to south. **Fl:** May–Jul. **Br Is dist:** Very rare and local, in E Sussex only.

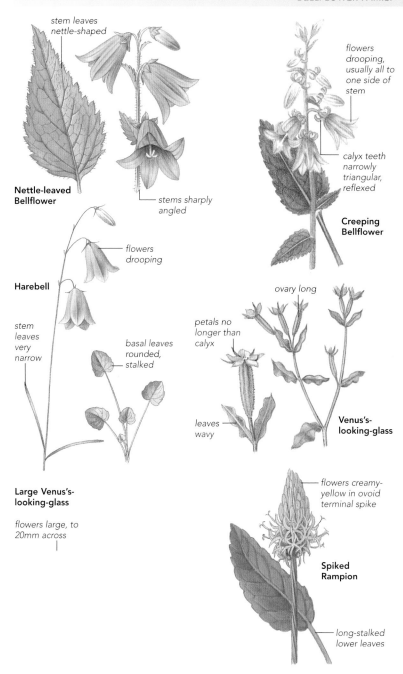

stem leaves nettle-shaped

flowers drooping, usually all to one side of stem

calyx teeth narrowly triangular, reflexed

Nettle-leaved Bellflower

stems sharply angled

Creeping Bellflower

flowers drooping

Harebell

stem leaves very narrow

basal leaves rounded, stalked

ovary long

petals no longer than calyx

leaves wavy

Venus's-looking-glass

Large Venus's-looking-glass

flowers large, to 20mm across

flowers creamy-yellow in ovoid terminal spike

Spiked Rampion

long-stalked lower leaves

Round-headed Rampion

Round-headed Rampion *Phyteuma orbiculare* (This name includes the form sometimes known as *P. tenerum*). A rather slender perennial herb, up to about 30cm tall. Basal leaves narrower, not usually heart-shaped at base. Flowers blue in a dense *rounded head*, 10–25mm in diameter, with bracts much shorter than inflorescence. In dry grassland and rocky areas, often calcareous; from Belgium and S England southwards. **Fl:** Jun–Aug. **Br Is dist:** Chalk downs, SE England west to Wiltshire only.

Ivy-leaved Bellflower

Ivy-leaved Bellflower *Wahlenbergia hederacea* Slender, hairless, trailing perennial up to 30cm long. Leaves rounded to kidney-shaped, 5–10mm in diameter, toothed or lobed, sometimes ivy-like, all stalked, alternate, pale green. Flowers solitary or paired from leaf axils, with slender stalks to 40mm long; corolla pale blue, bell-shaped and somewhat nodding. In damp, humid and shady places, on acid soil; from Belgium and Scotland southwards but predominantly western, local. **Fl:** Jul–Aug. **Br Is dist:** Local, commonest in SW England, but widespread in W Britain, and east to Kent.

Sheep's-bit

Sheep's-bit *Jasione montana* Downy, spreading or erect biennial or perennial herb to 30cm. Basal leaves in rosette, linear-lanceolate, to 50m long, wavy-edged and hairy; stem leaves shorter and narrower. Flowers in dense rounded scabious-like heads, to 35mm in diameter; corolla pale blue, 5mm long, with 2 broad stigmas. Differs from scabious in that the stamens do not protrude. In dry grassy places, usually avoiding lime-rich soils, commonest near coasts; almost throughout except the far north. **Fl:** May–Aug. **Br Is dist:** Throughout, but local and predominantly coastal.

Heath Lobelia

Heath Lobelia *Lobelia urens* Erect, usually hairless, perennial herb to 60cm, with solid, angled stems. Leaves spoon-shaped or ovate, to 70mm, irregularly toothed, shiny dark green and barely stalked; upper stem leaves narrower. Flowers in a loose long inflorescence, with narrow bracts; corolla blue-purple, 10–15mm long, 2-lipped, with 2 upper and 3 lower lobes; calyx teeth long, narrow and spreading. On grassy heaths, open woods and acid grasslands; from Belgium and S England southwards. **Fl:** Jul–Sep. **Br Is dist:** Very local and declining in SW England west of Sussex.

Water Lobelia

Water Lobelia *Lobelia dortmanna* Has similar flower spikes to Heath Lobelia, but differs in habit and habitat. Basal leaves in a rosette of numerous linear, blunt and untoothed leaves, producing leafless flower stems to 60cm. Corolla pale lilac, 15–20mm long. Grows with rosettes normally submerged in stony, acid, still waters, usually in upland areas, to a depth of 3m, with flower spikes emerging above water level. A distinctive plant. Locally common southwards to NW France. **Fl:** Jul–Sep. **Br Is dist:** A northern and western plant, becoming more common from S Wales northwards.

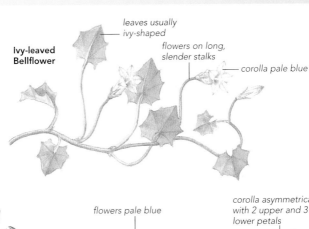

Ivy-leaved Bellflower

leaves usually ivy-shaped

flowers on long, slender stalks

corolla pale blue

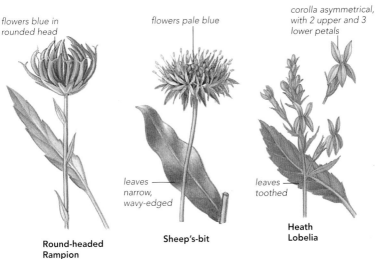

flowers blue in rounded head

flowers pale blue

corolla asymmetrical, with 2 upper and 3 lower petals

leaves narrow, wavy-edged

leaves toothed

Round-headed Rampion

Sheep's-bit

Heath Lobelia

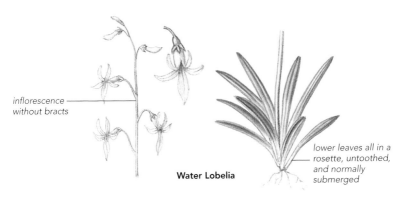

inflorescence without bracts

Water Lobelia

lower leaves all in a rosette, untoothed, and normally submerged

Hemp-agrimony

DAISY FAMILY Asteraceae (formerly Compositae)

Mainly herbs, with flowers in distinctive compound heads, the florets seated on a disc surrounded by a whorl of bracts, often like sepals. The form of the florets varies, and those in a head may be all the same or of 2 clearly different types ('ray' and 'disc' florets), producing the typical daisy-flower. Calyx varies: it may be a parachute-like pappus of hairs, small and scale-like or wholly absent. The stamens are joined into a tube attached to the inside of the corolla; the style forks into 2 stigmas. Some groups are particularly difficult, with many very similar species.

Daisy

Hemp-agrimony *Eupatorium cannabinum* Large erect perennial, to 1.75m. Basal leaves roughly ovate, stalked; stem leaves 3- or 5-lobed, pointed toothed, opposite, more or less unstalked. Flowers in numerous small heads, 2–5mm across, each with 5–6 florets, in extensive, lax, rounded, branched terminal inflorescences; florets reddish-mauve, or pale pink, with purple-tipped bracts; seeds with hairy pappus. Most of N Europe except far north, in damp grassy places and fens; common. **Fl:** Jul–Sep. **Br Is dist:** Common in England, Wales and parts of Ireland; rare or absent elsewhere.

Goldenrod *Solidago virgaurea* Variable, erect perennial, with stems to 1m in height. Basal leaves narrowly spoon-shaped, to 10cm long, stalked and usually weakly toothed; stem leaves narrowly lanceolate and unstalked. Flower heads numerous, in long, leafy, branched or unbranched heads; individual heads 6–10mm in diameter, made up of yellow ray and disc florets. Pappus dirty brown and hairy. Almost throughout the area, common in dry grassy and rocky places on most soil types. **Fl:** Jun–Sep. **Br Is dist:** Widespread and generally common throughout, rarest in the south-east.

Daisy *Bellis perennis* Perennial herb, with a rosette of leaves and erect flower stems to 15cm. Leaves oblong to spoon-shaped, to 60mm, downy when young, 1-veined, narrowed to stalk. Flowers in clearly defined heads on slender leafless stalks, thickened below the flower head; flower head 15–30mm in diameter, with a yellow disc and numerous slender outer white rays, often purplish-red below. Involucral bracts 3–5mm long and blunt. Widespread and common in grassy places from S Scandinavia southwards (naturalised farther north). **Fl:** March–Oct. **Br Is dist:** Abundant everywhere.

Sea Aster *Aster tripolium* Rather similar to Daisy, often taller, to 1m, and with fleshy leaves to 12cm; ray florets usually mauve (occasionally completely absent), heads 10–20mm in diameter; involucral bracts blunt, appressed and membranous at tips. In salt-marshes, coastal mud and cliffs, occasionally inland on saline soils, throughout where suitable habitats exist. **Fl:** Jul–Oct. **Br Is dist:** All round the coast, very rare inland, in English Midlands.

Blue Fleabane *Erigeron acer* Annual or biennial herb; flower stem to 40cm, often branched near top. Basal leaves stalked, spoon-shaped to 80mm; stem leaves lanceolate, unstalked. Flower heads 12–18mm across, varying from 1 (rarely) to many in a loose inflorescence; ray florets short, pale purple, barely exceeding yellow disc florets, erect not spreading; bracts often purplish. In dry grassy and rocky places, sand-dunes; almost throughout, locally common. **Fl:** Jun–Aug. **Br Is dist:** Widespread in England and Wales; rare elsewhere.

Canadian Fleabane *Conyza canadensis* Variable, erect, hairy annual to 1.5m (usually 0.6–1m). Leaves numerous, narrow, usually broader and more noticeably stalked towards the stem base. Flower heads small, 5–9mm, white or pinkish ray florets, in long, loose, many-flowered inflorescence. Native of N America, widely naturalised in waste places and dunes except extreme north. **Fl:** Jul–Oct. **Br Is dist:** Abundant in south, spreading northwards.

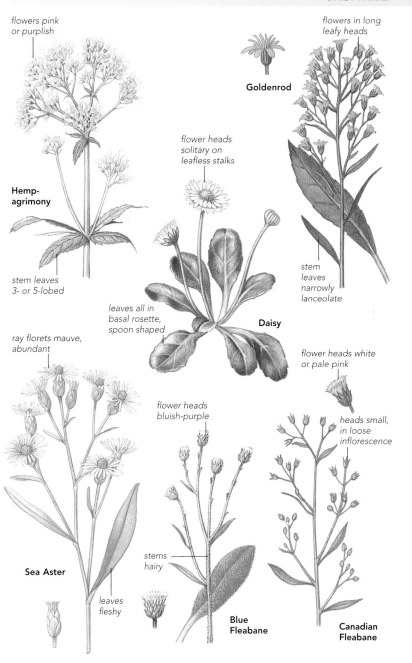

flowers pink or purplish

flowers in long leafy heads

Goldenrod

flower heads solitary on leafless stalks

Hemp-agrimony

stem leaves 3- or 5-lobed

stem leaves narrowly lanceolate

leaves all in basal rosette, spoon shaped

Daisy

ray florets mauve, abundant

flower heads white or pale pink

flower heads bluish-purple

heads small, in loose inflorescence

Sea Aster

stems hairy

leaves fleshy

Blue Fleabane

Canadian Fleabane

285

Common Cudweed

Small Cudweed

Marsh Cudweed

Immortelle

Mountain Everlasting, Cat's Foot

CUDWEEDS *Filago, Logfia* and *Omalothecia, Filaginella* and *Gnaphalium* A difficult group of small, usually woolly, plants with inconspicuous flowers, needing close examination of bracts, flower heads and leaves for identification.

Common Cudweed *Filago vulgaris* Erect annual, with white-woolly stems and leaves, to 30cm, branched or unbranched at base, but always branching above into 2–3 forks. Leaves erect, strap-shaped, 10–20mm long, wavy-edged, untoothed and woolly. Flower heads in dense, rounded clusters both in branch axils and terminal, each made up of 20–35 heads, 10–12mm in diameter, not exceeded by the leaves immediately below them; bracts of flower heads narrow, straight, outer ones woolly, inner ones bristle-tipped, erect; florets yellow. From S Sweden southwards in dry grasslands and open habitats on sandy and acid soils; locally common. **Fl:** Jul–Aug. **Br Is dist:** Locally common in S Britain, rare in the north, but generally decreasing.

Small Cudweed *Filago mimima* Slender grey-woolly annual to 30cm, (usually less), with ascending branches from above the middle. Leaves linear-lanceolate, to 10mm long. Flower heads ovoid to pyramidal, to 3.5mm long, 5-angled, in clusters of 3 to 6 in angles of stem and at tips, exceeding their basal leaves; overall appearance yellowish; *outer bracts woolly at base, but with hairless yellow chaffy tips,* spreading when in fruit. In sandy fields, on heaths and other acid open areas, from S Scandinavia southwards. **Fl:** Jul–Sep. **Br Is dist:** Widespread and locally common, though rare in Ireland, and absent from N Scotland.

Marsh Cudweed *Gnaphalium uliginosa* Spreading or ascending woolly annual, *much-branched from the base,* to 20cm. Leaves linear-lanceolate to oblong, up to 50mm long, woolly on both sides. Flower heads individually ovoid, 3–4mm long, clustered in terminal inflorescences of 3–10, well exceeded by the leaves at their base (which give the impression of green ray florets); florets yellowish-brown, flower-head bracts woolly at base, darker and hairless at tip. Widespread and common in damp, often disturbed places; almost throughout. **Fl:** Jul–Sep. **Br Is dist:** Common throughout.

Immortelle *Helichrysum arenarium* Erect white-downy perennial to 40cm. Leaves ovate-oblong, woolly on both sides, *flat,* to 70mm long and 1-veined; upper leaves much narrower. Flower heads individually 3–4mm in diameter, grouped together in a loose, branching inflorescence 20–50mm in diameter; flowers bright yellow to orange, with yellow, blunt bracts that spread widely when in fruit. In dry sandy places from S Sweden and Denmark southwards; local. **Fl:** Jun–Aug. **Br Is dist:** Absent.

Mountain Everlasting, Cat's Foot *Antennaria dioica* Creeping, downy, perennial herb, with woody stems and leafy runners with rosettes, producing erect unbranched flower stems to 20cm. Basal leaves spoon-shaped and rather blunt, up to 35mm long; stem leaves narrower and erect; all leaves green and virtually hairless above, downy below. Flower heads white-woolly in a dense umbel-like head of 2–8 flower clusters. Male and female plants separate: female flowers with larger heads, to 12mm in diameter, with pink-tipped bracts; male heads to 6mm in diameter, with white-tipped bracts, spreading outwards; all florets pink. Widespread and generally common, though local in lowland areas; on heaths, upland habitats and moors. **Fl:** Jun–Aug. **Br Is dist:** Common in N Britain, increasingly uncommon southwards.

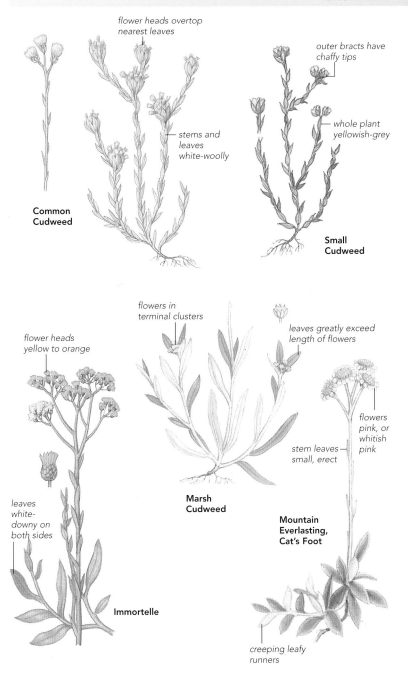

flower heads overtop
nearest leaves

outer bracts have
chaffy tips

stems and
leaves
white-woolly

whole plant
yellowish-grey

**Common
Cudweed**

**Small
Cudweed**

flowers in
terminal clusters

leaves greatly exceed
length of flowers

flower heads
yellow to orange

flowers
pink, or
whitish
pink

stem leaves
small, erect

leaves
white-
downy on
both sides

**Marsh
Cudweed**

**Mountain
Everlasting,
Cat's Foot**

Immortelle

creeping leafy
runners

287

INULAS *Inula* A group of perennial herbs with undivided alternate leaves. Flower heads solitary or in small groups, yellow, large, and with separate disc and ray florets, though rays sometimes very short.

Elecampane *Inula helenium* Robust, erect, hairy perennial to 2m, occasionally more. Leaves roughly ovate, up to 40cm long, basal ones long-stalked; stem leaves unstalked; all leaves virtually hairless above, softly downy below. Flower heads large, 60–80mm across, 1–3 together, with deep yellow disc and paler yellow, long, narrow rays. On roadsides, waste ground, plantations and other habitats; naturalised throughout except the far north, originally from C Asia. **Fl**: Jul–Aug. **Br Is dist**: Naturalised throughout, but never common.

Ploughman's-spikenard

Fleabane, Meadow Fleabane *Inula britannica* Rather similar to Common Fleabane, but leaves *more narrowly lanceolate*, softly hairy below; *outer flower bracts linear* and softly hairy. From S Scandinavia southwards, in damp meadows, streamsides and wet woods. **Fl**: Jul–Aug. **Br Is dist**: Formerly in Leicestershire, now extinct.

Golden-samphire

Ploughman's-spikenard *Inula conyzae* Erect, downy, often reddish biennial or perennial herb to 1m. Lower leaves oval to oblong, to 15cm long, narrowed into a flattened stalk (rather similar to Foxglove leaves, *see* p. 252); upper leaves stalkless, wedge-shaped at base and narrower. Flower heads ovoid, about 10mm long, numerous in tight, branched heads; florets dark yellow, ray florets very short or absent; inner bracts purplish, outer ones green and spreading. From Denmark southwards, in dry or calcareous grasslands and banks. **Fl**: Jul–Sep. **Br Is dist**: Locally common in England and Wales only.

Common Fleabane

Golden-samphire *Inula crithmoides* Fleshy, tufted, erect perennial herb, or small shrub to 1m. Leaves linear, to 50mm, numerous, fleshy, untoothed or with a 3-toothed tip. Flower heads 20–30mm in diameter, in a loose, roughly flat-topped inflorescence; ray florets to 25mm, much longer than bracts; outer flower-head bracts linear and erect. From S Britain and N France southwards, coastal only, in salt-marshes, on cliffs or shingle. **Fl**: Jul–Sep. **Br Is dist**: Coasts of S and W Britain only; local.

Small Fleabane

Common Fleabane *Pulicaria dysenterica* Creeping, perennial herb, with downy or woolly, erect, branched stems to 60cm. Basal leaves oblong, withered by flowering time; stem leaves alternate, downy, heart-shaped at base and clasping. Flower heads 15–30mm in diameter, numerous in loose inflorescences, orange-yellow; ray florets numerous, much longer than disc florets; bracts below head narrow, sticky and hairy, with long, fine tips. In damp grasslands and roadsides, on heavy soils; common generally as far north as Denmark. **Fl**: Jul–Sep. **Br Is dist**: Common and widespread north to S Scotland.

Small Fleabane *Pulicaria vulgaris* Rather similar to Common Fleabane, but annual, much-branched, to 40cm; *stem leaves round-based* not heart-shaped. *Flower heads smaller, 10mm in diameter*, numerous, *with short ray florets* and spreading outer bracts; all florets pale yellow. From S Sweden southwards, very local and declining, mainly in winter-wet grasslands and grazed hollows. **Fl**: Aug–Oct. **Br Is dist**: Very rare in S England only (mostly New Forest); on grazed commons.

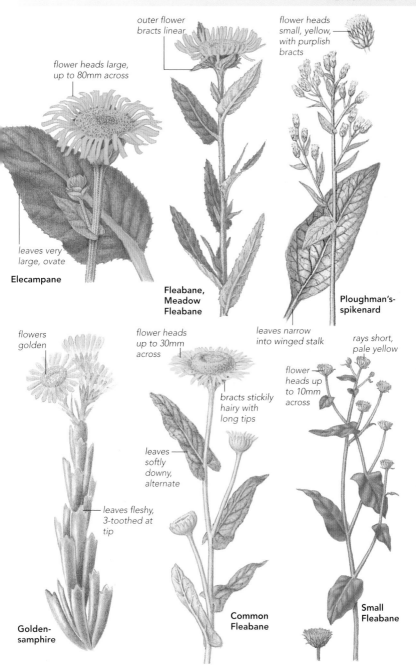

outer flower bracts linear

flower heads large, up to 80mm across

flower heads small, yellow, with purplish bracts

leaves very large, ovate

Elecampane

Fleabane, Meadow Fleabane

leaves narrow into winged stalk

Ploughman's-spikenard

flowers golden

flower heads up to 30mm across

rays short, pale yellow

bracts stickily hairy with long tips

leaves softly downy, alternate

flower heads up to 10mm across

leaves fleshy, 3-toothed at tip

Golden-samphire

Common Fleabane

Small Fleabane

289

Trifid Bur-marigold *Bidens tripartita* Hairless or slightly hairy annual to 60cm. Leaves 3-lobed (occasionally 5-lobed), coarsely toothed, with a short, winged stalk. Flower heads yellow, erect, 10–25mm in diameter, in branched clusters, *usually without ray florets, with 5–8 leaf-like spreading bracts below heads.* In damp places, especially where winter-flooded; widespread throughout but absent from the far north. **Fl:** Jul–Oct. **Br Is dist:** Locally common in S Britain, much rarer to the north.

Trifid Bur-marigold

Nodding Bur-marigold *Bidens cernua* Similar to Trifid Bur-marigold, except that the leaves are in opposite *undivided lanceolate pairs; flower heads drooping;* occasionally short, broad, yellow ray florets present. In similar habitats, widespread except in the far north. **Fl:** Jul–Oct. **Br Is dist:** Locally common in the south, much rarer to the north.

Sneezewort

Gallant Soldier *Galinsoga parviflora* Much-branched annual herb, with erect, more or less *hairless stems,* to 75cm. Leaves ovate, in opposite pairs, stalked, few-toothed, pointed, up to 50mm long. Flower heads small, 3–5mm in diameter, in much-forked inflorescences; disc florets yellow, ray florets usually 5 only, about 1mm long and 1mm wide, 3-lobed at tip, white; bracts few. Originally from S America, but now widely naturalised in waste places and cultivated land, almost throughout. **Fl:** May–Oct. **Br Is dist:** Widespread, though uncommon except in the south-east. Absent from Ireland.

Corn Chamomile *Anthemis arvensis* Aromatic annual herb, with spreading or ascending branched downy stems to 50cm. Leaves up to 50mm long, roughly oval in outline, but very divided, up to 3 times-pinnate with narrow pointed segments, *hairy or woolly below* especially when young. Flower heads solitary, long-stalked, 20–30mm in diameter, with yellow disc florets in a cone shape, and white rays with styles. Widespread throughout except the far north; in cultivated and waste ground, on calcareous soils. **Fl:** Jun–Jul. **Br Is dist:** Frequent in England, but rare elsewhere and absent from Ireland.

Sneezewort *Achillea ptarmica* Erect, tufted, branched or unbranched perennial, normally to 75cm, but occasionally more, downy on upper parts. Leaves lanceolate, to 70mm, *undivided but finely and sharply toothed,* unstalked. Flower heads 10–20mm in diameter, with central greenish-white disc florets, and white oval rays borne in a loose few-flowered, branched cluster. Throughout in wet meadows, marshy areas and damp woods, usually on acid soils. **Fl:** Jul–Aug. **Br Is dist:** Locally common throughout, rare in calcareous areas.

Yarrow *Achillea millefolium* Strong-smelling, creeping perennial producing erect, downy, furrowed, unbranched stems to 60cm. Leaves lanceolate in outline, but *highly divided, feathery,* twice to 3 times-pinnate, to 15cm long, lower ones stalked, upper ones unstalked. Flower heads numerous but small, 4–6mm in diameter, aggregated into dense flat-topped or gently rounded inflorescences; ray florets white or pink, 5 per head; disc florets yellowish white. Widespread and common throughout in grassy places, waste ground and hedgerows. **Fl:** Jun–Sep. **Br Is dist:** Common throughout.

Sea Mayweed *Tripleurospermum maritimum* A sprawling annual or perennial herb with feathery much-branched leaves with fleshy blunt cylindrical segments. Flowers solitary, long stalked with white rays and a yellow disc. In coastal habitats, throughout except the far north. **Br Is dist:** throughout, commoner in the north.

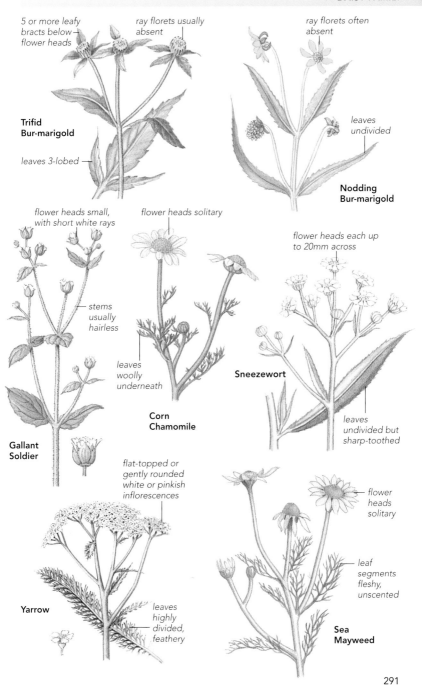

5 or more leafy bracts below flower heads

ray florets usually absent

Trifid Bur-marigold

leaves 3-lobed

ray florets often absent

leaves undivided

Nodding Bur-marigold

flower heads small, with short white rays

stems usually hairless

flower heads solitary

leaves woolly underneath

Corn Chamomile

flower heads each up to 20mm across

Sneezewort

leaves undivided but sharp-toothed

Gallant Soldier

flat-topped or gently rounded white or pinkish inflorescences

Yarrow

leaves highly divided, feathery

flower heads solitary

leaf segments fleshy, unscented

Sea Mayweed

291

Pineappleweed *Matricaria discoidea* Hairless annual to 40cm, *whole plant smells strongly of pineapple when crushed*; flower heads with conical hollow receptacle covered with greenish-yellow disc florets, *ray florets absent*. Widespread throughout in waste places, tracks and cultivated ground; probably an ancient introduction. **Fl:** May–Nov. **Br Is dist:** Throughout.

Cottonweed

Cottonweed *Otanthus maritimus* Erect or ascending perennial with white-woolly stems to 50cm. Leaves oblong-lanceolate, to 20mm long, toothed or untoothed, white-woolly, fleshy and unstalked. Flower heads in dense terminal clusters, individual heads globose, 6–9mm in diameter, with woolly bracts; florets yellow, ray florets absent. A distinctive plant. On sand and shingle shores; only in SE Ireland and W France southwards; local. **Fl:** Aug–Oct. **Br Is dist:** Now extinct, except 1 locality in Ireland.

Corn Marigold

Corn Marigold *Glebionis segetum, Chrysanthemum segetum* Erect or ascending hairless annual to 60cm, unbranched or branched, rather greyish-green. *Leaves oblong, but deeply lobed or toothed and slightly fleshy;* upper leaves barely toothed and clasping. Flowers solitary, 35–60mm in diameter, with both ray and disc florets golden-yellow, disc flat. Widespread and locally common, though decreasing, in cultivated ground, usually on acid soil, but absent from the far north. Probably an ancient introduction. **Fl:** Jun–Oct. **Br Is dist:** Widespread and locally common.

Sea Wormwood

Tansy *Tanacetum vulgare* Erect or ascending aromatic perennial, to 1m or more. Leaves alternate, oblong, to 20cm, but pinnately divided, with segments further divided, sparsely hairy. *Inflorescence a dense umbel-like head*, up to 15cm in diameter, made up of 10–70 heads each 7–12mm in diameter, golden yellow; ray florets absent. Roadsides and waste places; common throughout. **Fl:** Jul–Oct. **Br Is dist:** Common and widespread.

a

Oxeye Daisy *Leucanthemum vulgare* Erect perennial to 70cm, hairless or slightly hairy. *Basal leaves spoon-shaped*, to 10cm, long-stalked, with rounded teeth (a); stem leaves variable, becoming stalkless up stem, oblong and toothed. Flowers solitary or several together, 25–40mm in diameter, with white rays and yellow disc florets; involucral bracts variable in shape, overlapping, with dark purplish edges. Widespread and generally common in meadows, pastures, roadsides and, less frequently, in disturbed sites. **Fl:** May–Sep. **Br Is dist:** Common throughout.

MUGWORTS and WORMWOODS *Artemisia* A small group of tall herbaceous or slightly woody plants, unlike other *Asteraceae* superficially. Leaves alternate and divided pinnately to a greater or lesser degree. Inflorescences normally made up of numerous small flower heads in long, branching, spike-like masses, without ray florets.

b

Sea Wormwood *Seriphidium maritimum* Strongly aromatic perennial, with clusters of spreading to erect, partly woody stems to 60cm, g*rey or white-downy*. Lower leaves twice-pinnate with very narrow blunt segments (**b**), white woolly on both sides, withering at flowering time; upper leaves similar but smaller and short-stalked. Flower heads individually 1–2mm in diameter, ovoid, numerous in long leafy branched inflorescences, florets yellow-orange. Mainly coastal habitats from SE Norway and S Sweden southwards (rare inland on saline soils in C Germany). **Fl:** Aug–Oct. **Br Is dist:** Frequent around most coastal areas, rare in the north and in Ireland.

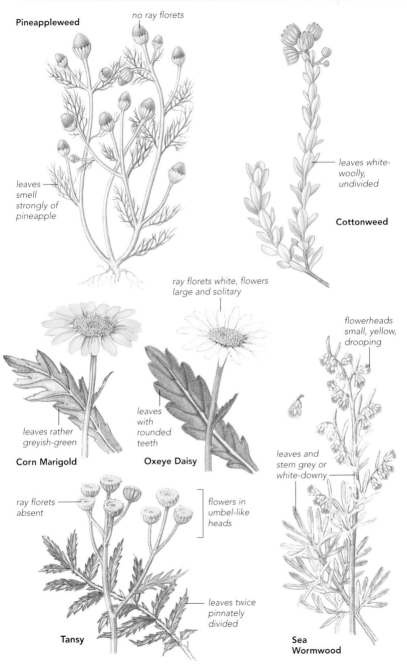

Pineappleweed

no ray florets

leaves smell strongly of pineapple

leaves white-woolly, undivided

Cottonweed

ray florets white, flowers large and solitary

leaves rather greyish-green

Corn Marigold

leaves with rounded teeth

Oxeye Daisy

flowerheads small, yellow, drooping

leaves and stem grey or white-downy

ray florets absent

flowers in umbel-like heads

leaves twice pinnately divided

Tansy

Sea Wormwood

293

Field Wormwood

Wormwood

Butterbur

Purple, or Alpine, Colt's-foot

Field Wormwood *Artemisia campestris* Similar to Sea Wormwood (*see* p. 292), but *unscented and virtually hairless* or slightly silky hairy when young; leaf segments pointed (**a**). Ssp *maritima* has leaf lobes shorter and fleshy. Widespread but local in dry, often heathy, places, except the far north. Ssp *maritima* occurs on coastal sands from the Netherlands southwards. **Fl:** Aug–Sep. **Br Is dist:** E Anglian Brecklands only; rare.

Mugwort *Artemisia vulgaris* Erect perennial, tufted, aromatic, to 1.2m, hairless or downy, usually with *reddish stems* that have a large area of white pith inside. Leaves to 80mm long, pinnately lobed, with deeply cut lobes (**b**), *dark green and hairless above, white-downy below*; lower leaves stalked, upper ones smaller and unstalked. Flower heads oval, 2–3mm in diameter, erect, red-brown, in dense branched inflorescences; bracts woolly, with chaffy margins. Throughout, though rare in the far north, in disturbed ground, roadsides and waste places. **Fl:** Jul–Sep. **Br Is dist:** Common throughout.

Wormwood *Artemisia absinthium* Perennial, aromatic plant with erect, silkily hairy stems to 90cm. Similar to Mugwort, but *leaf segments blunter, silky hairy on both surfaces* (**c**). Flower heads bell-shaped, hanging, with yellow florets. Widespread but local throughout; often naturalised from cultivation, on waste ground, roadsides and coastal habitats. **Fl:** Jul–Aug. **Br Is dist:** Not uncommon in England and Wales, rarer and more coastal elsewhere.

Colt's-foot *Tussilago farfara* Creeping perennial with runners producing erect, scaly, leafless flower stems to 15cm tall. Leaves appear separately, after flowers are over, and are roughly triangular, with heart-shaped base, shallowly and irregularly toothed, up to 20cm long, stalked, slightly downy above and very downy below. Flower heads 1 per stem, in clumps, 15–35mm in diameter, with very narrow yellow ray florets, and yellow disc; flower stems elongate when in fruit, which is a white 'clock'. Common and widespread throughout, usually on damp and clayey soils, especially where bare. **Fl:** Feb–Apr. **Br Is dist:** Common throughout.

BUTTERBURS *Petasites* A small group of distinctive plants, with large basal leaves, erect cylindrical flower spikes with scale-leaves on the stems and separate male and female plants.

Butterbur *Petasites hybridus* Perennial herb with creeping rhizome, producing erect flower spikes to 40cm (reaching 80cm when female spikes are in fruit), and large, rounded, heart-shaped leaves to 90cm in diameter, stalked, distantly toothed, downy below. Flowers in cylindrical spikes on stout stems with reddish or green scale-leaves; *heads pinkish red*. Female flowers individually 3–6mm, males 7–12mm; female spikes lengthen greatly as fruit matures. Widespread and common from N Scotland and N Germany southwards (naturalised in S Scandinavia); on riverbanks, damp woods and grasslands. **Fl:** Mar–May. **Br Is dist:** Common and widespread except in N Scotland; female plants very local.

Purple, or Alpine, Colt's-foot *Homogyne alpina* Creeping hairy perennial. Basal leaves kidney-shaped, to 40mm, dark green above, paler and hairy on veins below. Flowers 10–15mm in diameter, purple-pink, with tubular florets, in solitary heads on erect stems to 30cm. In damp places in mountains; Scotland and from the Alps southwards. **Fl:** Jun–Sep. **Br Is dist:** Presumed introduced; very rare in Scotland.

Mugwort

stems reddish

leaves dark green above

leaves white below

leaf segments pointed

Field Wormwood

Wormwood

flowers yellow

leaves greyish-hairy above and below

ray florets very narrow and numerous

flower stalks erect, with scales

Colt's-foot

flowers pinkish-red

basal leaves small, kidney-shaped

Purple, or Alpine, Colt's-foot

basal leaves very large

whole flowering spike pinkish, including scale leaves

Butterbur

295

Leopard's-bane

Leopard's-bane *Doronicum pardalianches* Erect, hairy perennial to 90cm. *Basal leaves heart-shaped* to ovate, long-stalked, to 12cm long (**a**); stem leaves alternate, becoming narrower and less stalked upwards. Flower heads 30–50mm in diameter, with bright yellow rays and disc florets, in loose, branching inflorescence of 2–6 heads; bracts below flower heads narrowly triangular with hairy margins. Southwards from the Netherlands and Belgium; in woodland areas or as a naturalised plant, rare in the north of range. **Fl:** May–Jul. **Br Is dist:** Scattered almost throughout, as naturalised introduction.

Broad-leaved Ragwort

RAGWORTS and GROUNDSELS *Senecio* Annual or perennial herbs (including shrubs, trees and climbers elsewhere), usually downy, with alternate, spirally-arranged leaves, and flower heads aggregated into flattish-topped umbel-like clusters, always yellow; bracts below flower head in 1 row, with a few short outer bracts at base of head; ray florets almost always present.

Broad-leaved Ragwort *Senecio fluviatilis* Creeping perennial with long stolons, and erect stems to 2m, densely leafy, hairy near top, hairless below. Leaves elliptical to linear-lanceolate, to 20cm, *hairless*, pointed, toothed, and unstalked (**b**). Flower heads numerous, 15–30mm in diameter, ray florets few (6–8 only). In damp meadows, fens and woods; native from the Netherlands southwards, though naturalised elsewhere. **Fl:** Jul–Sep. **Br Is dist:** Introduced; locally naturalised throughout.

Field Fleawort

Field Fleawort *Tephroseris integrifolia* Erect perennial to 70cm, usually less, with more or less downy stems. *Basal leaves in a flat rosette*, rounded-ovate, 5–10cm long, short-stalked and untoothed; *stem leaves few*, narrower, unstalked and rather clasping. Flower heads 15–25mm in diameter, orange-yellow, with about 13 ray florets, solitary or in few-flowered inflorescence of up to 12 flowers; involucral bracts with tuft of hairs at tip. In dry close-grazed grassland, usually on calcareous soils; throughout except the far north, but local. **Fl:** May–Jul. **Br Is dist:** Local, mainly on downland in S and E England. Plants from Anglesey have toothed basal leaves and more stem leaves, and are described as ssp *maritimus*.

Marsh Ragwort

Common Ragwort *Senecio jacobaea* Biennial or perennial herb. Highly poisonous. Hairless or slightly hairy, with stout, erect, leafy, *furrowed stems* to 1.5m (usually less), not creeping. Basal and lower stem leaves 10–20cm long, *pinnately lobed with large blunt end-lobe*; upper stem leaves often more divided, with smaller end-lobe; all slightly hairy below. Flower heads 15–25mm in diameter, yellow, in much-branched *flat-topped clusters*; ray florets 12–15, rarely absent altogether (var. *flosculosus*). A common weed of pastures, waste ground and other places, on almost any soil; widespread except in the extreme north. **Fl:** Jun–Oct. **Br Is dist:** Abundant throughout.

a

Marsh Ragwort *Senecio aquaticus* Similar to Common Ragwort, differing in that it has *undivided or little-divided basal leaves*, with much larger end-lobe; stem leaves with large oval end-lobes. *Inflorescence spreading*, not dense and flat-topped; individual heads 20–30mm in diameter; bracts never black-tipped. Poisonous. In marshy places and damp grassland; from S Scandinavia southwards. **Fl:** Jul–Aug. **Br Is dist:** Widespread and moderately common throughout.

b

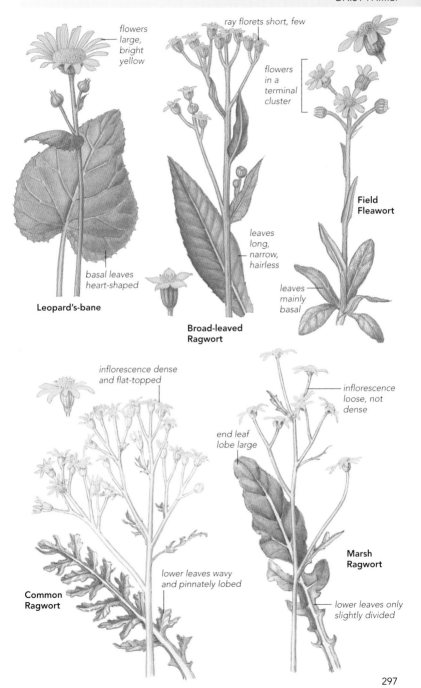

flowers large, bright yellow

ray florets short, few

flowers in a terminal cluster

Field Fleawort

leaves long, narrow, hairless

basal leaves heart-shaped

Leopard's-bane

leaves mainly basal

Broad-leaved Ragwort

inflorescence dense and flat-topped

inflorescence loose, not dense

end leaf lobe large

Marsh Ragwort

lower leaves wavy and pinnately lobed

Common Ragwort

lower leaves only slightly divided

297

Sticky Groundsel

Oxford Ragwort *Senecio squalidus* Annual, biennial or perennial plant, *usually branched at the base to form a spreading bushy plant.* Leaves once or twice pinnately lobed, with narrow, pointed leaflets, lower ones with a winged stalk, upper ones clasping. Flower heads 15–25mm in diameter, bright yellow, with *all bracts black-tipped.* Native to S Europe as far north as S Germany, but widely naturalised, especially in France and Britain; on walls, waste ground, railway lines, etc. **Fl:** May–Dec. **Br Is dist:** Widely naturalised and common in England and Wales; rare in Scotland and Ireland.

Groundsel *Senecio vulgaris* Familiar annual weed, with erect or spreading, branched, rather fleshy stems to 45cm. Leaves pinnately lobed with short blunt lobes, usually downy below, shiny above, lower leaves stalked, upper leaves clasping the stem. *Flower heads cylindrical,* roughly 4mm in diameter, 10mm long, in dense clusters at first; florets yellow, *ray florets absent or few,* curling back; short outer flower-head *bracts black-tipped.* Abundant throughout except the far north, in cultivated and bare areas. **Fl:** 1–12. **Br Is dist:** Abundant throughout.

Sticky Groundsel *Senecio viscosus* Similar in form to Groundsel, but usually taller, to 60cm, with stiffer, more erect, branches, *stickily hairy all over,* and *strong-smelling.* Flower heads , to 12mm in diameter, long-stalked, with about 13 longer, rather curled, pale yellow ray florets. Locally common from S Scandinavia southwards on waste ground, railway lines, sand-dunes and other dry, open habitats. **Fl:** Jul–Sep. **Br Is dist:** Common throughout, except the far north.

Carline Thistle *Carlina vulgaris* Erect, spiny, biennial plant, branched or unbranched, hairless or cottony-downy, to 70cm. Leaves ovate to oblong, to 15cm, wavy and spinily lobed, cottony below, the lower ones with a short stalk, upper ones clasping stem. Flower heads solitary or 2–3 together, 15–40mm in diameter; florets yellowish-brown, all disc, but surrounded by long yellowish bracts, spreading out like ray florets, with outer green spiny bracts – a distinctive combination. Throughout except the extreme north, locally common in dry grasslands, usually calcareous. **Fl:** Jul–Oct. **Br Is dist:** Locally common throughout except N Scotland.

BURDOCKS *Arctium* Robust, erect, downy, branched biennial plants. Leaves large, alternate, roughly heart-shaped, downy, not spiny. Flower heads globose, solitary in lax clusters; florets red-purple, bracts numerous, with hooked spiny tips, forming the familiar burs in fruit, aiding dispersal by animals. Much hybridisation and overlap can occur in the group.

Lesser Burdock *Arctium minus* Up to 1.5m tall. Basal leaves broadly ovate, to 50cm, *longer than wide,* heart-shaped at base, *with hollow stalks.* Flower heads 15–20mm wide, to 35mm when in fruit, globose, narrowed at top in fruit; cottony-downy at first, but becoming hairless later, short-stalked, with petals usually longer than bracts. Widespread throughout except the Arctic; common in scrub, open woods, waste ground and roadsides. **Fl:** Jul–Sep. **Br Is dist:** Common throughout.

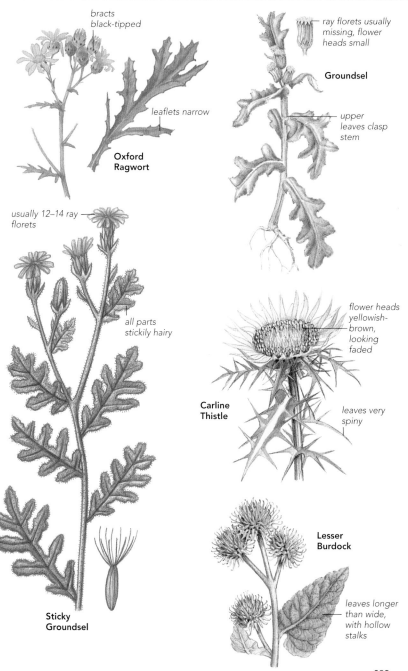

bracts
black-tipped

ray florets usually
missing, flower
heads small

Groundsel

leaflets narrow

upper
leaves clasp
stem

**Oxford
Ragwort**

usually 12–14 ray
florets

all parts
stickily hairy

flower heads
yellowish-
brown,
looking
faded

**Carline
Thistle**

leaves very
spiny

**Lesser
Burdock**

**Sticky
Groundsel**

leaves longer
than wide,
with hollow
stalks

299

Greater Burdock

Greater Burdock *Arctium lappa* Similar in form to other species (*see* p. 298). Basal leaves *as wide as long* (a), *leaf stalks solid*. Flower heads large, 30–40mm in diameter, in very few-flowered inflorescence, becoming opened widely when in fruit; bracts greenish-yellow. Widespread and fairly common throughout except the far north; in open woods, scrub and roadsides, on heavy soils. **Fl:** Jul–Sep. **Br Is dist:** Common in much of England and Wales, but rare or absent farther north.

Alpine Saw-wort

Alpine Saw-wort *Saussurea alpina* Creeping perennial producing erect grooved, rather downy flower stems to 50cm. Basal leaves ovate to lanceolate, to 18cm long, untoothed or slightly toothed, with narrowly winged stalk; upper leaves narrower and unstalked; all leaves more or less hairless above, white downy below. Flower heads egg-shaped, to 20mm long, more or less unstalked in a tight terminal inflorescence; florets all tubular, purplish at top, yellow-white below, greatly exceeding bracts; inner bracts grey-hairy. In grassland, open woods, rocky places, cliffs, mainly in mountains, though widespread in the Arctic. **Fl:** Jul–Sep. **Br Is dist:** Very local in mountain areas from N Wales and C Ireland northwards.

THISTLES *Carduus* and *Cirsium Carduus* species annual to perennial herbs with spiny-winged stems, and spine-edged leaves that are usually green above and cottony below. Flower heads solitary or in clusters, with masses of overlapping spine-tipped bracts. Florets all tubular, usually red to purple in colour. *Cirsium* (*see* pp. 302–4) very similar, differing mainly in that the flowers have a feathery-hairy pappus.

Musk, or Nodding, Thistle

Musk, or Nodding, Thistle *Carduus nutans* Erect biennial plant up to 1.2m, with cottony spiny-winged stems, branched above, and *spine-free for a section below the flower heads*. Leaves pinnately lobed, with segments lobed and spine-tipped, cottony below, especially along veins. Flower heads rounded-cylindrical, large (40–60mm in diameter when fully opened), *drooping, solitary on long spineless stalks*; florets deep red-purple, surrounded by an involucre of long, narrow, recurved, spiny-tipped, often reddish bracts; flowers fragrant. From Denmark southwards, frequent (except in the north of range) in dry grasslands, dunes and roadsides. **Fl:** May–Aug. **Br Is dist:** Common in England and Wales; much less common in Scotland; rare in Ireland.

Welted Thistle

Welted Thistle *Carduus crispus* Erect, branched biennial up to 1.2m, *with virtually continuous narrow spiny wings on all stems, except for a very short section below flower heads*; stems cottony. Lower leaves elliptical in outline, deeply pinnately lobed, 3-lobed and spiny; upper leaves narrower, stalkless, with base running down stem. Flower heads roughly 20–30mm long, globose to cylindrical, usually *in small clusters*; florets red-purple; involucre of bracts roughly oval, with numerous narrow, cottony, spreading bracts, with weak spine-tips. From S Sweden southwards; in waste places, scrub, grassland and open woodland; common. **Fl:** Jun–Aug. **Br Is dist:** Common throughout except N Scotland.

Slender Thistle

Slender Thistle *Carduus tenuiflorus* Similar to Welted Thistle, to 1m tall. Differs in that it is more erect and narrowly branched, with *stems broadly winged right up to flower heads, very cottony* and greyish. Flower heads more slender, to 20mm long but only 5–10mm wide, in dense terminal clusters; *florets pale pinky red*. In dry grassy and open habitats, often near the sea. Native from the Netherlands southwards, naturalised locally farther north. **Fl:** May–Aug. **Br Is dist:** Widespread, except in N Scotland; mainly coastal.

a

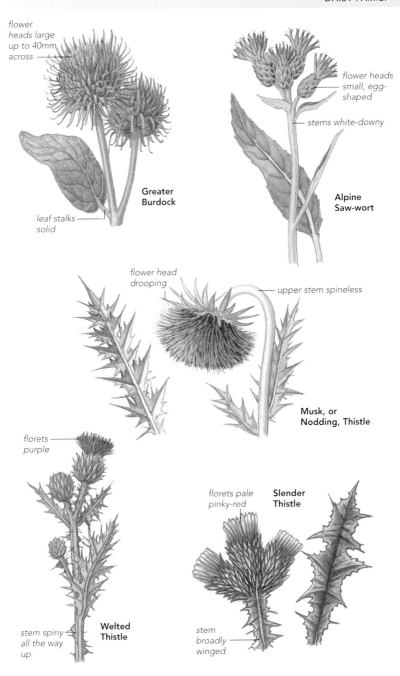

flower heads large up to 40mm across

flower heads small, egg-shaped

stems white-downy

Greater Burdock

leaf stalks solid

Alpine Saw-wort

flower head drooping

upper stem spineless

Musk, or Nodding, Thistle

florets purple

florets pale pinky-red

Slender Thistle

stem spiny all the way up

Welted Thistle

stem broadly winged

301

Woolly Thistle

Woolly Thistle *Cirsium eriophorum* Stout erect biennial plant, with *unwinged, cottony, furrowed stems to 1.5m*, branched in upper part. Basal leaves large, to 60cm long, pinnately divided into narrow 2-forked segments, *usually with 1 segment pointing upwards, the other downwards* (giving a distinctive 2-rowed effect); stem leaves smaller and stalkless; *all white-cottony below*, all lobes spine-tipped. Flower heads solitary, very large, globular, up to 70mm in diameter, with very *cottony bracts*; florets red-purple. From the Netherlands and N England southwards on calcareous grassland and scrub. **Fl**: Jul–Sep. **Br Is dist**: England and Wales only, north to Co Durham; local.

Meadow Thistle

Spear Thistle *Cirsium vulgare* Erect biennial, with cottony stems with interrupted spiny wings; branched in upper part, to 1.5m tall. Basal leaves to 30cm long, deeply pinnately lobed, with lobes forked and spiny, and a *single, long, stout, pointed end-lobe* (the spear); upper leaves smaller; all leaves bristly-prickly above, matt. Flower heads ovoid, 30–50mm long, with more or less cottony bracts; florets red-purple; *outer bracts with long, yellowish spine-tips*. Very common and widespread almost throughout, in waste places, grassland and disturbed ground, as a persistent weed. **Fl**: Jul–Oct. **Br Is dist**: Common throughout.

Cabbage Thistle

Meadow Thistle *Cirsium dissectum* Perennial, with *creeping stolons* producing simple, erect, unwinged, downy, ridged stems to 80cm. Basal leaves elliptical to lanceolate, to 25cm long, either pinnately lobed, or with widely separated teeth, *green and hairy above, white-cottony below*, with soft marginal prickles; stem leaves similar, but narrower and barely clasping stem. *Flower heads solitary* (rarely more) on *long, spineless stalks*, roughly 30mm long; florets red-purple; bracts of head narrow lanceolate, pressed close to head, outer ones spine-tipped. From the Netherlands and N Germany southwards, rare in the north; in damp, peaty meadows and bogs. **Fl**: Jun–Aug. **Br Is dist**: Locally common northwards to N England; frequent in Ireland.

Dwarf, or Stemless, Thistle

Cabbage Thistle *Cirsium oleraceum* Erect perennial to 1.2m, with unwinged, almost hairless, furrowed stems. Basal leaves to 40cm, elliptical in outline, but usually toothed or pinnately divided; upper leaves undivided, clasping the stem with heart-shaped bases; all leaves weakly spiny, pale green. Flower heads oval, 25–40mm in diameter, erect and in clusters exceeded by soft leaf-like bracts; *florets pale yellow*. On roadsides, fens and damp woods; from S Scandinavia southwards; locally common. **Fl**: Jul–Sep. **Br Is dist**: An occasional introduction only.

Dwarf, or Stemless, Thistle *Cirsium acaule* Perennial with a basal rosette of leaves, and *stemless or short-stemmed flower heads* from the centre. Leaves oblong, to 15cm long, deeply pinnately divided, with divided, wavy, very spiny lobes. Flower heads usually stalkless and solitary, but sometimes several together, sometimes stalked to 30cm; heads oval, 30–40mm long, florets red-purple. In dry calcareous grasslands; from Denmark southwards, rare in the north of range. **Fl**: Jun–Sep. **Br Is dist**: Locally common in S and E England and S Wales; absent from Scotland and Ireland.

flower head
very large,
spherical

leaves end
in long
stout spine

**Woolly
Thistle**

**Spear
Thistle**

leaves white-
downy underneath

flowers pale
yellow

flower head
solitary up to
30mm long

long leaf-
like bracts
surround
flower
head

stem downy
and without
prickles

**Cabbage
Thistle**

flower heads sit
directly on rosette,
without a stalk

leaves very
spiny, all in a
basal rosette

**Meadow
Thistle**

**Dwarf, or
Stemless, Thistle**

Melancholy Thistle

Cotton, or Scotch, Thistle

Melancholy Thistle *Cirsium heterophyllum* Rather like a large version of Meadow Thistle (*see* p. 302). Tall perennial to 1.2m, with cottony, unwinged, spineless stems. Leaves roughly oblong, 10–25cm long, unlobed to pinnately lobed, flat, with softly prickly teeth, *green and hairless above, but thickly felted below*; upper leaves similar, but smaller, with rounded clasping bases. Flower heads solitary, or (rarely) in clusters of 2–4 on long stems; up to 50mm long, 30–50mm wide; florets red-purple. Widespread in damp pastures, open woods and roadsides; common in the north, more confined to mountain areas in the south. **Fl:** Jun–Aug. **Br Is dist:** Absent from S England and S Wales; locally common from N England northwards.

Marsh Thistle *Cirsium palustre* Erect biennial, with stems to 1.5m, often branched above the middle, *all stems continuously spiny-winged; whole plant often reddish-tinged*. Leaves linear-lanceolate, pinnately divided, wavy, *very lobed and spiny*, hairy above but shiny green. Flower heads in crowded leafy clusters both on main stem and branches; flowers 15–20mm long, with *dark red-purple* (occasionally white) florets, and purplish-green bracts. The reddish colour of the plant, and the dark small florets, make identification easy. Very common in damp grassy places; throughout except the extreme north. **Fl:** Jul–Sep. **Br Is dist:** Common throughout.

Creeping Thistle *Cirsium arvense* Far-creeping perennial herb, with erect leafy stems to 1m, *unwinged*. Leaves not in distinct basal rosette, oblong, deeply pinnately divided, with triangular spiny lobes, very wavy, hairless above; upper leaves similar, but clasping, sometimes running a short way down stems as a spiny wing. Flower heads in open clusters, narrowly cylindrical, 20mm long, 10–15mm wide; *florets pale pinkish-purple or whitish, involucral bracts purplish*. Very common throughout in grasslands, cultivated land and waste places; a persistent weed. **Fl:** Jun–Sep. **Br Is dist:** Very common throughout.

Cotton, or Scotch, Thistle *Onopordum acanthium* Erect, robust biennial to 3m, with *white-cottony, continuously broad-winged stems*, branched in upper parts. Leaves oblong to ovate, unstalked, toothed or wavy-lobed, with strong spines, white-cottony on both surfaces. Flower heads solitary or in clusters of 2–5, roughly globose, 30–50 x 30–50mm; florets purplish-pink, bracts narrow, green and tipped with strong yellowish spines. From S Sweden southwards in waste places, roadsides and dry banks, but probably not native in the north part of range. **Fl:** Jul–Sep. **Br Is dist:** Reasonably common in S and E England, becoming rarer to the north and west. Probably not native.

Milk Thistle *Silybum marianum* Erect, robust, annual or biennial to 1m, hairless or cottony, often branched, stems unwinged. Basal leaves to 50cm, pinnately lobed or wavy-edged, spiny, hairless and *shiny green, marked with conspicuous whitish network of veins above*. Flower heads large, 40–50mm long, with red-purple florets and *surrounded by long, triangular, spiny-toothed bracts*. In waste places, roadsides and on coastal cliffs; native from France southwards, but naturalised farther north. **Fl:** Jun–Aug. **Br Is dist:** Possibly native on S coast, naturalised locally elsewhere.

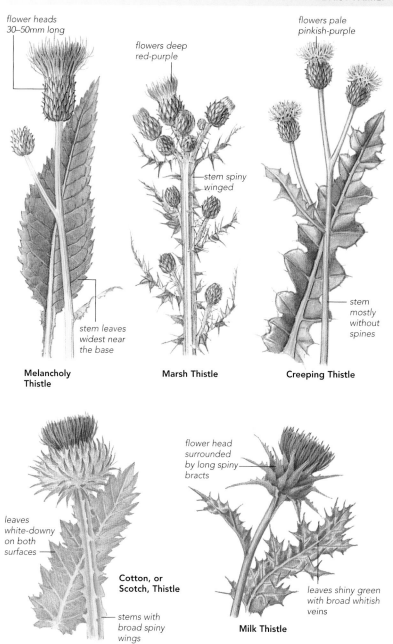

flower heads
30–50mm long

flowers deep
red-purple

flowers pale
pinkish-purple

stem spiny
winged

stem leaves
widest near
the base

stem
mostly
without
spines

**Melancholy
Thistle**

Marsh Thistle

Creeping Thistle

leaves
white-downy
on both
surfaces

flower head
surrounded
by long spiny
bracts

**Cotton, or
Scotch, Thistle**

stems with
broad spiny
wings

leaves shiny green
with broad whitish
veins

Milk Thistle

305

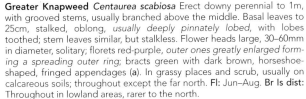

Saw-wort *Serratula tinctoria* Hairless perennial, *without prickles*, with erect wiry grooved stems to 1m, usually less. Leaves to 20cm, very variable in shape from undivided to deeply pinnately lobed, with finely toothed margins; lower leaves stalked, upper leaves clasping. Flower heads small, 15–20mm long in lax inflorescences; florets reddish-purple, involucre of bracts narrowly cylindrical in shape, with *closely pressed purplish bracts*. From S Scandinavia southwards in permanent pastures, heaths and open heathy woods, on mildly acid or calcareous soils. **Fl**: Jul–Sep. **Br Is dist**: Locally common north to S Scotland, rare in N Scotland and Ireland.

Saw-wort

KNAPWEEDS and CORNFLOWERS *Centaurea* Annual or perennial plants, with alternate bristly (but not spiny) leaves. Flower heads rather thistle-like, but surrounded by distinctive head of bracts, each consisting of a normal bract topped by an appendage that is frequently bristly or toothed; the shape of these appendages is often diagnostic. Florets all tubular, but outer ones sometimes greatly enlarged.

Common Knapweed,
Hardheads

Greater Knapweed *Centaurea scabiosa* Erect downy perennial to 1m, with grooved stems, usually branched above the middle. Basal leaves to 25cm, stalked, oblong, *usually deeply pinnately lobed*, with lobes toothed; stem leaves similar, but stalkless. Flower heads large, 30–60mm in diameter, solitary; florets red-purple, *outer ones greatly enlarged forming a spreading outer ring*; bracts green with dark brown, horseshoe-shaped, fringed appendages (**a**). In grassy places and scrub, usually on calcareous soils; throughout except the far north. **Fl**: Jun–Aug. **Br Is dist**: Throughout in lowland areas, rarer to the north.

Red Star-thistle *Centaurea calcitrapa* Biennial herb, with branched erect or ascending hairless stems to 70cm. Lower leaves deeply pinnately divided, with narrow lobes; upper leaves toothed. Flower heads 8–10mm in diameter, reddish-purple, but surrounded by a ring of long-spined, yellowish, spreading bracts, each about 20–30mm long. Native in S Europe, but naturalised locally throughout N Europe as far north as the Netherlands and Germany; in grassland and waste habitats, especially on chalky soils. **Fl**: Jul–Sep. **Br Is dist**: Well established on chalk on the Sussex coast; casual elsewhere.

Rough Star-thistle *Centaurea aspera* Erect plant to 50cm, downy. Leaves pinnate. Flower heads pink-purple, but distinctive by the appendages which consist of *3–5 chaffy palmately arranged recurved spiny teeth* (**b**). Sand-dunes and dry habitats; W France and Channel Islands, naturalised elsewhere. **Fl**: Jul–Sep. **Br Is dist**: Channel Islands, naturalised in S Wales.

Common Knapweed, Hardheads *Centaurea nigra* Erect, roughly hairy perennial to 1m, with grooved stems, branched in upper part. Leaves oblong to linear-lanceolate, unlobed or slightly lobed but *not pinnate*; upper leaves narrow and unlobed. Flower heads solitary or few together, 20–40mm in diameter; florets red-purple, *outer florets usually not enlarged*; bracts of head have brown to black, *triangular, deeply fringed appendages with bristly, often forked*, teeth (**c1**). Very common in grassy areas north to S Sweden. **Fl**: Jun–Sep. **Br Is dist**: Common almost throughout. The form known as ssp *nemoralis* differs in being very slender, often more branched, with stem not swollen below flower heads; florets paler pink-purple, commonly with enlarged outer ray florets; *teeth of bract appendage longer than undivided portion* (**c2**) (equal or shorter in nominate species), but nowadays it is generally incorporated into the nominate species as the distinctions are not consistent. **Fl**: Jun–Sep. **Br Is dist**: Local in England and Wales, mainly on lighter, calcareous soils.

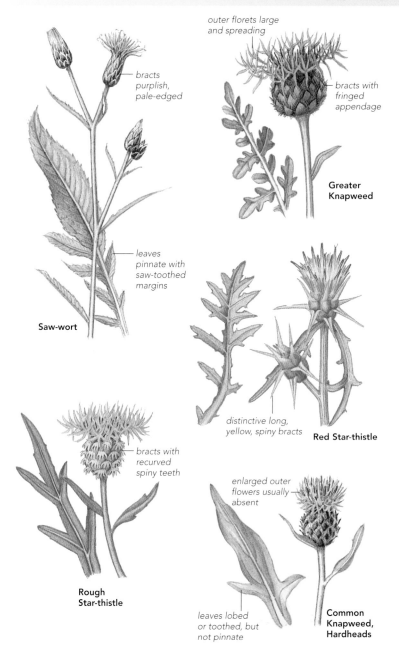

outer florets large
and spreading

bracts with
fringed
appendage

**Greater
Knapweed**

bracts
purplish,
pale-edged

leaves
pinnate with
saw-toothed
margins

Saw-wort

distinctive long,
yellow, spiny bracts

Red Star-thistle

bracts with
recurved
spiny teeth

**Rough
Star-thistle**

enlarged outer
flowers usually
absent

leaves lobed
or toothed, but
not pinnate

**Common
Knapweed,
Hardheads**

307

Perennial Cornflower

Perennial Cornflower *Centaurea montana* Creeping, downy perennial, with erect stems to 80cm, winged where leaf stalks run down. Leaves ovate to oblong, unlobed or occasionally somewhat toothed or lobed, cottony below. *Flower heads large, 60–80mm in diameter, blue or pinkish blue*, inner florets usually redder than outer, with long, spreading outer florets; bracts with black fringes. In open woods and meadows, especially in mountain areas; from the Ardennes southwards. Often cultivated. **Fl:** Jun–Aug. **Br Is dist:** Casual introduction only.

Cornflower

Cornflower *Centaurea cyanus* Superficially similar to Perennial Cornflower, but annual, with an erect, wiry, grooved stem to 90cm. Lower leaves undivided or pinnately divided and narrow; upper leaves linear and unlobed. Flower heads smaller, *15–30mm in diameter, with bright blue outer florets* and reddish inner ones; bracts with brown or silvery fringes. A weed of cultivated ground and disturbed areas; occurring almost throughout, but not native in the region, and generally declining. **Fl:** Jun–Aug. **Br Is dist:** Once a common arable weed, now virtually extinct.

Lamb's Succory

Lamb's Succory *Arnoseris minima* Distinctive plant to 30cm, resembling the cat's-ears, but easily recognised in flower by the hollow flower stalks strongly swollen at the top. Leaves in rosette, pinnately lobed. Flowers yellow, 7–10mm across, and solitary. In cultivated land, usually sandy; from S Sweden southwards; local. **Fl:** Jun–Aug. **Br Is dist:** Formerly in S and E England, but probably extinct.

CAT'S-EARS *Hypochaeris* Annuals or perennials with basal leaf rosettes, erect unbranched or somewhat branched stems, and yellow flowers, with ray florets. Very similar to hawkbits (*see* p. 310) differing in having membranous scales between the florets (absent in hawkbits).

Spotted Cat's-ear

Spotted Cat's-ear *Hypochaeris maculata* Perennial herb with all leaves in basal rosette, roughly ovate, bristly, wavy-toothed, distinctive by *blotching of dark red-purple spots*. Flower stems bristly, usually unbranched, with scale-leaves only (or none); flower heads solitary, 30–50mm in diameter, *lemon yellow*; bracts narrow, blackish. In grasslands, open woodland and cliffs; widespread except in the far north, though local, mainly on calcareous soils. **Fl:** Jun–Aug. **Br Is dist:** Rare and declining, in scattered localities throughout England and Wales.

Cat's-ear

Cat's-ear *Hypochaeris radicata* Perennial, with basal rosette of lanceolate to oblong, bristly, wavy-edged leaves to 25cm long; stems to 60cm, almost hairless, *usually branched once or twice, thickened below flower heads*, with few scale-like, dark-tipped leaves along them. Flower heads 25–40mm in diameter, solitary, with bright yellow florets; bracts in bell shape, narrowed abruptly to stem, with numerous hairless, purple-tipped, individual bracts. Widespread and common generally throughout, except the far north; in grasslands, dunes and roadsides, usually avoiding strongly calcareous soils. **Fl:** Jun–Sep. **Br Is dist:** Common throughout.

Smooth Cat's-ear

Smooth Cat's-ear *Hypochaeris glabra* Rather similar to Cat's-ear, but smaller, to 20cm; leaves shorter, hairless or slightly bristly, and glossy. *Flower heads small, 10–15mm, with the yellow florets barely longer than the bracts*; rays about twice as long as broad, opening fully only in sunshine. From S Norway southwards; in sandy grasslands. **Fl:** Jun–Oct. **Br Is dist:** Frequent only in S and E England; rare or absent elsewhere.

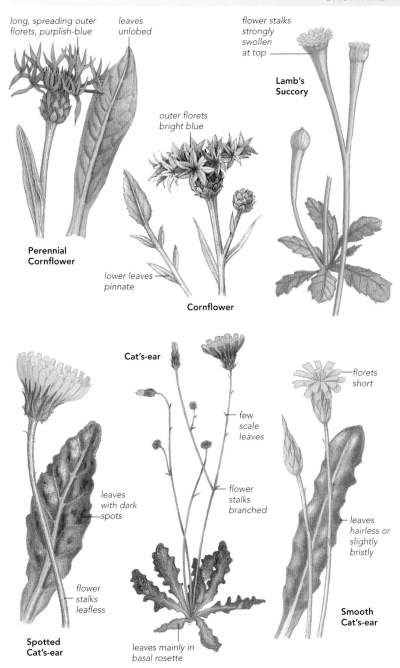

long, spreading outer florets, purplish-blue

leaves unlobed

flower stalks strongly swollen at top

Lamb's Succory

outer florets bright blue

Perennial Cornflower

lower leaves pinnate

Cornflower

Cat's-ear

florets short

few scale leaves

flower stalks branched

leaves with dark spots

leaves hairless or slightly bristly

flower stalks leafless

Spotted Cat's-ear

leaves mainly in basal rosette

Smooth Cat's-ear

309

Bristly Oxtongue

Goat's-beard,
Jack-go-to-bed-at-noon

HAWKBITS *Leontodon* Very similar to cat's-ears (*see* p. 308), but lacking the scales between the florets.

Autumn Hawkbit *Leontodon autumnalis* Hairless or slightly hairy (*with unforked hairs*), perennial herb, with basal rosette of leaves and *2–3 times branched, erect flower stems*. Basal leaves variable, oblong-lanceolate, usually deeply pinnately lobed, sometimes wavy-edged, with few simple hairs, or hairless; stems bear *numerous small scale-leaves just below heads*. Flower heads 12–35mm in diameter, erect in bud, yellow, with *involucre gradually tapering into stem*. In dry grasslands, throughout, usually on more acid soils, common. **Fl:** Jun–Oct. **Br Is dist:** Common throughout. Ssp *pratensis* has the bracts covered in long dark hairs; it occurs mainly in mountain pastures, including Britain.

Rough Hawkbit *Leontodon hispidus* Perennial herb, *covered with rough white hairs*. Basal rosette has oblong-lanceolate leaves, narrowing to base, wavy-toothed, very hairy. Flower stems to 40cm, hairy throughout with forked hairs, unbranched; flower heads 25–40mm in diameter, *solitary*, with golden yellow florets much longer than bracts; involucre narrows abruptly into stalk. In dry grasslands, usually calcareous; throughout the area except the extreme north. **Fl:** Jun–Sep. **Br Is dist:** Widespread and common except in N Scotland.

Bristly Oxtongue *Picris echioides* Erect annual or biennial, with furrowed bristly branched stems, to 90cm. Basal leaves oblong, narrowing into stalk; upper leaves narrower, with clasping basal leaves *covered with robust swollen-based bristles* (a) (only Teasel leaves look at all similar, *see* p. 276). Flower heads 20–25mm in diameter, in loose groups, florets yellow; outermost 3–5 bracts leaf-like, triangular, much broader than, but not as long as, inner bracts. Locally common from Denmark southwards, though not native over northern part of range; in grassy areas, disturbed ground and drier coastal habitats, usually on heavy soils. **Fl:** Jun–Oct. **Br Is dist:** Locally common in S Britain, especially near coasts, but rare farther north.

Cut-leaved Viper's-grass *Scorzonera laciniata* Almost hairless perinnial to 60cm, with *pinnately divided leaves*, and small flowers. Mainland Europe from Belgium southwards; in dry grasslands. **Fl:** May–Jun. **Br Is dist:** Absent.

Goat's-beard, Jack-go-to-bed-at-noon *Tragopogon pratensis* Variable annual to perennial, with erect, simple or slightly branched, stems to 70cm or more, downy when young, hairless and rather grey-green later. Lower leaves narrow, linear-lanceolate, to 30cm, with distinct keel, broadened and slightly clasping at base; stem leaves similar but smaller, with long fine point. Flower heads solitary, long-stalked, to 50mm in diameter, with yellow florets. Bracts 8–10, in 1 row only (compare with Cut-leaved Viper's-grass). Fruit is a large white 'clock', to 80mm in diameter. Two subspecies occur in N Europe. Ssp *pratensis* has *involucral bracts as long as or shorter than florets*, and the flowers remain open in dull weather. Throughout most of Europe in grassland. Ssp *minor* has *flower bracts much longer than florets*, and flowers close in dull weather and at midday. Similar habitats; W Europe only. **Fl:** May–Jul. **Br Is dist:** Ssp *minor* is the widespread subspecies, frequent throughout England and Wales; rare elsewhere. Ssp *pratensis* is not native.

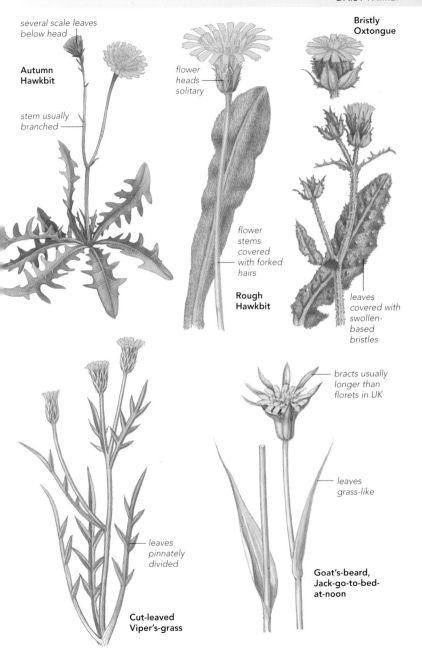

several scale leaves
below head

**Autumn
Hawkbit**

stem usually
branched

flower
heads
solitary

**Bristly
Oxtongue**

flower
stems
covered
with forked
hairs

**Rough
Hawkbit**

leaves
covered with
swollen-
based
bristles

bracts usually
longer than
florets in UK

leaves
grass-like

leaves
pinnately
divided

**Cut-leaved
Viper's-grass**

**Goat's-beard,
Jack-go-to-bed-
at-noon**

311

Marsh Sow-thistle

Prickly Lettuce

a

b

SOW-THISTLES *Sonchus* Annual or perennial herbs with stout, hollow, milk-containing stems. Leaves pinnately lobed or with wavy, spiny margins; stem leaves clasping. Flower heads in umbel-like clusters.

Prickly Sow-thistle *Sonchus asper* Erect, hairless annual or biennial (except for inflorescence, which may be glandular-hairy), to 1m, with simple or branched stem. Lower leaves roughly spoon-shaped in outline, sometimes pinnately lobed, with triangular, toothed lobes, and *rounded auricles at base*, deeply toothed all round margins, *glossy green above*; upper leaves narrower, firmly clasping stem with rounded bases (a). Flower heads 20–25mm in diameter, golden yellow. Very common in cultivated ground and waste places; throughout. **Fl:** Jun–Oct. **Br Is dist:** Common throughout.

Smooth Sow-thistle *Sonchus oleraceus* Rather similar to above, but leaves are usually pinnately lobed, with triangular lobes, and end-lobe distinctly wider than next pair of leaflets down; *auricles at base of leaves pointed*, not rounded. *Leaves matt*, not glossy, on upper surface (b). Flowers pale yellow. In similar habitats; throughout. **Fl:** Jun–Oct. **Br Is dist:** Common throughout.

Marsh Sow-thistle *Sonchus palustris* Tall robust perennial to 2.5m (occasionally even taller), with stout erect 4-angled hollow stems, glandular-hairy above and hairless below. Basal leaves oblong, with *arrow-shaped bases*, pinnately lobed blade, and a long pointed terminal lobe; margins finely spiny-toothed, leaves hairless; upper leaves narrow, with long, pointed, clasping basal lobes. Flower heads large, 30–40mm in diameter, and pale yellow; involucral bracts covered with *blackish sticky glandular hairs*. In marshes, fens and uppermost parts of salt-marshes; from S Scandinavia southwards; local. **Fl:** Jul–Sep. **Br Is dist:** Only in S and E England, from E Anglia to Hampshire; very local.

Perennial Sow-thistle *Sonchus arvensis* Similar in form to Marsh Sow-thistle. Differs in that the leaves have *rounded bases*, and are pinnately lobed with round short lobes. Florets deep yellow; bracts and inflorescence branches all covered with long, *yellowish, glandular hairs*. Widespread and common throughout on arable and disturbed land, and coastal sands. **Fl:** Jul–Oct. **Br Is dist:** Common throughout.

LETTUCES *Lactuca* Annual or perennial erect herbs, with milky latex. Flower heads with all ray florets; involucre cylindrical.

Prickly Lettuce *Lactuca serriola* Stiffly erect, hairless annual or perennial to 1.8m, branched above. *Leaves stiffly erect*, oblong-lanceolate, lower ones usually pinnately divided, with narrow, well-separated lobes, hairless but spiny on pale midrib underneath, and on margins; upper leaves less deeply divided, with clasping bases; all thick and waxy grey-green. Flower heads in loose inflorescence, with branches at acute angle to main stem; individual heads 11–13mm in diameter, with 7–12 yellow florets. On waste ground, roadsides and railways; widespread except in much of Scandinavia. **Fl:** Jul–Sep. **Br Is dist:** Common in the south and east, but rare or absent elsewhere.

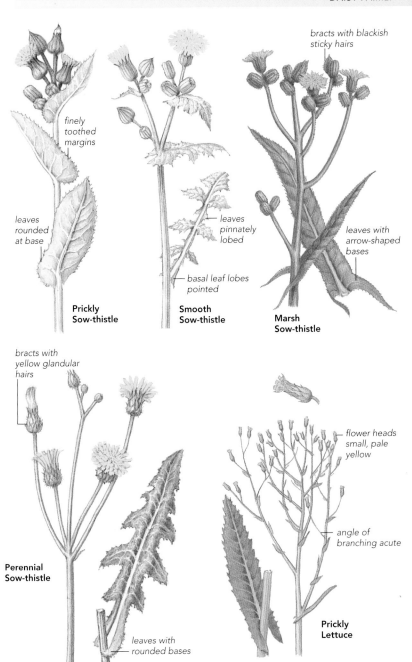

bracts with blackish
sticky hairs

finely
toothed
margins

leaves
rounded
at base

leaves
pinnately
lobed

basal leaf lobes
pointed

leaves with
arrow-shaped
bases

**Prickly
Sow-thistle**

**Smooth
Sow-thistle**

**Marsh
Sow-thistle**

bracts with
yellow glandular
hairs

flower heads
small, pale
yellow

angle of
branching acute

**Perennial
Sow-thistle**

leaves with
rounded bases

**Prickly
Lettuce**

Least Lettuce *Lactuca saligna* Slender annual to 1m. Leaves linear-lanceolate, bases arrow-shaped and clasping, untoothed, held vertically. *Flower heads in a narrow spike-like inflorescence with short branches*; florets pale yellow, 10–15mm long, reddish below. From S England and C Germany southwards; dry banks near the sea; very local. **Fl:** Jul–Aug. **Br Is dist:** Very rare and decreasing; near coasts in SE England.

Blue, or Mountain, Lettuce

Blue, or Mountain, Lettuce *Lactuca perennis* Erect, hairless perennial to 80cm, branched above. Leaves grey-green, pinnately lobed with very narrow, pointed segments. Flower heads few, in a branched inflorescence, long-stalked, 30–40mm in diameter, with bluish-purple florets. In rocky and dry places, on lime-rich soils, from Belgium southwards. **Fl:** May–Aug. **Br Is dist:** Absent.

Alpine Blue Sow-thistle *Cicerbita alpina* Tall perennial herb with erect, furrowed stems to 2m, reddish-glandular above. Lower leaves pinnately divided, with large, triangular, end-lobe; upper leaves narrower, with winged stalks broadening out into heart-shaped clasping base. Flower heads 20mm in diameter, pale violet-blue, in long raceme, with sticky hairy bracts and stalks. Widespread in N Scandinavia in moist shady and grassy habitats; confined to mountains farther south. **Fl:** Jul–Sep. **Br Is dist:** Very rare, in Scottish Highlands only.

Alpine Blue Sow-thistle

Wall Lettuce *Mycelis muralis* Erect hairless perennial to 1m. Lower leaves pinnately lobed, lyre-shaped, with a large end-lobe, and winged stalks; upper leaves smaller, less divided, with clasping bases; all leaves thin in texture, often red-tinged. Flower heads small, 7–10mm in diameter, in a large open inflorescence with branches at right angles to main stem; florets yellow, usually with 5 rays; involucre of bracts narrowly cylindrical. In woods, on old walls and rocks, often on lime-rich soil; throughout except the far north. **Fl:** Jun–Sep. **Br Is dist:** Throughout, though less common in Scotland and Ireland.

Wall Lettuce

DANDELIONS *Taraxacum* Perennial herbs with tap root, a basal rosette of leaves, and *solitary flower heads on leafless, hollow stems with abundant milky latex*; florets bright yellow, all rayed. Although easy to recognise as a group, dandelions are extremely difficult to recognise individually – more than 1,200 species are recorded from Europe altogether. The description below is that of *T. officinale*, the Common Dandelion, but this name includes numerous microspecies within it. Readers should refer to specialist texts for more details.

Common Dandelion *Taraxacum officinale* Variable perennial, with a basal rosette of pinnately lobed leaves, roughly spoon-shaped in outline, with winged stalks. Flower heads 20–60mm in diameter, on stalks to 40cm, rays usually having a brown or grey stripe below. Outer flower bracts curved back. Widespread and common throughout in grasslands. **Fl:** Mar–Oct. **Br Is dist:** Common throughout.

Nipplewort *Lapsana communis* Erect annual to 1m, with leafy much-branched stems lacking latex. Basal leaves oval, often pinnately lobed with large oval end-lobe; upper leaves oval to diamond-shaped. Flower heads small, 10–20mm in diameter, much-branched loose inflorescence; florets all rayed, 8–15, yellow, short; involucre narrowly cylindrical, with 1 row of equal bracts and a few shorter ones, nipple-like in bud. Widespread and common throughout; in waste and cultivated ground, woodland margins, etc. **Fl:** Jul–Oct. **Br Is dist:** Common throughout.

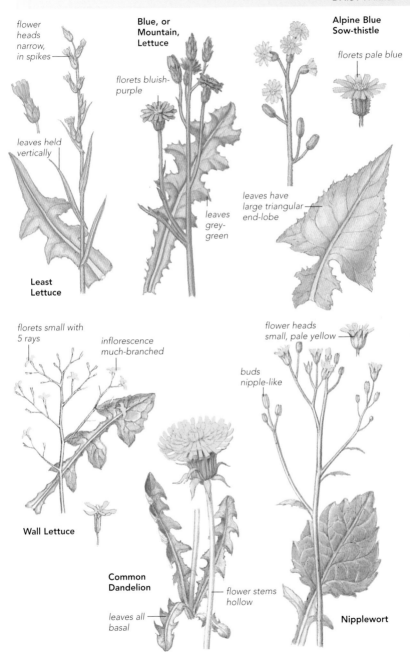

flower heads narrow, in spikes

Blue, or Mountain, Lettuce

florets bluish-purple

leaves held vertically

Alpine Blue Sow-thistle

florets pale blue

leaves grey-green

leaves have large triangular end-lobe

Least Lettuce

florets small with 5 rays

inflorescence much-branched

Wall Lettuce

Common Dandelion

flower stems hollow

leaves all basal

flower heads small, pale yellow

buds nipple-like

Nipplewort

315

Marsh Hawk's-beard

Smooth Hawk's-beard

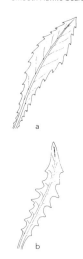

a

b

HAWK'S-BEARDS *Crepis* A small group of erect plants, annual to perennial, with branched stems. Leaves alternate, lobed or pinnately divided with backward-pointing lobes. Florets all rayed, yellow, strap-shaped; flower bracts in 2 rows, with outer ones shorter, often spreading.

Marsh Hawk's-beard *Crepis paludosa* Perennial herb with erect *hairless stem* to 90cm, branched above. Basal and lower stem leaves lanceolate to ovate, narrowed into a *short*, winged stalk (**a**); upper leaves narrower, clasping, with *arrow-shaped bases*; all leaves shiny, hairless and wavy-toothed. Flower heads 15–25mm in diameter, in few-flowered clusters; florets yellow, bracts woolly with black glandular hairs. Throughout N Europe, though local; in wet meadows and woods. **Fl:** Jul–Sep. **Br Is dist:** N Britain only, from N England and Wales northwards.

Smooth Hawk's-beard *Crepis capillaris* Erect, hairless annual or biennial to 1m, branched from the base or above. Leaves more or less hairless, glossy, irregularly pinnately lobed, with large triangular end-lobe and narrow side-lobes (**b**); upper leaves similar but smaller, stalkless *with clasping arrow-shaped bases*. Flower heads 10–15mm in diameter, erect in bud, in loose inflorescences; involucral bracts downy, often with black hairs on outer faces, hairless within, all appressed. Widespread, though absent or only locally naturalised in Scandinavia; in waste places, grassland, roadsides and banks. **Fl:** Jun–Oct. **Br Is dist:** Common throughout in lowland areas.

Beaked Hawk's-beard *Crepis vesicaria* Similar to Smooth Hawk's-beard, but *downier*; leaves have broader lobes, *downy all over*. Flower heads 15–25mm in diameter, *florets orange-yellow*, outer ones striped reddish outside; outer involucral bracts spreading. Fruit have long beaks. From the Netherlands southwards, in grasslands, waste ground and roadsides; common. **Fl:** May–Jul. **Br Is dist:** Probably not native; common and widespread in England, except in the north; absent from Scotland; rare in Ireland.

HAWKWEEDS *Hieracium* and *Pilosella* A large and highly complex group of plants, with several hundred very similar species. Perennials, without stolons (except in *Pilosella*), with erect, usually leafy, stems. Leaves toothed but not pinnately lobed. Flower heads with rays only, strap-shaped, usually yellow; flower bracts narrow, unequal, in overlapping rows. Identification is exceptionally difficult, and those interested in a more detailed treatment are referred to *Flora Europaea Vol. 4*. A very small selection of the more recognisable species is given.

Orange Hawkweed, Fox-and-Cubs *Pilosella aurantiaca* Similar to Mouse-ear Hawkweed, except the stem is taller, to 40cm, with blackish hairs, and bears several leaves. Flowers in clusters of 2–12 heads; *florets orange-red*, bracts covered with dark hairs. Widespread through N Europe, though probably not native in many western areas; local in grasslands, on banks, roadsides and often in mountains. **Fl:** Jun–Jul. **Br Is dist:** Not native, but widely naturalised.

Mouse-ear Hawkweed *Pilosella officinarum* Distinctive perennial herb with leafy runners, forming extensive patches, and erect, leafless stems to 30cm. Leaves in rosettes, spoon-shaped, to 80mm long, green and hairy above, but white-downy below. Flower heads solitary, 25–25mm wide, florets lemon-yellow, red-striped below. Throughout, except the extreme north; in dry, grassy places, banks and heaths. **Fl:** May–Aug. **Br Is dist:** Common throughout.

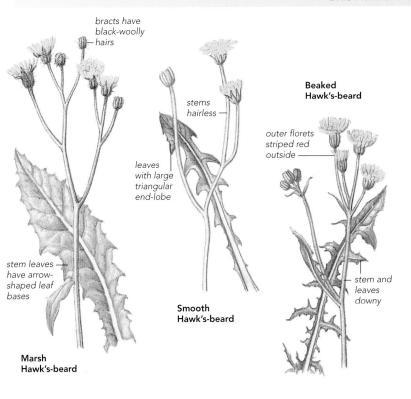

bracts have black-woolly hairs

stems hairless

Beaked Hawk's-beard

leaves with large triangular end-lobe

outer florets striped red outside

stem leaves have arrow-shaped leaf bases

stem and leaves downy

Smooth Hawk's-beard

Marsh Hawk's-beard

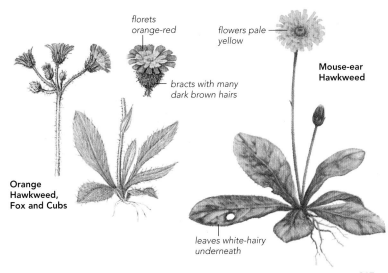

florets orange-red

flowers pale yellow

Mouse-ear Hawkweed

bracts with many dark brown hairs

Orange Hawkweed, Fox and Cubs

leaves white-hairy underneath

Arrowhead

Leafy Hawkweed *Hieracium umbellatum* Tall, erect, perennial plant to 80cm, softly hairy. *Leaves all on stem*, numerous, stalkless, narrowly linear-lanceolate, barely toothed, sometimes with rolled-under margins. Flower heads clustered in an *umbel-like inflorescence,* roughly flat-topped; bracts hairless, with recurved tips, blackish green (**a**). Widespread almost throughout; in woods, roadsides, heaths and banks, on dry soil. **Fl:** Jun–Oct. **Br Is dist:** Throughout, except the extreme north.

ORDER LILIIDAE (MONOCOTYLEDONS)

The second major group of flowering plants, generally easy to distinguish from Magnoliidae (Dicotyledons) by the presence of only 1 seed-leaf in the developing seedling; flowers with parts in multiples of 3, most commonly 3 or 6; and leaves with veins that are roughly parallel. The order includes many familiar bulbous plants, especially in the lily family.

WATER-PLANTAIN FAMILY Alismataceae
A small family of aquatic herbs. Leaves usually mainly basal and untoothed. Flowers have 3 separate petals and sepals, distinct from each other, and numerous carpels ripening into single-seeded achenes.

Lesser Water-plantain

Arrowhead *Sagittaria sagittifolia* Erect, hairless, aquatic perennial to 90cm. Aerial leaves distinctive, broadly arrow-shaped, long-stalked, erect, to 20cm long; submerged leaves linear and translucent; floating leaves, if present, oval to lanceolate. Flowers in a whorled raceme, individual flowers white, with purple blotch at base of petals, 20–25mm in diameter; lower flowers female with numerous carpels, upper flowers male. Widespread and generally common, though rare in the north; in still or slow-flowing water with muddy substrates. **Fl:** Jul–Aug. **Br Is dist:** Locally common in lowlands of England and Wales; absent from Scotland; rare in Ireland.

Floating Water-plantain

Lesser Water-plantain *Baldellia ranunculoides* Variable plant, erect, ascending or spreading, though rarely taller than 20cm. Leaves mostly basal, linear-lanceolate, to 10cm long, tapered at both ends, with long stalks. *Flowers solitary* (especially in creeping plants) or in few-flowered clusters, *petals pale pink*, flowers 12–16mm wide, with numerous carpels. From S Scandinavia southwards, widespread, though local; in fens, ponds, ditches and dune-slacks, etc., often calcareous. **Fl:** Jun–Aug. **Br Is dist:** Locally common in the south, becoming rarer in the north, absent from the far north.

Common Water-plantain

Floating Water-plantain *Luronium natans* Aquatic with horizontal stems, floating or submerged, rooting at nodes. Floating leaves are elliptical, blunt, to 40mm long on long stalks; submerged leaves linear, very narrow, to 10cm. Flowers normally solitary, long-stalked, 12–15mm in diameter, *white with yellow central spot*. From S Scandinavia southwards, local; in lakes and canals with rather acid water. **Fl:** Jul–Aug. **Br Is dist:** Very local, mainly in Wales and NW England; introduced elsewhere.

a

Water-plantain *Alisma plantago-aquatica* Erect hairless aquatic perennial to 1m. Leaves elliptical to ovate, up to 20cm, long-stalked, with rounded or wedge-shaped base, emergent (**b**). *Flowers in much-branched whorled inflorescence*, small (to 10mm in diameter), white to pale lilac, with yellow centre; carpels numerous, *with style arising from below the middle of each*. Common in water and on mud; throughout except the far north. **Fl:** Jun–Aug. **Br Is dist:** Common generally, though rarer to the north, absent from the far north.

b

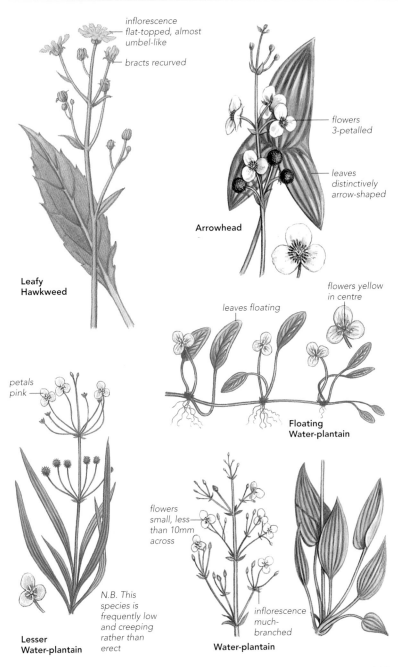

inflorescence flat-topped, almost umbel-like

bracts recurved

Leafy Hawkweed

flowers 3-petalled

leaves distinctively arrow-shaped

Arrowhead

flowers yellow in centre

leaves floating

Floating Water-plantain

petals pink

Lesser Water-plantain

N.B. This species is frequently low and creeping rather than erect

flowers small, less than 10mm across

inflorescence much-branched

Water-plantain

319

Starfruit *Damasonium alisma* Annual plant to 30cm. Leaves long-stalked, floating, blunt-tipped, heart-shaped at base, to 50mm long. Flowers white, about 6mm in diameter, in 1 to several whorls at top of stem. *Fruit distinctive, with 6–10 carpels spreading in a star-like whorl.* From S England and W France southwards; in ponds, especially where grazed and muddy. **Fl:** Jun–Aug. **Br Is dist:** Very rare in a few localities in SE England only.

Starfruit

FLOWERING-RUSH FAMILY Butomaceae

Perennial aquatic herbs, with leaves all linear, basal only. Flowers in terminal umbels, with 3 petals, 3 sepals and 9 stamens.

Flowering-rush *Butomus umbellatus* Very distinctive plant when in flower. Erect hairless aquatic perennial to 1.5m. Leaves all basal, linear, pointed, 3-angled, almost as tall as flower stems. Flowers pink, 15–27mm in diameter, in terminal umbel with brownish bracts, on tall rounded stems. In still and slow-moving fresh or slightly brackish water; throughout, except the far north. **Fl:** Jul–Sep. **Br Is dist:** Locally common in lowland England and Wales; rare or absent elsewhere.

Frogbit

FROGBIT FAMILY Hydrocharitaceae

Submerged or floating aquatic herbs. Flowers with 3 sepals, 3 petals and a variable number of stamens.

Frogbit *Hydrocharis morsus-ranae* Hairless floating plant with runners producing tufts of leaves. Leaves rounded and kidney-shaped, 20–30mm in diameter, often bronze-green, long-stalked, with large stipules. Flowers long-stalked, 20mm in diameter, white with crumpled petals, and yellow spot near base of each; female flowers solitary, male flowers 2–3 together. Widespread throughout except the far north; in ditches, ponds and other still waters. **Fl:** Jun–Aug. **Br Is dist:** Local in England, rare or absent elsewhere.

Water-soldier

Water-soldier *Stratiotes aloides* Stoloniferous aquatic perennial, submerged for much of year but rising to the surface to flower. Leaves in a coarse rosette, like a pineapple top, numerous, lanceolate, to 40cm, rigid, spine-edged, slightly brownish-green. Flowers erect, females solitary, males clustered 2–3 together, 30–40mm in diameter, 3-petalled, white. Widespread though absent from the far north and parts of the west, occasionally naturalised outside its range; occurs in ponds, canals and ditches. **Fl:** Jun–Aug. **Br Is dist:** Probably native, and locally abundant, only in E England; rare and naturalised elsewhere. British native plants are all female.

Canadian Pondweed,
Canadian Waterweed

a

Canadian Pondweed, Canadian Waterweed *Elodea canadensis* Submerged perennial aquatic herb, with brittle stems to 3m long (usually much less). Leaves translucent green, up to 10mm long (occasionally more), *blunt*, oblong to linear (a), unstalked, in whorls of 3. Male and female plants separate, males very rare: female flowers 5mm in diameter, with 3 tiny white to purplish petals floating on long thin stalks. Naturalised in still and slow-moving waters throughout N Europe except for Arctic areas, originally from N America. **Fl:** May–Oct. **Br Is dist:** Naturalised throughout.

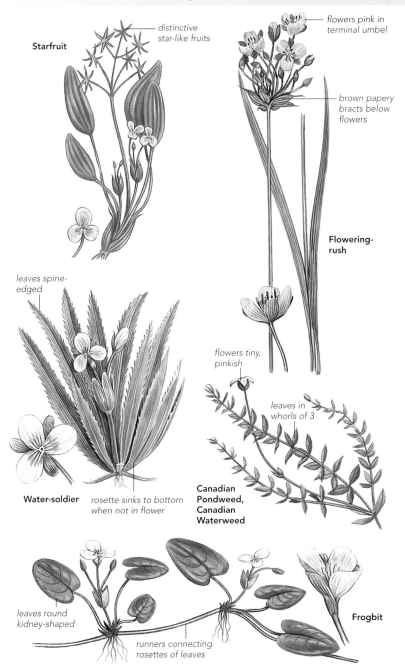

Starfruit

distinctive star-like fruits

flowers pink in terminal umbel

brown papery bracts below flowers

Flowering-rush

leaves spine-edged

flowers tiny, pinkish

leaves in whorls of 3

Water-soldier

rosette sinks to bottom when not in flower

Canadian Pondweed, Canadian Waterweed

leaves round kidney-shaped

runners connecting rosettes of leaves

Frogbit

Bog Pondweed

Beaked Tasselweed

a

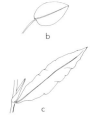

b

c

PONDWEED FAMILY Potamogetonaceae
Aquatic herbs with opposite or alternate leaves, usually with stipules. Flowers in stalked spikes from the leaf axils. Individual flowers small, numerous, in 4 parts with only 1 perianth whorl, usually greenish. Some species are difficult to identify, and many hybrids occur, complicating matters farther.

Broad-leaved Pondweed *Potamogeton natans* Submerged and floating leaves both present, stems cylindrical to 2m. Floating leaves dark green, opaque, blade length up to 12cm, *with a discoloured flexible joint* (**a**) *close to where the stalk and blade meet* (the only species with this); submerged leaves long, narrow, linear, to 30cm; stipules 5–15cm long, persistent, with close-set veins. Flower spikes cylindrical, dense, to 80mm long, emerging from water on stout stalk. Fruits greenish. Common throughout in still or slow-moving fresh water. **Fl:** May–Sep. **Br Is dist:** Widespread and common.

Bog Pondweed *Potamogeton polygonifolius* Similar to Broad-leaved Pondweed; *often reddish in colour. Floating leaves lacking flexible joint* (**b**), stipules 20–40mm, membranous, with well-separated slender veins. Flower spikes cylindrical, to 40mm, with stalk much longer than spike. Fruits brownish. Widespread and common, except in the far north; in bogs and acid waters, though absent from large areas. **Fl:** May–Oct. **Br Is dist:** Widespread throughout, generally common except in more calcareous or highly farmed lowlands.

Shining Pondweed *Potamogeton lucens* Wholly submerged aquatic. *Leaves all of similar type*, translucent, oblong-lanceolate, short-stalked, but with *blade running down stalk* (**c**); wavy-edged, to 20cm long, with minutely toothed margins. In lime-rich still or slow-flowing water; throughout, except the far north. **Fl:** Jun–Sep. **Br Is dist:** Mainly southern and eastern; rare elsewhere.

TASSELWEED FAMILY Ruppiaceae
A small family of submerged aquatic herbs of saline or brackish waters. Flowers hermaphrodite, lacking petals or sepals, in pairs on long stalks.

Beaked Tasselweed *Ruppia maritima* Slender aquatic perennial, wholly submerged, with hair-like stems. Leaves very fine, less than 1mm wide, light green, alternate or opposite, pointed. Flowers in umbel-like heads (actually several close-set pairs), with the common *stalk less than 60mm long*, less than twice the length of individual flower stalks; petals absent, 2 stamens to 0.7mm long. In saline or brackish water, usually coastal; throughout. **Fl:** Jul–Sep. **Br Is dist:** Widespread around coasts, very local in the north, commoner in the south.

distinct visible joint

stipules very long 5–15cm

Broad-leaved Pondweed

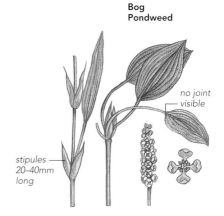

Bog Pondweed

no joint visible

stipules 20–40mm long

Shining Pondweed

leaves wavy-edged

blade of leaf continues down stalk

flowers and fruits in umbel-like clusters

leaves very narrow

Beaked Tasselweed

Eelgrass

Holly-leaved Naiad

Slender Naiad

Scottish Asphodel

German, or Tofield's, Asphodel

EELGRASS FAMILY Zosteraceae

A small family of perennial grass-like herbs, unusual in being wholly marine in habitat. Flowers reduced to bare necessity of 1 stamen and 1 style, in separate male and female flowers.

Eelgrass *Zostera marina* Submerged perennial herbaceous marine plant. Leaves to 50cm long (occasionally much longer), and 10mm wide, with 3 *to 9 veins* and broad, rounded, *bristle-tipped points*; basal sheaths entire, not split; leaves on flower shoots similar but smaller. Flowers greenish, in much-branched terminal inflorescences, enclosed in base of a sheath; stigma twice the length of style. Locally common around all coasts, on fine sand or silt substrates, from low water down to 10m depth. Varies in abundance through disease. **Fl:** Jun–Sep. **Br Is dist:** Widespread though local.

NAIAD FAMILY Najadaceae

A very small family with 1 genus. Leaves virtually opposite. Male and female flowers separate.

Holly-leaved Naiad *Najas marina* Distinctive submerged aquatic, with opposite pairs, or whorls, of narrowly lanceolate leaves (to 6mm wide), *with strongly spiny margins*, and scattered teeth on the stems; leaf sheaths without hairs. Flowers tiny, in leaf axils. In clear fresh or brackish water; widespread except in the north, though local. **Fl:** Jul–Aug. **Br Is dist:** Rare and declining, in Norfolk Broads only.

Slender Naiad *Najas flexilis* Similar in form to Holly-leaved Naiad, leaves in 2s or 3s, *very minutely toothed*, narrower (to 1mm wide), with few-haired leaf sheaths. From Britain and Germany northwards, in acid still waters, but very local. **Fl:** Jul–Sep. **Br Is dist:** From N England northwards, and in W Ireland; very local.

LILY FAMILY Liliaceae

A very large family of herbaceous plants (at least, in N Europe), usually with bulbs or tubers. Leaves normally narrow, linear, untoothed and parallel-veined, except for May Lily, which is in 4 parts (*see* p. 334). Flowers normally with 6 roughly equal and similar perianth segments, in 2 whorls (equivalent to petals and sepals). Stamens normally 6, ovary 3-celled and superior. Modern DNA work has subdivided the Lily family into at least 12 separate families, though for convenience we have grouped them all together in one family here.

Scottish Asphodel *Tofieldia pusilla* Erect hairless perennial herb to 20cm. Leaves mainly basal in flattened fan, like miniature iris leaves, to 80mm long. Inflorescence is a dense short-stalked spike, with 5–10 flowers; *flowers greenish or whitish*, about 2mm in diameter, with a 3-lobed bract at base. In damp flushes and boggy areas, mainly in mountains; throughout but very local and confined to mountains in the south. **Fl:** Jun–Aug. **Br Is dist:** Upper Teesdale and Scottish Highlands only, locally common.

German, or Tofield's, Asphodel *Tofieldia calyculata* Similar to Scottish Asphodel, but a larger plant to 35cm, with a longer spike of up to 30 *yellowish flowers*. In wet places, usually calcareous, in S Sweden and Alpine areas. **Fl:** Jun–Aug. **Br Is dist:** Absent.

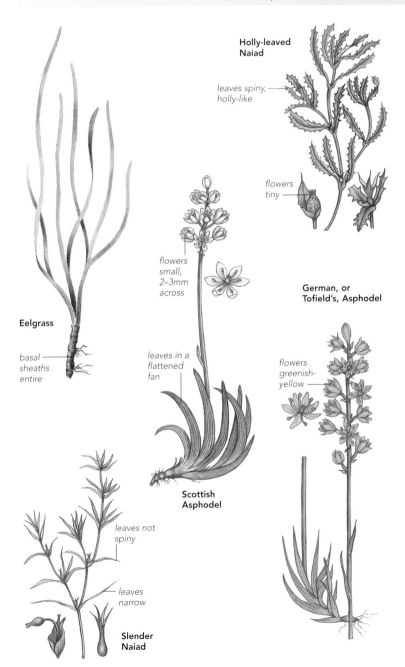

Holly-leaved Naiad

leaves spiny, holly-like

flowers tiny

Eelgrass

basal sheaths entire

flowers small, 2–3mm across

leaves in a flattened fan

German, or Tofield's, Asphodel

flowers greenish-yellow

Scottish Asphodel

leaves not spiny

leaves narrow

Slender Naiad

325

Bog Asphodel

Bog Asphodel *Narthecium ossifragum* Similar in form to the Scottish and German Asphodels (*see* p. 324), but with erect spikes of *larger (to 15mm in diameter) starry orange-yellow flowers* in a spike up to 10cm long; anthers orange-red, with conspicuously orange-woolly filaments. Leaves and fruits all become orange-red in late summer. In bogs, flushes and on wet heaths; from S Scandinavia southwards, locally common. **Fl:** Jun–Aug. **Br Is dist:** Widespread but local, and absent from many lowland areas.

St Bernard's Lily

St Bernard's Lily *Anthericum liliago* Slender hairless perennial to 70cm, with leaves in basal cluster. Leaves linear, narrow, up to 40cm long, but only 3–7mm wide, flat or channelled. Inflorescence is a *few-flowered, usually unbranched, raceme*; petals white, flowers 25–50mm in diameter, flower bracts 10mm long; *style curved*, and ascending. In dry grassland, rocky banks and open woods; from S Sweden southwards, though local. **Fl:** May–Jul. **Br Is dist:** Absent.

Meadow Saffron, Autumn Crocus

Meadow Saffron, Autumn Crocus *Colchicum autumnale* Hairless perennial herb, with an underground corm producing leaves in spring and flowers in autumn. Leaves oblong-lanceolate, bright glossy green, to 30cm long x 40mm wide, erect in spring, dying well before flower. Flowers arise directly from ground in autumn, without leaves, with long stalk-like perianth tube and 6 pink-purple perianth lobes, very like *Crocus* species (*see* p. 340) but with 6 (not 3) stamens. Fruits appear with leaves in following spring. In meadows and open woods; north to the Netherlands and Germany, local, naturalised farther north. **Fl:** Aug–Oct. **Br Is dist:** Mainly in the Midlands, rare elsewhere.

Meadow Gagea

GAGEAS, STARS-OF-BETHLEHEM *Gagea* Small bulbous perennials with erect, unbranched stems; leaves basal and on stem. Flowers erect, yellow (with a green stripe down back of each perianth segment), in umbel-like clusters (or solitary), with leaf-like spathe at base of inflorescence.

Meadow Gagea *Gagea pratensis* Basal leaf up to 6mm wide, flat; stem leaves in 1 opposite pair. Flowers large (20–30mm in diameter), greenish yellow, in groups of 2–6; *stigmas 3, yellow*. In meadows and disturbed ground; from S Sweden southwards, though local. **Fl:** Mar–May. **Br Is dist:** Absent.

Yellow Star-of-Bethlehem

Yellow Star-of-Bethlehem *Gagea lutea* Very similar to Meadow Gagea, but basal leaf wider, to 15mm, with hooded tips. Flowers in groups of 1–7, sometimes with hairy flower stalks; *only 1 stigma, green*. In damp grassland and open woods, often on basic and heavy soils; local. **Fl:** Mar–Apr. **Br Is dist:** Widespread north to S Scotland, but very local and absent from many areas.

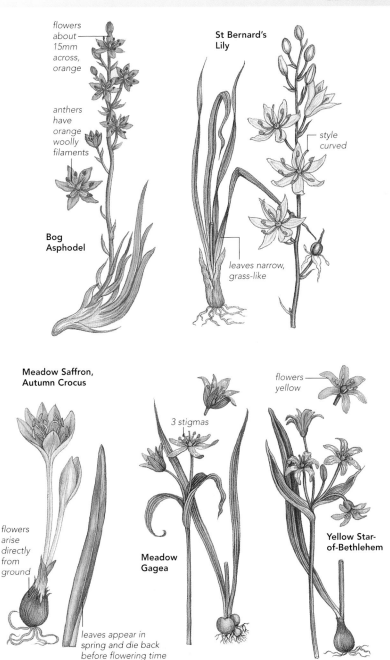

flowers about 15mm across, orange

anthers have orange woolly filaments

Bog Asphodel

St Bernard's Lily

style curved

leaves narrow, grass-like

Meadow Saffron, Autumn Crocus

flowers arise directly from ground

leaves appear in spring and die back before flowering time

3 stigmas

Meadow Gagea

flowers yellow

Yellow Star-of-Bethlehem

327

Field Gagea

Wild Tulip

Fritillary, Snake's-head Fritillary

Martagon Lily

Spiked Star-of-Bethlehem, Bath Asparagus

Least Gagea *Gagea minima* Has *basal leaf only 1–2mm wide, not keeled* like above 2 species. Flowers in groups of 1–7, with *pointed (not blunt) perianth segments*, becoming reflexed. Widespread almost throughout in similar habitats, but local. **Fl:** Mar–May. **Br Is dist:** Absent.

Belgian Gagea *Gagea spathacea* All parts of plant hairless. Basal leaves 2, narrowly linear, to 4mm wide. Flowers in groups of 2–4, *with single spathe-like bract at base of inflorescence;* flowers 18–20mm in diameter, yellow. From S Sweden south to N France; local; in open woods, scrub and damp grassland. **Fl:** Apr–May. **Br Is dist:** Absent.

Field Gagea *Gagea arvensis* Greyish, slightly hairy plant. Basal leaves 2, narrowly linear, channelled; *stem leaves 2, in an opposite pair.* Flowers numerous, *5–12 together,* with narrow, *pointed perianth segments.* From the Netherlands and S Sweden southwards in dry open habitats, arable land. **Fl:** Apr–May. **Br Is dist:** Absent.

Wild Tulip *Tulipa sylvestris* Distinctive bulbous perennial, with erect stems to 45cm. Leaves linear-lanceolate, up to 30cm long, greyish green on upper surface, channelled. Flowers normally solitary (or 2), nodding in bud, erect when open, 30–50mm long, yellow, often greenish outside; stigmas 3. In meadows and grassy places; probably native only in NW France (and farther south), but widely naturalised north to S Scandinavia. **Fl:** Apr–May. **Br Is dist:** Introduced, naturalised locally; northwards to S Scotland, declining.

Fritillary, Snake's-head Fritillary *Fritillaria meleagris* Erect, hairless rather grey-green perennial to 30cm. Leaves alternate, not basal, narrow-linear. Flowers very distinctive within N Europe, large drooping lantern shape, 30–50mm long, chequered pink and brownish purple (less commonly all white), solitary or paired, with a nectary at the base of each segment inside. From the Netherlands southwards (naturalised farther north) in damp alluvial meadows, especially if winter-flooded. **Fl:** Apr–May. **Br Is dist:** Very local, though often abundant where it grows, in a band across S and E England, mainly in Thames Valley.

Martagon Lily *Lilium martagon* Robust, erect perennial to 1.8m, with rough stems. Leaves oval-lanceolate, up to 16cm long (usually less), mainly in *separated whorls up stem.* Flowers large, 40–50mm in diameter, *reddish purple with darker spots, with perianth segments strongly recurved,* in a loose terminal raceme. In woods, scrub and grassy places; native from NE France southwards, but widely naturalised farther north. **Fl:** Jun–Jul. **Br Is dist:** Naturalised widely, possibly native in a few southern localities. Very local.

Spiked Star-of-Bethlehem, Bath Asparagus *Ornithogalum pyrenaicum* Erect, hairless perennial, with stout stems to 1m. Leaves linear, to 60cm, grey-green, all basal, withering early. *Flowers pale greenish-yellow* to greenish white, starry, to 20mm in diameter, in long terminal raceme with short whitish bracts to each flower. Developing inflorescence resembles Asparagus, and is eaten locally (hence the name). Meadows, scrub and roadsides; from Belgium and S England southwards; local. **Fl:** May–Jul. **Br Is dist:** Very locally common in a small area from Bath eastwards to Bedfordshire.

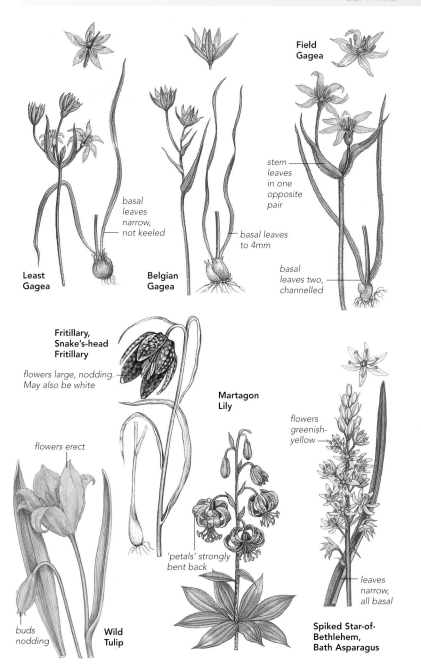

Field Gagea

Least Gagea

basal leaves narrow, not keeled

Belgian Gagea

basal leaves to 4mm

stem leaves in one opposite pair

basal leaves two, channelled

Fritillary, Snake's-head Fritillary

flowers large, nodding. May also be white

flowers erect

Martagon Lily

flowers greenish-yellow

'petals' strongly bent back

leaves narrow, all basal

buds nodding

Wild Tulip

Spiked Star-of-Bethlehem, Bath Asparagus

329

Spring Squill

Alpine Squill

Bluebell

Tassel Hyacinth

Star-of-Bethlehem *Ornithogalum angustifolium* Low hairless bulbous perennial to 30cm tall. Leaves narrowly linear, to 30cm, with white stripe down central channel. *Flowers in an umbel-like terminal raceme,* with lower flowers on longer stalks than upper so that inflorescence is almost flat-topped; *perianth segments white,* with green stripe on back, in starry flowers 30–40m in diameter. In dry grassland, roadsides and cultivated ground; from the Netherlands southwards, though naturalised farther north. **Fl:** Apr–May. **Br Is dist:** Widespread, local, probably native only in E Anglia. Most of the British plants are thought to be *O. angustifolium* rather than the closely-related *O. umbellatum,* though more work is needed on this difficult group.

Spring Squill *Scilla verna* Small hairless bulbous perennial to 15cm. Has from 3 to 6 linear leaves, to 4mm wide and 20cm long, curly, produced before flowers. Flowers in a 2-to 12-flowered erect terminal cluster; perianth segments pale blue or violet-blue, pointed; *each flower has 1 bluish-purple bract, usually longer than flower stalk.* In dry rocky grassy coastal sites; mainly western; local. **Fl:** Apr–May. **Br Is dist:** Locally common on the coasts of W Britain, rare in the east.

Alpine Squill *Scilla bifolia* Similar to Spring Squill, but has *only 2 leaves,* wider (to 12mm), appearing with flowers; flowers bright blue, *without bracts.* In meadows and woods, not particularly coastal; from Belgium and Germany southwards. **Fl:** Mar–Apr. **Br Is dist:** Absent.

Autumn Squill *Scilla autumnalis* Very similar to Spring Squill, most readily distinguished by flowering time. Leaves produced in autumn, with or after flowers; *flowers dull purple, bracts absent.* In dry grassy and rocky places, mainly coastal; from S England and France southwards. **Fl:** Jul–Sep. **Br Is dist:** Coastal sites in S England only.

Bluebell *Hyacinthoides non-scripta* Familiar, hairless bulbous perennial to 50cm. Leaves all basal, linear, to 15mm wide, glossy green, hooded at tip. Inflorescence is a 1-sided raceme, with up to 16 drooping, narrowly bell-shaped flowers; perianth segments blue or blue-violet (rarely pink or white), joined at base, with 6 lobes curled back at tips; anthers cream. In woods, scrub, grassland and coastal cliffs; from Scotland and the Netherlands southwards, but predominantly western. **Fl:** Apr–Jun. **Br Is dist:** Common throughout except on higher mountains and in the extreme north. Spanish Bluebell *H. hispanica* is widely naturalised as a garden escape. It has more open flowers, and blue anthers. It hybridises with the native bluebell producing a plant that is intermediate in floral characteristics.

Tassel Hyacinth *Muscari comosum* Distinctive plant; an erect bulbous perennial to 50cm, usually less. Leaves linear, to 40cm long, 15mm wide and channelled. Flowers in a long loose spike, with lower flowers pale brownish-green, flask-shaped, closed at mouth; *upper flowers sterile, purplish, in an erect tuft; all flowers long-stalked.* In dry grassland and disturbed ground, from N France and S Germany southwards, naturalised farther north. **Fl:** Apr–Jun. **Br Is dist:** Introduced; occasionally naturalised in the south.

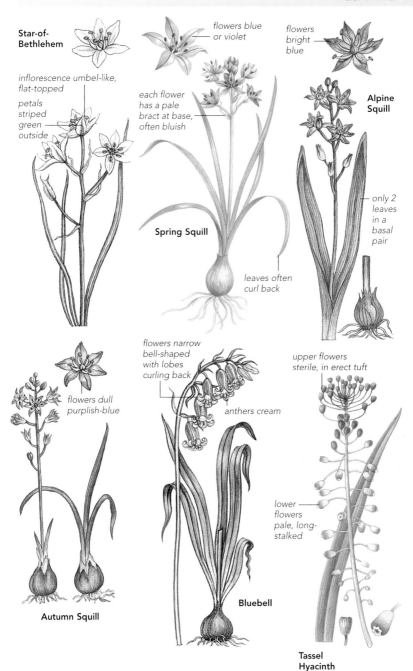

Star-of-Bethlehem

inflorescence umbel-like, flat-topped

petals striped green outside

flowers blue or violet

each flower has a pale bract at base, often bluish

Spring Squill

leaves often curl back

flowers bright blue

Alpine Squill

only 2 leaves in a basal pair

flowers dull purplish-blue

flowers narrow bell-shaped with lobes curling back

anthers cream

upper flowers sterile, in erect tuft

lower flowers pale, long-stalked

Autumn Squill

Bluebell

Tassel Hyacinth

331

Ramsons

Grape Hyacinth *Muscari neglectum* Variable, erect, hairless, bulbous perennial to 30cm. Leaves linear, semicircular in section, channelled, bright green, and up to 30cm long, *to 6mm wide*, all basal. Flowers in a dense cylindrical terminal spike, 20–30mm long; flowers dark blue, oval, inflated, 3–5mm long, constricted at mouth, with 6 small white teeth at opening; uppermost flowers smaller, paler and sterile. In dry, often calcareous, grassland areas; from Britain and N France southwards, naturalised to the north of range. **Fl:** Apr–May. **Br Is dist:** Probably native in E Anglia; naturalised elsewhere.

Chives

Compact, or Small, Grape Hyacinth *Muscari botryoides* Similar to Grape Hyacinth, but *leaves wider (to 12mm), hooded or wider at tip*; flowers pale violet, globular, 2–4mm long, in loose conical heads. In dry grasslands; from Belgium and Germany southwards, though possibly not native in the north of range. **Fl:** Mar–Jun. **Br Is dist:** Absent.

GARLICS, LEEKS AND ONIONS *Allium* Perennial bulbous herbs, smelling of garlic or onion when bruised. Leaves variable, flat or cylindrical, sheathing at base. Flowers in terminal umbels, with 1 or more papery bracts below head. Flowers small with 6 similar perianth segments; bulbils are often mixed in with flowers in some species. A difficult group, with 13 species in the area.

Field Garlic

Ramsons *Allium ursinum* Distinctive erect bulbous perennial. Leaves basal, stalked, ovate to elliptical, up to 25cm long and *70mm at broadest*, pointed. Flower stalk to 45cm, with spathe of 2 papers bracts, shorter than flower stalks, and globular head of up to 20 white flowers; individual flowers to 20mm in diameter; bulbils absent. Locally abundant in woods, especially on damp or calcareous soils; from S Scandinavia southwards. **Fl:** Apr–Jun. **Br Is dist:** Locally abundant throughout except NE Scotland; rare in Ireland.

Sand Leek

Chives *Allium schoenoprasum* Tufted plant to 40cm. Leaves cylindrical, *hollow*, greyish-green, to 25cm long. Inflorescence stalks up to 40cm, cylindrical, with small dense umbel, 20–40mm in diameter, with 8–30 lilac-purple flowers; bulbils absent; *anthers yellow, not protruding; spathe made up of 2 bracts*, less than 15mm, shorter than umbel. In rocky and grassy habitats, or damper sites in mountains; throughout except the far north, often naturalised. **Fl:** Jun–Aug. **Br Is dist:** Very local as native, on limestone; mainly western.

Field Garlic *Allium oleraceum* Tall perennial to 1m. Leaves linear, to 4mm wide, up to 25cm long, sheathing stem in lower half, channelled above, strongly ribbed on underside. *Spathe consists of 2 long pointed bracts, with longer one up to 20cm long*. Inflorescence has a mixture of bulbils and long-stalked flowers, with whitish, bell-shaped flowers, sometimes pink or green-tinged, *stamens not protruding*. Throughout except the far north; in rocky, grassy and disturbed situations. **Fl:** Jul–Aug. **Br Is dist:** Local, widespread but mainly eastern; absent from N Scotland; rare in Ireland.

Sand Leek *Allium scorodoprasum* Similar to above, with flat, solid, keeled, rough-edged leaves. Spathe with *2 bracts, shorter than flower stalks (to 15mm)*; umbel 10–50mm in diameter; perianth ovoid, reddish-purple, with *stamens not protruding; purple bulbils present*. In dry grasslands, roadsides and sandy habitats; from S Scandinavia southwards, though local. **Fl:** May–Aug. **Br Is dist:** N England to C Scotland only.

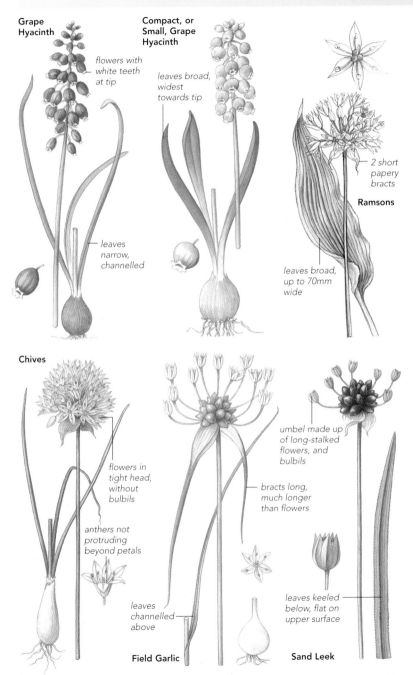

Grape Hyacinth

flowers with white teeth at tip

leaves narrow, channelled

Compact, or Small, Grape Hyacinth

leaves broad, widest towards tip

2 short papery bracts

Ramsons

leaves broad, up to 70mm wide

Chives

flowers in tight head, without bulbils

anthers not protruding beyond petals

umbel made up of long-stalked flowers, and bulbils

bracts long, much longer than flowers

leaves channelled above

Field Garlic

leaves keeled below, flat on upper surface

Sand Leek

Round-headed Leek *Allium sphaerocephalon* Tall plant to 90cm. *Leaves semicircular in section, but grooved on upper side,* up to 60cm long, but very narrow (1–2mm). Umbel dense, small (20–30mm in diameter, rarely more), spherical, *without bulbils; spathe of 2 bracts, short, less than 20mm;* perianth segments pink to reddish-purple, *stamens protruding.* From Belgium and England southwards; in dry open habitats, such as limestone rocks and sand-dunes. **Fl:** Jun–Aug. **Br Is dist:** Avon Gorge and Jersey only.

Wild Leek

Crow Garlic, Wild Onion *Allium vineale Leaves semicircular in section, hollow, channelled* to 60cm long, to 4mm wide. Spathe of a *single papery bract, not longer than flowers,* falling early. Umbel variable, usually with few long-stalked pink, red or white flowers, and *numerous greenish-red bulbils;* may also be all bulbils, or almost all flowers; *stamens protruding.* Throughout in dry grasslands and disturbed habitats, except the far north. **Fl:** Jun–Jul. **Br Is dist:** Common in the south, becoming rarer to the north.

May Lily

Wild Leek *Allium ampeloprasum* Tall robust plant, with cylindrical stem up to 2m. Leaves linear, grey-green, waxy, to 50cm long by 40mm wide, flat, channelled, with rough margins. *Spathe a single papery bract,* falling as flowers open. *Umbel large, to 90mm in diameter,* globose, with hundreds of flowers; perianth segments pale purplish, 6–8mm long, stamens slightly protruding; bulbils normally absent. Var. *babingtonii* (Babington's Leek) has *numerous large bulbils, and few flowers.* In disturbed, open, and rocky places, especially coastal; from S Britain and N France southwards. **Fl:** Jun–Aug. **Br Is dist:** The type is rare in SW Britain; var. *babingtonii* is rare in Cornwall and W Ireland.

Whorled Solomon's-seal

Lily-of-the-valley *Convallaria majalis* Creeping, hairless perennial with rhizomes. Leaves arise in pairs or in 3s, direct from rhizome, with green or reddish-purple scales at base; blade ovate to lanceolate, pointed, to 20cm long, 60mm wide. Flowers produced in 1-sided, nodding racemes on leafless stalks, to 30cm; perianth bell-shaped, white (rarely pink), fragrant; fruit a globose red berry, 8–10mm in diameter. In woods, scrub, mountain meadows and limestone rocks; throughout except the far north. **Fl:** May–Jul. **Br Is dist:** Local in England; rare elsewhere. Widely cultivated and naturalised.

May Lily *Maianthemum bifolium* Perennial with creeping rhizome, and erect stems to 20cm, hairless except at top. Leaves deeply heart-shaped at base, alternate, stalked, pointed, 30–60mm long, usually both basal and on stem. Flowers in short, erect, cylindrical spike to 40mm, with up to 20 small white flowers, 2–5mm in diameter and in 4 parts. Fruit a red berry about 5mm in diameter. Widespread almost throughout in woods, often rather acid or humus-rich; local. **Fl:** May–Jun. **Br Is dist:** Very local in woods in a few localities in England; absent elsewhere.

SOLOMON'S-SEAL *Polygonatum* Three species (in this area) of creeping perennials with arching or erect stems bearing whorled or alternate leaves, with clusters of white tubular flowers from the axils.

Whorled Solomon's-seal *Polygonatum verticillatum* Erect perennial, with angled stems to 80cm. Leaves linear-lanceolate, to 15cm long, *in whorls of 3–6.* Flowers in pendulous clusters in leaf axils, bell-shaped, constricted in middle, greenish-white, to 10mm long. Throughout, though local; in woods and rocky ground, especially in mountains. **Fl:** Jun–Jul. **Br Is dist:** Rare, only in N England and S Scotland.

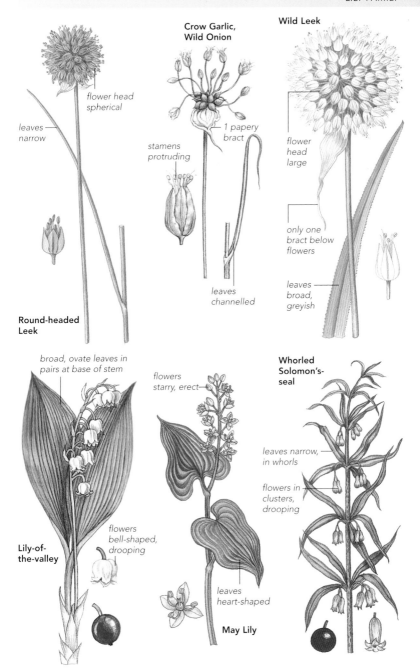

Crow Garlic, Wild Onion

Wild Leek

flower head spherical

leaves narrow

stamens protruding

1 papery bract

flower head large

only one bract below flowers

leaves channelled

leaves broad, greyish

Round-headed Leek

broad, ovate leaves in pairs at base of stem

flowers starry, erect

Whorled Solomon's-seal

leaves narrow, in whorls

flowers in clusters, drooping

Lily-of-the-valley

flowers bell-shaped, drooping

leaves heart-shaped

May Lily

Solomon's-seal

Solomon's-seal *Polygonatum multiflorum* Hairless, clump-forming perennial, with arching round stems to 80cm. *Leaves alternate*, ovate to lanceolate, to 15cm long, stalkless or short-stalked, tending to spread out on each side of the stem. Flowers stalked, *in clusters of 2–6*, pendulous, from leaf axils; perianth greenish-white, tubular bell-shaped, somewhat contracted in middle of tube. Widespread almost throughout; in dry woods and scrub, often on lime-rich soils. **Fl:** May–Jun. **Br Is dist:** Curiously localised, mainly in C S and NW England, and S Wales.

Herb-paris

Herb-paris *Paris quadrifolia* Highly distinctive plant. Perennial, with erect stems to 40cm, bearing a single whorl of 4 (or more) net-veined, roughly diamond-shaped leaves at the top. Flowers solitary, with 4 or more narrow green sepals, and 4 or more very narrow petals, topped by a conspicuous purple ovary, and 6–10 yellow stamens. Widespread almost throughout in woods, often on damp or calcareous soils. **Fl:** May–Jul. **Br Is dist:** Widespread almost throughout, but local.

Wild Asparagus

Wild Asparagus *Asparagus prostratus* Hairless perennial, with prostrate or ascending stems to 40cm, rarely 60cm. Leaves reduced to tiny membranous bracts, which may have clusters of short green cladodes (much-reduced stems) in their axils, producing the overall effect of a feathery much-divided leaf. Flowers tiny, 4–6mm long, in axils of leaves, greenish-yellow, bell-shaped, separate male and female. Fruit a red globose berry, 6-10mm in diameter. In grassy coastal habitats, sand dunes,and cliff tops from Germany to W France. **Fl:** Jun–Sep. **Br Is dist:** Rare in S England, Wales and SE Ireland only.

Butcher's-broom

Butcher's-broom *Ruscus aculeatus* Highly distinctive plant. A hairless, much-branched, shrubby, erect plant to 1m, with separate male and female plants. Leaves are reduced to tiny membranous scales, with leaf-like cladodes in their axils; these are ovate-lanceolate, dark green, tough, spiny-pointed, to 40mm long. Flowers are produced, usually solitary, on the upper side of the cladodes; about 5mm in diameter, greenish, with 6 perianth segments. Fruit a globose red berry, 10–12mm in diameter. In woods, hedge banks, normally on dry calcareous soils; from C England and N France southwards. **Fl:** Jan–Apr. **Br Is dist:** Locally common in S England, rarer northwards, naturalised in Scotland.

Spring Snowflake

DAFFODIL FAMILY Amaryllidaceae (now considered to be a family within Liliaceae)
Hairless, bulbous perennials with basal, usually linear leaves and leafless flower stems. Unlike others in lily family, daffodils have an inferior ovary, and flowers always enclosed in a spathe. Stamens 6, style single. In *Narcissus*, the flowers have a conspicuous cup, the corona, inside the petals.

Spring Snowflake *Leucojum vernum* Bulbous perennial to 35cm. Leaves strap-shaped, bright green, to 25cm long and 20mm wide. *Flowers usually solitary, rarely 2 together*, nodding at tip of stem; spathe green with papery border, up to 40mm long, usually forked at tip; flowers with 6 perianth segments all alike, in bell shape, white with greenish patch near the tip of each, 20–25mm long. In damp, shady places or meadows; native from Belgium and S England southwards, though naturalised elsewhere. **Fl:** Feb–Apr. **Br Is dist:** Possibly native in 2 localities, Dorset and Somerset only.

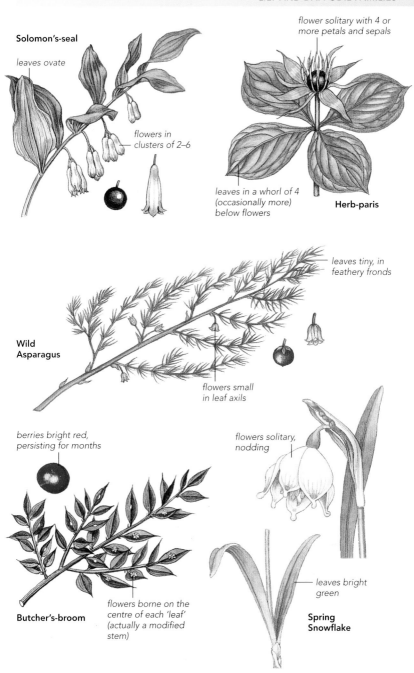

Solomon's-seal

leaves ovate

flowers in clusters of 2–6

flower solitary with 4 or more petals and sepals

leaves in a whorl of 4 (occasionally more) below flowers

Herb-paris

leaves tiny, in feathery fronds

Wild Asparagus

flowers small in leaf axils

berries bright red, persisting for months

flowers solitary, nodding

Butcher's-broom

flowers borne on the centre of each 'leaf' (actually a modified stem)

leaves bright green

Spring Snowflake

337

Summer Snowflake

Wild Daffodil

Black Bryony

Summer Snowflake *Leucojum aestivum* Rather similar to Spring Snowflake (*see* p. 336), but a taller more robust plant to 60cm. Leaves similar but longer, equalling the flower stem. *Flowers in an umbel of 2–5*, with a 40–50mm spathe, green at apex, undivided; perianth segments white, with green tip, 14–18mm long. In marshes and wet woods, including tidal ones; from the Netherlands and S Ireland southwards; local. Also widely cultivated. **Fl:** Apr–Jun. **Br Is dist:** Very local as native in S England and S Ireland (as ssp. *aestivum*); absent elsewhere except if naturalised.

Snowdrop *Galanthus nivalis* Small bulbous herb to 30cm, often confused with *Leucojum* species (*see* p. 336 and above). Differs in the *greyish-green linear leaves*, to 6mm wide. Flowers 1 per stem, drooping, with 3 outer segments to 25mm long, white, and 3 inner segments to 11mm long, white with green patch near the tip. In damp broad-leaved woodland; from N France and Germany southwards; naturalised elsewhere. **Fl:** Jan–Mar **Br Is dist:** Locally naturalised almost throughout, possibly native in SW England and Welsh borders.

Wild Daffodil *Narcissus pseudonarcissus* ssp *pseudonarcissus* Hairless perennial, with erect, flat, linear, grey-green leaves to 50cm. Flowers solitary (rarely more), turned sideways, at tip of stems up to 50cm. Flowers 50–60mm in diameter, consisting of outer whorl of 6 pale yellow perianth segments, and an inner, deeper yellow cup, 25–30mm long (the corona). From N England, the Netherlands and W Germany southwards; in woods and meadows. **Fl:** Apr–May. **Br Is dist:** Locally common in England and Wales, though absent as native from large areas.

YAM FAMILY Dioscoreaceae
Twining climbers, with leaves that look more like those of dicotyledons than monocotyledons. Flowers unisexual, in small spikes.

Black Bryony *Tamus communis* Climbing, herbaceous, hairless, perennial, twining clockwise, lacking tendrils. Leaves heart-shaped, 8–15cm long, bright glossy green, net-veined. Male and female plants separate; flowers greenish-yellow, open bell-shaped, small (4–5mm in diameter), with males in cylindrical long racemes, females in small clusters. Fruit a red, globose, poisonous berry, 10–12mm across. From England and Germany southwards; in hedgerows, wood margins, scrub and commons. **Fl:** May–Jul. **Br Is dist:** Common in lowland areas of England and Wales; absent elsewhere.

IRIS FAMILY Iridaceae
Bulbous, rhizomatous or cormous plants. Similar to daffodil family, though with 3. style3-lobed , and petals joined at base.

Blue-eyed Grass *Sisyrinchium bermudiana* Hairless perennial with erect or ascending, flattened, winged stems from short rhizome. Leaves all basal, linear, to 5mm wide, 15cm long. Flowers in 2 (occasionally 1 or 3) terminal inflorescences, 2–4 in each, with leaf-like bracts below each; perianth light blue, 15–20mm in diameter, lobes ovate with distinct bristle-point. In damp grassland and lake-margins; native only in N and W Ireland; naturalised elsewhere. **Fl:** Jul–Aug. **Br Is dist:** As above.

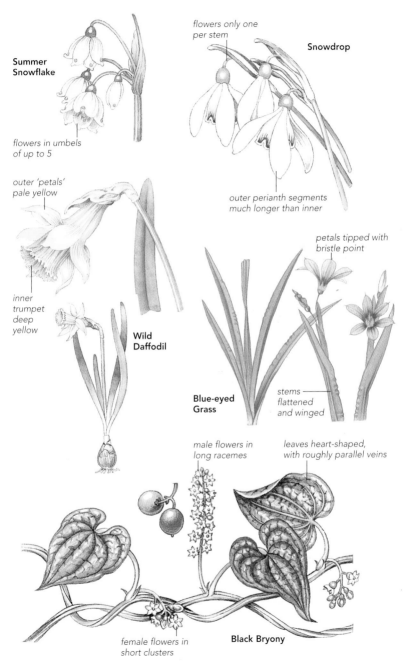

Summer Snowflake

flowers only one per stem

Snowdrop

flowers in umbels of up to 5

outer 'petals' pale yellow

outer perianth segments much longer than inner

inner trumpet deep yellow

petals tipped with bristle point

Wild Daffodil

Blue-eyed Grass

stems flattened and winged

male flowers in long racemes

leaves heart-shaped, with roughly parallel veins

female flowers in short clusters

Black Bryony

Stinking Iris,
Roast Beef Plant

Stinking Iris, Roast Beef Plant *Iris foetidissima* Tufted perennial herb, with erect stems from slender rhizomes. Leaves sword-shaped, dark green, evergreen, up to 70cm long and 20mm wide, about as long as flower stems. *Plant smells strongly of meat when crushed.* Flowers 60–80mm in diameter, *dull purplish with brownish yellow towards centre*, unbearded, with purple veins, in characteristic iris shape. Brown capsule splits into 3 segments when ripe, exposing large orange seeds. From N France and N England southwards; in woods, hedge banks and scrub. **Fl:** May–Jul. **Br Is dist:** Common on calcareous soils in S England and Wales, becoming rarer to the north; absent from Scotland and far N England.

Siberian Iris

Yellow Iris, Yellow Flag *Iris pseudacorus* Perennial hairless herb, with erect stems to 1.2m, from rhizomes. Leaves sword-shaped, to 90cm long and 30mm wide, rather greyish-green. Flowers in clusters of 2–3, each with a spathe below, green with papery margins towards the tip. Flowers large, to 10cm in diameter, *bright yellow with red-purple veins*, unbearded. Capsule similar to Stinking Iris, but seeds duller brown. Throughout, except the extreme north; in marshes, riversides and other wet places. **Fl:** May–Jul. **Br Is dist:** Common throughout.

Siberian Iris *Iris sibirica* Has narrow grass-like leaves to 10mm wide, *flowers violet-blue with yellow*, 60–80mm across, on stalks to 1.2m. In damp grassland; mainly eastern, but reaching Germany and E France and 1 place in W France. **Fl:** Jun–Jul. **Br Is dist:** Absent.

Blue, or Butterfly, Iris

Blue, or Butterfly, Iris *Iris spuria* Perennial herb, with erect stems to 60cm, unpleasant-smelling. Leaves linear, to 20mm wide, usually shorter than inflorescence. Flowers to 50mm in diameter; *falls have almost round blue-violet tip, contracted abruptly to yellowish, winged stalk*; standards shorter, violet and erect. In damp places on calcareous or saline soils; from S Sweden southwards, but very local. **Fl:** May–Jun. **Br Is dist:** Probably introduced, but long-established in Lincolnshire and Dorset.

Dwarf Iris *Iris aphylla* Low perennial to 30cm, leafless in winter. Flowers in groups of 3–5, violet-purple, to 70mm across; *falls with yellowish beard*. An eastern species, extending into Germany; in dry rocky grasslands. **Fl:** May–Jun. **Br Is dist:** Absent.

Spring Crocus

Spring Crocus *Crocus vernus* Familiar crocus type flower. Leaves linear, 2–4 from corm, 4–8mm wide, with central white stripe, still short at flowering time. Flowers goblet-shaped, up to 20cm tall, opening more widely in bright sunshine, purple, white or striped; style branched, orange. In grassland and open woods, commonest in mountain pastures; from Jura and S Germany southwards, though widely naturalised elsewhere. **Fl:** Mar–May. **Br Is dist:** Naturalised locally in grasslands; declining.

Sand Crocus

Sand Crocus *Romulea columnae* Very small cormous perennial. Leaves 3–6, narrowly cylindrical, curly, to 2mm wide and 10cm long, all basal. Flowers solitary or 2–3, 7–10mm in diameter, opening only in sun; perianth starry, purplish-white inside, yellow towards the base, dark-veined, greenish outside, all equal in size and shape. In sandy and rocky coastal turf; from SW England and N France southwards. **Fl:** Mar–May. **Br Is dist:** In Devon and the Channel Islands only; locally common.

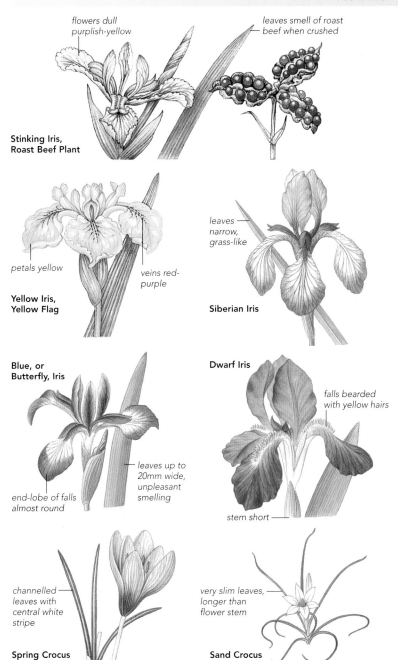

flowers dull purplish-yellow

leaves smell of roast beef when crushed

Stinking Iris, Roast Beef Plant

petals yellow

veins red-purple

Yellow Iris, Yellow Flag

leaves narrow, grass-like

Siberian Iris

Blue, or Butterfly, Iris

Dwarf Iris

falls bearded with yellow hairs

leaves up to 20mm wide, unpleasant smelling

end-lobe of falls almost round

stem short

channelled leaves with central white stripe

Spring Crocus

very slim leaves, longer than flower stem

Sand Crocus

341

Pipewort

Bog Arum

Lords-and-ladies,
Cuckoo-pint

Wild Gladiolus *Gladiolus illyricus* Slender erect hairless perennial to 90cm, from corms. Leaves to 30cm long and 10mm wide, long-pointed, grey-green, all flattened in the same plane. Flowers in long, loose, rather 1-sided raceme of 3–10 flowers, with alternate ones pointing in different directions, each with a spathe of 2 green, often purple-tipped, bracts. Perianth bright rosy purple, with 6 unequal segments, 30–40mm long, the upper 3 forming a loose hood, all more or less streaked with white and red. On heaths, scrub and open woodland, mainly on acid soils; from S England and W France southwards, very local. **Fl:** Jun–Jul. **Br Is dist:** Now only in the New Forest; locally common under bracken.

PIPEWORT FAMILY Eriocaulaceae
A small family of herbs with rosettes of leaves and tight heads of mixed male and female flowers.

Pipewort *Eriocaulon aquaticum* Distinctive, rather slender aquatic herb, with erect tufts of leaves produced at intervals from creeping rootstock. Leaves narrow, 3–5mm wide, to 10cm long, somewhat flattened and tapering gradually to a fine point. Flower stems erect, angled, to 60cm, emerging above water surface. Flowers in dense flattened sphere, to 20mm in diameter, surrounded by a whorl of tiny grey bracts, described as resembling 'whitish-headed knitting needles'. In shallow peaty lakes and pools; in W Ireland and W Scotland only; very local. **Fl:** Jul–Sep. **Br Is dist:** As above.

ARUM FAMILY Araceae
A distinctive family with leaves broader than most monocotyledons, often lobed, sometimes net-veined. Flowers tiny, crowded into a spadix (short, dense spike), wholly or partly enclosed by a large fleshy bract, the spathe.

Sweet-flag *Acorus calamus* Large, rhizomatous, aquatic perennial. Leaves long, linear, to 1.2m, 10–20mm wide, pointed, with margins wavy in parts, and with an off-centre, pronounced midrib. Flower stem 3-angled, as tall or taller than leaves, with a long spathe and an apparently lateral cylindrical greenish-yellow spadix of flowers, to 90mm long. Naturalised in shallow water and wet places; throughout N Europe except the extreme north; originating from SE Asia. **Fl:** Jun–Jul. **Br Is dist:** Locally naturalised.

Bog Arum *Calla palustris* Aquatic perennial with a stout rhizome and stout stems to 30cm. Leaves rounded to oval, up to 12cm long, heart-shaped at base, with long stalks. Spathe broad, white on upper surface, not enfolding spadix, spadix short and squat, to 30mm long, flowers yellowish-green. Fruit a red berry, about 5mm across. In swamps, marshes and lake margins; C Europe, extending westwards to Belgium, Denmark and France. **Fl:** Jun–Aug. **Br Is dist:** Very locally naturalised.

Lords-and-ladies, Cuckoo-pint *Arum maculatum* Erect, hairless, tuberous perennial to 50cm. Leaves basal, arrow-shaped, shiny green, often purplish-spotted, with long petiole 15–25cm, *appearing in spring before flowers*. Spathe consists of rolled basal section, and unfurled, cowl-shaped erect upper part, to 25cm high, pale green-yellow; spadix enclosed in spathe, with *purple-brown (rarely yellow)* club-shaped upper part visible in cowl. Fruit a red berry in a dense spike. Common as far north as Scotland and N Germany, in woods and hedgerows, often rather damp. **Fl:** Apr–May. **Br Is dist:** Common in S Britain, increasingly rare to the north.

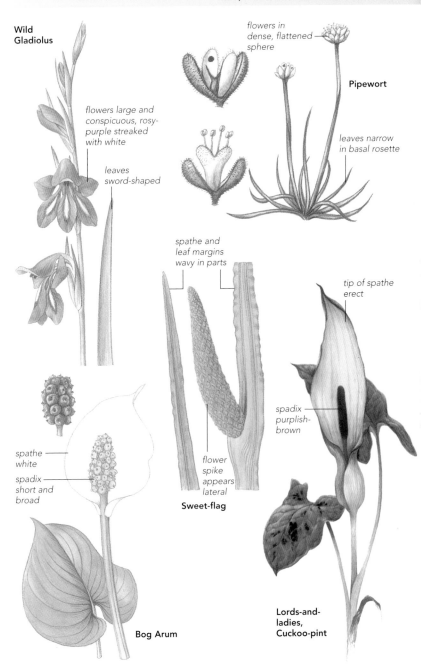

Wild Gladiolus

flowers large and conspicuous, rosy-purple streaked with white

leaves sword-shaped

flowers in dense, flattened sphere

Pipewort

leaves narrow in basal rosette

spathe and leaf margins wavy in parts

tip of spathe erect

spadix purplish-brown

spathe white

spadix short and broad

flower spike appears lateral

Sweet-flag

Bog Arum

Lords-and-ladies, Cuckoo-pint

343

Italian, or Large, Lords-and-ladies *Arum italicum* ssp *neglectum* Similar to Lords-and-ladies (*see* p. 342), differing in that *some leaves appear in autumn;* leaves are less pointed, more leathery, not spotted, less wrinkled. Spathe up to 40cm high, with *tip hanging forwards over spadix when fully open; spadix always yellow.* In woods and shady places, mainly coastal; from S England southwards. **Fl:** May–Jun. **Br Is dist:** S England and Wales only, mainly near coasts. Locally common.

*Italian, or Large,
Lords-and-ladies*

DUCKWEED FAMILY Lemnaceae
A family of floating or submerged perennial herbs, often forming carpets on surface. No clear division into stem and leaves, merely a frond with or without roots. All species small. Flowers tiny, reduced to stamens or ovary only.

Rootless Duckweed *Wolffia arrhiza* One of the smallest flowering plants in N Europe. Consists of tiny ovoid green frond, to 1mm long, without roots. Flowers in cavity on surface of frond, never produced in Europe. Local, from the Netherlands and Germany southwards; in still fresh water. **Br Is dist:** Very local (though easily overlooked!) in S England only.

Rootless Duckweed

Ivy-leaved Duckweed *Lemna trisulca* Occurs slightly below surface of water. Consists of thin translucent elliptical fronds, 5–15mm long, tapering into short stalks and *joined into colonies, with terminal trio of fronds looking rather like miniature ivy leaves.* Flower fronds smaller and floating. Widespread and generally common in still fresh water, except in the extreme north. **Fl:** May–Jul. **Br Is dist:** Common in the south, rare in the north.

Fat Duckweed *Lemna gibba* Frond oval, opaque, up to 5mm, green and convex above, usually *strongly swollen and white spongy below,* each with *1 root* (a). Widespread except in N Scandinavia; in still fresh water. **Fl:** Jun–Jul, rarely produced. **Br Is dist:** Local in S Britain; absent from Scotland.

Common Duckweed *Lemna minor* Fronds elliptical to rounded, symmetrical, *flat on both surfaces,* up to 5mm across, floating, with a *single long root* hanging below (**b**). Common almost throughout, except the extreme north; in still or slow-moving fresh water. **Fl:** Jun–Jul. **Br Is dist:** Common throughout, except the extreme north.

Greater Duckweed *Spirodela polyrhiza* Fronds to 10mm, rounded ovate, opaque, *flat on both sides,* often purplish below, *with several roots* (**c**) (up to 15 per frond). Widespread throughout except the extreme north, locally common; in still fresh water. **Fl:** Jun–Jul, but rarely produced. **Br Is dist:** Locally common in the south, rare or absent in the north.

BUR-REED FAMILY Sparganiaceae
Perennial aquatic herbs, with leafy stems. Flowers unisexual, in dense spherical heads.

Branched Bur-reed *Sparganium erectum* Erect, hairless perennial to 1.5m. Leaves usually all erect, occasionally floating, triangular in section, *keeled* and linear. *Inflorescence branched,* with the globular, yellow male heads borne above the female on each branch; flower clusters individually unstalked; perianth segments thick, with dark tip. In water and marshy places, not tolerant of grazing; throughout. **Fl:** Jun–Aug. **Br Is dist:** Common almost throughout.

**Italian, or
Large, Lords-and-ladies**

*tip of spathe
usually flops
forward*

*spadix
yellow*

**Rootless
Duckweed**

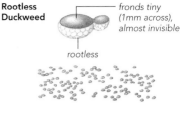

*fronds tiny
(1mm across),
almost invisible*

rootless

**Ivy-leaved
Duckweed**

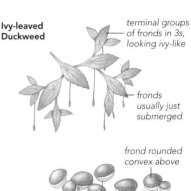

*terminal groups
of fronds in 3s,
looking ivy-like*

*fronds
usually just
submerged*

*frond rounded
convex above*

*frond rounded
and white
below, with 1
root per frond*

Fat Duckweed

**Common
Duckweed**

*fronds flat on
both surfaces*

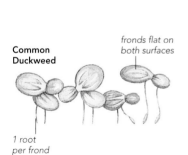

*1 root
per frond*

**Greater
Duckweed**

frond flat above

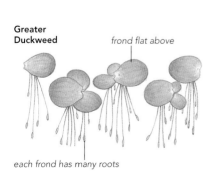

each frond has many roots

*male flowers
at top*

*female
flowers
below*

*inflorescence
branched*

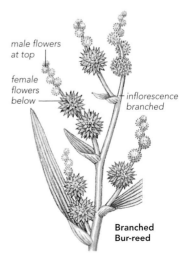

**Branched
Bur-reed**

Lady's-slipper

Unbranched Bur-reed *Sparganium emersum* Rather similar to Branched Bur-reed (*see* p. 344). Leaves erect or floating, *triangular but not keeled*. *Inflorescence unbranched*, with several female clusters at base, and 3–10 separated male clusters on the main axis above them; style straight. In fresh water, still or slow-flowing; throughout. **Fl**: Jun–Aug. **Br Is dist**: Locally common throughout.

REEDMACE FAMILY Typhaceae
A small family with 1 genus. Mainly aquatic, with flowers crowded into dense cylindrical inflorescence, with female flowers towards base.

Bulrush, Common Reedmace *Typha latifolia* Stout robust perennial to 2.5m. Leaves mainly basal, 10–20mm wide, very long, often overtopping flower spike, grey-green, set in 2 distinct opposite rows. Inflorescence is the familiar dense cylindrical spike, with the *lower part very stout (up to 15cm long and 30mm in diameter)*, deep brown, made up of female flowers, topped by *immediately adjacent narrower yellowish male section*. In still water and wet places; wide-spread and common throughout. **Fl**: Jun–Aug. **Br Is dist**: Common throughout.

Lesser Bulrush *Typha angustifolia* Similar to Bulrush, but slenderer; leaves only 3–6mm wide, darker green; male and female parts of inflorescence *distinctly separated by a stalk 10–90mm long*, whole inflorescence more slender. In similar habitats, though more local; absent from the north. **Fl**: Jun–Jul. **Br Is dist**: Locally common in England and Wales; rare or absent farther north, uncommon in Ireland.

ORCHID FAMILY Orchidaceae
A huge mainly tropical family, with about 30,000 species worldwide. Perennial herbs, usually with rhizomes or tubers. Many have unusual modes of life, especially as saprophytes, living without green pigment (chlorophyll) and therefore dependent on rotting vegetation which they utilise with the aid of a fungus; many tropical species are epiphytes, growing on trees, but all N European species are terrestrial. Flowers are produced in spikes or racemes; they have the perianth in 2 whorls of 3, of which the outer 3 are usually all similar, while the inner 3 have 1 much larger than the other 2, known as the lip or labellum, which is usually on the lower part of the flower, and is often quite different from the other segments, which may themselves be modified greatly. The ovary is inferior, generally forming part of the flower stalk. The anthers and stigma are borne on a distinctive central column.

Lady's-slipper *Cypripedium calceolus* Very distinctive plant, unlikely to be confused with any other N European native. Stems to 50cm, rather downy. Leaves oval to elliptical, pointed, sheathing, strongly veined. Flowers usually solitary (rarely 2) per stem, with large leaf-like bract at base; outer perianth segments narrow, maroon, to 90mm long; lip is shorter, but greatly inflated and yellow with red spots in hollow interior. In woods and grassy places, mainly on limestone soils; from C Scandinavia southwards, but very local and declining. **Fl**: May–Jun. **Br Is dist**: Very rare in N England only.

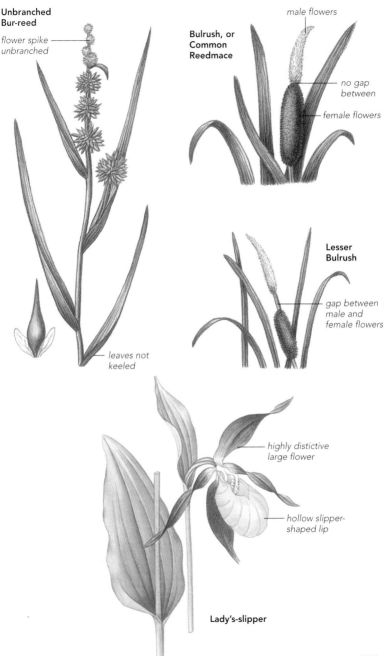

Unbranched Bur-reed

flower spike unbranched

Bulrush, or Common Reedmace

male flowers

no gap between

female flowers

Lesser Bulrush

gap between male and female flowers

leaves not keeled

highly distictive large flower

hollow slipper-shaped lip

Lady's-slipper

347

Marsh Helleborine

Narrow-lipped Helleborine

Green-flowered Helleborine

Dark-red Helleborine

HELLEBORINES *Epipactis* and *Cephalanthera* Plants without basal rosette, but with numerous stem leaves. *Epipactis* flowers stalked in loose cylindrical racemes, usually twisted so that all face in roughly the same direction. Flowers have inner perianth whorl of 2 similar upper segments, and a 2-part lip, consisting of the inner hypochile and outer, roughly triangular, epichile; ovary straight, not twisted. *Cephalanthera* flowers have less marked separation of the lip into 2 parts, and the perianth segments fold forwards to form a bell shape.

Marsh Helleborine *Epipactis palustris* Erect plant to 50cm, downy near top. Leaves oblong-oval to lanceolate, pointed, largest ones at base of stem, upper ones held erect. Flowers in loose raceme with up to 14 flowers; outer perianth segments ovate-lanceolate, brownish or purplish green; inner upper 2 shorter, whitish with red-purple streaks; lip has *heart-shaped white epichile, with frilly edges* and yellow spot at base; flowers open widely. In marshes and fens; widespread but absent from the far north. **Fl:** Jul–Aug. **Br Is dist:** Local in England, Wales and Ireland; rare or absent farther north.

Broad-leaved Helleborine *Epipactis helleborine* Erect plant to 80cm, with 1–3 stems in clump. Lowest leaves scale-like, largest leaves around centre of stem, ovate-elliptical, to 17cm long, strongly veined, dull green on both sides, all leaves spirally arranged. Raceme 7–30cm long, with up to 100 flowers; flowers (a) open wide, held horizontally or slightly drooping; outer perianth segments ovate-elliptical, green tinged purple; hypochile cup-shaped, dark red-brown, unspotted inside; epichile heart-shaped, broader than long, with curved-back tip, varying from green to red-purple; ovary hairless. Widespread in woods, shady banks and dune-hollows; throughout except the extreme north. **Fl:** Jul–Sep. **Br Is dist:** Locally fequent throughout except N Scotland.

Narrow-lipped Helleborine *Epipactis leptochila* Tall slender plant to 70cm. Leaves oval-lanceolate, to 10cm long, often yellow-green. Flowers (b) wide open, yellow-green, outer perianth segments pointed, with *epichile very narrowly heart-shaped* with flat tip, long-pointed, *yellowish-green with white margin*. In woods and scrub, often very shady, usually on calcareous soils; rare or local from Denmark southwards. **Fl:** Jun–Jul. **Br Is dist:** S England only; very local.

Green-flowered Helleborine *Epipactis phyllanthes* Small, slender, downy, erect plant to 45cm. Leaves light green, ovate-lanceolate, not strongly veined, up to 70mm long. *Flowers pendent, normally not fully open; all perianth segments yellowish-green*, except hypochile which is white inside, and epichile which is greenish-white. Very local from S Sweden southwards, but absent from many areas; in woods and on dunes on calcareous soils. **Fl:** Jul–Sep. **Br Is dist:** Local in England and Wales; rare in Ireland; absent elsewhere.

Dark-red Helleborine *Epipactis atrorubens* Stems usually solitary, downy, erect, to 60cm. Flowers all *reddish-purple to brick-red*, hypochile spotted inside with red. A distinctive species. In woods, scrub and rocky slopes on chalk and limestone; throughout, except the far north. **Fl:** Jun–Aug. **Br Is dist:** Very local, mainly in N England and N Wales, also W Ireland and NW Scotland.

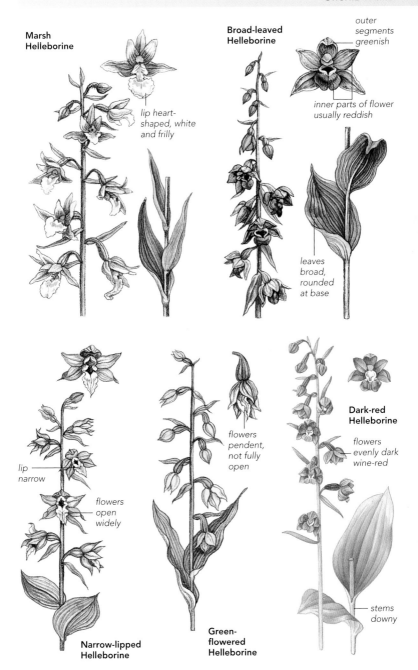

Marsh Helleborine

lip heart-shaped, white and frilly

Broad-leaved Helleborine

outer segments greenish

inner parts of flower usually reddish

leaves broad, rounded at base

Narrow-lipped Helleborine

lip narrow

flowers open widely

Green-flowered Helleborine

flowers pendent, not fully open

Dark-red Helleborine

flowers evenly dark wine-red

stems downy

White Helleborine

White Helleborine *Cephalanthera damasonium* Erect hairless perennial, with angled stems to 60cm. Leaves oblong-lanceolate to lanceolate at top, up to 10cm long. Flowers 3–12 in a spike up to 12cm long, each with a leaf-like bract at base; perianth *creamy white*, about 20mm long, *partially open*, erect, segments blunt; hypochile has an orange blotch, and epichile has orange ridges along it. Widespread from S Sweden southwards, in woods and scrub; commoner in the south. **Fl:** May–Jul. **Br Is dist:** Local in southern half of England only, mainly in beechwoods on chalk and limestone.

Red Helleborine

Narrow-leaved, or Sword-leaved, Helleborine *Cephalanthera longifolia* Similar to White Helleborine, but stems less angled, with whitish (not brown) scales below; leaves long, narrow, linear, with tips slightly drooping. *Flowers purer white*, in a denser spike with shorter bracts, *opening more widely*; perianth segments pointed. Widespread except in the extreme north; in woods and other shady places. **Fl:** May–Jun. **Br Is dist:** Widespread in scattered localities, but very local, and absent from many areas; declining. Least rare in C S England.

Violet Limodore

Red Helleborine *Cephalanthera rubra* Rather like Narrow-leaved Helleborine in form, with shorter straight leaves, few in number. Flowers all *reddish-pink*, opening widely, with whitish lip marked with red and yellow; ovary and upper parts of stem sticky and hairy. In open woods and scrub; from S Scandinavia southwards, rare in the north of range, commoner in the far south. **Fl:** Jun–Jul. **Br Is dist:** Very rare, in a few S England localities only.

Violet Limodore *Limodorum abortivum* Highly distinctive plant. Erect, rather cane-like stems to 80cm, lacking green leaves (saprophytic, or possibly partially parasitic). Flower spike lax, with 4 to 25 flowers; perianth segments long, to 20mm, all violet or whitish; lip triangular, wavy, yellowish and violet. Woods and shady areas, often associated with pine; mainly S Europe but extending into N France, Belgium and S Germany. **Fl:** May–Jun. Appearance and timing very variable according to spring rainfall. **Br Is dist:** Absent.

Ghost Orchid

Ghost Orchid *Epipogium aphyllum* Saprophytic plant with erect pinkish-yellow leafless stems to 20cm, rarely more. Leaves reduced to brownish scales. Flowers in loose raceme of 1–5 flowers; these are pendent, 15–30mm across, relatively large for size of plant, with linear, pale yellow perianth segments, and a 3-lobed white to pinkish, red-spotted lip. Throughout, extending inside the Arctic Circle; in woods and shady places, but always very local. **Fl:** May–Sep. **Br Is dist:** Very local, rare and sporadic in appearance, in a few S England beechwood localities.

Bird's-nest Orchid

Bird's-nest Orchid *Neottia nidus-avis* Erect plant to 45cm, with pale brown stems, lacking chlorophyll. Leaves reduced to brownish sheathing scales. Inflorescence moderately dense, 5–21cm long, with numerous flowers; bracts shorter than ovaries; perianth segments all brown, 4–6mm long, curled together to form a hood over the flower; the lip is 8–12mm long, divided into 2 lobes. Widespread in shady woodland, especially on humus-rich soils; throughout except the extreme north. **Fl:** May–Jul. **Br Is dist:** Local throughout except N Scotland, but rare in the north of range.

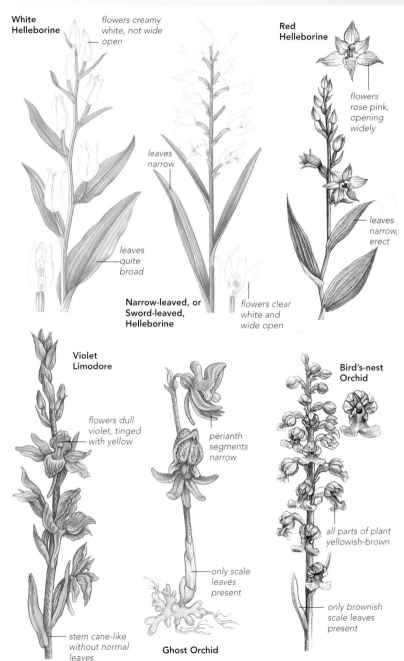

White Helleborine

flowers creamy white, not wide open

leaves quite broad

Red Helleborine

flowers rose pink, opening widely

leaves narrow, erect

leaves narrow

Narrow-leaved, or Sword-leaved, Helleborine

flowers clear white and wide open

Violet Limodore

flowers dull violet, tinged with yellow

stem cane-like without normal leaves

perianth segments narrow

only scale leaves present

Ghost Orchid

Bird's-nest Orchid

all parts of plant yellowish-brown

only brownish scale leaves present

351

Lesser Twayblade

Autumn Lady's-tresses

Creeping Lady's-tresses

Musk Orchid

Common Twayblade *Neottia ovata (Listera ovata)* Erect plant to 60cm. There is a *single unstalked pair of broad ovate leaves*, up to 18cm long, *near the base of the stem*, forming a distinctive feature (hence the English name). Inflorescence is a dense or lax raceme, with numerous green flowers with short bracts; perianth segments form a hood, lip hangs down below, yellowish-green, 10–15mm long, forked to half-way. Occurs in a wide range of habitats; throughout except the extreme north; generally common. **Fl:** Jun–Jul. **Br Is dist:** Throughout, except in high mountain areas.

Lesser Twayblade *Neottia cordata (Listera cordata)* Similar in form to Common Twayblade, though quite obviously different. Plant much smaller, to 20cm at most, with a *reddish stem*. Leaves ovate to heart-shaped, up to 40mm long, in a single, opposite pair near base of stem, dark green and shiny above. Flowers *in short, loose raceme of 4–12, much smaller than those of Common Twayblade*; perianth segments 2–2.5mm long, reddish, not in such a distinct hood; lip reddish, with 2 diverging lobes. Widespread; on moorland, in pinewoods and boggy areas, but local, and surprisingly inconspicuous, often growing under heather. **Fl:** Jun–Sep. **Br Is dist:** Mainly N England and Scotland, becoming more frequent northwards; also on Exmoor, but very rare there.

Autumn Lady's-tresses *Spiranthes spiralis* Erect plant with flower stems to 20cm, bearing only small, green scale-leaves; rosette of leaves withers long before flowering time, and the rosette for following year's flower spike is produced near base of spike. Inflorescence is in the form of a *tight single spiral* of 6–25 flowers, each small (6–7mm), barely open, and white; lip has green centre and frilly edges, curved downwards. From E Denmark southwards; in dry grasslands, stabilised dunes and coastal turf; local. **Fl:** Aug–Sep. **Br Is dist:** Local in S England, Wales and S Ireland; rare in N England.

Creeping Lady's-tresses *Goodyera repens* Differs from Autumn Lady's-tresses in having *creeping stems*, and *evergreen leaves with conspicuous cross-veins* between the longitudinal ones. Stem to 25cm, with narrow, slightly twisted spike of dull white, barely opened flowers; perianth segments blunt, sticky-hairy, in tight hood; lip short and narrow. In mossy coniferous or mixed woods; throughout N Europe, though local. **Fl:** Jul–Aug. **Br Is dist:** In coniferous woods, mainly old pinewoods, in N England and Scotland, and 1 colony in Norfolk.

Musk Orchid *Herminium monorchis* Erect plant to 25cm, from tubers. Leaves 2–3, close to base of stem, yellow-green, lanceolate to oblong, with bract-like leaves higher up stem. Flower spike 20–60mm long, with numerous small yellowish-green, slightly pendent flowers, sometimes all facing in 1 direction; perianth segments 2.5–3.5mm long, converging slightly to form hood; lip 3-lobed, 4mm long, all yellowish-green. In dry and moist grasslands, usually calcareous; throughout, except the extreme north; local. **Fl:** Jun–Jul. **Br Is dist:** S and E England, local; S Wales very rare; absent elsewhere.

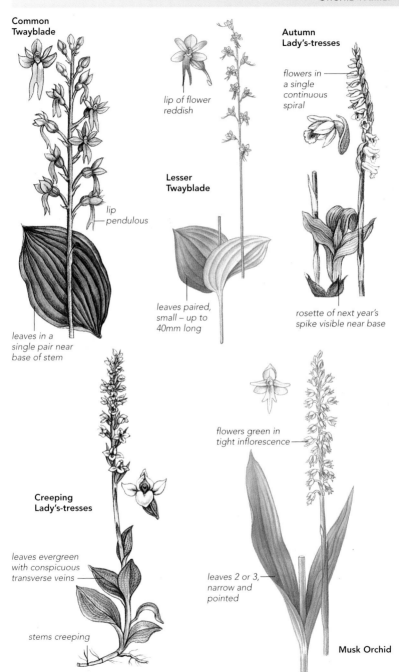

Common Twayblade

lip of flower reddish

Autumn Lady's-tresses

flowers in a single continuous spiral

lip pendulous

Lesser Twayblade

leaves in a single pair near base of stem

leaves paired, small – up to 40mm long

rosette of next year's spike visible near base

Creeping Lady's-tresses

leaves evergreen with conspicuous transverse veins

stems creeping

flowers green in tight inflorescence

leaves 2 or 3, narrow and pointed

Musk Orchid

353

Small-white Orchid

BUTTERFLY-ORCHIDS *Platanthera* Tuberous plants, with paired or few leaves near base of stem. Flowers white or greenish, with lateral lobes spreading, lip long and strap-like and a spur.

Lesser Butterfly-orchid *Platanthera bifolia* Erect stems to 45cm, with 2, almost-opposite, oval leaves near base of stem, up to 80mm long. Stem has only scale-leaves up it. Flowers (a) in dense or loose cylindrical spikes, up to 20cm long; perianth segments white, and 2 inner segments form a hood with upper outer segment; lip 6–10mm long, broadly strap-shaped; *the anther lobes run parallel;* the spur is long (25–30mm), slender and *horizontal.* Widespread almost throughout in open woods, moors, heaths, bogs and grassland, with little soil preference. **Fl:** May–Jul. **Br Is dist:** Throughout, but local.

a

Greater Butterfly-orchid *Platanthera chlorantha* Similar to Lesser Butterfly-orchid, but taller, in larger spike. Flowers (b) larger, in larger spike, usually more greenish-white in colour; the *anther lobes diverge downwards,* the spur is shorter (18–25mm long), thicker, and swelling towards tip, usually held pointing downwards; lip broader and shorter, more triangular in shape. In woods, scrub and grasslands, usually on calcareous soils; throughout, except the far north. **Fl:** May–Jul. **Br Is dist:** Local, throughout.

b

Fragrant Orchid *Gymnadenia conopsea* Erect plant to 45cm, with 4–8 linear, glossy green, unspotted leaves near the base, and a few small, narrow leaves up the stem. Flowers numerous in a *dense cylindrical spike,* up to 16cm long; *flowers all pink to reddish-lilac* (rarely white); lateral outer segments spread out horizontally, while remaining 3 curve up to form a hood; the *lip has 3 blunt equal lobes,* and there is a *long slender downward-pointing spur,* almost twice the length of ovary. Widespread almost throughout in damp or dry grassy places, fens, etc. usually calcare-ous; plants of more acid sites may be slenderer and with longer, barely lobed lip, these plants are sometimes distinguished as *G. boreale.* **Fl:** Jun–Jul. **Br Is dist:** Locally frequent throughout,

Small-white Orchid *Pseudorchis albida* Slender erect plant to 35cm. Leaves 3–5, broadly lanceolate, becoming narrower up stem, up to 80mm long. Inflorescence a dense cylindrical spike, up to 70mm long, with numerous tiny greenish-white flowers; flowers 2–3mm, with perianth seg-ments curving in to form a hood, and lip markedly 3-lobed; spur about as long as ovary, curved down. In pastures, heaths and mountain areas; throughout, but very local and absent from many lowland areas. **Fl:** Jun–Aug. **Br Is dist:** Increasingly frequent from N England northwards and westwards; probably extinct in S England.

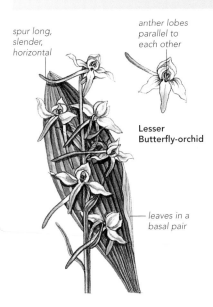

spur long, slender, horizontal

anther lobes parallel to each other

Lesser Butterfly-orchid

leaves in a basal pair

anther lobes diverging

spur pendant, broad, often broadest at tip

Greater Butterfly-orchid

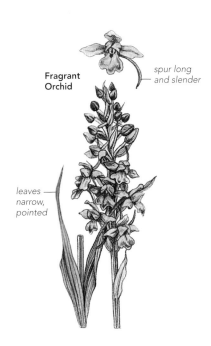

Fragrant Orchid

spur long and slender

leaves narrow, pointed

flowers plain yellowish-white

lip 3-lobed

Small-white Orchid

Black Vanilla Orchid

Northern Marsh-orchid

Southern Marsh-orchid

Black Vanilla Orchid *Nigritella nigra* Slender, erect plant to 25cm, with angled stem. Leaves linear-lanceolate, channelled and pointed. Flower spike dense, conical becoming ovoid, with numerous *blackish-crimson* (rarely paler) *tiny flowers;* perianth segments spread widely, and unlobed lip is at top of flower. In meadows and pastures, mainly in mountains, but at lower altitudes in N Scandinavia. Absent from most of area. **Fl:** Jun–Aug. **Br Is dist:** Absent.

Frog Orchid *Dactylorhiza viridis (Coeloglossum viride)* Erect, small plant to 30cm. There are 2–6 leaves, broadly lanceolate at base, narrower higher up. Inflorescence loosely cylindrical, with 5–25 flowers, with lower bracts exceeding flowers; the 5 upper perianth segments converge to form a hood; the lip hangs down, 6–8mm long, with 2 long marginal lobes and a very short central lobe; all segments yellowish-green to reddish. Widespread almost throughout, locally common in calcareous grass-lands, including hilly areas. **Fl:** May–Aug. **Br Is dist:** Throughout, though rare, except in a few areas such as chalk downs in S England, and hill pastures in N Britain.

MARSH-ORCHIDS *Dactylorhiza* An extremely difficult group of plants, which appear still to be evolving. The boundaries between species are very blurred, and numerous fertile hybrids occur. The main characteristics are: tubers palmately lobed; leaves plain or often spotted; flowers have perianth segments all separate, equal or with inner lobes smaller; lip generally 3-lobed; spur present. Differs from the closely related *Orchis* species (*see* pp. 358–60) in the tuber shape, the leaf-like bracts that are as long as, or longer than, flowers; and in *Orchis* species, the developing flower spike is sheathed by the leaves.

Northern Marsh-orchid *Dactylorhiza purpurella* Up to 75cm. *Lower leaves lanceolate,* unspotted or spotted towards the tip, upper ones reaching or exceeding base of inflorescence, bracts long, usually exceeding flowers; flowers deep magenta *lip small* (5–9mm long), *almost entire, broadly diamond-shaped,* with regular deep crimson streaks all over. Local from S Scandinavia southwards; in fens and wet meadows. **Fl:** Jun–Jul. **Br Is dist:** N Wales and N England northwards, except for 1 site in S England.

Southern Marsh-orchid *Dactylorhiza praetermissa* Taller than Northern Marsh-orchid, up to 75cm. Lower leaves lanceolate, unspotted (or ring-spotted in the var. *pardalina*), in 2 roughly opposite ranks up stem. Flowers pale pink-red to purplish; lip 10–14mm long, broader than long, *3-lobed with side-lobes very shallow and mid-lobe short and blunt;* centre of lip marked with light crimson dots and streaks. In fens, wet meadows and dune-slacks, etc. often calcareous; from Denmark to N France, commonest in the south. **Fl:** Jun–Jul. **Br Is dist:** The southern equivalent of Northern Marsh-orchid; widespread in the south, rare in N England; absent elsewhere.

Heath Spotted-orchid *Dactylorhiza maculata* ssp *ericetorum* Differs from similar marsh-orchids. An erect plant to 60cm. Leaves lanceolate and dark-spotted. Flowers in dense slightly pyramidal spike, varying from whitish to pale purple; *lip broad, triangular, shallowly 3-lobed,* with *central lobe small and not longer than side-lobes* (a); lip marked with streaks and loops. Throughout, on heaths, moors and damp, usually acidic, habitats. **Fl:** May–Aug. **Br Is dist:** Locally common throughout.

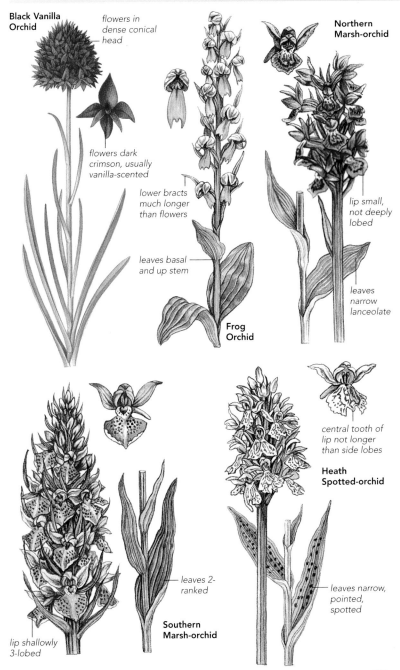

Black Vanilla Orchid

flowers in dense conical head

flowers dark crimson, usually vanilla-scented

lower bracts much longer than flowers

leaves basal and up stem

Frog Orchid

Northern Marsh-orchid

lip small, not deeply lobed

leaves narrow lanceolate

central tooth of lip not longer than side lobes

Heath Spotted-orchid

leaves narrow, pointed, spotted

leaves 2-ranked

Southern Marsh-orchid

lip shallowly 3-lobed

Green-winged Orchid

Bug Orchid

Burnt, or Burnt-tip, Orchid

Early Marsh-orchid *Dactylorhiza incarnata* Very variable species, with several named subspecies. *Stem very hollow,* erect, to 70cm. Leaves lanceolate, *yellowish-green, unspotted,* keeled and *usually hooded at tip.* Inflorescence cylindrical, dense, with lower bracts much longer than flowers; the lip is small, entire or shallowly 3-lobed, but *strongly reflexed on either side,* making it appear very narrow from the front, and with a U-shaped line on either side in most forms; colour variable, from cream to deep purple, normally flesh-pink. Ssp *cruenta* is pale purple, with leaves spotted both sides; ssp *coccinea* is brick-red, leaves unspotted; ssp *pulchella* has flowers deep purple, streaked red; ssp *ochroleuca* has cream or yellow unmarked flowers. Widespread throughout, except the far north; in a range of wet habitats, from acid to alkaline. **Fl:** May–Jul. **Br Is dist:** Local throughout.

Common Spotted-orchid *Dactylorhiza fuchsii* Similar to Heath Spotted-orchid (*see* p. 356), except that basal leaves tend to be broader, elliptical and blunt. Flower spike generally more evenly cylindrical when flowers open; flowers pale pink, with numerous darker streaks and spots; *lip more deeply and evenly 3-lobed,* with lobes rather pointed, and central lobe at least as long as lateral lobes. Widespread and common throughout, except the extreme north; in neutral to calcareous damp or dry grasslands, scrub and woods. **Fl:** Jun–Aug. **Br Is dist:** Locally common throughout.

Orchis A large genus, rather similar to the marsh-orchids, but differing as described under marsh-orchids (*see* pp. 356 and above). For simplicity, we have kept the old *Orchis* grouping despite the name changes.

Green-winged Orchid *Anacamptis morio, Orchis morio* Erect plant to 50cm, but very variable in height according to conditions. Leaves in a rosette, glossy green, *unspotted* and crowded up the stem. Flowers variable in colour, from reddish-purple, through pink, to white, but always having *outer perianth segments strongly veined and suffused with green;* lip broad, bluntly 3-lobed, with central pale patch dotted with red; spur about length of ovary. Widespread and locally common, except in N Scandinavia; in pastures and other long-established grasslands. **Fl:** Apr–Jun. **Br Is dist:** Locally frequent, though declining, in much of England and Wales, but rare or absent elsewhere.

Bug Orchid *Orchis coriophora* Rather similar to Green-winged Orchid, but has *narrower leaves, lacks the green veins,* and has the lip longer than wide, deeper red-purple with greenish streaks, with long central lobe. In damp grasslands; from Belgium and S Germany southwards; rare. **Fl:** Apr–Jun. **Br Is dist:** Absent.

Burnt, or Burnt-tip, Orchid *Neotinea ustulata, Orchis ustulata* Small plant, usually to 20cm, occasionally more. Flower spike distinctive, with the *unopened flowers appearing very dark purple,* giving the burnt tip in contrast to the white and red opened flowers; the lip is 4–8mm long, 3-lobed, man-shaped, white with red spots. In dry grasslands, usually calcareous; as far north as S Sweden. **Fl:** May–Jun, with a few populations flowering in Jul. **Br Is dist:** In England only, but rare except on S England chalk downs.

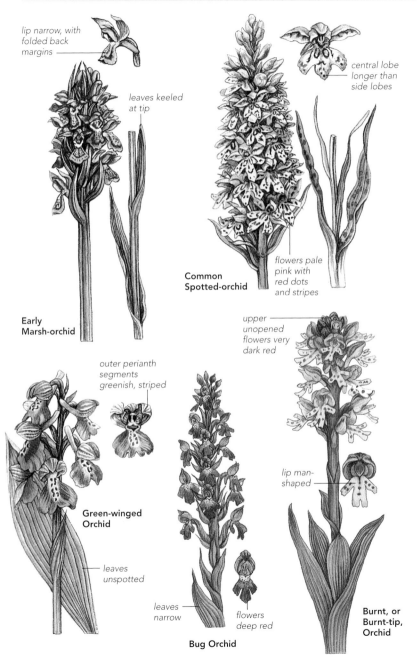

lip narrow, with folded back margins

leaves keeled at tip

central lobe longer than side lobes

Common Spotted-orchid

flowers pale pink with red dots and stripes

Early Marsh-orchid

upper unopened flowers very dark red

outer perianth segments greenish, striped

lip man-shaped

Green-winged Orchid

leaves unspotted

leaves narrow

flowers deep red

Bug Orchid

Burnt, or Burnt-tip, Orchid

Monkey Orchid

Monkey Orchid *Orchis simia* Erect plant to 45cm. Lower leaves broadly lanceolate and unspotted. Flower spike cylindrical, with f*lowers opening from top downwards* (the opposite to most *Orchis* species). Flowers whitish pink, with an upswept hood; lip distinctive, in shape of a monkey with white body (dotted with minute reddish tufts of hair), and crimson arms, legs and minute tail, with arms and legs narrow and curved; spur cylindrical, downward-pointing, as long as ovary. In grasslands, scrub and open woods, usually on calcareous soil; from S Sweden southwards, but rare in the north of its range. **Fl:** May–Jun. **Br Is dist:** Very rare, in S England and Yorkshire only.

Military Orchid

Military Orchid *Orchis militaris* Rather similar to Monkey Orchid. *Hood greyish outside*; the labellum is similarly shaped to Monkey Orchid, but with *shorter, wider legs and arms*, less distinctly different in colour from the body, and the legs diverge widely; the *flowers open from the base of the spike first*. In grassland, scrub and open woods, often calcareous; from S Scandinavia southwards, though rare in the north of its range. **Fl:** May–Jun. **Br Is dist:** Very rare, in a few protected sites in SE England only.

Lady Orchid

Lady Orchid *Orchis purpurea* Close to Monkey Orchid and Military Orchid in general form, though often larger, to 80cm high. Flower spike up to 15cm long, becoming cylindrical, flowers opening from bottom upwards. The helmet of the flower is deep reddish-purple outside; the lip is much broader than in the above 2 species, with the *broad central lobe divided into 2 further broad lobes, resembling a Victorian lady in a wide skirt*, coloured pale pink-white with red dots and suffusions. In woods, scrub and grasslands, from Denmark southwards, becoming commoner in the south of its range. **Fl:** Apr–Jun. **Br Is dist:** Virtually confined to Kent and adjacent areas, where it is locally abundant; very rare elsewhere.

Early-purple Orchid *Orchis mascula* Medium-sized orchid to 40cm. Leaves oblong-lanceolate, to 10cm long, *glossy green with numerous dark purplish blotches*, extending lengthwise (compared with transversely on matt leaves of spotted orchids), occasionally unspotted. Flowers in loose cylindrical spikes, red-purple; the lip is 8–12mm long, shallowly 3-lobed, with the central lobe notched, and the sides of the lip folded back to a variable degree; the central part of the lip is whitish, speckled red; spur stout, curved upwards, as long as ovary. In grasslands, woods and scrub; throughout except the far north and east; probably the commonest orchid of the area. **Fl:** Apr–Jun. **Br Is dist:** Throughout, locally common, in a wide range of habitats.

Loose-flowered, or Lax-flowered, Orchid *Anacamptis laxiflora, Orchis laxiflora* Rather similar to Early-purple Orchid, but usually taller, up to 1m. *Leaves unspotted*, lanceolate, under 20mm wide. Flowers red-purple, lip with central lobe very short or absent; spur shorter than length of ovary, and flower bracts with 3–7 veins (usually 1 (to 3) in Early-purple Orchid). In marshes and damp meadows; as far north as S Sweden (only as ssp *palustris*), though absent from the Netherlands, Denmark and N Germany. **Fl:** Apr–Jun. **Br Is dist:** Only in the Channel Islands, where it has declined considerably. Ssp *palustris* (sometimes distinguished as a separate species, *O. palustris*) differs in the paler flowers, tighter narrower inflorescence and more distinctly 3-lobed lip, with central lobe as long as marginal lobes. Similar habitats and flowering time, in S Sweden and Germany. **Br Is dist:** Absent.

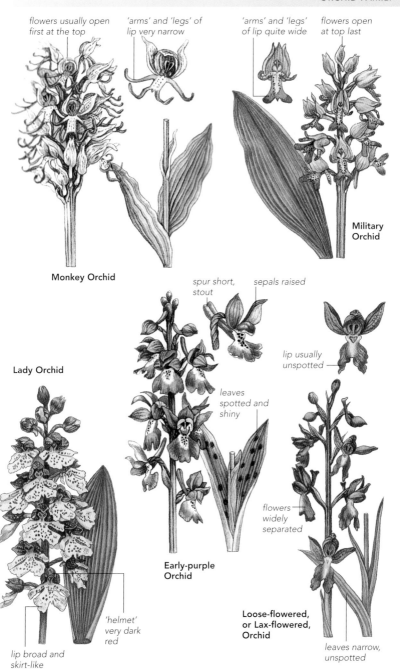

flowers usually open first at the top

'arms' and 'legs' of lip very narrow

'arms' and 'legs' of lip quite wide

flowers open at top last

Military Orchid

Monkey Orchid

Lady Orchid

spur short, stout

sepals raised

lip usually unspotted

leaves spotted and shiny

Early-purple Orchid

flowers widely separated

Loose-flowered, or Lax-flowered, Orchid

'helmet' very dark red

lip broad and skirt-like

leaves narrow, unspotted

361

Pyramidal Orchid

Fly Orchid

Early Spider-orchid

Bee Orchid

Pyramidal Orchid *Anacamptis pyramidalis* Erect plant to 30cm. Leaves lanceolate, slightly greyish-green, unspotted. Flowers in a short dense spike, up to 80mm long (usually less), *distinctly conical or dome-shaped.* Perianth and lip all deep pink; lip broad, deeply 3-lobed, with 2 ridges at its base; spur very long and slender, longer than ovary. Readily distinguished from Fragrant Orchid (*see* p. 354) by the shape of the inflorescence. On dry, often calcareous, grasslands and stabilised dunes; from S Sweden southwards. **Fl:** Jun–Aug. **Br Is dist:** Mainly southern, extending locally to NW Scotland.

Ophrys A distinctive group, with few-flowered inflorescences; flowers have greatly enlarged lip, furry, and often resembling an insect, with spreading outer perianth segments, and remaining 2 inner segments often reduced. In S Europe, there are many confusing species, but the 4 that occur in N Europe are reasonably distinctive.

Fly Orchid *Ophrys insectifera* Tall slender plant to 60cm, with leaves both basal and on stem. Inflorescence open, with 2–14 well-spaced flowers; outer perianth segments greenish-yellow and roughly equal; *inner 2 blackish-purple, thin and short like an insect's antennae;* lip narrow, 6–7mm wide, 3-lobed with a notched central lobe, furry brown except for a central bluish patch (like a reflection on the 'fly's' wings), soon fading. In grasslands, open woods and scrub, occasionally in fens, on calcareous soils; widespread but absent from the far north. **Fl:** May–Jun. **Br Is dist:** Local in England and Wales, mainly southern; rare in Ireland; absent from Scotland.

Early Spider-orchid *Ophrys sphegodes* Leaves mainly in basal rosette. Stems to 40cm, usually less. Flowers larger and broader than Fly Orchid, with lip 8–12mm wide, in a loose 2- to 10-flowered spike. *Perianth segments all yellow-green,* with inner 2 not reduced to antennae-like structures; lip large, velvety brown, without appendages, *marked with bluish H- or X-shaped speculum mark.* From S England and C Germany southwards; in short turf and open rocky areas, usually on calcareous soils. **Fl:** Apr–May. **Br Is dist:** In S England only; local and mainly coastal.

Bee Orchid *Ophrys apifera* Rather similar to Early Spider-orchid. Flowers differ mainly in that the 2 *inner perianth segments are narrow, greenish* (or reddish); the outer perianth segments are pinkish-purple; the lip is narrower and smaller, with 2 distinct, but small, furry side-lobes; *centre of lip marked with a rough U-shape;* lip appendage present, but curved back underneath. From the Netherlands and N Ireland southwards; in dry grasslands, dunes and old quarries, usually on calcareous soils. **Fl:** Jun–Jul. **Br Is dist:** Local throughout England, Wales and Ireland, but rare or absent in the north.

flower spike pyramidal

Fly Orchid

inner two petals reduced to look like a fly's antennae

lower lip furry, with central bluish patch

flowers pink, without spots

Pyramidal Orchid

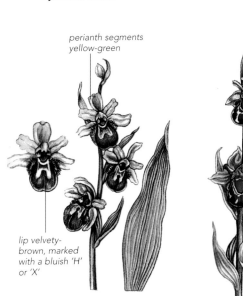

perianth segments yellow-green

lip velvety-brown, marked with a bluish 'H' or 'X'

Early Spider-orchid

inner 2 petals narrow, usually greenish

sepals pink

U-shaped mark in centre of lip

Bee Orchid

Man Orchid

Man Orchid *Orchis anthropophorum (Aceras anthropophorum)* Rather yellowish-green plant to 30cm. Leaves oblong-lanceolate, glossy green and unspotted. Inflorescence is long, narrow and cylindrical, with as many as 90 flowers. All perianth segments greenish-yellow, streaked and edged with red-brown; lip pendent, 12–15mm long, of similar colour, with very distinctive, narrow, man shape; no spur. From the Netherlands southwards; in calcareous grasslands and scrub. **Fl:** May–Jun. **Br Is dist:** Rare, only in S and E England., most frequent on the North Downs.

Lizard Orchid

Lizard Orchid *Himantoglossum hircinum* Tall, stout, highly distinctive plant to 1m. Basal leaves roughly oval, withered by flowering time, stem leaves narrower. Inflorescence long, up to 30cm, cylindrical, with numerous large flowers. Flowers have 5 perianth segments forming a hood that is greenish-grey outside, striped red inside; the lip is unlike that of any other N European orchid, with the central lobe prolonged into a ribbon-like tongue, up to 50mm long, twisted and forked at the tip. In grassland, scrub, wood margins and stabilised dunes; from the Netherlands and England southwards. **Fl:** May–Jul. **Br Is dist:** Only in S England in a few scattered sites, where it often appears and persists for a few years only.

Calypso

Coralroot Orchid *Corallorhiza trifida* Small, erect, saprophytic orchid to 30cm, lacking normal green leaves. Stem yellowish green, often clustered, with brownish scales. Inflorescence is lax, with 2–12 pendent flowers. Perianth segments greenish-yellow, lip pendent, white with red lines, unlobed or with 2 small side-lobes. Widespread, though local, throughout, commoner in the north or in mountain areas farther south; mainly in damp boggy woods, wet moorland and dune-slacks. **Fl:** May–Jul. **Br Is dist:** Northern, mainly in N England and E Scotland.

Calypso *Calypso bulbosa* Beautiful and very distinctive orchid. It has 1 stalked, oblong, basal leaf, and a single stem bearing a solitary large flower, up to 50mm across. This has 5 long, narrow, pink-purple sepals held erect, and a large inflated pink- or whitish-speckled lip. In damp woods and boggy areas; N Scandinavia only. **Fl:** May–Jun. **Br Is dist:** Absent.

Fen Orchid

Fen Orchid *Liparis loeselii* Small, erect perennial, with roughly triangular stems to 20cm, from a bulb-like structure. Leaves normally 2, basal, in opposite pair; oblong in shape, yellowish-green, greasy in appearance. Flowers in a loose spike with 2–10 flowers; perianth segments yellow-green, narrow, linear, 5–8mm long, and spreading but curving inwards; lip broader, at top of flower, since the ovary is not rotated at all; no spur. In fens, bogs, dune-slacks and other wet places; from C Scandinavia southwards. **Fl:** Jun–Jul. **Br Is dist:** Rare, in scattered localities in E Anglia, SW England and Wales.

Bog-orchid

Bog-orchid *Hammarbya paludosa* Differs from the above species in its much smaller size, rarely exceeding 12cm, though often only 60–80mm high, with 3–5 leaves. The inflorescence is a small, narrow spike, up to 60mm long, with numerous tiny yellow-green flowers; the ovary twists through 360°, so the ovate lip faces upwards; perianth segments narrow and spreading; spur absent. In acidic marshes, bogs and flushed areas; throughout, though very local and absent from many areas. **Fl:** Jul–Sep. **Br Is dist:** Scattered, mainly northern, though locally common in the New Forest and Purbeck area.

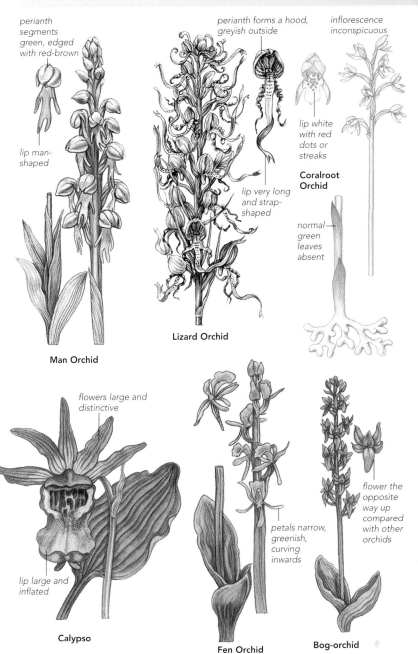

perianth segments green, edged with red-brown

lip man-shaped

Man Orchid

perianth forms a hood, greyish outside

lip very long and strap-shaped

Lizard Orchid

inflorescence inconspicuous

lip white with red dots or streaks

Coralroot Orchid

normal green leaves absent

flowers large and distinctive

lip large and inflated

Calypso

petals narrow, greenish, curving inwards

Fen Orchid

flower the opposite way up compared with other orchids

Bog-orchid

365

INDEX OF LATIN (BINOMIAL) NAMES

INDEX OF COMMON NAMES

INDEX OF FAMILY NAMES

AUTHORS' ACKNOWLEDGEMENTS

The high standard of the maps is due to the knowledge and toils of Martin Walters and John Akeroyd, to whom we are extremely grateful.

We also thank the artists Chris Orr, Robin Soames, Tiffany Passmore and Robin Walls for the splendid line drawings.

Finally, we would like to thank our families, again, for their patience and forbearance during our long hours of field work and writing.